AMERICAN ARCHITECTURE:

INNOVATION · AND · TRADITION

A M E R I C A N
A R C H I T E C T U R E:

INNOVATION · AND · TRADITION

Edited by
David G. De Long
Helen Searing
Robert A.M. Stern

The Temple Hoyne Buell Center
for the Study of American Architecture
Columbia University in the City of New York

RIZZOLI
NEW YORK

AMERICAN ARCHITECTURE: INNOVATION AND TRADITION

Edited by David G. De Long, Helen Searing, Robert A. M. Stern

This volume documents the symposium and exhibition inaugurating the Temple Hoyne Buell Center for the Study of American Architecture. A publicly and privately supported not-for-profit study organization, the Buell Center was founded in 1982 as part of Columbia University in the City of New York. The symposium and exhibition were held at Columbia University, April 21–24, 1983.

SYMPOSIUM VOLUME: AMERICAN ARCHITECTURE: INNOVATION AND TRADITION

Editors
David G. De Long
Helen Searing
Robert A. M. Stern

Managing Editor
Lisa Friedman

Editorial Consultants
Julia Bloomfield
Sylvia Lavin
Joan Ockman

Editorial Assistants
Bruni Burres
Barbara Genova

This book has been made possible by a grant from the National Endowment for the Humanities.

First published in the United States of America in 1986 by
RIZZOLI INTERNATIONAL PUBLICATIONS, INC.
597 Fifth Avenue, New York, NY 10017

Copyright © 1986 by the Temple Hoyne Buell Center for the Study of American Architecture, Columbia University, New York

Library of Congress Cataloging-in-Publication Data
Main entry under title:

American architecture.

1. Architecture—United States—Addresses, essays, lectures. I. Stern, Robert A. M. II. Searing, Helen. III. De Long, David Gilson, 1939-
NA705.A49 1986   720′.973   85-42952
ISBN 0-8478-0645-6

Designed by Heidi Humphrey/H+
Set in type by Eastern Typesetting and Trufont Typographers
Printed and bound in the U.S.A.

Cover:
The old and new Transamerica buildings, San Francisco, California. Photograph by Ken Collins.

CONTENTS

FOREWORD

by Helen Searing

The aim of the inaugural symposium of the Temple Hoyne Buell Center for the Study of American Architecture was an open-ended, timely, and provocative examination of mainstream American architecture in the context of American culture. Among the general topics initially considered as themes for the symposium were the alternating claims of regional and international vocabularies in the making of American architecture, and the persistent and often percipient transformations by American designers and builders of received models, imported or indigenous. It was, however, the theme of the clashing and complementary forces of innovation and tradition that was ultimately selected as the one that would raise the largest number of important issues. It is intended that future sessions will address more specific questions, such as the interplay between native American and colonial building practices, and investigate areas that have been less consistently developed, such as the contributions of groups that, because of race, ethnic makeup, class, or gender, have remained at the margins of research.

The swings of the pendulum between innovation and tradition can be charted everywhere in the world, but perhaps the oscillation has nowhere been more extreme than in the relatively young United States, with its plural constituencies and cultural discontinuities. Settlers stirred by revolutionary aims and utopian dreams brought with them, from vastly different sources, an enormous variety of collective memories that had to be acknowledged and addressed. The desire for roots was a counterforce to the urge toward liberation. An entrepreneurial pragmatism fostering technical invention was often checked by a cultural insecurity that took refuge in proven traditions. The dialectic of these contradictory forces in American architecture offers potent opportunities for study.

If the story of American architecture told in terms of the positive and negative tensions between innovation and tradition is not a novel one, neither is it uncontroversial. This is particularly so at present, when the modernist impulse to jettison all reminders of the past in the name of a permanent revolution is being challenged by voices that vigorously, even shrilly, reassert the claims of history. Ideology strongly colors these debates, but it would be a mistake to label a preference for innovation or tradition obviously left or right, populist or elitist. There are also many who seek an equilibrium between the two forces, and they too must be heeded.

Certainly there was no consensus at the symposium among the speakers or the audience; whether one looked to those making architecture or those analyzing it, criticism and history could be seen to reflect the disagreement to the same degree as architectural practice. Some speakers thus focused on the inventive proclivities in the development of American architecture while others emphasized its overriding continuities. While in the past commentators from abroad, especially, have tended to laud the innovative technology of America while castigating, or at least patronizing, its architectural design as retardataire or irrelevant—an attitude that pervades histories of the skyscraper, for example—several speakers at the symposium revealed this point of view as flawed.

As already suggested, the heterogeneity of viewpoint, was deliberately sought; the organizers looked for a broad spectrum of perspectives and methodologies among the participants. The central theme was meant to incorporate the investigations of those for whom social issues were paramount no less than those whose interests were formalistic or iconographic. Speakers, moderators, and curators were invited from a variety of institutions, while respondents were drawn from the faculty of the Graduate School of Architecture and Planning of Columbia University. Brought together in a single forum, in keeping with the syncretic goal of the center, were professionals involved in practice, criticism, and history. While the theme clearly accommodated those who found it especially applicable to the experiences of a colonial nation, it also invited the viewpoint of those who believe it artificial and chauvinistic to isolate American architecture as a unique phenomenon and to ask, in effect, what is American about American architecture.

In keeping with the effort to promote the broadest possible inquiries on this inaugural occasion the decision was made to address the central theme at a variety of scales and over different time spans. Sessions were structured around the object, the building, and the place, although concerns and insights expressed in the various sessions overlapped and intermingled. Objects were seen as both enduringly relevant and instantly obsolete, purposely functional and purposely symbolic; buildings were seen as monumental and impermanent, grandiose and vernacular, abstract and representational, costly and cheap, directed toward public realms and private ones; settlements—rural, urban, suburban—were examined that were generated by communitarian ideals or by individual greed, that fostered democracy or appealed to false bourgeois sentiment, that engendered the sense of place for which we yearn or denied it. Failures no less than successful ventures were carefully, even lovingly, limned.

The exhibitions, put together by different curators, were arranged according to region, with one section devoted to "America as a Region," and made visible factors of topography and demography, myth and folklore, local specialization and national aspiration; depending on the curator's agenda, the selections were broadly interpretive or narrowly focused according to building type or race and class of user. Similarly, the architects who were invited to discuss their own work represented firms that ranged in size from tiny to huge, and demonstrated dramatically differing views on what constitutes a viable architecture today.

Finally, the respondents reminded the directors and speakers how much had been ignored or forgotten—in the consideration of the symposium's theme in particular, and of American architecture in general. Their comments not only provided a healthy critique of the symposium, but suggested directives for future gatherings.

The study of American architecture as an expression of American institutions is an ongoing project, not only because in the present we are adding to the stock of the future, but also because the heritage of the past is continuously being reevaluated. As we lose we also gain, with new objects, buildings, places, makers, and users coming into view. Tradition and innovation characterize the study as well as the creation of American architecture, and the celebration of these basic forces fittingly commences the activities of the Temple Hoyne Buell Center.

INTRODUCTION AND ACKNOWLEDGMENTS

by James Stewart Polshek

The Temple Hoyne Buell Center for the Study of American Architecture was founded in 1982 to advance the understanding and interpretation of American architecture, landscape, and urbanism. To achieve this goal, the Buell Center has embarked on an ambitious program of publications, exhibitions, and symposia designed to engage architects, scholars, and the general public. These rich and varied programs make the Buell Center one of the world's most important focal points for the study of American architecture.

The title of this symposium, "American Architecture: Innovation and Tradition," is highly appropriate to our great friend and benefactor, Temple Hoyne Buell. Sandy Buell epitomizes every word in the title: he is an American, an architect, an innovator, and a respecter of tradition. We are deeply grateful for his generosity. I also want to thank the charter sponsor of this symposium, Knoll International, whose generosity made this event possible. Knoll, as many of you are aware, has been a leader in the design world for years. Under the corporate leadership of Stephen Swid and Marshall Cogan, they have been extraordinarily generous in supporting symposia and other kinds of public discourse that have generated both controversy and enlightenment. We hope this event will justify their confidence in us.

I also want to thank Nan Swid for her profound interest in architecture and design and her friendship to all of us here at the Graduate School of Architecture and Planning (GSAP). Her assistance in planning many of the events related to this inauguration has been invaluable. There have also been others who have supported this event, and I wish gratefully to acknowledge their generosity: Lily Auchincloss, who is one of the true patron saints of architecture; the Charrette Corporation, without whom architects would all have to stop drawing; Rose Associates, who build so much of what we do draw; the A.I.A. College of Fellows Fund; the A.I.A. Foundation; the Formica Corporation; the George Gund Foundation, the LAW Fund; the National Endowment for the Arts; and the Graham Foundation. I also want to thank the Center's Board of advisors, Henry-Russell Hitchcock, Ada Louise Huxtable, Edgar Kaufmann, Phyllis Lambert, I. M. Pei, Adolph Placzek, and Vincent Scully. Finally, I wish to thank the co-directors of the symposium. All three of these eminent scholars have been associated with the GSAP in a number of important ways—Helen Searing,

Alice Pratt Brown Professor of Art History at Smith College; Robert A. M. Stern, architect and Professor of Architecture in the GSAP; and David De Long, architect and Chairman of the Division of Historic Preservation at the GSAP.

I would like to say a few words about this symposium and the new Center. Architecture would be little more than a group of semipermanent artifacts but for our collective cultural memories. It is to the proposition that the appreciation, understanding, and use of architecture is a profound and humanizing experience that this new center is dedicated. It must be a primary mission of the Center to bring together architectural scholarship and the practice of the art of building—that is, to encourage the one and to inform the other.

The idea for the Center grew out of two concerns of mine. The first was the nonrecognition, by teachers of history and theory in architecture schools, of the influence of Hispanic and Japanese culture on American architecture. Part of the reason for this obviously has to do with the "Renaissance" syndrome and part with plain, old-fashioned American chauvinism.

My second concern arises from a more recent phenomenon. It is the alarming degree to which urbanism is coming to be informed by real-estate development, historic preservation by regulatory politics, and architecture by commercial marketing pressures. A place is needed for scholars and practitioners to gather together to take the "long view." I hope that the Temple Hoyne Buell Center for the Study of American Architecture is just such a place. If successful, this intellectual center can play a large role in addressing these concerns, and can go far beyond them to reinforce the teaching and the practice of architecture in a fundamental way.

SYMPOSIUM

SYMPOSIUM
AMERICAN ARCHITECTURE: INNOVATION AND TRADITION

April 21–24, 1983

Co-Directors
David G. De Long
Helen Searing
Robert A. M. Stern
James Stewart Polshek
*Dean, The Graduate School of
Architecture and Planning,
Columbia University*

Executive Director
Ann Kaufman

Assistant Director
Sylvia Lavin

Designer
Heidi Humphrey/H+

The symposium was made possible by generous contributions from:

Charter sponsor
Knoll International

Lily Auchincloss
Charrette Corporation
The George Gund Foundation
The L.A.W. Fund
Rose Associates
College of Fellows Fund—AIA

KEYNOTE ADDRESS:

AMERICAN ARCHITECTURE: THE REAL AND THE IDEAL

by Vincent Scully

AMERICAN ARCHITECTURE:
THE REAL AND THE IDEAL

by Vincent Scully

We are met in a city on a hill, appropriately named "Columbia." We are here in a rotunda of enormous scale under the dome which is that city's crowning glory. If we were to stand at the entrance to Butler Library, below its colossal colonnade, and were to look back at this dome, we would feel the regulating axis of classical architecture passing through our bodies, while the high, hard blocks of the surrounding buildings are deployed symmetrically on either side. If we were to move forward along that axis, toward the dome, we would come, with some surprise, to a wide cross-axis, an extensive avenue which runs westward out and down toward the river, eastward out and up toward the sky. It is the climactic release of the classical garden, the broad transept before the dome. The sky which crowns the eastern arm of that transept may well be black with the smoke of burning buildings, fired in anger in the city that smoulders below it in the plain. That city is one which was never envisaged or imagined by those Puritan clergymen who compared their American community to a "city on a hill." It is another city, one of pain and deprivation, sorrow and despair. When those who live in it look up to the western sky the city on the hill shines unattainable before their eyes.

It must be one of the primary goals of the Center whose foundation we are celebrating today to bring those two cities together, to embody each in the other and to make the vision of the American community better than it was before. In the end each city needs the other, in simplest truth cannot survive without the other, since envy could destroy the first and fear obliterate the second. Such concern is right and proper for the Center because architectural history, like architecture itself, is not concerned primarily with individual buildings but with the city as a whole. It is concerned with all man-made objects in relation to all others and to nature itself. The human environment entirely shapes its focus. In order to study the character of the contemporary American environment we need to examine its past, which may be, and should be, studied in the Center from as many different points of view as individual scholars may bring to bear. The one essential is that we have confidence in the reality of architecture as an art and in the capacity of architectural history to expand our knowledge of ourselves and our environment through the experience of works of art. Given that, all ways are open, and all can help us confront our history, which means, of course, our future as well.

I would suggest, in a most preliminary fashion, that there are four areas, or categories, of historical study which seem to be of particular relevance in our attempts to explore the American city at the present time. The first is that of this continent itself, what Francis Jennings called this "widowed land," and the architecture our Amerindian predecessors built upon it. The second category is that of the pervasively American colonial experience, with what Neil Harris called its "materialist, craftsman culture." That culture, decisively revived in the 1870s, has been integral to the creation of the United States. It played a part in the formation and development of the third category which, I would like to suggest, is that of our realist tradition. That tradition produced America's basic and most significantly inventive contributions to the architectural environment during the nineteenth century: the suburban house and its partner, the center-city office building. During the past generation that tradition has been in a state of reassessment and revival, and is in fact helping to shape some of our most important contemporary work. Finally, the fourth category is the persistent American Classical ideal which has acted sometimes as an adversary, sometimes as a complement, to the realist tradition itself. The Classical ideal has always had special power in America because it was, from the beginning, so closely linked to our revolution and our national independence. Of all the categories I have mentioned it is the one which has most recently been revalued.

We may never again have, on this continent, an urbanism which is as grand, or as fatal, as that which was created by those who preceded us here. In the Aztec capital of Tenochtitlan, the Temple of Quetzalcoatl, the god of civilization, stood in the center of the Great Plaza. It was shaped like a gigantic seated figure with a distinct, rounded head. It looked toward the notch between the Temple of Tlaloc, the god of rain, on the left, and the Temple of Huitzilopochtli, the god of war, on the right. At the equinox, the sun rose in that notch, so that when the sun was behind Tlaloc it was the season of rain and agriculture, and when it was behind Huitzilopochtli, it was the dry season of hunting and war. Far beyond the city the axis that extended from the notch fell between the twin peaks of Popocatepetl and Ixtaxihuatl, which bounded the Valley of Mexico on that side. Each peak rose on the majestic horizon along the arc that swung out from its temple in the city far below. The man-made and the natural were one.

Tenochtitlan is gone now, but one of its models, to which the last Aztec king, Montezuma, paid ritual visits throughout the year, was Teotihuacan, still extant as an archaeological site. From the Temple of Quetzalcoatl at the Teotihuacan, the pyramids of the Sun and the Moon echo the shape of the notched mountain behind them. The arrangement at Tenochtitlan was simply a variant of that relationship, of which the essentials may also be seen at Taos Pueblo in New Mexico. This continent, unlike Europe, is fortunate to

*1 Pyramid of the Moon
Teotihuacan, Mexico.*

*2 Water goddess
Teotihuacan.*

3 Tikal, Guatemala.

*4 Postcard of the Empire State
Building.*

possess not only archaeological remains of premodern civilizations but also those civilizations still alive among us today. At Taos, for example, the North House is still used as a pyramid base for ritual, much as the Temples of the Sun and the Moon were used at Teotihuacan. Although the pyramid at Taos is asymmetrical in shape, it also, like the temples of Teotihuacan, echoes in its own forms the shapes of the sacred mountain beyond it.

The principle at Teotihuacan and Taos is nothing mystical, but rather pragmatically American: it has to do with the drawing force from nature itself. The Pyramid of the Moon at Teotihuacan is on the axis of the main street of the town, which is the Street of the Dead, and the mountain looms directly beyond it, notched and running with springs (fig. 1). The mass of the pyramid is compressed, with long horizontal fracture lines, like those fissures in a natural mesa from which subsurface water is squeezed. The Water Goddess at Teotihuacan is herself an image of maximum compression and horizontal fracture (fig. 2). The great block on her head seems dropped from a great height upon her, and it is notched in the center, exactly like the mountain behind the Temple of the Moon. Its pressure forces water out of the goddess. It flows from her hands. The whole arrangement of temples and mountains is an image of this act at landscape scale. Nature is being helped along by human ritual, as it is invigorated by the blood of human sacrifice which is poured out there.

In the south, among the Classic Maya, the principle upon which the pyramids were designed seems at first to be rather different (fig. 3). The mass is made to seem not compressed but as if leaping up like a great spring. The temple at the top is of concrete, dark and severely restricted in interior space, but lifted up and shaped like the rain clouds above it. When we climb the steep steps to the temple and come finally before its face we discover that the thick concrete has kept the interior moist and cold, so that it literally breathes out upon us the dank rain breath of its companion clouds. In one of the most curious of the alchemies that make art, these Mayan temples had not a little to do with suggesting the setbacks and the roof combs of the Art Deco skyscrapers of New York, such as the Paramount Building and the Empire State Building (fig. 4). So while the temples at Tikal are in fact skyscrapers, being literally intended to touch the clouds and to release their water, they also played a part in releasing the skyscrapers of the twentieth century, with their springy bases, to lift up and rise free. Those latter-day American "temples of commerce," as they were so often called, reflect the worship of something far beyond simple material concerns, something deeply felt but otherwise vaguely formulated, here embodied in a passionate leap to the sky.

Teotihuacan, on the other hand, worships a very definite divinity— Quetzalcoatl, the Plumed Serpent, who is water in its two basic

5 *Taliesin West*
Near Scottsdale, Arizona
Frank Lloyd Wright, 1938.

forms. He is the horned serpent from the ground, like the water pressed from the mesa; and he is the plumed bird and horned divinity, like the rain and lightning that come from the sky. He is squeezed out like springs of water by the pressure of the *tablero* structure of his own temple, and his great head, all lightning and rain, stands out against the temples and the mountain in the distance. His divinity is still recognized today in the snake dances of the Hopi. The principle is the same. The snake, who is consigned to the dust in Western culture, is "befriended," as the Hopi say; they lift him into space and touch him with the feathers of the eagle, the most majestic of birds. He becomes the Plumed Serpent himself, and as he is returned to his hole in the desert, he also brings with him the rain from the sky. The same God is worshiped at Taos, where the North House calls to the mountain from which the water descends into the pueblo. The house seems simultaneously to hold the mountain and to complete its forms, but, as we move in around it, it also stands out from the mountain to become an altar of the sky. Thus, while the house is inflected toward the shapes of the mountain beyond, it also reflects those of the clouds and is therefore double, just as the great plumed serpent is. The beat of the dance, of which the climactic sets take place directly across the front of the North House, echoes the syncopation of the forms of the house itself, which are in tune with those of the mountain. At these dances one feels the most intense relationship imaginable between the natural, the man-made, and the human act. Indeed, environment and act are one.

As European-Americans we have built very few temples to this paramount American divinity, who in our rather pallid terms is, I suppose, the ecology of the land. Taliesin West is surely the major example (fig. 5). There, as at Taos, the shapes are inflected to the shapes of the surrounding landscape, and the recollection of pre-Columbian forms is strong, obviously intentional on the part of Frank Lloyd Wright. The structure is open to the divinity who is the embodiment of things as they are, including the terror and death which form part of our natural world. Neil Levine now tells us that the later work of Wright was largely based on his doctrine of "imitation," and this may well have been suggested to him first by the pre-Columbian architecture which appealed to him so strongly. At the same time, James O'Gorman has shown that a similar principle was at work in Henry Hobson Richardson's design. So there is at least a strong undercurrent of ancient instinct in some of America's most powerful works.

The dominant European-American tradition, however, is a colonial one and it is Spanish and French as well as English in character. For our purposes, though, its roots can be traced most easily in New England. Here we turn inside, away from nature. Ideally, the fireplace is directly in the middle of the house, giving off heat to warm the closed box of rooms around it (fig. 6). Every detail consciously shuts out the outside, in direct opposition to the topographical, even cosmic, urbanism of Tenochtitlan. It is the tight family group, in the closed spaces surrounding the hearth, which forms the focus of this tradition. The environment is totally built, created by the central fireplace and the beams of the skeletal structure of the house. A completely hermetic family environment is sought rather than one which is open to communal values. That overall integration of the house as a discrete social unit was reaffirmed and recreated during the Colonial revival of the 1870s, and was of enormous importance in the personal integration of the environment carried out by Frank Lloyd Wright from the 1890s onward. The dining room chairs of Wright's Martin House, for example, make a special environment around the table, one which echoes the frame that is created by the stripping of walls and ceiling, so that all is woven together into a unity. These forms came to Wright from the Colonial Revival, through the work of Shingle style architects, and from Japan as well. They permitted a new interweaving of the whole which Wright orchestrated into symphonic form. His expansive and releasing spaces, images of the modern nation as a whole, were anchored by the fire "burning in the heart of the house." The harmony is, in the end, "colonial," despite the fact that Wright himself used that adjective as one of ultimate abuse.

6 Interior, Parson Capen House Topsfield, Massachusetts, 1683.

But the colonial interior itself had given rise to beings whose power has never since been equaled or surpassed in American culture; they may be called, as John Russell once did, the "household gods." They are the furniture. Many pieces of furniture, such as the enormous cupboards which were typical in scale of late medieval work and of Renaissance Mannerism thereafter, were originally brought from England and placed in the low, dark colonial interiors (fig. 7). Immediately, there was a disjunction in scale, intensified by the placement on those sideboards of the objects most precious to the Puritan culture. These prized possessions were above all of silver.

7 Court cupboard, oak Newbury, Massachusetts, 1680.

It might be said that silversmithing was the first, and among the greatest, of the colonial arts. During the seventeenth century American painting, for example, hardly existed, but American silversmiths were as good as any in the world. It is, therefore, the craftsman who was the absolute artist of the time, and silver was the ideal Puritan art. Its forms were thin, linear, bright, lucid, fleshless, devoid of the dull Papist gleam of gold; more than that; useful—"functional," a later age would say. Most of all, they constituted the actual wealth of the household, the primary material possession, shaped into sculptural forms.

In fact, during the early eighteenth century, with the so-called Queen Anne style, silver pieces become ever more sculptural and figurally active, taking on monumental power (fig. 8). They became Baroque beings, figural embodiments of physical force, endowed with a special iconic intensity as they shone from the tops of their dark cupboards in the shadows of the house. They were the sacred furniture of the Puritan household altar. They deified, or at least sanctified, the house.

A parallel evolution occured in chairs. The early chairs, such as the Brewster Great chair or the ladder-back, are primarily environmental, making no gesture to the sitter. Their framed structure is like that of the house itself, and like the house they simply contain their human inhabitant. This begins to change late in the seventeenth century with the William and Mary style, when the Renaissance-Baroque concept of the human figure as dominating the world begins to make itself felt in chairs as in silver. The arms of the chair turn over and down and the back lifts up, and the shape of the person who occupies it begins to be visible. This figural quality becomes even stronger with the Queen Anne style (fig. 9). The craftsman's preoccupation with the structural joint unites with the wholly Baroque cabriole leg to transform the leg of the chair into that of an animal. Meanwhile, the back rises up, curves over and down, transfers its energy to the seat and then to the legs, so that the chair as a whole seems to become a living being. It is figural sculpture which embodies the human presence which brought its shape into being. It is precisely this compact sculptural intensity which tends to distinguish the American Queen Anne chair from its English contemporaries. It is often called more "linear" than English examples, and it is true that its contours are strikingly continuous in a linear sense, but that linearity is used by the American craftsman to outline a sculptural figure: in fact, another household god, masquerading as a thing of utility and simple material prestige.

At this moment of special intensity in the development of the materialist craftsman culture as exhibited by the Queen Anne, what can be called the first American painting appears in the work of Robert Feke (fig. 10). It is, of course, portrait painting, hence dou-

8 *Two-handled silver cup*
Jacob Hurd, ca. 1744.

9 *Queen Ann armchair, walnut*
Philadelphia, 1740–1750.

10 Portrait of James Bowdoin II
Robert Feke, 1748.

11 Spindle-backed armchair, maple
Lisbon, Connecticut, 1770–1800.

12 High chest of drawers, cherry
and pine
Connecticut, 1740–1760.

bly a possession and a physical embodiment. A portrait by Feke and a Queen Anne chair alike flaunt their craftsman origins. Feke is part of the colonial craftsman tradition and is proud of it. His paintings can be contrasted with those of such English practitioners in the colonies as John Smibert precisely in the way that the American Queen Anne chair can be contrasted with the English one. The American painting is more linear and taut, and the work shines with the exactitude and the pride of the craftsman tradition. A comparison is also useful with the Windsor chair, which originates in England, comes to the colonies in the 1740s, and then becomes an American specialty (fig. 11). The fundamentally crude English beginnings are transformed into thin, daring creations of skeletal structure, of a kind which later becomes characteristic of American architecture in general. Feke's paintings are equally thin, stretched, and tensile. They also make us think of Queen Anne silver, figural, taut, and shining, but the analogy goes deeper. In all likelihood, Feke himself had been a craftsman, probably a tailor, and he was famous for the way he painted clothes, all sheen and sharp points and exquisite cut. One can see in Feke the beginnings of that American image which Theodore Dreiser later sought to identify, in which, having no titles, it is what one wears and how one carries oneself that communicates to others what one is. The materialism of the American position, here visible in its early purity, shines out of Feke's painting. Smibert's people are still English, and tend to look rather disheveled as Smibert applies to them his own journeyman-Baroque line. Feke's are all pristine bandbox American. Much the same stance is visible in the highboy, which by the middle of the eighteenth century was no longer fashionable in England, but which had become the ultimate household god of the American interior (fig. 12). It stands upright on its legs, with shining brass pulls, exactly akin to the details of the costumes painted by Feke. His painting also closely resembles the luminous, two-dimensional facades of the provincial Baroque houses of America in the mid-eighteenth century (fig. 13). Feke's work, the furniture, and the

13 Wentworth-Gardner House
Portsmouth, New Hampshire,
1760.

14 Chippendale armchair
Eliphalet Chapin, 1760–1780.

15 Mrs. John Winthrop
John Singleton Copley, 1773.

16 Paul Revere
John Singleton Copley, ca.
1768–1770.

silver are therefore all part of an integrated American colonial style—a phenomenon very much of the Queen Anne: the Baroque made personal, domestic, and middle class.

Later in the century, with the Chippendale chair, the stance becomes even more fully Baroque, spatial, and three-dimensional (fig. 14). The back no longer curves in upon itself but explodes into space. The chair grows larger: the seat is set lower but becomes bigger, and the legs spread out as it takes command of its environment. Indeed, the space is virtually devoured by the craftsman's object. Similarly, the contemporary paintings of John Singleton Copley create persons who are physically three-dimensional in a way that Feke's were not. Their possession and control of space is analogous to that exerted by the Chippendale chair. Copley is also the first American painter who is as skilled in his craft as the colonial craftsmen had been in theirs for almost a hundred years. He paints with the strength of this tradition, and notwithstanding his exact knowledge of anatomy, distorts his figures to give them the expressive power that colonial furniture had achieved long before. Mrs. Winthrop is as real as her furniture, jammed in between her polished table and her upholstered chair (fig. 15). Copley's people thereby identify themselves through their objects and, where applicable, through their crafts. His *Paul Revere* is the best example of that. The figure holds his round, smooth chin just as he holds the round, smooth teapot he has made (fig. 16). His body, as truncated by the table, is itself pot-like. He is what he does, and this identification through work was later to become a typical American adjustment to reality. Similarly, Copley's painting of Samuel Adams, the most violent of the revolutionaries, derives its power from similar distortions. The shortened arm makes the body like an armless chair, causing the eye to leap from the figure to the document, and then to the face with its glaring eyes. When another artist copied the painting and corrected the proportions of the arm, the power of the composition was lost. Samuel Adams is as potent as a Chippendale chair and as explosive in his sculptural being.

This materialist realism, in which the human being is identified in relation to objects, remains a constant in American painting. The best complement to Copley, and the only other American painter of persons to rank with him, is Thomas Eakins. Almost one hundred years after Copley, Eakins painted his fiancée Katherine as intensely in relation to objects as Copley had painted Mrs. Isaac Smith. But there is a difference, one that is absolute (figs. 17, 18). Mrs. Smith *is* the chair and is in command of it. She knows herself to be the beneficiary of the materialist culture as well as its dragon guardian, and she swells with pride in owning the objects which are contained in her house. Katherine, however, does not dominate the objects around her. They close in upon her in the dark interior; they eat her up. It is as if a hundred years of confinement in the house, spent caring for and surrounded by objects, had destroyed

the woman. The enormous bookcase looms heavily above her head, the knobbed chair arms embrace and threaten her, and her body dissolves into pure nervous vibration. She is present only through her nerves and her uneasiness: the monumental mass of Mrs. Isaac Smith has been worn away. Other paintings of the period, such as Eastman Johnson's *Hatch Family,* strongly suggest the complexity of what Sigmund Freud called the "family romance," the interaction between late nineteenth-century middle-class people and their possessions within the hermetic house. It is Eakins, however, who understands this best, and who endows Copley's materialist objectivity with the technical means, the Rembrandtesque light and shadow, which can explore the ambiguities of the self in the new, industrialized, urban age.

During this period, the same realist tradition also creates the new American house itself. Realism in architecture begins in the 1830s and 1840s and is an international phenomenon. In England it is explored largely through the Gothic Revivalists, in France by the Neo-Grecs. In America it has a decisive effect on the construction of wooden houses (fig. 19). They join this tradition in the sense that for the first time since the Renaissance the building is examined systematically, not in terms of proportion but in terms of how it is made. As Andrew Jackson Downing said, "the main timbers that go into the support of a house are vertical" so that vertical board-and-batten siding "properly signifies," in the associational vocabulary of the period, a wooden house. It extends to the skeleton of the porch, creating the archetypal American screened porch, a

19 Board-and-batten house Newport, Rhode Island, ca. 1846.

21 The Coming Storm
Martin Johnson Head, 1859.

20 *Drawing of a veranda*
Andrew Jackson Downing, 1853.

basic platform and frame from and through which the nineteenth-century American comes to view the world (fig. 20). The romantic realism which created it extends to the painting of the American landscape to which it opens. As evinced by the Hudson River school, American painters found in the landscape not only religion and science, as European painters did, but nationalism as well, and an American antiquity which American cultural institutions did not themselves possess. In his *Ox Bow*, Thomas Cole depicts the storm of barbarism passing away, while the smiling agrarian garden of the new America opens out, transcendentally, to infinity. At the same time, American genre painters, such as William Sidney Mount, at once shaped the kind of views which might be seen from a Stick Style porch itself and constructed them in ways which recall the structure of that porch. They are full of light, but are defined by a clearly linear organization through which the luminous atmosphere expands. What is seen from the porch is not the romantic castle that Downing loved to put there but, most often, a still and silent landscape held together by a skeleton of lines, the ghost of the architectural frame. It is this which defines a human stance in relation to the still American light on the water which the Luminist painters loved (fig. 21).

Like Luminist painting, with its genre antecedents, the lightly framed wooden house, too, became a nineteenth-century vernacular and constituted even a viable urban way of building at moderate scale.[1] The characteristic two-family houses in New Haven are built in what can be called Stick Style, Shingle Style, and Colonial Revival modes, but what seems of importance is that they all constitute a vernacular type, adjusted to the urban situation. The standard organization shows a narrow lot and a high, two-family house, with a strong frontal gable and a skeletal front porch (fig. 22). This opens to a lawn, a sidewalk, a strip of grass planted with elm trees, and then the street. Here is an urbanism in which, as always, the buildings are only part of the overall structure. The porch, for example,

22 *Stick and Shingle style street*
New Haven, Connecticut

23 *Watts Sherman House
Newport, Rhode Island
H. H. Richardson, 1874.*

is both inside the house and out in the street, and it unites all the elements of inside and outside into one complex and satisfying environment. It is an urbanism complete in vernacular terms. The frontal gable, for example, has a history extending from the Greek temple to the Palace of Augustus on the Palatine to the American Greek Revival house, which, in contrast to Colonial houses, begins to be entered at the gable end like a temple. It is also integral to the creation of the Shingle Style. In the Watts Sherman House by H. H. Richardson, of 1874, it becomes stretched and horizontal, not vertical and linear but spatial and volumetric (fig. 23). The influence of Norman Shaw's late medieval forms is also apparent, but the long slope of the shingle roof that Richardson uses was clearly derived from American colonial architecture, specifically from the Bishop Berkeley House, a photograph of which was published in an architectural magazine in 1874, the first colonial house to be so distinguished.

24 Cannon Rock
Winslow Homer, 1895.

The Shingle Style also contains the kind of epic power—so different from the calm silence of mid-century Luminism—which we find in the paintings of Winslow Homer. Homer, too, is moved by New England, and can, in part, be regarded as a product of the Colonial Revival. His *Cannon Rock,* in which the ocean seems to flood forward from the canvas to drown us all, is the reverse triangle of the Shingle style's looming gable (fig. 24). Such archetypal shapes have always had decisive historical effect. That of the Low House in Bristol, Rhode Island, for example, with some admixture of the Watts Sherman House and other buildings, was a direct inspiration for Robert Venturi's Beach House project of 1959, with its pure gable shape, its horizontal shadow lines, and its shingled surface (fig. 25), and that project initiated the revival of the realist Shingle style vernacular which continues today. Once again, though, the ancient American doctrine of "imitation" seems to play a part: the gable in Richardson's hands *is* a breaking wave, and up through it leaps Venturi's fire.

25 *Elevation of Beach House
Robert Venturi, 1959.*

At the end of the nineteenth century, Frank Lloyd Wright also played a central role in furthering the realist tradition through his condensation of Shingle Style elements in the frontal gable. In his own house in Oak Park, of 1889, he combined two houses by Bruce Price in Tuxedo Park, of 1885-1886, the Chandler and Kent Houses. The symmetrical organization of the terrace of the Kent House is made asymmetrical by Wright; Price's perspective drawing, published in *Building* in 1886, may have suggested this. Moreover, Price's frontal, symmetrical buildings on their pedestal porches, were clearly influenced by Charnay's renderings of Yaxchilan and Palenque in his book *Les Anciennes Villes du Nouveau Monde* of 1885—a book which had been paid for by Pierre Lorillard, Price's client at Tuxedo. Lorillard's own house is closely adapted from Charnay's rendering of the Temple of the Sun at Palenque. To go further: Wright's Charnley House of 1892 and his Winslow House of 1893 both use Mayan mask motifs to frame the front door. Wright then leaves pre-Columbian forms until he comes to need them again after he definitely breaks with his suburban culture in 1914. During his great suburban years, of course. Wright got rid of the shingles and the gable, adopted stucco, horizontal stripping, and the lowest possible hipped roof, and the resultant forms, as published in Germany by Wasmuth in 1910 and 1911, clearly helped to create the International Style. But when Venturi begins his revolt against that style it is also to Wright that he turns. In his house for his mother, Venturi transforms Wright's frontal gable with its Neo-Palladian half circle into the suggestion of a total circle framing a square central opening (fig. 26). Tiny as the building is, we feel in it some enormous power bursting the circle apart, stretching the lintel and splitting the gable. Venturi so explodes the archetypal,

*26 Vanna Venturi House
Germantown, Pennsylvania
Robert Venturi, 1962.*

Neoplatonic image of a circle in the square, upon which Le Corbusier's architecture, not to say that of the International Style as a whole, had fundamentally been based. Venturi also sets them within a third basic shape, the Shingle Style triangle of the gable itself. He then goes on to return to the vernacular even more fully, and to its shingles themselves. Most of all in the Trubeck and Wislocki Houses on Nantucket, he goes all the way back to the Oriental type: to the frontal gabled building with a porch, and thereafter, in domestic architecture, he works by extending the language of this and other vernacular types. This is supremely important, because when buildings are created within the same type the differences between them can be seen as absolute. They can be understood as differences between creatures of the same species. It is only through respect for types that ultimate intensity, permanence, and directness can come into architecture. Different examples of a single type constitute a language, without which poetry is impossible. This is what Greek temples were about. So Melville wrote of them:

> Not magnitude, not lavishness
> But form, the site;
> Not innovating wilfulness
> But reverence for the archetype.

That archetype, embodied in houses, marks one of the most important achievements of the American realist tradition, because through it the strength of preindustrial, precapitalist ways of building were adapted to modern conditions and so made available for contemporary use. Those Marxist scholars and architects who would withhold recognition from this American achievement of the late nineteenth century, renewed in the late twentieth, are, in my opinion, misreading the material.

A similar adaptation of traditional forms to modern functions and materials takes place in the American skyscraper, the center-city office building. Again, to return to an Eakins painting of 1900, *The Thinker,* we find that working only with the profile of the dark suit Eakins makes tangible the skeleton underneath, the inner structure of the body. The stance of the feet on a slanting surface suggests the image of a thinly clad skeleton standing tall in space. Here Eakins assesses the reality of the American situation, as defined by Baudelaire in the early days of European realism, to "make us heroic in our varnished boots." Louis Sullivan's skyscraper office buildings can be seen as much the same thing. The Wainwright, for example, is an everyday red-brick mass articulated in terms of skeletal structure; the thin cladding serves to intensify the interweaving of the skeleton beneath it. As the buildings get taller, growing from the Wainwright to the Guaranty, they become even more like Eakins's *Thinker:* tall, stretched, thin—lanky Americans. Sullivan himself would have welcomed the figural analogy, in so far as he believed in Empathy, which is the experience of works of art through associating them with our own physical stance. Indeed, empathy followed Associationism as the major nineteenth-century contribution to our understanding of the aesthetic process. So Sullivan said of a building by Richardson, "Here is a man for you to look at...[who] stands on two feet, stretches and stirs," which exactly describes the image of a standing body that Sullivan's Guaranty Building itself achieves. The building *is* Eakins's man of the period in terms of the American realist tradition.

Another determinant of the office building is its urban situation, its setting in the American grid plan. The grid is itself colonial, indeed colonial Greek in origin. It goes back in America to such seventeenth-century plans as those for New Haven and Savannah. In the early nineteenth century it becomes the plan of New York, and as the century goes on it shapes the continent everywhere, from Chicago to Salt Lake City to San Francisco, and imposes an increasingly orthogonal clarity on the map of the states. At first, as in New Haven, the buildings are small on large lots, and this remains the suburban pattern, but when the streets of the center of the city are filled up with building a very old and traditional way of constructing architecture comes into play. All buildings are fundamentally alike, simple cubical boxes respecting the street, filling the space; but each is decorated differently. An urban order is created by the volumetric uniformity, but the distinct surface treatment enables every building to remain individual enough. The architects of the Chicago Loop and Sullivan himself worked accordingly, respecting the grid and filling it with buildings articulated in somewhat different but closely related ways. Palladio's *palazzo* blocks in Vicenza are eloquent demonstrations of these principles; Sullivan's Wainwright Building in St. Louis shows him to be a master of them as well (fig. 27). The building is intended neither to stand alone nor to scrape the sky. Although it is an articulated skeleton, it is also a solid block, like a Renaissance *palazzo*, and it is not much higher than such a building might be. It should be seen in its context of similar buildings, each a similar block, each decorated differently. The Wainwright is in fact very similar to Palladio's Palazzo Valmarana in Vicenza, where the stretching of the pilasters is like the stretching of Sullivan's piers. It is too bad that the buildings immediately adjacent to the Guaranty in St. Louis have been torn down, and it is to be hoped that the two which remain across the street will not fall before the ill-conceived scheme for a Mall which has been hanging over the city for some years.

27 *Wainwright Building St. Louis, Missouri Dankmar Adler and Louis Sullivan, 1890–1891.*

The doctrine of the International Style, despite its urbanistic pretensions, was not urban at all. Rather, as stated in the first Bauhaus manifesto, its goal was the "building," not, as Aldo Rossi now so eloquently insists, the "city." In practice the style came to exhibit its exemplars as distinct from all other buildings, especially from all traditional buildings in their urban contexts. This iconoclasm began to break down the traditional order of the city. It was first exemplified in America by Lever House, whose slab turned side-

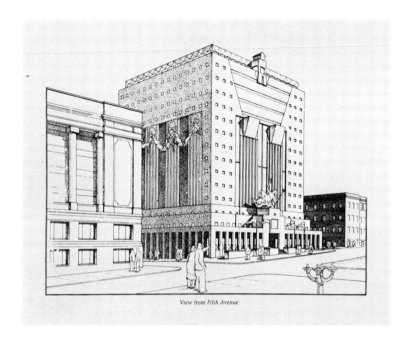

*28 Public Services Building
Portland, Oregon
Michael Graves, 1982.*

ways and broke up the marvelous shape of Park Avenue. Michael Graves has reacted against this almost universal and highly destructive trend in Portland, where the basic fact of the center of that beautiful city is a small, square grid, in which, indeed, many buildings can be perfect *palazzi,* filling whole blocks (fig. 28). Each fills its grid space and is scaled in relation to the other buildings, their solid masses defining the streets. Graves uses colors and motifs in his decoration which are similar to those of the blocky office-building types of the early twentieth century in Portland's downtown, now being rehabilitated. This movement toward the rehabilitation of the inner city office building of the realist tradition is now in full swing throughout the United States, countering the attempts to destroy it which are still being mounted by the International Style out of its pirate's lair in Houston.[2]

Over the last generation we have also learned to appreciate the skyscrapers of New York. Although the public has always loved them, architectural historians tended for many years to agree with Le Corbusier, who said that they were too many and too small; he wanted them to be in large measure, like the skyscrapers of Chicago, "Cartesian" blocks, though blown up in scale and set in the center of vast super blocks with the old system of streets destroyed. But New York skyscrapers were based on premises and prototypes wholly different from those of Chicago. Their models included the spires of colonial churches as well as the *palazzo.* Like Trinity Church in New York and the churches of colonial Boston, the main body of the building is embedded in the city, while the spire points up, meant to be seen from great distances, in these cases from the sea.

So, from the very beginning in New York, the skyscraper was meant to act not only as rentable space but as a gesturing symbol. Its lower floors respected the street while the upper stories leaped and pointed upward with all a spire's fantasy. We now know that Sullivan himself would have built in this way if he had been given buildings as tall as the skyscrapers of New York to construct. His drawing of such a group keeps the block on the street and then allows fancy free rein in the towers that rise higher than any buildings before them had done, exactly as the genial giants at the tip of Manhattan were eventually to do. That greatest of all groupings of skyscrapers began to be destroyed by the International Style. The inert slab of Chase Manhattan, for example, smothered the life in the pointing spires and demolished their scale. It and its followers certainly took all the fantasy out of the skyscraper, not to mention the glory. Today, of course, all that has changed, and the skyscraper vernacular, if I may employ that term, has been revived like that of the house. This is surely as it should be, because the old skyscrapers of New York were, in their inimitable way, the most moving buildings of modern times. Despite everything, they are still beloved throughout the world for exactly what they were: the romantic climax of the American materialist tradition.

29 Colonnades, University
of Virginia
Charlottesville, Virginia
Thomas Jefferson, 1825.

These buildings stand in opposition to America's other kind of city, that which embodies the Classical idea. The specific model for this city was the French Classical garden, toward which a few moments' attention should be directed here. A word might be said first about the language of Classicism, which we, in this generation, are only now relearning. We can watch Thomas Jefferson himself trying to master that incomparable language of columns, entablatures, and pediments and seeking to graft it onto vernacular speech in order to express the grandeur of the new republic and of the humanistic learning which he believed to be the only hope for its future (fig. 29). For many years we have regarded Jefferson's work as the record of an ideal long gone by, never to be directly available to us again. Today, at last, his language, like the vernacular it complemented, can be understood anew as a matter of type, as a means of communication capable of saying many different things precisely because it *is* a language, with the rules of language shaping its thought and making its meaning clear. The foundation of Classicism as a modern language is the Classical plan, which may be said to have been shaped by a growing confidence on the part of humanity in its ability to control the landscape, so developing from Delphi to Athens, to Lindos, ancient Rome, Baroque Rome, Vaux, and Versailles. There, finally, the triumphant spatial axes explode the original grid of the *parterres* into great stars at cosmic scale, whose rays rush out across the countryside. Eventually such garden plans became regional in application, and from them, as Louis XIV hoped, the shape of modern France was born. By the middle of the nineteenth century, railroads radiate from Paris to the fortifications of Vauban on the natural frontiers, so defining a shape, an intrinsic

*30 Aerial view of Washington,
D. C., 1930s.*

order, and a centralized organization for France as a whole which
is like that originally conceived at Versailles. Paris, of course, takes
over the central position from Versailles, but under Baron Haussmann in the nineteenth century it is the principle of the classic
garden which shapes that city itself. The axes radiating from the
Étoile, for example, cut through solid blocks of buildings which
are not simply sliced-off Classical blocks but massive, rounded
clumps beneath their great mansards. They are thick stands of forest, irradiated by their magical *allées*. Paris is thus the ultimate
garden, the consummate work of art of modern times. It is the
environment beyond all others which has most formed the mind
of modern man through the experience of itself.

The other great garden is Washington, D.C. (fig. 30). The original
plan by Pierre Charles L'Enfant was directly in this French Classical
tradition, but it retained the American grid at Jefferson's insistence—the Classical and vernacular languages sustaining and enriching each other once more. Radiating avenues take off from the
two centers of power, the Capitol and the White House, and pass
through the grid, setting up all the electric tensions which are common to intersecting systems. Yet the scheme was truncated by the
position of the Potomac, which cut deeply into the body of the
city and cut off the projected axis from the Capitol all too abruptly.
The Capitol building itself kept on growing throughout the first
half of the nineteenth century. Like Versailles, it spread out laterally
but, unlike Versailles, it needed a visible democratic symbol; hence
the dome. What had signified a church in Europe came to mean a
public building in the United States. It too grew as the century

progressed, but its progress was vertical until, in 1863, during the darkest days of the Civil War, the cast-iron frame finally rose to completion and the statue of Freedom was placed on its top. The Capitol was joined in the 1880s by the Washington Monument in the form of a pure obelisk, much simpler and more archetypally Classical than any of the earlier proposals. It stood on the very bank of the river, in a plan as yet incomplete.

Only in the revival of Classicism with the City Beautiful movement of the late nineteenth and early twentieth centuries did the plan of Washington take on its appropriate scale, surpassing that of Versailles. Eventually all the major heroes of the Republic found Classical memorials in it: Abraham Lincoln by 1922, Thomas Jefferson in 1943. In 1901, the Senate Park Commission, of which Charles Follen McKim was the most important member, directed its attention primarily to the axis of the Mall, from the Capitol to the projected Lincoln Memorial at the end of the new reflecting pool, the latter recalling the Grand Bassin at Versailles. The iconography of this great project was that of the American Civil War. The ordeal of the nation provided the mythic material which was to be embodied in symbolic form. Classical sculpture, centered on the human figure, was the vehicle of that embodiment. Below the Capitol, crowned with Freedom, Grant sits on his horse, as if contemplating a field of battle, with cavalry and artillery coming up to his support. He is immovable and implacable as Fate, the very image of War and Death, looking down the axis of the Mall toward Virginia, and toward the effigy of his commander-in-chief in his Memorial. The Lincoln Memorial, designed by Henry Bacon, is, like the Washington Monument, a kind of miracle of Classicism in its purest form, and it won a competition over some impressive proposals. One of them, by John Russell Pope, looks deceptively pre-Columbian in perspective. Bacon's, as built, manifests Classicism's ancient duality. On the outside it is clear, taut, beautifully crafted, and blazing white in the sunlight. Within, the image of Lincoln, like Zeus, sits brooding in the shadows. It is enormous; seen from the outside between the columns it fills the hard, bright shell with a dark, looming, superhuman presence. The language of Classicism is as public and religious, dealing with deep human memories, beliefs, and sorrows. Its forms grow with the events that are associated with them, and the buildings of Washington have taken on much more intense meaning during the past generation than they had for my generation, when we hardly understood the ways in which we needed them, or what public sorrow might be. All of us who watched the Kennedy funerals pass before the assassinated Lincoln in his Memorial and then go on to the burial ground in Arlington across the water now see the building with a passion lacking before.

But there is more than that; the emotions aroused by Classical forms are historically stabilized by the literature which has gathered around them over centuries. That literature, too, is public as well as religious. It suggests the basic meaning of public acts. So in this Classic setting the Kennedy funerals can hardly help but be seen as those of the Gracchi, the Tribunes of the people, slaughtered, after which more conservative forces progressively took command. Later, when Martin Luther King cried "Free at last!" before Lincoln's temple, the words echoed with splendors and ironies they could not have possessed in any other setting. In the massive demonstrations against Vietnam, a half-million people formed a base for the Washington Monument, so that it leaped out of a sea of humanity toward the sun.

All of this is mythic enough, as Washington is mythic, and feeds the incorrigible desire that all historians share, to bring the past to life in some newly effective way, so that fate may be hoodwinked in the future and the fatality which we know lies upon human institutions may, for the first time in history, finally be set aside.

NOTES

[1] "Vernacular" has proved so successful and durable a word that I cannot confine its application to the architecture of abject poverty as my colleague J. B. Jackson would apparently have us do.

[2] This situation has changed recently as the oil business has faltered.

THE OBJECT:
DECORATIVE AND INDUSTRIAL ARTS

INTRODUCTION

by Mildred Friedman

The object is our topic, our beginning today. Defined as an aspect of the decorative and industrial arts, it is certainly both an open-ended and ambiguous one. The question of when an object is art is similar to that of when a building is architecture. When we talk about objects do we mean that they are enduring or ephemeral, designed or found, custom-made or ready-made? Dada provided a most profoundly cynical definition of the object as art in Marcel Duchamp's explanation of his famous ready-mades as common objects raised to the level of art through the process of appropriation. He demonstrated his thesis by selecting, among other things, a bicycle wheel, a wine rack, and, as his first American ready-made, a snow shovel, to which he gave the ominous title *In Advance of the Broken Arm*. Asked how he made these apparently banal selections, Duchamp replied, "The choice of ready-mades was never dictated by an aesthetic delectation. Such choice was always based on a reaction of visual indifference, and at the same time on a total absence of good or bad taste.... When all is said and done a complete anesthesia."

We are here now not to select or design, but to examine the object within the larger context of architecture. For it is not the isolated object but the sensibility with which objects are brought together that creates an environment and a quality or spirit appropriate to an architectural idea. Yet if it is possible to see the universe in a drop of water, it may be possible, at the very least, to increase our awareness of building and place through an initial search for meaning in the more portable elements of the designed environment. Whether a hand-finished, one-of-a-kind folding screen by Eileen Gray, or an anonymous, industrially produced borax chair, the isolated object can signify everything from individual expression to family history to cultural bias. Given that, we can go on to ask a question essential to the purpose of this symposium. What do we mean when we describe an object as distinctively American? In a relatively homogeneous society, Japan for example, one can trace cultural and social history by looking at artifacts over time. But America's heterogeneity has provided an aesthetic history with such a broad sweep that it is difficult to define what is or is not American. Vincent Scully has demonstrated this very clearly in the examples of American design he chose that have their derivation if not their form in European forerunners. It may, in fact, be this diffuse background that has created our need to search out an American tradition.

Therefore, in beginning this search, the Buell Center should look at similarities and differences between, for example, Heppelwhite and Shaker, Lalique and Tiffany, Aalto and Eames. It may be that only minor stylistic differences will emerge because, of course, a chair is a chair is a chair. If, on the other hand, it is possible to identify attitudes and forms indigenous to America—whether with respect to process or product, craft or industry—we will move a little closer to an understanding of ourselves.

To that end, three papers will be presented this morning. Edgar Kaufmann, jr., will discuss what he terms ". . . utterly neutral but familiar objects: pyramids." From these he believes we can learn something of the meaning of design. His contention is that the pyramid—like all objects—conveys different meanings to different observers because perception is essentially subjective. Consequently, visual communication is partial at best. Nonetheless, as a way to begin to understand the mutations of meanings, Mr. Kaufmann proposes that we investigate American design in the context of what he believes to be worldwide universal form.

Edgar Kaufmann, jr., is a member of the Board of Advisors to the Buell Center for the Study of American Architecture at Columbia and Adjunct Professor of the History of Architecture at Columbia University. He is a distinguished author and critic who was a director of industrial design at the Museum of Modern Art from 1940–1955, where he was responsible for that institutions's groundbreaking Good Design program. His provocative exhibition and book, *The Rise of an American Architecture*, place him at the center of today's discussion.

Our second speaker, David Handlin, has chosen to focus on tradition, and obligingly, Arthur Pulos, our third speaker, will concern himself primarily with innovation. Handlin traces the European literary tradition of the object from Molière through Robbe-Grillet and Barthes. He finds no comparable tradition in American letters, as he believes Americans are untroubled by philosophical design issues. We are, he insists, united in a quest for material plenty, as reflected in the trade fairs and expositions of our early history followed by today's department stores and mail-order catalogues. Yet beneath the surface of consumerism Handlin sees two American experiences as pivotal: transplantation from the Old to the New World and change from home craft to factory production. These themes come together for him in Frank Lloyd Wright's essay "The Art and Craft of the Machine."

David Handlin is Associate Professor of Architecture in the Harvard Graduate School of Design and the author of *The American Home: Architecture and Society from 1915 to 1950*. He practiced architecture in Italy and England, where he was a lecturer in the Department of Architecture at the University of Cambridge from 1973–1978.

He is currently teaching and practicing architecture in Cambridge, Massachusetts.

While David Handlin looks at tradition, Arthur Pulos chooses to emphasize the significance of technological innovation in understanding objects in American architecture. In fact, he sees innovation in vernacular objects as defining the American tradition. Arthur Pulos urges us, instead of looking elsewhere for cultural guidance, to examine the things of our daily lives. He views manufactured objects as a true American expression: democratic, humble, unpretentious. They are the purest manifestation of the machine and the model for what he terms the "contrived minimalism" of modern decorative art. Pulos maintains that Americans prefer the useful to the beautiful and that the essential forms of objects are tied to their performance.

Arthur Pulos is Chairman Emeritus of the Department of Design at Syracuse University and President of Pulos Design Associates. He is the author of, among many writings, a new history of industrial design in America, *The American Design Ethic*.

THE OBJECT AS ELUSION

by Edgar Kaufmann, jr.

The key words of this symposium, as contained in its title, are *place, architecture,* and *object,* and innovation and tradition. When I first heard these commonplace words, I felt uneasy. To clear my thoughts I decided to consider a real, familiar, but remote example. What might help in understanding it? Could it lead to a fresh understanding of American design?

Objects have meaning only according to how they are seen, through the senses and through the particular "mental set" of the observer/user. To study American objects as something other than sociological evidence requires applied research, for useful guidelines are not available. Thus I proposed to conduct a sketchy research about *pyramids*. From this research I hoped to learn some crude, salient facts about the meaning of design and products, and the mutations of such meaning. This knowledge then might serve to guide research into American objects—decorative, industrial, elitist, or vernacular. My proposal was criticized because the exemplary object, a pyramid, was not American.

What remarkable ignorance of historic relationships and of the history of styles! Most Americans pay some attention to that paltry object, the one-dollar bill. On it one sees the Great Seal of the United States, featuring a three-dimensionally depicted pyramid crowned by the all-seeing eye of the Deity. The seal was adopted after careful debate even before a peace with Britain was settled in mid-1782. The pyramid has been a central symbol of American life for two centuries.

Let me consider the pyramid of Khufu at al Jizah. What is this pyramid—a place marker, a work of architecture, an object? Its form probably began with a great heap of sand over the subterranean tomb of a king. Then came the mastaba, a shelter for repeated rituals. In order that the king's Ka might communicate with the gods above, one mastaba was raised over another, stepwise. Finally the whole was enveloped smoothly in polished ashlar in a form much like the original sand heap.

What did the form mean? To the builders, it was the Ka's home; to the tomb robbers, who promptly arrived, a treasure trove; to Alexander, one of the regalia of empire; to the Christian eremites, an abomination; to the Moslems, a quarry; and then it was nothing.

With the fifteenth-century revival of Classicism the pyramids took on importance once again; they were acclaimed as one of the few remaining wonders of the ancient world, embodiments of eternity. Then came Napoleon, aping Alexander. Today, what does the Great Pyramid mean to the university students, the film stars, the souvenir vendors with their inkwells and paperweights at al Jizah? Each one has seen something different.

This brief history lesson demonstrates that it is not enough to say that what is seen is a product of the ability to see. It is equally affected by what one wants to see, expects to see. Does that mean that perception is so subjective that there can be no visual communication? Clearly not, but visual communication must be recognized as partial at best.

I have veered far away from American design, but I believe that one might posit here that it is useful to have some idea of what lies at the core of the perception of objects, of the history of their perception. One might think of the object as a pearl, a grain of sand around which are deposited layers of iridescence forming an ever-growing structure with new qualities, new depth.

If such notions hold up under testing, the study of American design might proceed along ways as yet untrodden, and categories like place, architecture, and object might have another importance than they do now. The duality of innovation and tradition might vanish. I hope that the Buell Center will be liberal enough to try out new approaches as well as accepted ones in the study of American design, and to conceive of American design as one significant aspect of a vaster experience. In fact, it is only in the context of worldwide design and architecture that the characteristic vitality and poetry of American work can be fully appreciated.

BETWEEN SUBJECT AND OBJECT

by David P. Handlin

The history of objects is virtually the history of the world. It encompasses household industries and high technology. It includes the processes of production, distribution, and consumption. It takes place in the home, workshop, factory, warehouse, marketplace, world exposition, department store, shopping mall, and museum. It involves craftsman, artist, housewife, worker, entrepreneur, and bureaucrat. It can be written about from many points of view and ideological perspectives. One need only think of the meaning of "craft," "machine," "market," "commodity," "consumer," or "bourgeoisie" to understand that objects are not detached; they are inextricably engaged with vital and often antagonistic issues.

The history of objects can and should be discussed in these terms and indeed there is a substantial literature in which this has been attempted. But the danger in connecting objects to processes, places, and people is that the focus will be diverted from the objects themselves. In that event something fundamental will be missed, because the history of objects also has to illuminate those moments when all of our preknowledge, predispositions, and prejudices evaporate, as we are engulfed in the aura that at times appears to surround and pervade them. In these rare but revealing instances, as the ordinary becomes extraordinary and the physical resonates with the metaphysical, objects bring us into contact with irreducible truths.

Like works of art, objects can touch our deepest thoughts and feelings. But the quality that distinguishes objects from works of art (at least as they are conventionally defined) is the very ordinariness that is part of their usefulness. The object's seemingly unprepossessing nature, its commonness, can render all the more dramatic and powerful the revelation of its transcendent message. Hence, the role of the "found object" in recent art movements. Equally, it was this special capacity of the ordinary that Ralph Waldo Emerson had in mind when he wrote in "The American Scholar": "I embrace the common, I explore and sit at the feet of the familiar, the low."[1]

The experiences that can result from such encounters are too profound to ignore, but since the relationship between subject and object can be so direct and intimate, it is tempting to say that it touches upon or springs from something either highly personal or universal and simply leave it at that. Certainly responses of this kind can be understood as such, but it should also be possible to describe them in more specific terms. There are many ways of doing so, but given that objects have been made and used in America, at some point it is necessary to ask whether the sensations, emotions, associations, impressions, and ideas that are elicited from and projected onto objects can be discussed in terms of an American experience.

Anyone attempting to do so will initially encounter one puzzling condition: Americans have rarely commented about objects in such terms. Indeed the analysis of the culture in general has usually been made within certain restricted boundaries. Europeans have frequently noted this fact, given explanations for it, and sometimes even seized upon it as a point of envy. For example, Goethe once wrote, "America, you are better off than our old nations. You have no ruined castles and rock formations. Your soul and mind are untroubled, and in modern times they are not stirred by vain and useless memories and by idle strife."[2] In effect, the tacit argument has been that the brief history of the United States has run an essentially smooth course; hence there has been no need to indulge in any deep soul-searching. Consequently, what William Dean Howells described as the "smiling aspects" of American life have commanded the most scholarly and critical attention. The history of objects has thus been dominated by an art-historical perspective that has emphasized connoisseurship and stylistic categorization, or by accounts of the activities and inventions of a sequence of Poor Richard—Benjamin Franklin figures—tinkerers, inventors, and entrepreneurs who made ingenious devices, especially those that save time and labor and thereby further the pursuit of material progress.[3]

These studies have been useful and illuminating, but they constitute only a partial history. There is another side to the story, one that may in part be darker, but is certainly deeper and more complex. What emerges from this other interpretation is that speculation about objects may have been more a forbidden than a neglected or uninteresting subject. In effect, Americans may have been reluctant to talk about the complex web of thoughts and feelings that surrounds objects not because there was nothing remarkable or unusual about which to comment but instead because this subject touches upon experiences that are so fundamental, so profound, and so poignant as to be virtually unmentionable.

Of these experiences two have been pivotal. Both have to do with the transition from the Old World to the new one. The first experience is transplantation. Objects have always been integral to the process of immigration because even before the voyage started decisions had to be made about what was to be taken and what was to be left behind. If Salzbergers of the eighteenth century or Russian Jews of 1900 could bring to the New World only what

Salzburgische Emigranten.

Nichts als das Evangelium
Vertreibt uns ins Exilium.
Verlaßen wir das Vaterland,
So sind wir doch in Gottes Hand.

1 *The Salzbergers on their way to the New World, 1732.*

they could carry on their backs, they had to sift out their possessions and subject them to an unaccustomed scrutiny (fig. 1). This process called into question established and unchallenged assumptions about the value of objects and hence about the nature of an established order. At the same time, it made the immigrants reflect upon their own condition—upon their past, their aspirations for the future, and the complex reasons why they were about to make this momentous journey. Inevitably objects became symbols of, and all but synonymous with, these highly charged thoughts and feelings.

Each unanticipated experience in the new world again called into question assumptions about the value of objects and, by extension, about the position and potential of a person in the larger order. When a plow that had coped with the English soil had to be discarded or changed to cope with the American terrain, it became not just a plow, but a witness to, a symbol of, much more far-reaching processes.

2 *LaSalle at the source of the Mississippi.*

This kind of revaluation was not only initiated by changes in the operational capacities of objects. Iconographic characteristics could also be altered or called into question by the change in context. The French coat of arms that LaSalle left at the mouth of the Mississippi is a case in point (fig. 2). That coat of arms traveled thousands of miles from France in order to give Louis XIV title to what was described as a "stupendous accession from the fertile plains of Texas to the bare peaks of the Rocky Mountains." But it was only after making this extraordinarily difficult journey and planting the coat of arms that La Salle, at least according to Francis Parkman, suddenly understood that the stupendous accession was established only by virtue of "a feeble human voice, inaudible at half a mile." Divorced by thousands of miles from its place of origin, the coat of arms had not simply lost its power to communicate: placed as it was in a seemingly endless wilderness, LaSalle also had to come to terms with the fact that there was virtually no one there to receive its message.[4]

Such conditions were not encountered only in the seventeenth and eighteenth centuries, and transplantation did not take place only from the Old World to the new. In settling their continent Americans have been highly mobile, and at the beginning of the nineteenth century the complex range of experiences and emotions that was produced by transplantation was further extended by a second pivotal experience, the transition from what one commentator called the "Age of Homespun" to the "Day of Roads," from an economy of scarcity to one of abundance, from a traditional to a modern society.[5] As the factory replaced the household as the primary source of production, the nature of objects changed, but equally important, the relationship of people to those objects also changed, as did their sense of themselves (fig. 3).

We can gain some sense of the response to this change in one of the rare acknowledgments of it, a story by Harriet Beecher Stowe entitled "The Ravages of a Carpet." Ostensibly this is a simple tale about how a family replaced a tattered old hand-made carpet with a new factory-produced, store-bought one. On the surface this was a happy, self-contained event. But as soon as the decision was made, doubts arose. Some of them arose because of residual ideas about frugality and waste, which seemed at odds with the very notion of discarding anything, no matter how dilapidated or outdated. But the more important reservations had to do with the sense that, no matter how threadbare it was, the old carpet was virtually a part of the family in a way that no machine-made, mass-produced carpet would ever be. In the eighteenth century the carpet had been either a treasured family possession or an unquestioned part of the family background (fig. 4). In the nineteenth century, when carpets were made by large companies and large machines, the age-old position of this venerable object was called into question.

4 Portrait of Isaac Royall and Family
Robert Feke, 1741.

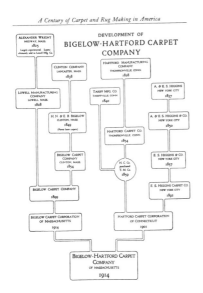

Above, left:
5 *The Development of the Bigelow-Hartford Carpet Company.*

Above, right:
6 *Axminster broad loom.*

In Stowe's story the initial doubts grew when unanticipated consequences of the purchase emerged. Once the new carpet took its place in the living room, the rest of the furniture began to look shabby, and soon there was subtle pressure to replace it. Even more consequential was the effect that the carpet had on social relationships. To make room for it, the arrangement of the living room had to change. The members of the family consequently had to change their behavior toward each other, and also toward their friends, some of whom no longer felt they could drop in as they had done before. The use of the word ravages in the title was, therefore, not inappropriate; Stowe understood that the carpet symbolized and in its perhaps small way participated in the family's passage from a traditional to a modern world—a process filled with both opportunities and pitfalls, but certainly involving far more drama than is usually expressed in simple words about progress (figs. 5, 6).[6]

While there seems to have been little direct comment about these experiences, the objects that were so intertwined with them could not help but bear their imprint. Some have done so more clearly than others. Most are only denotative of a direct and specific issue. Others, however, have an especial fascination because they have more connotative meanings. Such objects have been produced in every period of American history, but the themes suggested above can perhaps best be exemplified by a few objects that were made between 1900 and 1914. Contemporaries thought this period unique because it marked a transition between the past of the nineteenth century and the unpredictable future of the twentieth. Our perspective is, of course, different, but we may still find this period, and its products, of great interest because of its transitional nature. The turn of the century occupies a special position because it is neither part of a remote past nor decisively of our own era.

7 *Tiffany Studios window glass shop, 1913.*

8 *Tiffany glass vase, 1897.*

9 *Title page of* Box Furniture. *Louise Brigham, 1909.*

The glasswork of Louis Comfort Tiffany is one good example (fig. 7). In terms of the experiences described above, the most fascinating pieces are not those produced for specific clients and commissions, but instead those made for a general market, almost on a mass-produced basis, in Tiffany's enormous workshop. Almost thirty years ago Edgar Kaufmann wrote about the significance of Tiffany's attempts at mass production. In these objects Tiffany had to accentuate qualities that were inherent in his more specialized work, but which perhaps the very specificity of that work prevented him from developing. Because they had to be produced quickly, they had decorative patterns that were characterized by an elusive, almost random quality, which accentuated an inherent uncertainty about whether what was being suggested was a growing form or one encrusted with age (fig. 8). Were these abstract patterns, or was it possible to read through and into them the amalgamation of decorative motifs from the Orient, Byzantium, Rome, and American Indian sources? By the same token, were these glass objects clear or opaque? Did they belong to the world of the hand-made or to that of the mass-produced? Tiffany developed techniques that suggestively raised but did not definitively answer these questions.[7]

Louise Brigham's furniture achieved the same result (fig. 9). At one level the task she set herself was to find a way that the poor of American cities could build well-designed and serviceable furniture for themselves. In doing so Brigham was not motivated by sentimental beliefs about the value of handwork. An associate of Jacob Riis, she had lived for many years in one of New York City's settlement houses, and she well understood that there were still large segments of America's working population who could not afford anything from a store. What she proposed in a book called *Box Furniture* and also in a program to teach the principles of box furniture in New York City's public schools was a method by which people could make furniture out of used packing crates (fig.

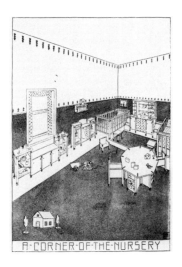

13 *"Interior Decoration"*
supplement to Modern Art
Collector, *1915.*

14 *Interior of Frank Lloyd*
Wright studio
Oak Park, Illinois, 1906.

10). In effect, Brigham seized upon one of the central characteristics of modern production—the apparent necessity of ephemerality, disposability, and obsolescence—and she made this the subject of her designs.[8]

Yet it is not simply the inversion—of that which should contain the furniture becoming the furniture—that gives what Louise Brigham proposed its distinctive properties. Study in Europe with Charles Rennie Mackintosh and Josef Hoffmann had introduced her to a language of form that helped her to give expression to her undertaking. Brigham and several other designers such as Edward Aschermann, who had also been a pupil of Hoffmann, attempted to put these ideas into a broader context. In articles in a pioneering magazine, the *Modern Art Collector,* they tried to define what one designer, Beatrice Irwin, called, in her book of the same title, "the new science of color" (fig. 11). They believed that disparate sources of ornament and imagery could be unified and vitalized by a new approach to design that emphasized bold colors (fig. 12). In doing so they were looking for a language of form suitable for a mass audience, especially one that was composed of people from diverse ethnic origins. At the same time they saw no conflict in applying these principles to special commissions. The new science of color was as appropriate for the dining room of the well-to-do as for a room in a Lower East Side tenement. It could also give energy to the advertisements that announced the products of modern industry (fig. 13).[9]

The themes of representation and abstraction, the permanent and the ephemeral, a respect for ancestral traditions and a faith in the new, the inert and the organic, and the capabilities of craft and machine are all best summarized in the furniture designs and decorative works of Frank Lloyd Wright. His chairs still seem strikingly original, but at the same time they almost appear to embody the skeletal remains of ancient ancestors (fig. 14). His lighting fix-

tures are integral to an architecture of masonry and wood, and yet they also illuminate and give expression to a new world of electricity (fig. 15). Indeed, in considering the range of decorative sources upon which Wright drew and the way he manipulated and amalgamated them, it is difficult not to conclude that Wright synthesized for his clients, and hence for all Americans, this momentous transition from an old world to a new one.[10]

If we examine any aspect of Wright's prodigious output, it is possible to understand something about how he produced work that was both his own and a response to the broad culture of architecture and design. Many aspects of Wright's achievement remain elusive, but one hint may be found in his own essay, "The Art and Craft of the Machine," in which, unlike most other designers of the period, Wright outlined an approach to the decorative and industrial arts that could partake of the best of both the craft tradition and the capabilities of modern machines, while still being true to the ideals of art.

"The Art and Craft of the Machine" is justifiably famous, but equally suggestive is a line Wright wrote in his article "In the Cause of Architecture" of 1908. In that essay he said that in formulating the principles that had guided his work, the question uppermost in his mind had been "not 'what style,' but 'what is style?' "[11] If the members and associates of the Buell Center for the Study of American Architecture also keep this question uppermost in their minds—if they forthrightly ask "not 'what style,' but 'what is style?' " and try to understand the depths of experience embodied in style—then there is every reason to be confident that they will begin to illuminate the heretofore obscure nature of American objects.

NOTES

[1] Ralph Waldo Emerson, "The American Scholar," in *Nature, Addresses, and Lectures* (Boston, 1883), p. 110. This concept of the common or ordinary has a long lineage, aspects of which are discussed in Lionel Trilling, *Sincerity and Authenticity* (Cambridge, Mass.: Harvard University Press, 1973), pp. 90–95.

[2] Quoted and translated in Samuel Bing, *Artistic America* (Cambridge, Mass.: MIT Press, 1970), p. 186.

[3] Kenneth S. Lynn, *William Dean Howells: An American Life* (New York: Harcourt, 1971), p. 3. The history of the collecting of objects, both by individuals and by museums, is a fascinating subject that has not been treated in a sustained manner. Nor has another intriguing topic, the relationship of scholarship to the activities of the antiques trade. Sigfried Giedion's *Mechanization Takes Command* (New York, 1948) is still the work that best chronicles and celebrates the American propensity for invention.

[4] Francis Parkman, *LaSalle and the Discovery of the Great West* (Boston: Little Brown, 1897), vol. 2, pp. 50–52.

[5] Two of Horace Bushnell's most illuminating speeches were titled the "Age of Homespun" and the "Day of Roads." They are published in *Work and Play* (London, 1864), pp. 39–76 and 78–115. Many economists have discussed the distinction between, and attendant anomalies of, scarcity and abundance. Simon Patten was one of the earliest and most eloquent American economists to do so. See Simon Nelson Patten, *The New Basis of Civilization* (New York: Macmillan, 1907); Daniel M. Fox, *Simon N. Patten and the Transformation of Social Theory* (Ithaca, N.Y.: Cornell University Press, 1967).

[6] Harriet Beecher Stowe, "House and Home Papers," *Atlantic Monthly*, vol. 13 (1864), pp. 40–47.

[7] Edgar Kaufmann, jr., "Tiffany, Then and Now," *Interiors*, vol. 14 (1955), pp. 82–85.

[8] Louise Brigham, *Box Furniture* (New York: Century, 1909).

[9] The *Modern Art Collector* was published between 1915 and 1917. Beatrice Irwin, *The New Science of Color* (San Francisco: Union Lithograph, 1915); *The Pagan Trinity* (London: John Lane, 1912).

[10] Wright's decorative works are discussed in David A. Hanks, *The Decorative Designs of Frank Lloyd Wright* (New York: Dutton, 1979). "The Art and Craft of the Machine," is in Edgar Kaufmann and Ben Raeburn, eds., *Frank Lloyd Wright: Writings and Buildings* (New York: Horizon, 1960), pp. 55–73.

[11] Frank Lloyd Wright, "In the Cause of Architecture," *Architectural Record*, vol. 23 (1908), p. 58.

THE OBJECT:
A SEARCH FOR FORM

by Arthur Pulos

> "For a while, it seems to me, our near solution will lie
> in the steady pursuit of the vernacular."
> *Lewis Mumford, 1926*

In this paper I take the position that innovation in design is closely tied to technology and that modern technology must be democratic and serve everyone in order to justify its cost. Technological form tends to be "innocent" because the tools of design and manufacture demand directness of method and material. In fact, the naïvete of technological form, which is most often characteristic of vernacular objects, has arguably provided the base upon which American culture has been building for more than two centuries. By this line of reasoning, innovation in vernacular objects may be the American tradition.

A more conventional concept of tradition claims that Americans are culturally impotent, doomed forever to look to the past or elsewhere for aesthetic inspiration. According to this line of thought, tradition operates within carefully defined formalist limits, established by scholars with examples taken from the cultural vaults of museums. It is also possible that a more dynamic kind of tradition exists, one which like nature's own force—homeostasis—is ever changing to maintain a viable equilibrium with its environment. Nothing threatens cultural life so much as the assumption that it is passive. If culture encompasses all of the arts of life, it is the dynamism of change that allows it to breathe and be vital.

Americans who have looked elsewhere for cultural guidance for many years will perhaps find it difficult to admit that their own culture may be vested in the vernacular objects that serve their daily lives—in what Vincent Scully has called "the dignity of the vernacular tradition." It is possible that the commitment of the vernacular to maximum utility with a minimum of investment of material and energy has produced forms that constitute a true folk base for American expression. Horace Greeley recognized that "we have democratized the means and the appliances of a higher life ... we have brought and are bringing more and more the masses of the people up to the aristocratic standards of taste and enjoyment and so diffusing the influence of splendor and grace over all minds."[1] The roots of American tradition may thus reside in the discovered arts of survival rather than the borrowed arts of luxury.

Designers are aware that objects are in a constant state of evolution, driven forward to perfection by the inexorable advance of technology, changing social patterns, and personal aspirations for a better life. They recognize that technology, as evident in energy systems, in systems for nutrition, shelter, transportation, communication, and entertainment, depends upon all classes for support, and thus, everyone has equal access to its benefits.

It is very much in the nature of the vernacular manufactured object that it should be humble rather than pretentious, for it serves as only one element in a larger service system. In this context, it is set apart from objects that are created as art forms—as ends in themselves—as well as from other products that may have had their origins in utility but have been transformed into art objects to be admired for their formal qualities but never disgraced by use. The latter tend to be endowed with the name of their creator and enshrined as cultural artifacts, sometimes serving as metaphors of the vernacular.

The vernacular product, however, continues to fulfill its purpose in a modest way, balancing economy of means against human needs and expectations. George Wallis, who was sent from England to report on manufacturers in the American Crystal Palace Exhibition in 1853, wrote that the American consumer typically expected a manufactured article to last for only a short time and was therefore reluctant to pay a premium for either quality or durability. The taste for short-lived articles, he reported, "is said to run through every class of society and has, of course, a great influence upon the character of goods generally in demand ..."[2] This bias in favor of a short life-expectancy in products stimulates rapid changes in fashion and is highly receptive to the introduction of newer manufacturing techniques.

1 Faucet set
George Sakier, 1933.
Designed for the American Standard Company, Sakier's faucet set has been called the best of the functional modern, despite Sakier's conviction that function follows form.

It does not necessarily follow, however, that a more rapid turnover of products is synonymous with lower quality. Rather, industry is challenged to maintain product quality at the same time as it uses materials and energy more efficiently. Manufactured objects constantly seek the simplest and most unassuming level that is acceptable to the consumer. It is in this sense that the vernacular object is often taken as the purest expression of the machine and becomes a model for the contrived humility and self-conscious minimalism of modern decorative and industrial arts.

There is an inescapable correlation between the tools of the designer and the machines of manufacture (fig. 1). His straight edge and compass find their surrogates in the milling machines, shapers, and lathes that have for years been at the heart of the tool-making industries. The geometric action of such tools and machines determines the form of not only the final product but also the basic materials upon which production depends. Planar and linear ma-

2 *Furniture for D. D. Martin House*
Buffalo, New York
Frank Lloyd Wright, 1908.
The vertical lines were in direct contradiction to Wright's avowed commitment to the horizontal. The furniture is mechanical in character and as uncomfortable visually as it must have been in fact.

3 *Ice water pitcher*
Reed and Barton Company, 1876.
This silver-plated pitcher was commended at the Centennial Exhibition for being just as beautiful as its solid silver equivalent, its lower cost making it more favorable than the plated ware.

4 *Automatic piano*
Pierre Legrain for Auto-Pleyeia, ca. 1925.
Although not considered outstanding in its time, this automatic piano was a valid attempt to turn a functional product into a piece of abstract technological sculpture.

terials derive their form from rolling mills, brakes, shears, extruders, and drawing machines, all of which operate geometrically. Even if the final object is to be produced from a liquid or viscous material, the molds and forms in which the casting is done are normally produced by machines that act geometrically.

Every architectural student is familiar with Frank Lloyd Wright's observation, "From the very beginning my T square and triangle were easy machines of expression for my geometric sense of things."[3] The same rather naïve empathy for tools as a source for form was behind machine-age styles in products and architecture. Even so, Wright was aware that formalist geometry was not necessarily charitable to the human body. "I have been black and blue in some spot, somewhere," he writes, "almost all my life from too intimate contact with my own furniture" (fig. 2).[4]

Thus it was relatively easy in the past to conclude that Platonic forms were the natural expression of the machine age. The fact that the shapes that resulted were devoid of human qualities notwithstanding, early machine-age technology, with its commitment to geometric tools, machines, and materials certainly dictated the form and therefore the aesthetic expression of the result. It is interesting to note that a century ago machines were being used to make products that would give the appearance of having been made by hand (fig. 3). Half a century later the craft shops of the Bauhaus and the artisans of Paris were using hand methods to make products that pretended to have been made by machines (fig. 4). Today, while many manufactured products have moved on to the next level of technology, buildings are still being made by handicraft methods. In this context, a building constructed from so-called modern materials—concrete, steel, and glass—is not much different from an earlier one built of wood, stone, and brick.

The principles of standardization and interchangeability at the heart of the American system of manufacturing separated workman from manager. The ensuing depersonalization of worker and product further supported geometricity. In buildings, the modular systems which developed promised infinite variation in form. However, this resulted in a Gordian knot of specialized occupations, each cloaked with layers of defensive trade, industry, and government controls. Thus any system that served originally as an inspired methodology in the forefront of technology became less flexible in time and slowly slipped back, deterring progress in the very area that it served so brilliantly in the beginning (fig. 5).[5] It was Henry-Russell Hitchcock who warned that standardization tended to hold progress back.

It is possible that today, with access to computer-driven tools of design and manufacture, dependence upon Euclidean geometry may no longer be necessary. Products and buildings seem to be

5 *Balloon framing*
Designed by George W. Snow,
ca. 1835.
The balloon frame, so-called be-
cause of the lightness of the struc-
ture, was conceived as a method
of prefabrication to take advan-
tage of standardized lumber sizes,
manufactured nails, and unskilled
labor. After a century and a half
it continues to dominate the build-
ing of private houses in the
United States, despite the expec-
tation of mass-produced homes.

6 *"Dollar" pocket watch*
American Watch Company,
ca. 1880.
The dollar pocket watch became a
typeform for the product as well
as a leading example of an
American product that was ma-
chine-made from inexpensive
products, yet equal in functional
quality to the vastly more expen-
sive foreign competition's
products.

entering a realm of innovative forms that may be expected to be tuned more closely to human needs. Designers may also be able to escape the security and trap of three-dimensional model-making that has produced so much "foam-core" architecture, reminiscent of M. W. Baldwin's locomotives that were in reality enlarged versions of the jeweler's models made for his clients.

There is a design ethic in the United States according to which problems of survival solved by the most direct means are believed to result in forms that are beautiful as well as functional. From Benjamin Franklin's "nothing is good or beautiful but in the measure that it is useful"[6] to Tocqueville's observation that "Americans will habitually prefer the useful to the beautiful, and they will require that the beautiful shall be useful,"[7] the presumption has been that aesthetic value is to be measured by the degree to which a product approaches the perfection of its species. Parenthetically, it was Franklin who brought fire out of the fireplace and made it a portable domestic appliance—property of the tenant rather than the dwelling.

In 1869, James Jackson Jarves recognized that objects for mass manufacture would have to observe rules of economy in labor and materials and strive for efficiency and dependability of service. This would result in a machine aesthetic distinct from that of industrial arts and handicraft products. He doubted that a manufactured object should be given a cloak of aesthetic respectability with stylistic mannerisms. He did not doubt, however, that "the American, while adhering to his utilitarian and economical principles has, unwittingly . . . developed a degree of beauty in [objects] that no other nation equals."[8] Thus humble vernacular utilitarian objects devoid of applied decoration and borrowed style were being manufactured long before they were discovered by artists and architects and elevated to the exalted status of a machine style (fig. 6). In Europe the style emerged as a functionalist dogma and had overtones of socialism. In the United States, when the movement was brought back home, it was sterilized of political content and emerged as the "pure" formalism of the International Style. Objects and buildings became further dehumanized and served in the end as monuments to themselves. Today selected historical examples, mostly in the area of furniture and accessories, are being treasured for their unique expression at the same time as their uniqueness is being violated by reproduction for profit.

In other areas where one dared to champion more advanced technologies, products and even buildings often donned a more familiar costume of style in order to allay public suspicion. Beneath this masquerade one could glimpse the basic innocence of the utilitarian form and sense the fact that it would one day achieve its own typeform. The automobile in the guise of a carriage, the kitchen range as a Baroque altar, the cash register as a Renaissance treasure

DESIGN.

No. 35,932.   Patented June 3, 1902.

T. R. KENNEDY & E. J. KING.
STOVE OR RANGE.

7 *Kitchen range*
Thomas Kennedy and Edward
King, 1902.
The cast-iron products of Ken-
nedy and King show a rhythmic
consistency that is suited to the
structural requirements of cast-
iron stoves.

8 *Wisteria lamp*
Tiffany and Company, ca. 1900.
Made for Mrs. Curtis Freshel ac-
cording to her original design, this
is probably the best of the Tif-
fany lamps. It captures a certain
naturalism without compromising
the more romantic tendencies of
Art Nouveau.

9 Clarkesville Diner
John Baeder, 1978.
The painting depicts the station-
ary diner, a logical extension
from dining on a moving train
to dining at a fixed site.

10 *Outdoor religious shrine, 1983.*
This example illustrates an adap-
tive use of a bathtub.

box, and even the lamp as a glass garden—no matter how attractive their decoration—sooner or later either shed their past for a unique typeform or, as with many lighting fixtures and appliances, have disappeared into the architecture (figs. 7, 8).

Furthermore, today, in a curious functional and aesthetic crossover, it is believed to be innovative as well as profitable to adapt objects and buildings that have outlived their original purpose to other interesting, and not always illogical, uses. Abandoned churches are secularized as artists' studios and design and architectural offices; schools are renovated into condominiums; gasoline stations are reclaimed as beauty parlors and grocery stores; ocean liners become hotels; street cars are salvaged as diners and cabooses as bars; airplanes, tractors, and locomotives serve as playground equipment; bathtubs are elevated to lawn shrines while truck tires contain flower beds—all in a wave of contemporary nostalgia driven by the wind of expediency (figs. 9, 10). One may draw an interesting parallel between this practice characteristic of developed countries with that of developing countries, where tires become sandals, butter cans become stoves, and oil drums fill the air with music.

One may also presume that it is in the name of blending innovation and tradition that a certain new building in Manhattan provides a grand Roman arch for the faithful at its feet at the same time as it sports the broken-cross pediment of a highboy as a hat; while nearby another building suggests that its sloping roof accepts the advantages of solar energy at the same time as its feet straddle a clutch of old world restaurants.

11 Empire State Building,
New York
Shreve, Lamb and Harmon
Architects, 1930–1931.
The additive massing of the Empire State Building established
a typeform for the American
skyscraper that has not been
equaled by any other building.

12 Scale
Joseph Sinel, 1930.
This scale was designed in the
skyscraper style for the International Ticket Sales Corporation.
Sinel recalls, ". . . I made a
model from a Del Monte fruit
case [and took it] to show the ex-
ecutives of the company and they
immediately okayed it and paid
me a fee of $10,000 and royalties
for twenty-five years."

13 TV house cartoon
W. Mack, 1983.
The cartoon caption, "You tell
them to go away. You built this
ridiculous house," calls attention
to the cross-fertilization of form.

14 Alcoa Building
Pittsburgh, Pennsylvania
Harrison and Abramowitz,
Architects, 1952.
Note the stamped curtain wall
sections. Technological and
functional needs result in the TV
shape as the logical form.

15 IBM Selectric typewriter, 1970.
The use of the TV shape in three
dimensions seems to humanize the
form of the typewriter. It is also
a logical choice for the die-casting
process.

Buildings and manufactured objects have had a close but cautious association over the years. The decorative and industrial arts have been for the most part under the control of architects who see them essentially as extensions of their own obligation to recommend furnishings that enhance the character of their buildings. However, mass-produced products have tended to follow an independent course of development under the direction of engineers abetted by the young profession of industrial design. Such products have en-joyed a contrapuntal relationship with architecture. *The Bremen* and other great ocean liners of the early years of this century, with their porthole windows, horizontal pipe railings, and white rounded surfaces, certainly influenced the forms of German and French mod-ernism and its American echo, the International Style. The ominous economic realities of the early thirties were challenged by the soar-ing optimism of the neo-Gothic Chrysler Building, the Art Deco classicism of Radio City, and the sheer scale of the setback volume of the Empire State Building (fig. 11). These buildings and others like them, enhanced by Hugh Ferriss' renderings of dreamy castles in the air, became symbols of hope, and for a time their skyscraper style was emulated by manufactured products, from scales and gasoline pumps to furniture and even packaging (fig. 12). Today, in a reprise of this monumental theme, the skyscraper is once again raising its unique finger to the sky, complete with the dramatic lighting evoked in the hazy renderings of the 1930s. In reprisal the unique shape of the television screen has burned itself into the minds of designers and architects alike so deeply that it constantly emerges as the characteristic shape of fenestration (Arthur Drexler has written that the windows of the Alcoa building in Pittsburgh look "like several thousand television sets"), furniture, automobile grilles, wristwatches, typewriters, and countless other products (figs. 13–15).

16 *Douglas DC-3 aircraft, 1936.*
More than any other aircraft, the
Douglas DC-3 became the type-
form for 1930s airliners. It set the
form for aerodynamic design and
influenced many other products.

17 *Pencil sharpener*
Raymond Loewy, 1934.
Loewy's whimsical application of
the streamlined form to a pencil
sharpener was much criticized.

Below, left:
18 *Chrysler Airflow automobile,*
1934.
The Chrysler Airflow was the
first production automobile to be
designed according to aerodynamic
principles. It made a clean break
with earlier designs and estab-
lished an aesthetic base for the
Lincoln Zephyr and other cars.

Below, right:
19 *Locomotive train engine*
Raymond Loewy, 1938.
Loewy designed the streamlined
shell for the Pennsylvania Rail-
road's Engine 3768 after exten-
sive wind tunnel tests showed the
engine's wind resistance could
be lowered by one-third. The
locomotive was used to pull the
Broadway Limited for two
years, and was then put on dis-
play at the 1939 New York
World's Fair.

However, the vertical thrust of the skyscraper was not the machine age's only expression of the drama of dynamism and progress (fig. 16). As monocoque aircraft began to dominate the airways, their smooth shapes, real and imagined, began to dictate the form of other manufactured products. The decorative and industrial arts began to abandon their enriched surfaces for the smooth, clean shapes of the teardrop and its free-form variants (fig. 17). Steamships, locomotives, and automobiles hastened to adopt aerodynamic shells—in the style now referred to as "streamline moderne" (figs. 18, 19). In this they were simply following one of the fundamental laws of the design ethic by which a product nearing the end of its period in history will often take on the form of its successor in order to stave off oblivion. This same desperate behavior forced many handsome nineteenth-century buildings to wrap their lower stories with black glass and streamlines in the twenties and thirties. "Streamlines" became the distinguishing mark of the moment and for a time were applied more or less arbitrarily to buildings, interiors, and products (fig. 20). Thus, modern architecture emphasized the horizontal plane as a unique expression of the machine age. In the process the solid mass of traditional architecture was transformed into airy volumes defined by thin, floating planes of stucco or glass.

Since Sputnik, a new constructivism has been developing that combines a replay of the machine-age ship shapes of the 1920s with the hard geometry of space-age hardware. While high technology erects mammoth gantries as well as airy television towers and daring drilling platforms, a High-Tech style proves to be little more than its lowbrow echo.

In such ways technology continues to have an impact on buildings and objects. Things continue to convey symbolic meaning and aesthetic value to their users. The gold striping of the nineteenth century and the chrome bands of the early twentieth are in no ways different from the decorative graphics and streamers that enrich modern airliners and other products of man. They add nothing to operation and performance, but they are indispensable to the pride of their makers and the confidence of their users. Nevertheless, beneath these marks of communication, there remains the essential form of the vernacular object, our surest guide to innovation and tradition.

20 *Texaco gas station
Walter D. Teague, 1937.
Teague and his staff standardized
gasoline stations with three parallel lines as the main ornament.*

NOTES

[1] Horace Greeley, *Art and Industry as Represented in the Exhibition at the Crystal Palace* (New York: Redfield, 1853), p. 52.

[2] Nathan Rosenberg, *The American System of Manufacturing* (Edinburgh: Edinburgh University Press, 1969), p. 10.

[3] Frank Lloyd Wright, *An Autobiography* (New York: Horizon, 1977), p. 125.

[4] Ibid., p. 145.

[5] Arthur J. Pulos, *The American Design Ethic: A History of Industrial Design* (Cambridge, Mass.: MIT Press, 1983), p. 107.

[6] Constance M. Rourke, *The Roots of American Culture and Other Essays* (New York: Harcourt-Brace, 1942), p. 3.

[7] Alexis de Tocqueville, *Democracy in America* (New York: Schocken, 1961), vol. 2, p. 56.

[8] James Jackson Jarves, *Art Thoughts* (New York: Hurd and Houghton, 1869), p. 323.

RESPONSE

by Catherine Lynn

I share David Handlin's interest in the American home and a great enthusiasm for the quantity of wonderful material he has brought together in his book *The American Home*. However, when I read the paper he prepared for this conference, I began to wonder if we had been reading the literature of two different countries. According to Mr. Handlin, objects have always been all but omnipresent in American life. However, studies of the seventeenth- and early eighteenth-century American houses that other colleagues have been presenting and publishing during the past few years, especially those drawing on early inventories, reveal a surprising dearth of furnishings and useful objects in houses of all but the very rich. The scarcity of objects continues well into the eighteenth century.[1] Not only is that symbol of status and masculine authority, the chair, a rare item in many houses, but so is the basic cooking equipment that made variety in food preparation possible. Also missing from most houses are sets of individual dishes so that each might eat from his own plate.[2] The consumer revolution that took hold in America during the eighteenth century and transformed the character of everyday life for all but the poorest during the early nineteenth century seems even more dramatic in light of the fact that things had so recently been scarce. Largely for that reason, there was in this country, as in Europe, an outpouring of contemporary comment about "the broader meaning and significance of objects," to use Mr. Handlin's phrase.

Unlike Mr. Handlin, I find in America none of what he calls "reluctance to speculate about the complex web of thoughts and feelings that surrounds objects," but rather a rushing into print to explore those meanings. Like Emerson, many Americans felt that things were in the saddle. The initial reaction of many American descendants of the Puritans was to interpret those things as the vain seductions of a materialist world and to urge transcendence over and past them, to a world of God's nature and spirituality. The will to purge the world of objects is so essential to Thoreau's *Walden* and so familiar that I will only remind you of it. In another vein was the enthusiastic nineteenth-century response of Horatio Greenough to the simple forms of racing sulkies[3] and sailing ships, which were still being celebrated in the writings of John Kouwenhoven in 1948 and in the writings of many others who hailed the purified forms of an American vernacular.[4] I find in the literature of America, particularly mid-nineteenth-century America, that the symbolic and mythic valences of objects are central, especially in the novels of James Fenimore Cooper, Herman Melville, and Nathaniel Hawthorne. In a later generation, realistic novelists such as William Dean Howells and Henry James seem to be virtually consumed with an interest in interpreting and exploring the meaning of objects. And these are only a few of the best-known examples.

Less familiar in the recent writings about nineteenth-century America is Emerson's little essay of 1859 called "Domestic Life."[5] I cite it because during the later nineteenth and early twentieth centuries, Americans who wrote about furnishings so often referred to it, and also because Emerson provides a basis for the faith in the power of objects, indeed, of visual forms, not only to reflect, but also to influence human character. In "Domestic Life" Emerson asserts that "the secret power of form over the imagination and affection transcends all our philosophy. The first glance we meet may satisfy us that matter is the vehicle of a higher power than its own. And that no laws of line or surface can ever account for the inexhaustible expressiveness of form." Emerson goes on to encourage Americans to acquire objects, at the same time warning them against doing so. For the home, he advises, "whatever brings the dweller into a finer life, what educates his eye or ear or hand, whatever purifies and enlarges him may well find place there. And yet, let him not think that a property in beautiful objects is necessary to his apprehension of them, and seek to turn his house into a museum."

How may Americans tried to do just that—to turn their houses into museums? I'm sure that for many of you, as for me, pictures of late nineteenth-century rooms crowded with objects are familiar images which represent a failure to heed Emerson's warning. Looking at the pictures, I have been provoked to question what happened to the earlier puritanical fear of objects. I doubt that such a fear was simply overwhelmed by indulgence in "conspicuous consumption," to use the term coined by Thorstein Veblen in the 1890s. Veblen's ideas are certainly applicable and helpful to our understanding of those rooms, but it is too easy to apply his term, reduce them to nothing more than displays of conspicuous consumption, and dismiss them.

These rooms and the many objects in them have more to reveal. Americans, particularly in the 1870s and 1880s, took too seriously the English urge, derived from Pugin and Ruskin, to theorize about the meanings of objects and to read moral values into the forms of objects. When John Ruskin's lamp of truth was taken to heart in the nineteenth century, it seemed to shed a light on what had become a major activity of American women: house furnishing. It gave that activity moral value. Ruskin transformed aesthetic choices. He made them moral choices. He made it possible to see tables and chairs as potential tools of moral influence. Emerson and the American novelists lent weight to the proposition that objects revealed character and formed it. In a society that did not offer women active roles as producers, this line of thinking justified and dignified women's roles as society's chief consumers. It encouraged them to regard the relatively passive activity of shopping as the active making of moral choices—indeed as art-making. They grasped the notion too eagerly. They took it too far.

Rather than failing to produce a literature that dealt with the meanings of objects, America in the nineteenth century produced not only a literature that dealt with such ideas, but also a vast commercial subliterature, much of it, again, derived from English theory. The subliterature included advertisements that paraphrased John Ruskin. It popularized the English habit of mind that insisted that objects have only one important kind of meaning, moral meaning. This was a reduction and weakening of Emerson's reading of objects.

In 1859 John Ruskin published *The Two Paths,* his only book devoted exclusively to the industrial arts.[6] It was a spirited rebuttal of the ideas of Owen Jones and of principles being taught in the English government's schools of design. Ruskin attacked the separation of design from fine art, and applied to the decorative arts many of the principles he had earlier introduced in his books on architecture. Ruskin described "direct falsity of assertion respecting the nature of materials or the quantity of labor is in the full sense of the word wrong. It is as truly deserving of reprobation as any other moral delinquency."[7]

I point particularly to Ruskin's *The Two Paths* because this book, first published in 1859, had gone through nineteen editions in this country by 1891, which renders it the book about objects—"industrial arts"—most republished in America during the nineteenth century. It was republished a great many more times than Eastlake's *Hints on Household Taste,* for instance. Ruskin's moralistic fulminations on the industrial and decorative arts begat countless commercial publications, including house decorating manuals, which appeared during the late 1870s and continued throughout the 1880s. Their authors charged readers to create "conscientious" rooms. Charles Wyllys Elliott, writing of furniture in New York's *Art Journal* of the 1870s, for instance, warned his readers to "avoid veneers as you do sin or drink."[8] And in the 1870s one perfectly intelligent woman, writing an otherwise very good book on the history of furniture, attested to her faith in the power of beautiful objects to influence the character of growing children by hazarding the following advice: "provided there is space to move about without knocking over the furniture there is hardly likely to be too much in a room."[9]

It is worth looking hard at this literature of the nineteenth century. Until very recently it has been difficult to recognize either its influence in its own day, or its aftereffects. Its tendency to get hold of one idea like morality, which dictated the necessity of applying ethical standards to design, and to ride that idea much too far, produced rooms against which the next generation reacted. Recognition that this in fact constituted overreaction to an overreading now helps in assessing the vehemence with which the modern movement rejected ornament and decoration.

NOTES

[1] Abbott Lowell Cummings, ed., *Rural Household Inventories, Establishing Names, Uses, and Furnishings of Rooms in the Colonial New England Home 1675–1775* (Boston: Society for the Preservation of New England Antiquities, 1964); Barbara Carson, "Styles and Standards of Living in Southern Maryland 1670–1752," talk delivered to the Southern Historical Association, Atlanta, 1976; and Gloria Main, *Tobacco Colony: Life in Early Maryland 1650–1720* (Princeton, N.J.: Princeton University Press, 1982).

[2] James Deetz, *In Small Things Forgotten* (Garden City, N.Y.: Anchor/Doubleday, 1977).

[3] Horatio Greenough, *The Travels, Observations, and Experiences of a Yankee Stonecutter* (first published 1852; Gainesville, Florida: Scholars' Facsimilies and Reprints, 1958).

[4] John A. Kouwenhoven, *Made In America* (New York, 1948); reprinted as *The Arts In Modern American Civilization* (New York: Norton, 1967).

[5] Ralph Waldo Emerson, "Domestic Life," a lecture first delivered in Boston in 1859, in *Collected Works*, vol. 7, *Society and Solitude* (Boston and New York: Houghton Mifflin, 1904); reprinted (New York: AMS Press, 1968), pp. 103–33.

[6] John Ruskin, *The Two Paths*, 1859, vol. 16 of *The Complete Works of John Ruskin*, ed. E. T. Cook and Alexander Wedderburn (London: George Allen, 1903).

[7] John Ruskin, *The Seven Lamps of Architecture*, in *The Complete Works*, vol. 8, p. 59.

[8] Charles Wyllys Elliot, "Household Art," *The Art Journal* (New York), vol. 1, no. 1 (1875), p. 298.

[9] Harriet Prescott Spofford, *Art Decoration Applied to Furniture* (New York: Harper & Brothers, 1877), p. 222.

RESPONSE

by Susana Torre

The object is an elusive subject indeed because the boundaries of an intellectual discourse regarding objects in general and the relationship of objects to architecture in particular remain to be established in our time. Perhaps the most useful work we can accomplish today, taking advantage of a forum on so forgotten a subject in architectural circles, will be to sketch, even if with faint lines or crude brush strokes, the limits of this discourse.

One of the obvious difficulties seems to be the lack of the kind of implicit agreements that we have regarding architecture: whatever our ideological position, we have come to share a belief that issues of context—the relationship of a building to the neighborhood or the city, the spatial hierarchy it establishes, the building and environmental technologies it makes use of, and the symbolic representation it embodies—constitute valid analytical categories forming the conceptual armature of architectural discourse. These concepts, in turn, provide points of contact between disciplines, allowing us to understand the relationships between architecture and the other arts or architecture and social life.

No such conceptual framework exists today for a discussion about objects and architecture, partly because the question of mass production that encompassed both buildings and objects in the early part of the century is no longer seen as a relevant issue. If anything, contextualism, regionalism, classicism, and postmodernism have returned architecture to the realm of the specifically crafted building, and objects to the realm of the custom-made *objet d'art*. Objects such as furniture accessories, lighting fixtures, and even clothing seem to embody the realm of the personal and the private. Historically, however, architecture has been mostly understood as a public and social art. Objects have been encompassed within architectural-artistic discourse only in three instances: first, when they have become accessories to an architect's aesthetic vision, and as such projected over the entire designed environment—examples include the interiors of some of the Viennese architects, as illustrated in Adolf Loos's story of the poor rich man, and Alexander Rodchenko's workers' uniforms; second, when planning, building, and objects have reinforced the entire value system of a community, as in the case of the Shakers; and third, when objects have entered into contact with the public space of the city as public monuments, commenting upon publicly held values or sentiments.

Just as problematic as the question of the essence of the object raised by Edgar Kaufmann, jr., or the question of taxonomy discussed in the first part of David Handlin's paper, is that of the object's status as commodity in the great consumer society, ostensibly avoided in Arthur Pulos's presentation. Because even as we grapple to bring some conceptual coherence to the ubiquitous world of objects as props for private or public rituals, this coherence eludes us. For all objects, no matter what their function, style, or purpose might be, share an almost universal condition as commodities. As such, they are perceived, manipulated, bought and sold according to social categories such as class, gender, race, or ethnic identification, or to marketing categories based on income level and consumer-interest profiles. This is why objects are so often useful as accessories for social analysis and commentary but so seldom remain as permanent icons of a culture.

The environment of shopping structures, beginning with the great European department stores of the mid-1800s, may be a useful point of departure to understand the relationship between architecture, objects, and consumption as a public activity. These buildings were designed with an extraordinary understanding of their public, institutional role. Owners of the nineteenth-century department stores and their architects experimented with totally flexible, modern plans that contained extravagant and luxurious atrium spaces, as well as with innovative programs that included restaurants, beauty parlors, and cultural activities in addition to shopping—primarily with a female audience in mind. The unsafe and chaotic environment of most nineteenth-century metropolitan streets and the inconvenience of traveling long distances to acquire objects sold in specialized districts were problems addressed by clever entrepreneurs in unprecedented ways. A controlled and safe environment with everything under one roof was not only convenient but provided the context for public intercourse among affluent clients. Much in the same manner that handcrafted objects could be displayed without reference to their origins, fragments of architecture could be lifted from their contexts and used to create desirable associations, as in the case of Bon Marché's grand stair, based on that of the Paris Opèra. Architectural features such as massive turrets at the building corners, large plate-glass windows at the street level, stairs and atriumlike spaces, and lavish ornamentation often based on feminine or masculine motifs were treated as autonomous objects to be placed for maximum effect within the total fabric of the building.

The social dispersion of the American context during the nineteenth century was echoed by the mail catalogue, which made it possible for most items to be conveniently selected and purchased from a catalogue; the benefits of public intercourse at a metropolitan scale were sacrificed in exchange for the availability of the contents of the catalogue to purchasers living in remote places. In the United

States, a close association between shopping and public intercourse came fully of age with the modern suburban shopping mall, replicating the environmental control and safety of the European department store, but enforcing the store's isolation from an urban context. In appropriating and defining the identity of whatever safe and controlled public realm we had left, the shopping mall raised questions regarding the current relationship of objects, buildings, and the urban, public realm for which no satisfactory answers yet exist.

- Perhaps the purpose of this symposium is best understood as that of providing a context for questions to be asked. Regarding the topic that has occupied our attention this morning, I would like to offer the following:

- In a nation where the same objects of consumption are universally accessible regardless of place and location, how can the object be integrated in a theory of regional identity for buildings and places?

- In the context of the suburban shopping mall, where traditional symbols of the architecture of town and square are appropriated by kitsch representations, how can the object be related to discussions about the role of the monument and monumentality in public places?

- Can objects only escape their status as commodities when they are primarily aesthetic explorations or the harbingers of technological advance?

KEYNOTE ADDRESS:

THE SKYWARD TREND OF THOUGHT: SOME IDEAS ON THE HISTORY OF THE METHODOLOGY OF THE SKYSCRAPER

by Thomas A. P. Van Leeuwen

THE SKYWARD TREND OF THOUGHT[1]:
SOME IDEAS ON THE HISTORY OF THE METHODOLOGY OF THE SKYSCRAPER

by Thomas A. P. Van Leeuwen

New York
The heart of all the world am I!
A city, great, and grim, and grand!
Man's monument to mighty man!
Superb! Incomparable! Alone!
Greater than ancient Babylon,
The giant walled! Greater than Tyre,
Sea-Queen! Greater than Nineveh!
Pearl of the East! Greater than Rome,
Stupendous reared, Magnificent!
Greater than Paris, city fey!
Greater than London, Fog-enmeshed!
Greater than Venice! Vienna!
Or Petrograd! Greater than these!
That I am! Mark my high towers!

Arthur Crew Inman

With few exceptions, it is a generally accepted opinion that the skyscraper is an unequivocal and explicable object: a tall commercial building. History, historical methodology, and criticism have all served to legitimize this opinion. The history in which the tall commercial building finds its proper and indisputable place is European modern and American positivist art history. Its traditional structure is a narrative of deterministic and evolutionary conviction, and it is frequently called a "story" (e.g., Thomas E. Tallmadge, The Story of Architecture in America, *1936, and Alfred Morgan,* The Story of Skyscrapers, *1934). Its objective is to give credence to the second half of the title of this symposium: Innovation.*

Yet I would suggest that we also introduce the first half, Tradition, into the history of the skyscraper, viewing it as a late, but rightly timed, example of paradigmatic architecture, indeed, as the tower of cosmogony.[2] Numerous testimonies to this larger view can be found in the initial European responses to the American tall commercial building.

Thus the French novelist Paul Bourget, finding himself in August 1893 in the heart of downtown Manhattan, at the intersection of Broadway and Wall Street, exclaims:

> *As soon as one feels oneself undergoing the total ensemble of these buildings, one experiences again and again this impression of Babylon, which indeed is splendid and, I must admit, puts a spell on you.[3]*

Other foreign responses were equally romantic and enthusiastic, if of somewhat limited imagination. That is, it is significant that such commentators as Jules Huret, Karl Lamprecht, A. A. Ampere, Paul de Rousiers, and André Maurois[4] were unable, or unwilling, to evaluate skyscrapers in their own right, but always interpreted and classified them within the range of paradigmatic architecture, such as represented in the books of Athanasius Kircher (most notably, Turris Babel, and the more familiar Entwurff einer historischen Architectur by J. B. Fischer von Erlach).[5]

In a time when visitors crossed the Atlantic by steamer, the passing of the Statue of Liberty must have seemed the preface to a picture book of architectural wonders of the past (figs. 1, 2), and from this point on historical fantasy might flow freely. When the German historian Karl Lamprecht visited Manhattan in 1904, he envisioned immediately the many-towered city of San Gimignano and he began to draw extensive parallels between the early-capitalist free-states of Tuscany and the high-capitalist city of New York. He illustrated his account, titled *Americana,* with only two photographs: one of Manhattan and one of San Gimignano (figs. 3, 4), of which he wrote:

> Do not your towers look like the skyscrapers of New York where the typewriters rattle all the way up to the twenty-fourth floor? . . . New York is the San Gimignano of today, its bankers and wholesalers playing Montagues and Capulets with each other.[6]

The Dutch architect Hendrik Petrus Berlage, who traveled to the United States in November 1910, shared Lamprecht's "Tuscan experience" but could not, on the other hand, suppress the resurgent image of Babel as he contemplated the skyscrapers of Manhattan; he wrote:

> They seem a consummation of that dream
> Of Babel's towers, these buildings that arise
> And towering seem almost to touch the skies[7]

whereas later visitors like Le Corbusier and Salvador Dali saw the resurrection of the Egyptian pyramids and the city of Babel.

Above, left:
3 *"New York as seen from the Hudson River." From Karl Lamprecht,* Americana *(Freiburg im Breisgau, 1906), p. 81.*

4 *"San Gimignano as seen from the Rocca." From Karl Lamprecht,* Americana, *p. 82.*

What makes these comparisons interesting is not so much that the commentators drew parallels with the past, but that they perceived, in one way or another, a historical continuum. The skyscraper was not, as one might expect, experienced as a shocking futuristic novelty, but as something overwhelmingly familiar. It must be admitted that for someone like Le Corbusier, there was almost certainly an element of jealousy; he was envious that it was not he who had created this most splendid vision of modern architecture.[8] But even this reaction shows at the same time the inevitability of the occasion: things were falling spontaneously into their proper places. And the inevitable happened, as the enactment of the fulfillment of earlier promises. These promises constitute another set of parallels: those of *Genesis Redivivus* and America as a New World.

5 *A brick from a "house in Leyden" set in the south wall of the Chicago Tribune Building.*

The expectations of the early emigrants were certainly grandiose, fed by mystical and religious impulses, and what they found when they got here was certainly not Mesopotamia or the Heavenly Jerusalem.[9] Yet their driving force, the determination to see a better world realized, makes parallels with historical, mythical, and biblical prefigurations not only apt but compulsory, even to a degree of tedium.

This new world was better in the sense that it was fresh and unspoiled, like the world in the time of the creation. The Pilgrim Fathers, coming from the "fair and bewtifull citie" of Leyden, knew that "this is the place where the Lord will create a new Heaven and a new Earth."[10] A brick from "a House in Leyden, Holland, used by the Pilgrims as a church before their voyage on the Mayflower to America" is set in the southern wall of the Chicago Tribune building (fig. 5), as if to give proof to a reality that, in the general confusion between mythology and history, might be lost. The voyage over the wild Atlantic was found so similar to the drifting on the waters of the Deluge that Columbus could be compared to Noah, the Mayflower to the Ark, and finally America to the land of Sanaar, where Noah's offspring finally settled after their descent

6 *Mount Ararat and the land of the Sanaar, showing the wanderings of Noah's offspring. From Athanasius Kircher,* Turris Babel *(Amsterdam, 1879), bk. 1, p. 13.*

7 *"And Oloffe hastened and climbed to the top of the tallest tree . . . he saw shadowed out palaces and domes and lofty spires. . . ."* From One Forty West Street Building—New York City *(New York, 1926), p. 3*

8 *Woolworth Building, New York. Cass Gilbert, 1913. From a post-card reading "The most beautiful office building in the world."*

from Mount Ararat (fig. 6).[11] After all, Washington Irving began his *History of New York* with the discovery of America by Noah, "at the time of the building of the tower of Babel," and he had one of his heroes, "the sage Oloffe," climb into a tree to see a vision of the Babylonic New York, in a persiflage of the biblical text: "We will build here for ourselves a city and a tower whose top shall reach into the sky" (Genesis 11) (figs. 7, 8).

Thus the skyscraper should be approached as the realization of a higher degree of building principles than pragmatic or deterministic ones, the discovery of which requires digging into that timeless reservoir of expressive means and didactic models of revelation, eternity, and, most importantly, cosmogony.[12] The performance of the skyscraper is that of a tower of cosmogony, so aptly illustrated by the American sacred mountains par excellence, the Grand Tetons (fig. 9).

Irving Pond, Claude Bragdon, Hugh Ferriss, Harvey Wiley Corbett, and Francisco Mujica, among others,[13] all made it their daily concern to search for what Walter Benjamin, Mircea Eliade, and Henri Bergson referred to as *L'éternel retour* of architecture[14] or, as Pond formulated it, "the constant search for the sublime essence of a spirit which has found embodiment in the great architecture of the past."[15] These notions of timelessness, of changeless change, seem strangely out of place in our standard art-historical treatment. The history of architecture as an evolutionary process seems radically opposed to the lifespan of the "timeless types." If we want to describe their historical presence, we have to measure their lifespan by a different historical time, one that encompasses much longer units than those we employ in our everyday art history.

It appears to be a stroke of luck that for this special case we can borrow from the historical discipline, in particular from Louis Althusser and Fernand Braudel, the division of historical time into several *durées,* from which I will reserve the *longue durée,* so-called "geological time," for paradigmatic architecture and the "timeless types" (e.g., Babel, the Pyramids, Solomon's Temple, etc.), and the short time-spans for the events (*les événements*) of which all of art history is made.[16]

It seems rather inappropriate that art history, which deals with the long lifespans of entire civilizations, has confined itself to a treatment of the past that much more appropriately seems to fit military operations than the slowly changing pattern of the history of ideas. Nevertheless, art history is composed of events and anecdotes, in which time is dealt with only in its physical sense,[17] compressed into still short spans and subordinated to senseless divisions, such as "nineteenth-century architecture" and the like. Interestingly, one attitude benefits by this method, that of evolutionary positivism. In modernist art history especially (i.e., history by and for the

American Architecture: Innovation and Tradition

9 *The modernist view of the sacred mountain Symposium poster, "American Architecture: Innovation and Tradition" New York, 1983.*

10 *"The Law of Polarity" From Claude Bragdon, The Beautiful Necessity (London, 1922), p. 24.*

modern movement), the evolution of art is made visible as a string of events, knotted together by the convincing logic of cause and effect. Thus we get one level on which events occur, brought forth in a single sweep of time, tolerating only those facts that appear as the logical constituents of such a model. These events are arranged sequentially, the only way possible within a linguistic construct, and an arrangement that in its turn affects not only the position of events but suggests a causality. *After* becomes *because of.* This system of causation relies on a multitude of natural laws, all centered around the themes of action-reaction and cause-effect.

Complementing the law of causation, although not a natural law but a modus operandi in interpretive historiography, is what I will call the Law of Polarity (fig. 10).[18] The function of this law is to reinforce and intensify presumably opposing forces. Its method relies on the modes of short time-span, anecdotism, and polarization, as used in extremely dialectical fields like diplomatic and military history. To protect themselves against the dictates of history, these modes have acquired built-in defense mechanisms. Movements and *isms* are prefabricated and attached to the product before it even arrives. For a period as history-conscious as that of modernism, it remains impossible to distinguish between what actually happened and what has been written down as having happened. In 1927, Walter Curt Behrendt published a bellicose pamphlet called *Der Sieg des neuen Baustils,* in which he suggested that a) there was something like an enemy (*die Gegner*), b) there was a battle, and c) that battle was won by the New Builders.[19] Comparable examples of paranoid historical consciousness may be found, naturally, but to an unexpectedly modest degree, in the manifestos of Le Corbusier, Giedion, and other CIAM members, and, in a much more unrestricted manner, in the quasi-histories of the movement such as Hitchcock's *Modern Architecture* (1929) and Cheney's *The New World Architecture* (1930). Here we find, even more than in the European accounts, probably because of an accumulative effect of American "new worldness" combined with European revolutionism, the most radical picture of architectural history. Architecture is seen as a military operation, ranging back all the way into the nineteenth century, where with a most convincing feeling for reality, the artists are pitched against the engineers, the traditionalists against the protomodernists, and so on.[20]

To illustrate the workings of anecdotal history and its auxiliary mechanisms I have selected the Chicago Tribune Competition of 1922 for several reasons. First, thanks to the fact that the Tribune Competition has become such a monumental cliché in art history, all of its constituent elements have been blown up to excessive proportions; second, its historical material can be interpreted in terms of the two methods that I have just expounded; and third, it is still one of the rare cases in which European concepts and American concepts can be observed under (almost) laboratory conditions. The Chicago Tribune Competition of 1922 offers good illustrations of the incongruity of both historical time and interpretative polarization.

The competition's program was simple and enigmatic: "To erect the most beautiful and distinguished office building in the world is the desire of *The Tribune*."[21] Undoubtedly, the winner would be the one who would interpret this ultimatum the most penetratingly. The key word was "world." It appears no less than eight times on the first page of the introduction to the *Tribune*'s 1923 catalogue of the competition's entries and a total of twenty-one times on its first eight pages. There are two possible interpretations. The first is that "world" was to be understood as the *Tribune's* world, which was Chicago and the state of Illinois, possibly including the other world, of New York, merely for the sake of rivalry.[22]

This is not bad reasoning. To be the most beautiful office building it had to be more beautiful than the most beautiful building then existing within the aforementioned "world." Obviously this was the almost ten-year-old Woolworth Tower, designed by Gilbert in 1913 (see fig. 8). That this was so is confirmed by the statement that a fellow competitor added to one of his sketches (fig. 11). It was the Japanese-American architect Richard Yoshijiro Mine:

> My tireless search for a building design at the famous Ricker Architectural Library from end to end brought me to the Woolworth Building of New York. My conviction was then, that it would be something.[23]

Mine won one out of ten honorable mentions, but not first prize because he was too close to Gilbert's design, and a straight copy was not desired. Hood and Howells revealed their similar conclusion in a much more subtle and attractively disguised intrepretation of the Gothic spirit, which was, if we may believe Frank Lloyd Wright, an irresistible topic in the Midwest: "It is alone in an atmosphere of this nature [in the West and the Middle West] that the Gothic Spirit in building can be revived."[24] Thus the jury had to succumb to that wonderful gimmick of the flying buttresses balancing the spire, reminiscent of the Butter Tower in Rouen.

The other intrepretation of "world" was probably the more acute of the two, that made by Eliel Saarinen, who received second prize but was generally acclaimed as the real winner.[25] One of the reasons the competition became so famous was its typical "competitive" character. Not only did it carry a very large sum of prize money, but also a widely and enthusiastically disputed verdict.

That European modernism did not get the representation the authors of the competition had expected it to get was a sad case of miscalculation. In progressivist eyes, Chicago was the El Dorado

11 "It would be something"
Design for the Chicago Tribune Tower Competition
Richard Yoshijiro Mine, 1922
From The International Competition for a New Office Building for the Chicago Tribune *(Chicago, 1923), plate 82.*

of the *Neue Sachlichkeit*—of merciless pragmatism, unscrupulous functionalism, and, above all, a territory where "artists" were not welcomed; was it not Giedion himself, quoting Bourget, who said that "Chicago [architecture] is the work of some impersonal power, irresistible, like a force of Nature," and that "the architect frankly accepted the condition imposed by the speculator," and then went on to speak of "the simple force of need as a principle of beauty"?[26]

And so, when the projects of Walter Gropius and Max and Bruno Taut were rebuffed they felt betrayed, firstly by America, but above all by time. What had seemed the logical continuation of the modern was not recognized, not regarded as fitting the purpose. The future was not part of the program. As we shall see, it was the celebration of the present that was the issue.

Disillusionment, mixed with resentment and indignation, fed the notion that an army of opposing forces was conspiring against the right course of history. Existing polarities such as architect versus engineer, visible construction versus "sham" or "bogus" decoration, nineteenth century—this time seen not as a periodization but as a being with human characteristics which was, according to Pevsner, "profoundly dishonest"—versus the new era: all of these were amalgamated with the local American oppositions, such as East versus West, academicism versus self-reliance, and so forth. In the ensuing "cold war," more than anything else the exhibition of the frame was the all-pervasive article of faith. And the frame, as Colin Rowe has said, was much more than a means to an end; it was the end itself.[27]

The voices of European arrogance and modernistic paternalism made it their vocation to point out to the Americans that they were losing their faith and that in the Chicago Tribune Competition it was clearly becoming apparent that the Europeans had stuck much more faithfully to the principles of the frame. Giedion proclaimed that the "foreign projects [were] closer to the Chicago school."[28] In other words, American architects were handling their heritage with increasing carelessness, and it required the higher intelligence of a Gropius to make them realize this. From that moment on, the Americans were degraded and at the same time idealized as noble savages, who created out of instinct rather than reason, and who were to be treated as natural artists, but always and exclusively in spite of themselves.

In this way, modernism discovered its unspoiled Eden, and the great myth was spun around Chicago. In a Rousseau-esque effort to crown the least artistic the noblest of savages, a man like William Le Baron Jenney was chosen to fulfill the role of inventor of the frame. That this was a dramatic case of miscasting, due to a rigorous lack of evidence, did not bother anybody at the time; nor did the election of Louis Sullivan as the omnipotent representative of American progressive architecture in general stir up questions of doubt. On the contrary, Sullivan was unanimously hailed as the savage genius, the isolated conscience of artistic truth, the victim of academic conspiracy, and also the man who had been monstrously neglected by his own countrymen. This, in particular, was an excellent occasion for the Europeans to adopt him as the ideal precursor of modernism in Paradise. Paul Frankl, who professed a lively interest in the skyscraper and even designed "skyscraper furniture," believed firmly that Sullivan was the inventor of the skyscraper: "The credit for this innovation goes to the distinguished architect Louis Sullivan."[29]

Wright had already conquered Europe with the Wasmuth publications in 1910. In 1911 Sullivan followed in his wake, and from 1913 on, when Hendrik Petrus Berlage had his *Amerikaansche Reisherinneringen* published, Sullivan's authority was firmly established in Europe.[30] Thus it was around Sullivan that the *"Künstler-Legende"* was woven. Sullivan acted as a *pars pro toto* for the Chicago school.

It was, of course, mere coincidence that when the Chicago school, for reasons of stylistic impurity, was declared clinically dead in 1922, Sullivan had to follow soon. It was all the fault of the Chicago Fair of 1893. The White City is an inevitable and vastly overrated oddity. Where other World Fairs have been treated with benevolence and even canonized, like those in London of 1851 and in Paris of 1889, the Chicago World's Fair has been regarded with something akin to hatred. Hitchcock, taking his cue from Sullivan's *Autobiography of an Idea,* in his 1929 *Modern Architecture,* called it "the white plague."[31] Yet ordinary people felt comfortably happy with it, and, as was common in world exhibitions, it disappeared after it was consumed. Therefore it was called "the vanishing city" (fig. 12), for it did vanish almost without a trace, but not quite: the park and the later reconstructed "Queen of the Fair," Charles Atwood's Fine Arts Building, remained. Thus the function of the fair in the "stories" is that of a sort of architectural bête noire. Modernists as well as many Americanists were convinced that the

Below, left:
12 *"The Vanishing City"*
Cover of a photographic guide-book to the 1893 Chicago World's Fair.

Below, right:
13 *"Die Gegner"*
Photo of the "dull and inert forces" (Mumford). Left to right: G. E. Graham, E. Butler, D. Burnham, a news-paper reporter, G. G. Fuller, C. Atwood From The Western Architect *(1924) p. 90.*

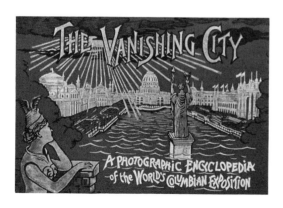

fair represented something evil, something America had to be protected against.

Lewis Mumford wrote in 1931 in his *The Brown Decades,* "So low had American taste sunk in the generation after the World's Fair that people habitually characterized as an advance what was actually a serious retrogression."[32] Mumford believed that the fair represented a collection of "dull and inert forces that stood in the way" of what he considered to be the natural course of architecture.[33] By general prejudice and traditional consensus, those "forces" were usually embodied by the architects "from the East." About the time of the fair several pictures were made of the architects responsible (fig. 13); later these served as snapshots of the enemy on maneuvers ("*die Gegner,*" as Walter Curt Behrendt called them).[34]

Thus, the same "dull and inert forces" were observed to be demonstrably at work in the years of 1922 and 1923, and it was logical and in the line of history to assume that the fair was an anticipation of the Tribune competition. Sullivan, the oracle, had said that "the damage wrought by the Chicago Fair would last half a century." Giedion, and Pevsner following him, believed that Sullivan had made an important prediction, although in fact the text comes from the 1924 *Autobiography of an Idea,* and not from 1893. Thus Pevsner wrote in his *An Outline of European Architecture* (1943): "Chicago might have become the international centre of modern architecture had it not been for the 'World's Fair'.... Of the Chicago Exhibition Sullivan said that the damage wrought by it would last for half a century. The prognostication has proved accurate."[35]

The prognostication was only accurate for Pevsner and Giedion in terms of their ideal line of history, and their idea of what was modern and youthful. In their view, what was modern and youthful, as being opposed to being dull and inert, was Sullivan and the frame. In their search for presages, oracles, and prognostications, they found that Gropius's Tribune Tower was foreshadowed in Sullivan's Carson, Pirie and Scott Store, which dates from the threshold period of transition between the nineteenth century and the New Age. In its exhibiting of the "neutral skeleton" Sullivan's monument was well chosen, but it turned out that its architect had been guilty of certain transgressions. The plot, as set out by the modernist historians, develops as follows. First, the building is described by Giedion as the realization of the ideal of true architecture: "The interior is still of the warehouse type, with continuous unbroken floor areas. The front is designed to fulfill its indispensable function, the admission of light."[36]

(The latter statement is, of course, an error. If there was one thing that was to be avoided in a department store, it was direct light from the street fronts) Giedion continues: "Its basic elements are the horizontally elongated 'Chicago windows', admirably homo-

geneous and treated to coincide with the framework of the skeleton."[37] Yet the edge where State and Madison streets converge and where "the world's busiest corner" is situated is elegantly curved and is therefore a blatant violation of the ideal. Giedion finds a way out. He explains that Sullivan was responding to the demands of his client: "The owners had asked for this curvilinear addition as a reminiscence of the pavilion attached to their old store."[38]

Apart from the fact that the curved access made most effective use of "the world's most profitable corner," and was, as Giedion suggested himself, "a stylistic remnant" of the owners' previous store, it seems highly inconsistent to attribute this design decision exclusively to the owners, since the Chicago style was predicated on the belief that "true beauty" was the result of "the simple force of need." Wasn't the architect or engineer supposed to "loyally accept the conditions imposed by the speculator/owner?" A similar dissimulation is evident in Giedion's attempt to downplay the use of ornament in the building: "The windows, with their thin metal frames, are sharply cut into the facade. The windows in the lower stories are connected by a narrow line of ornament pressed into the terra cotta. Too thin to be visible in the photograph...." (fig. 14).[39] In fact, the worst photograph available does not obscure this ornament, and although one can see a suspicious cut running from the lower left corner through the entrance pavilion, the thin line of ornament is still very much apparent. It is more apparent in any case than in the photo Walter Curt Behrendt used for his chapter on Sullivan in *Modern Building* of 1937, where the ornament, intentionally or not, has been eliminated (fig. 15).

For Behrendt, a year or so earlier, in his discussion of the Carson, Pirie, Scott Store, had taken a different approach. He too had noticed the discrepancy (especially for a European modernist) between the bareness of the upper stories and the exuberant detailing of the two lower stories. But instead of dissimulating it, he focused the reader's attention on it: "…the urge and pleasure of self-expression, never put fully to rest in an artist, is worked off on the two lower stories, the only ones which are really visible at a glance from the street." Yet in their symptomatic mistaking of functionalism for pure aesthetics, both men had a blind spot when it came to seeing functionalism as a system of finding optimal answers to specific needs, such as those of American business. Whereas Giedion in his excitement entirely forgot that the building was intended as a department store, Behrendt half-apologetically acknowledged that the prime need of the building was to attract windowshopping buyers who were not at all interested in those surfaces of the building beyond their range of vision. On the contrary, as every shopkeeper knows, the shopper's interest is almost exclusively directed to the windows at eye level; and it is precisely for this reason that the fanciful and—certainly for that time—wild ornament lines the windows like seductive eyelashes.

Quite rightly Behrendt noted the "obvious similarity to the abstract ornament of the Art Nouveau movement."[40] There can be little doubt that a client who borrowed its image so freely from the famous Parisian stores must have been quite pleased with a local architect who could design in the vein of men like Frantz Jourdain, who at that time was applying to the La Samaritaine Department Store a rich Art Nouveau ornamentation. Behrendt even went so far as to see a certain artistry in Sullivan's design, albeit still within the tradition of the nineteenth century, and when he considered the fact that he was judging the product of a culture in transition he could also forgive Sullivan's more regressive tendencies to a degree.

Not so Giedion. Not that he was more committed to the movement than Behrendt, but he was more committed to the idea of Sullivan as a leader, and as such Sullivan had to be infallible. Therefore he had to be "cleansed," and so Giedion wrote: "George Elmslie, whom we have already mentioned as one of Sullivan's staunchest collaborators, was the designer of most of the ornamentation on his building." And he went on to dispute Behrendt's lax judgment: "It was not influenced by the contemporary Art Nouveau."[41] (One must bear in mind that Art Nouveau was considered the most lethal of all nineteenth-century diseases.)

Nor was Berlage much impressed by Sullivan's ornamentation. In his *Travel Recollections* of 1913 he called him "too much of a decorator," especially in the Bayard Building in New York and in the Carson, Pirie and Scott Store.[42] Berlage too noticed the discrepancy between the undisguised mass of the building and the "superfluity

16, 17 "An attractive ensemble of two friendly tudor gables facing each other"
From H. P. Berlage, Ameri-kaansche Reiserinneringen *(Rotterdam, 1913), figs. 6, 7.*

of ornament"[43] but in the end he was not able to see clearly the essence of Sullivan's ornament, and it seems that his admiration for him was rather indiscriminate and without much real understanding. As a tribute to the great man, Berlage included in his book a picture of a typical Sullivanesque building, of which he wrote: "Masonic Temple at Chicago—Architect Sullivan" (fig. 16). It should not be alarming that even a foreigner as knowledgeable as Berlage could mistake a well-known Burnham and Root building for one by Sullivan, but it remains rather odd that Berlage should have accepted unquestioningly the hipped roof and the pointed gables as characteristic of Sullivan. Even odder is the inclusion of picture No. 6 (fig. 17). In the text Berlage recalls a pleasant lunch one day in a Chicago club, which must be the reason that he confuses this Burnham building with one by Sullivan. In any case, the presence of the Tudor gables in plates 6 and 7 of the modest picture section of his book throws an interesting light on Berlage's idea of Sullivan's architecture. It also proves how widely the intepretations of the great forerunner could differ, even when they come from the propagators of modernism themselves.

Thus it appears that both Giedion and Berlage were influenced by the authority of Sullivan's name and reputation, but when it came to recognizing his style and ideas, they failed dramatically. In Giedion's case this meant an unpleasant complication. His anecdotal-positivist treatment of history did not allow for insignificant or inexplicable occurrences, and therefore the conflicting character of Sullivan's architecture had to be resolved. So Giedion concluded in the mellow and understanding tone of the psychoanalyst:

> Even when architects of Sullivan's generation pressed on towards new solutions, they sometimes found themselves held back by nineteenth-century traditions. They suffered from a split personality.... The split personality of the nineteenth-century architect makes itself felt in Sullivan's Carson Pirie Scott building.[44]

A recurrent theme in the appreciation of the frame by the European modernists is the connotation of youth. The framed building is the image of the new age and the vehicle for new generations to express their youthfulness. But why? What makes the frame so easily understood as denoting youth? There seems to be no unequivocal explanation of this meaning, but there are enough instances to suggest a common conception. An enlightening commentary is to be found in the Dutch architectural magazine *Bouwkundig Weekblad* of 1923, written by J. J. P. Oud, precisely in the case of the Chicago Tribune Competition. Most Dutch competitors were, unlike their French and Italian colleagues, of a modernist inclination and their reflections on the competition's results were a mixture of old-world arrogance and modernist indignation. Dutch indignation, habitually more indignant than justified, concentrated itself upon a rigorous rejection of Hood and Howells' winning design and a fanatical rehabilitation of a Danish modernist design that was not even en-

18 *Design for the Chicago Tribune
Tower Competition
Knut Lönberg Holm, 1922.
From J. J. P. Oud, "Bij een
Deensch Ontwerp voor de
Chicago Tribune"
De Bouwtandig Weekblad,
vol. 44, no. 45 (1923), p. 457.*

19 *"With the religious fervor of St.
Thomas the Incredulous, he
poked his finger into the wounds
of the dying building"
From* The Origin of the
Skyscraper
(Chicago, 1931).

20 *Detail,* St. Thomas the
Incredulous
*Michelangelo de Caravaggio,
1598–1599.*

tered: Knut Lönberg-Holm's icon of the frame, with dominating horizontals and two Wrightian light-fixtures near the top (fig. 18). In his "oratio prodomo" Oud favored Lönberg-Holm's project and disapproved of Hood's as well as Saarinen's, writing:

> [Hood's design is] a 'pseudo-morphosis': modern requirements petrified in traditional, gothicising, counter moulds.... The Finn's design is a hybrid between American mercantilism and the devotional surrender to the 'sublime' in the religious sense of the Western world.[45]

In the appraisal of the Holm entry that followed, Oud wrote: "It is so much fresher and younger than the 'petrified' designs of 'those two elderly gentlemen' [i.e. Hood and Saarinen]."[46] Equating "petrified" architecture with "old," he coupled "fresh" and "young" with the diaphanous frame of Holm. In doing so he echoes a notion that pervades many cultures, from Socratean thought to Indo-Tibetan cosmology, that "man is created with a body that was diaphanous, and ... a counterforce tries to destroy it by progressive petrification."[47] Another equally important connotation of the frame is, besides its well-known analogy to the vertebrae, the anology to the psychical interior: Modernism regarded the frame as "the true self of architecture." Freudians like Giedion called it "the subconscious of architecture."[48] Truth, they thought, could be measured in the exposing of the frame.

In terms of our subject of the skyscraper it is important to know that this moral-theological criterion determined the distinction between skyscrapers and true skyscrapers. The skyscraper might be nothing more than a very tall building, for unless it had a steel frame it was not a *true* skyscraper. The skyscraper's truth was located in its interior. All this has to do with the question of the first skyscraper, authoritatively solved, decades ago, in favor of the Chicago Branch Building of the New York Home Insurance Company, by William Le Baron Jenney, from 1885, which is not very much a skyscraper from a visual point of view. From an ethical point of view, however, it was sufficiently true to be acknowledged the nation's first.

Thus, with almost religious fervor, Thomas Eddy Tallmadge in 1931 poked his finger into the wounds of the dying building, to ascertain that in the lifeless remains lay what he could not see in the living thing: the first skyscraper (figs. 19, 20).[49]

With the strong emphasis on the frame, the other aspects of the skyscraper—its awesome height, its towering presence, in brief, all the meanings that refer to sublimity and divinity—were neglected. The anecdotal history of cause and effect did not take these factors into consideration. The meaning of the word "world" in the competition program was aptly interpreted by Hood and Howells, but it was Saarinen whose response was most accurate and intuitive

21 *Design for the Chicago Tribune Tower Competition Eliel Saarinen, 1922.*

(fig. 21). Saarinen sensed that phrases like "the building of a world-city in a new world"[50] could refer to a different level of time. Thus, "world city" meant *cosmopolis, cosmic city;* and "new world" was not simply the United States of America, but indeed a *new* world. Everything had to both have a meaning in terms of Creation (cosmogony), and evoke geological time—*longue durée*.[51] Further, this world had to be understood and experienced in terms of radically different conceptions of time and space: as Heaven upon Earth, as the Pilgrim Fathers had foreseen, as the Heavenly Jerusalem.

On first consideration it may seem that such unworldly ideas are irrelevant in the context of the skyscraper, being a business structure and not a palace or a temple, the immediate result of commercial transactions. Indeed, business and businessmen dictated the programs out of which skyscrapers grew, their form as well as their decoration. In many cases it can be said that the creative power of the businessmen was more responsible for final results than that of the architect or the contractor. Nevertheless, although it always seems to be purely functional, business—and in particular big business and still more so American big business—contains a highly paradoxical and metaphysical element, in which extreme oppositions alternate, in which the practical and the frivolous, efficiency and waste, fight for priority and surprisingly often coexist harmoniously. In the American skyscraper, poetic imagination and brutal materialism are perfectly welded, and it would be a mistake to think that these two aspects are in contradiction; they are not. Dreams, while rooted in business, are the cornerstones of the skyscraper.

This seeming contradiction of motives was noted by the Dutch historian Johan Huizinga, author of *The Waning of the Middle Ages,* who visited the United States several times and who reflected upon his American experiences in two little volumes, published in 1918 and 1926.[52] Huizinga wondered how it could be that Americans had such a religious, mysterious, and even atavistic nature, but at the same time placed enormous emphasis on the practical and not, as would have been logical, on the metaphysical. He was an extremely well-read man, with a thorough knowledge of American culture, including the writings of William James and John Dewey, whom he frequently quotes, and he had no difficulty understanding American pragmatism, behaviorism, and the like. But what he could not understand was the violence with which the pragmatic attitude was professed. In the last chapter of his *Amerika, levend en denkend* (America, Living and Thinking) of 1926, he elaborated on what he called "the anti-metaphysical attitude of the American." After quoting one of the more irreverent and striking passages from J. B. Watson's *Behaviorism* ("No one knows just how the idea of a soul or the supernatural started. It probably had its origin in the general laziness of mankind"), he went on to wonder whether America had returned to the eighteenth century.[53] He then quotes from the "young American sociologist Elizabeth Ephrussi" to explain the mystique of American materialism:

> It would be a mistake to think that America is materialistic because of its strong proliferation of big business, which is so manifestly embodied in its skyscrapers. The substance of this reality is materialistic, no doubt, but so vehemently, so insistently, so fervently materialistic, that the very ardor of the devotion vouchsafed to the material rises to a new kind of spirituality. The impulse, overreaching itself, becomes transcendent.[54]

Transcendent materialism is indeed a most dominant constituent of the skyscraper story. The two-sidedness of Sullivan did not seem contradictory to his American public, even though it was an unsurmountable obstacle to his European interpreters. So it was with Chicago architecture in general. The early or "heroic" period was canonized for its uncompromising materialism, and was seen as clearly distinct from the following or "decadent" period, inaugurated by the Chicago Tribune Competition.[55]

But to staunch chauvinists such as Thomas E. Tallmadge, the dividing line was only a superficial one. Naturally, Tallmadge was too much of a mythographer not to make use of cause-and-effect anecdotism, and so his account of "the progress of the New Architecture" is completely in line with contemporary American progressivists like Mumford (1931), American modernists like Cheney (1930), and European modernists like Behrendt (1937) and Giedion (1941).[56] But unlike them he emphasizes not rupture and opposition but continuity. Instead of contrasting Hood's design to Saarinen's in terms of old to new, eclectic to modern, as is generally done, he singled out the Saarinen entry as the most logical and natural continuation of the Chicago spirit in the modern era. In his view, the hard-core matter-of-factness of the 1880s and 1890s was subtly transformed into the metaphysics of the 1920s. Tallmadge quotes Louis Sullivan to the effect that the Saarinen tower was like a tree of stone and steel that had sprung forth from "some titanic seed, planted deep in the earth," most probably planted there by himself in the late 1880s.[57]

Tallmadge also stressed the importance of the process of creation. He loved to picture Saarinen "tracing those fairylike outlines on some icy eyrie by the flashing lights of the Aurora Borealis or in a glacial grotto with myriad elves all about him, all busily engaged in making the thousands of curious little lines which gave his drawings a most uncanny feeling of enchanted inspiration and of superhuman assistance."[58] In other words, where the beauty of the older Chicago architecture resided mainly "in the simple force of need," the accent had imperceptibly shifted to enchanted inspiration and superhuman assistance. Even if the "true skyscraper" could have been erected with only the help of simple technology and Midwestern self-reliance, the "true tower" had to be resurrected

22 *Eliel Saarinen's Chicago
Tribune Tower
design in the halo of a rising sun
From the cover of Thomas Eddy
Tallmadge,* The Story of Ar-
chitecture in America *(New
York, 1936).*

23 *Reconstruction of the Temple
of King Solomon
Frank Helmle and Harvey
Wiley Corbett, 1925
Rendering by Hugh Ferriss
From* Pencil Points, *vol. 6
(Nov. 1925), p. 79.*

Below, left:
24 *Interior of King Solomon's
Palace—
Restoration of Temple
and Citadel
Helmle and Corbett, 1925.*

Below, right:
25 *"Le Cauchemar de l'Infini"
From John Martin,* Belshazzar's
Feast, *1821.*

from the "reservoir of ideas," guided by divine mediation. The divine origin of Saarinen's "true tower" is frequently suggested in drawings and vignettes in which the tower appears in a halo of the rays of the rising sun, as for example on the cover of Tallmadge's *The Story of Architecture in America* and as the new vignette of *The Western Architect* (fig. 22).[59]

Saarinen was not the only one who was superhumanly assisted in recreating a monumental architecture. A few years later, in 1925, Frank Helmle and Harvey Wiley Corbett were asked to carry out the reconstruction of the temple and citadel of King Solomon, according to the instructions of a certain John Wesley Kelchner, "who, inspired by religious zeal, has made the reconstruction of the Temple his chief object in life for over thirty years" (fig. 23).[60] As was also the case with the well-known multitowered Monument to the Republic by Erastus Salisbury Field of 1876, the project was meant to add luster to that celebration of American achievement, the Philadelphia Exhibition of 1926. Once more it was the Babylonian example that was taken up by Kelchner's architects Helmle and Corbett in their design for the forecourt of the Temple of Solomon, this time in a reconstruction of John Martin's Belshazzar's Feast of 1821 (figs. 24, 25).[61]

Whereas the "true skyscraper" was merely a building of nondescript appearance in a non-defined location in the chaos of the primaeval commercial city, the "true tower" was destined to be a conspicuous beacon, to define space and to bring order into chaos. As such it was the perfect *axis mundi*.[62] In the 1909 Chicago Plan, the chaotic primaeval city with its irregular skyline is razed as if by a gigantic lawn mower: the private skyscrapers are castrated and reduced to, and consequently represented by, a single, collective, artificial mountain. The Saarinen design is the exact fulfillment of that idea, as it was actually proposed in his plan of 1923 for the Chicago lakefront.[63]

Francis Swales and, to a lesser degree, Chester Price followed Saarinen's concept in their recreation of City Hall Square for the

27 *"Upper Manhattan from University Heights—a conception of the future"*
From Thomas Adams, Regional Plan of New York, *p. 25.*

28 *"Spectacula Babylonica"*
From J. B. Fischer von Erlach, Entwurff einer Historischen Architectur, *p. 16.*

29 *"Die Stadtkrone"*
From Bruno Taut, Die Stadtkrone *(Jena, 1919), fig. 49.*

26 *"A Monumental Building for the New York Civic Center"*
Francis Swales, 1931
From Thomas Adams, Regional Plan of New York and its Environs, *vol. 2 (New York, 1931), p. 385.*

Committee of the Regional Plan for New York City in 1931.[64] Swales's sketch of the "proposed building for the Civic Center" is certainly dependent on the Lakefront Grant Hotel (fig. 26), but more importantly, it tries to amalgamate the Babel archetype into a crushing Leviathan, composed of the traditional eight zones.[65] Swales presented himself as a man enamored of the grandeur of the Ancients. In his 1931 article "The Architect and the Grand Plan," he praised the great mythic and historical examples, from "the unified or monumental or civic plan, beginning in Egypt, extending to Babylon, Greece, Carthage, Rome..." to "Bologna at the time of Dante, a city of early skyscrapers,"[66] and strongly advocated these examples to those engaged in reorganizing the chaotic American cities.

The closest Swales ever got to his ideal was probably in his design for Upper Manhattan—"A Conception of the Future"—which features a central pyramidal monument, cenotaph, or temple, obviously dependent on examples from Boullée and Ledoux, but more importantly inspired by the *Spectacula Babylonia* from Fischer von Erlach's *Entwurff einer historischen Architektur* of 1721 (figs. 27, 28). The "father of modern art history" likewise influenced European planners on the "grand scale," like Bruno Taut in his *Stadtkrone* of 1919 (fig. 29).[67] Just as Kircher and Fischer von Erlach entertained a common fascination for the great buildings of the golden age of architecture and even frequented the same circles (they participated in the cultural life around Queen Christina of Sweden), architectural thinkers like Bruno Taut found in Irving Pond, Claude Bragdon, and, to a lesser degree, Louis Sullivan coeval spirits in the United States.[68] In all their writings they stressed the importance of continuity rather than change, "the cosmic being opposed to the anecdotal," as Adolf Behne put it in his contribution to Taut's book.[69]

It was the cosmic aspiration of a civilization to crown its "world cities" with one large tower or a cluster of towers which Taut illustrated with forty examples from the past and several from contemporary America, including the McKim, Mead & White Municipal Building of New York and the southern tip of Manhattan skyline.[70] It is in this light that what are usually interpreted as predictions or images of the future can now be seen as symptoms of an architectural continuum, the same vision that one finds in the city of towers described by Washington Irving or in the image of a skyscrapered Manhattan described by Edgar Allan Poe in 1849. Poe's story takes place after the year 2050, the year the New York area is destroyed by an earthquake. Archaeologists find that nine-tenths of Manhattan was covered with churches, or churchlike buildings. It explains that the "Knickerbocker Tribe" was "by no means uncivilized":

> It is related of them that they were ... oddly afflicted with a monomania for building what, in the ancient Amriccan, was denominated "churches"—a kind of pagoda instituted for the worship of two idols that went by the names of Wealth and Fashion.[71]

30 *Cartoon for* Harper's Weekly
Thomas Nast, 1881
From Charles Lockwood, Manhattan Moves Uptown
(Boston, 1976), p. 277.

Similarly, when Tom Nast made his "visionary" print of the clustered skyscrapers on the tip of Manhattan in 1881, it was probably less visionary than we are inclined to think (fig. 30).[72] The question of the first skyscraper, so eighteenth-century-like in character, now becomes less and less relevant.[73] So does the overpowering emphasis on Yankee technology and on the skyscraper as a constructional invention.

By now I have made it sufficiently clear that the skyscraper was not an invention, and certainly not an exclusively technological one. The "eternal return" of the tower was not dependent on mere technology. Whoever does not believe this has only to look back to the late 1950s and early 1960s, when that other perennial dream, the voyage to the moon, was finally realized with technological means hardly more sophisticated than the bullet Jules Verne had imagined for his moonshot.

A last point I want to stress is the position of the idea of the future within the perennial dream. Hegel was right to say that the future could never be a real future because it always had to be at least part

31 *"Urbs Turrita"*
From Athanasius Kircher,
Mundus Subterraneus/De
Onderaardse Weereld, *bk. 8*
(Amsterdam, 1682), p. 29.

of the present. In other words, the future can only be imagined in the terms of either the present or, however paradoxical, the past. In this sense the skyscraper realized two functions: it signified an optimistic belief in the future, and it did so with the help of a familiar significant image. In this way, belief in the future was transformed into confidence in the future. Cesar Pelli has said in a recent interview that the mainspring of present skyscraper building is "to express a strong confidence in the future."[74] Apparently, opinion has not changed over the last hundred years; the *Real Estate Record and Building Guide* of November 1875 states, in reaction to the appearance of two well-known proto-skyscrapers: "Look at the overgrown and oppressive Western Union and Tribune and Equitble buildings—types of unbounded confidence in our future, without regard to our present ability to pay."[75] This proves that skyscrapers are built especially in terms of economic depressions: 1875, 1929, 1982. They seem to serve as magic totems to ward off the evil turn of the economy.

This reference to totemism brings us to a wonderful gem from Kircher's collection of rarities, the *Mundus Subterraneus,* or *De Onderaardse Weereld,* of 1682. In this most curious book, Kircher exhibits pages profusely illustrated with intriguing images engraved on amber amulets and dug out of the Inner World, sometimes by innocent passers-by, sometimes by official prospectors, and brought to the attention of the author. The Inner World was considered to be the apocalyptic vault of creation, the place where all mysteries were revealed. On the wondrous ambers were messages containing clues to age-old problems as well as predictions of important things to come. One of Kircher's ambers contains the image of an Urbs Turrita, a towered city (fig. 31).[76] Looking at this enigmatic picture, can anybody deny that the Citicorp Building was prognosticated a long, long time ago?

NOTES

[1] I have borrowed this title from Moses King, who uses it in his 1905 *King's Views of New York* as a slogan to accompany "a design of a great 45-story structure, 650 feet high, planned by former Bridge Commissioner Gustav Lindenthal and Architects Henry F. Hornbostel and George B. Post." It will also be the title of a larger forthcoming study (conducted in conjunction with the American Council of Learned Societies and the University of Leyden, Holland) in which I trace the tradition, application, and justification of "thinking skyward" in American architecture ideologies.

[2] With the exception of M. Revesz-Alexander, *Der Turm als Symbol und Erlebnis* (The Haag, 1953), general studies on the iconography, ideology, and semantics of the tower have not yet come to my attention. There are, however, some interesting studies on specific types of towers, such as Wolfram Prinz, *Schloss Chambord und die Villa Rotonda in Vicenza* (Berlin: Franfurter Forschungen zur Kunst, 1980) and Johann-Christian Klamt, "Der Runde Turm in Kopenhagen als Kirchturm und Sternwart," *Zeitschrift für Kunstgeschichte,* 38 (1975), pp. 153–70. The commemorative tower expresses its necessary values of eternity by reaching to the heavens. See *Encyclopedia of Religion and Ethics,* James Hastings, ed. (New York, 1913), p. 745. The tower of progress, on the other hand, also reaches skyward, but for different reasons. It challenges the laws of gravity rather than connecting heaven and earth. Skyscrapers like the Woolworth tower were designed to glorify one man's achievement and often embodied these two motives: to secure life after death, as with Mr. Woolworth, and at the same time to demonstrate technological progress. See Thomas A. P. Van Leeuwen, "Sacred Skyscrapers and Profane Cathedrals," *A.A. Files, Annals of the Architectural Association School of Architecture,* no. 8 (Jan. 85), pp. 39–57. Leopold Eidlitz confirms this in his definition of architecture: "The origin of architecture must be thought in the desire of man to live after death." See Leopold Eidlitz, *The Nature and Function of Art, More Especially of Architecture* (New York, 1881), p. 333.

[3] Paul Bourget, *Outre-Mer (Notes sur L'Amerique),* vol. 1 (Paris, 1895), p. 39.

[4] The most complete study in this field is Lewis A. Dudley, "Evaluations of American Architecture by European Critics" (Ph.D. diss., University of Wisconsin, 1962). Thanks to the ample bibliography of this book I was able to determine the existence of the English translation of Bourget's *Outre-Mer.*

[5] Johann Bernhard Fischer von Erlach, *Entwurff einer historischen Architectur* (Vienna, 1721), reprinted (Dortmund, Germany: Harenberg Kommunkation, 1978).

[6] Karl Lamprecht, *Americana* (Freiburg im Breisgau, 1906), p. 81. Lamprecht's critical analysis of turn-of-the-century American culture is interesting and in some ways superior to Bourget's *Outre-Mer.*

[7] Hendrik P. Berlage, *Amerikaansche Reisherinneringen* (Rotterdam, 1913), p. 6. I have not yet been able to trace the poet's name.

[8] Le Corbusier, in his *Quand les Cathédrales étaient Blanches* of 1936, was convinced that the skyscraper should find its own style, in spite of its architects, and that its growth could only be explained as the Tower of Babel. He writes, "*ne possédait jusqu'ici qu'une légende: celle de la tour de Babel,*" p. 62.

[9] Dutch television recently presented a program which raised several interesting points about Dutch emigration to the United States. The main argument noted the unwillingness of immigrants to admit that their expectations of America were not fulfilled. Even in times of hunger and poverty, the letters they sent home were filled with desperate merriment and anecdotes boasting abundance and prosperity. Clearly, the immigrants' belief in the promise of material plenty triumphed over the physical realities. See Arthur Holitscher, *Amerika, Heute und Morgen, Raiseerlenbnisse* (Berlin, 1923), p. 98 ff.

[10] J. W. Schulte Norholt, *Amerika, Land, Volk, Cultuur* (Baarn, The Netherlands, 1965), p. 11. In the first chapter of this book, the author expounds his theories on America as the continent with "its mythical surplus value of a new world." I refer especially to the theories related to the notion of "the great circle" in which America is explained as the completion of the creation, as the final realization of all preceding great cultures and as the continent of death and resurrection.

[11] Washington Irving, *A History of New York, from the Beginning of the World to the End of the Dutch Dynasty ... by Diedrich Knickerbocker* (London, 1900), pp. 13, 61. Book 1 of Knickerbocker's narrative "Containing an account of a mighty ark, which floated, under the protection of St. Nicholas, from Holland to Gibbet Island—the descent of the strange animals therefrom ..." is a liberal treatment of Genesis 9 and part of Genesis 10.

[12] Werner Oechslin, *Skyscraper und Amerikanismus, Mythos zwischen Europa und Amerika,* pp. 4–12, and Manfredo Tafuri, " 'Neu-Babylon': das New York der Zwanzigerjahre und die Suche nach dem Amerikanismus," *Archithese,* 20 (1976), pp. 12–

25; "Amerikanismus, Skyscraper und Ikonografie," *Metropolis 3*. I am indebted to Professor Stanislaus von Moos who was so kind as to send me this important three-volume series on American architecture.

13 Assuming that their work is less well known than that of Sullivan, Ferriss, and Mujica, I will mention here Claude Bragdon's *The Beautiful Necessity* (London, 1910), Irving Pond's *The Meaning of Architecture* (Boston, 1918), and a rare contribution by Harvey Wiley Corbett, "America Builds Skyward," *America as Americans See It* (New York, 1932), pp. 44–52. It is a book intended for the European public. Bragdon's remarks about Ferriss are from *The Frozen Fountain* (New York, 1932), p. 32.

14 The fundamental study on this subject is Mircea Eliade, *Le Mythe de l'Éternel Retour* (Paris, 1949).

15 Irving Pond, *The Meaning of Architecture* (Boston, 1918), p. 11.

16 Louis Althusser, "Les défauts de l'économie classique. Esquisse du concept de temps historique," *Lire le Capital* (Paris, 1968), pp. 112–49.

17 I have borrowed the idea of "physical time" from P. T. Hugenholtz, *Tijd en Creativiteit* (Amsterdam, 1959). I am much indebted to the philosopher Fons Elders who brought to my attention several interesting publications such as the one mentioned above.

18 The term is taken from Claude Bragdon's *The Beautiful Necessity*, p. 34. Bragdon illustrates the law of opposing forces using a drawing based on a famous painting by Tiepolo.

19 Walter Curt Behrendt, *Der Sieg des neuen Baustils* (Stuttgart, 1927), p. 11.

20 The alleged animosity between architects and engineers in the nineteenth century seems to be the result of a mythical personification of architecture and construction, represented as two opposing powers. See Peter Collins, *Changing Ideals in Modern Architecture, 1750–1950* (Montreal, 1967), pp. 128–49.

21 *The International Competition for a New Administration Building for the Chicago Tribune 1922* (New York, 1980), p. 10.

22 The relative value of the term "world" in American usage did not remain unnoticed by Europeans. For example, Paul Bourget wrote, "*Le moindre produit est sur les annonces 'the best in the world'—le meilleur au monde! ... Un vainqueur de boxe devient 'le champion du monde'* (the champion of the world) ... *Où finit la naïveté? Où commence le charlatanisme?*" *Outre-Mer*, p. 54.

23 From a letter by Mine to the curator of the department of architecture at the Art Institute of Chicago, John Zukowsky, dated March 23, 1979. I thank Mr. Zukowsky for helping me to establish this informative link. Copyright The Art Institute of Chicago.

24 Frank Lloyd Wright, *Ausgeführte Bauten und Entwurfe/Studies and Executed Buildings* (Berlin, 1910), Introduction, n.p.

25 "Sullivan hailed this design as a return to, and a carrying forward of, those principles of which he had been the advocate and exemplar; Bertram Goodhue, himself a competitor, who had had an advance view of all the drawings, told me that Saarinen's design was in a class by itself and superior to all others, and such was the consensus of opinion, professional and lay." Claude Bragdon, *The Frozen Fountain*, p. 31.

26 Sigfried Giedion, *Space, Time and Architecture* (Cambridge, Mass., 1946), p. 303, and Montgomery Schuyler, "Architecture in Chicago: Adler and Sullivan" *The Architectural Record* (Dec. 1895), p. 8.

27 Colin Rowe, "Chicago Frame," *The Mathematics of the Ideal Villa and other Essays* (London, 1967), p. 90.

28 Giedion, *Space, Time and Architecture*, p. 314.

29 Paul T. Frankl, *New Dimensions, The Decorative Arts of Today in Words and Pictures* (New York, 1928), p. 52.

30 Berlage, *Amerikaansche Reisherinneringen*, p. 33: ". . . the credit for being the forerunner of modern architecture in America belongs to Sullivan." Henry-Russell Hitchcock, *Modern Architecture: Romanticism and Reintegration*, reprinted (New York, 1970), p. 110. Was he perhaps paraphrasing a quotation of Fiske Kimball? *Architecture as Nature, The Transcendentalist Idea of Nature* (Madison, Wisconsin, 1981).

31 Henry-Russell Hitchcock, *Modern Architecture, Romanticism and Integration*, reprinted (New York, 1970), p. 110.

32 Lewis Mumford, *The Brown Decades, A Study of the Arts in America 1865–1895* (New York, 1971), p. 64.

33 Ibid., p. 64.

34 Behrendt, *Der Sieg des neuen Baustils*. As the title of this booklet indicates, the field of architectural development was seen as comparable to military history. Battles could be fought, victories could be won, defeats could be suffered.

35 Nikolaus Pevsner, *An Outline of European Architecture* (Harmondsworth, 1963), p. 446.

36 Giedion, *Space, Time, and Architecture*, p. 311.

37 Ibid., p. 311.

38 Ibid., p. 312.

39 Ibid., pp. 311–12.

40 Walter Curt Behrendt, *Modern Building* (New York, 1937), p. 110. Juan Pablo Bonta demonstrated quite entertainingly in his *Architecture and its Interpretation* (New York, 1979) how photographs of buildings became the means of illusionistic manipulation in several cases of architecture in the process of canonization. The Carson, Pirie, Scott store is presented as a classic case of its genre. William Jordy was the first to show oblique views of the upper stories so that otherwise invisible ornaments could be seen in the recessed moldings framing the windows. See *American Buildings and Their Architects*, vol. 3: *Progressive and Academic Ideals at the Turn of the Twentieth Century* (Garden City, New York, 1976), pp. 140–41. The cracked photograph Giedion reproduced as figure 183 on p. 311 was most probably taken from Morrison's book from 1935 (see note 51) on which Giedion based his own account of Sullivan.

41 Behrendt, *Der Sieg des neuen Baustils*, and Giedion, *Space, Time, and Architecture*, p. 312. It was Hugh Morrison's idea to transfer the responsibility for the decoration to Elmslie, who, after all, was Morrison's "chief source of information." See also William Jordy, *American Buildings and their Architects* vol. 3.

42 Berlage, *Amerikaansche Reisheinneringen*, pp. 34–35.

43 Ibid., p. 35. Cf. Thomas A. P. Van Leeuwen, "De Commerciele Stijl," *Americana* (Otterlo, 1975), p. 78.

44 Giedion, *Space, Time, and Architecture*, p. 312. In their apparent failure to understand the artistic libertinism and tolerance of the preceding periods, Mumford, Pevsner, Giedion and Morrison believed that the nineteenth century was a time of "confusion" and "inner conflict." Giedion was convinced that France was full of inner contradictions. He wrote, "On the one hand it is the country of obstinate academism.... On the other, the course of painting and construction is inconceivable without France." Sigfried Giedion, *Mechanization Takes Command, a contribution to anonymous history* (New York, 1969), p. 496. The use of the term "inconceivable" is characteristic of their line of historical thinking. Carl Condit, the most loyal of Giedionists, continued this thought in *The Chicago School of Architecture* (Chicago/London, 1964), pp. 1–13.

45 J. J. P. Oud, "Bij een Deensch Ontwerp voor de Chicago Tribune," *Bouwkundig Weekblad* (Nov. 10, 1923), p. 457.

46 Ibid., pp. 456–58.

47 Jacob Needlebaum, ed., *The Sword of Gnosis* (Harmondsworth, 1974), p. 148.

48 Giedion, *Space, Time, and Architecture*, p. 24.

49 *The Origin of the Skyscraper, Report of the Committee Appointed by the Trustees of the Estate of Marshall Field for the Examination of the Structure of the Home Insurance Building* (Chicago, 1931). Tallmadge was chairman of the committee, which consisted of the architects Graham, Shaw, Schmidt, Reed, and Rebori. Also see Thomas Eddy Tallmadge, *The Story of Architecture in America* (New York, 1936), pp. 180–81. This quest for the first skyscraper is comparable to the somewhat naïve optimism of the *"esprits simples"* who thought that the origin of architecture could be revealed in the reconstruction of the primitive hut. See Joseph Rykwert, *On Adam's House in Paradise—The Idea of the Primitive Hut in Architectural History* (New York, 1972).

50 *The International Competition for a New Administration Building for the Chicago Tribune 1922* (New York, 1980), p. 3.

51 Dutch architect H. J. M. Walenkamp wrote in *De Bouwwereld*, vol. 23, no. 20 (1923), p. 1: "He [Saarinen] had designed a tower, as the towers of the old world ought to be." J. J. P. Oud's response was in the same vein (see note 44).

52 J. Huizinga, *Mensch en Menigte in Amerika* (Haarlem, 1928) and J. Huizinga, *Amerika—Levend en Denkend* (Haarlem, 1926).

53 Huizinga, *Amerika—Levend en Denkend*, pp. 173–74.

54 Ibid., p. 164.

55 This historical fact does not need explanation. A slight refinement may be added, however. "Derivative and eclectic architecture very nearly reached its end in the Tribune, but the passion for classical and medieval styles was to survive for two

more years before finally spending itself." Carl Condit, *Chicago 1910–29, Building, Planning and Urban Technology* (Chicago, 1973), p. 114.

56 Sheldon Cheney's *The New World Architecture* (New York, 1930), refers not to America, but to the modernist's utopia in general. The book was not widely publicized on the European continent.

57 Tallmadge, *The Story of Architecture in America,* p. 292.

58 Ibid., pp. 293–94.

59 Since Saarinen's victory as a loser, *The Western Architect* sported a new version of Saarinen's design against a backdrop of a rising sun.

60 "Dr. John Wesley Kelchner's Restoration of King Solomon's Temple and Citadel, Helmle & Corbett Architects," *Pencil Points,* vol. 6, no. 11 (1925) pp. 69–86.

61 The idea of linking Ferriss' drawings to those of John Martin is not new. See Oechslin, *Skyscraper und Amerikanismus,* pp. 6–7.

62 Mircea Eliade, *The Sacred and the Profane* (New York, 1961), p. 20 ff.

63 Eliel Saarinen, "Projects for Lakefront Development of the City of Chicago," *The American Architect and the Architectural Review,* 134 (1923) pp. 487–514; Manfredo Tafuri, "La Montagna Disincantata—Il Grattacielo e la City," *La Città Americana dalla Guerra Civile al New Deal* (Rome: Bari, 1973), p. 453; Mario Manieri-Elia, "Trois Architectes Européens en Amerique: Eliel Saarinen, Mendelsohn, Neutra," *Archithèse* 17, (1976), *Metropolis* I, pp. 16–17. Eliel Saarinen, *The City, Its Growth, Its Decay, Its Future* (New York, 1943), p. 193.

64 Thomas Adams, *Regional Plan of New York and its Environs,* vol. 2, *The Building of the City* (New York, 1931), pp. 384–85.

65 Athanasius Kircher, *Turris Babel* (Amsterdam, 1679). Kircher followed the descriptions of Strabo and Herodotus.

66 Francis Swales, "The Architect and the Grand Plan—An Important Discussion of a Vital Topic," *Pencil Points,* vol. 12, no. 3 (March, 1931), pp. 166–77. Passages quoted: pp. 167, 174.

67 David Watkin, *The Rise of Architectural History* (London, 1980), p. 1; Bruno Taut, *Die Stadtkrone* (Jena, 1919). Although he did not mention Fischer von Erlach, the source appears to be quite evident.

68 Harald Keller in Fischer von Erlach, *Entwurff einer historischen Architectur,* n. p.

69 Adolf Behne, "Wiedergeburt der Baukunst," in Taut, *Die Stadtkrone,* p. 116.

70 Taut, *Die Stadtkrone,* p. 93, figs. 60–61.

71 Edgar Allan Poe, "Mellonta Tauta," *Tales,* vol. 3 (New York, 1914), p. 341, originally published in *Godey's Lady's Book,* February 1849. It was Antoine Bodar who directed my attention to this important passage.

72 From a reproduction in Charles Lockwood, *Manhattan Moves Uptown* (Boston, 1976), p. 277. The cartoon was probably made a year earlier, in 1880. See William Bonner, *New York, The World's Metropolis* (New York, 1924) and Albert Bigelow Paine, *Thomas Nast: His Period and his Pictures* (Princeton, 1904), p. 444.

73 Giedion, *Space, Time, and Architecture,* p. 314.

74 Jan Rutten and Hans Wijnant, "Wolkenkrabbers zijn Uitdrukking van Vertrouwen in de Toekomst" (Skyscrapers are the Expression of Confidence in the Future), an interview with Cesar Pelli, *Bouw,* vol. 30, no. 11 (1983), special issue *Wolkenkrabbers in New York,* p. 25.

75 *Real Estate Record and Builders' Guide,* vol. 16, no 402 (November 27, 1875), p. 776.

76 Athanasius Kircher, *Mundus Subterraneus or De Onderaardse Weereld,* book 8 sterdam, 1682), p. 29.

THE BUILDING:
VERNACULAR AND MONUMENTAL

INTRODUCTION:
THOUGHTS ON THE GEOGRAPHY
OF AMERICAN ARCHITECTURE

by William Jordy

At first glance, the theme of the three papers that follow appears to be "Westward the Course of American Architecture Makes Its Way": from Boston in the 1870s and 1880s, to Chicago in the 1880s through the teens, and (with some overlap in the teens) on to Los Angeles thereafter. This pat progression is, of course, "happenstantial." It is less a matter of historical fact than a convenient format for providing a national gloss, with a changing chronological focus, on the American architectural scene.

Suppose the game were extended. Would one add Colonial Philadelphia, Federalist Salem (incorporating something on Bulfinch, because Boston has already been allocated to Richardson), and (following Talbot Hamlin's lead) Greek Revival Washington? Should New York (which has to be accommodated somewhere) arbitrarily fill the gap from 1840 to 1870, simply because no other city comes to mind to make the bridge? Or is New York better saved for McKim, Mead & White and the American Renaissance? Or for the period between the two world wars, when its skyline was most compelling and the idea of the skyscraper city most alluring? Should Philadelphia be reserved for Louis Kahn and the Venturis, and Colonial go to some other important, but more circumscribed, center such as Williamsburg? And who can be completely happy leaving current developments to Los Angeles?

So the format encourages its own queries, more musings than questions of serious historical inquiry. Yet the musing induces thoughts on the geography of American architecture, and calls up problems for fruitful investigation that directly or tangentially touch on this theme.

Of course, local and regional studies of American architectural history are numerous: on the most significant architecture of a locale, whether as guidebooks, or fleshed out with more substantial commentary; on the vernacular tradition of a particular area; and on the development of such local or regional episodes as the Chicago style of commercial buildings, Art Deco in New York, and the diffuse Bay Area style of redwood modernism around San Francisco after World War II. Except for the theoretical and comparative studies of vernacular architecture, however, historians have directed little beyond the most obvious (one is tempted to say most superficial) inquiry into those geographical and human factors that have sometimes substantially influenced buildings and their distribution within the country. Few large-scale historical studies have been significantly organized around centers of production. Some studies of Colonial architecture are an exception. So is Hamlin's pioneering volume on the Greek Revival, although his analysis of the role of local centers in the production of a national style possesses neither the detail nor sophistication that might be expected of any counterpart undertaken today.[1] There must be others, but not many.

The format of the following papers suggests that, as the country expanded westward, there were ambitious professionals ready to join in the migration and establish new centers for the making of architecture. For the most creative architects moving into them, these centers provided locales for starting afresh, for doing things in a different way. This theme of the West as the "newest white page turned for registration," to use Irving Gill's phrase,[2] appears, variously manifested in all three papers. So does the countertheme of holding onto remembered traditions even if, in Western centers, the traditional image may be scrappier in quality and more casually applied than in their Eastern counterparts. Uneasily pressed between the "new page" and the "old," Western production has had a difficult time of it in Eastern establishment history. Early on, Chicago could not be denied. Perceptions of the uniqueness of its progressive architecture go all the way back to the 1880s and 1890s, even as the buildings were going up.[3] But Chicago could be condescended to. Its most original architecture might be new, to be sure, but crude. Not until the thirties did historians begin to take Chicago seriously, and even then not really until the astonishment of a foreigner (Giedion) compellingly placed Chicago's accomplishments, as he saw them, into an international context.[4] Los Angeles fared worse. Not until well after World War II did it seriously count in the history books as a center for the creation of architecture. It was the devotion of a long-time resident (McCoy) and the appreciation of another foreigner (Banham) that decisively effected the change in attitude.[5]

Like all provincial phenomena (or those perceived as such by establishment spokesmen who do the judging), Western production has too often been viewed pejoratively; alternatively, portions of it have been received ecstatically. In both cases the judgment has tended to bolster various current establishment points of view. Characteristically, the more cosmopolitan center accepts its own complexity without question, but oversimplifies the allegedly provincial situation. Moreover, the West comes to view itself in terms of the establishment encapsulations. The papers that follow challenge, in part, some of these constructs and suggest more complex views of Western achievement.

One area, then, for future investigation evolving from the themes of these papers might be an examination of the history of attitudes toward the architecture of the West (or of the several Wests). It could serve as a means both to reassess Western architecture itself and to chart changing attitudes toward what is conceived to be quintessentially "American," in territory where "American qualities" in architecture are quintessentially supposed to reside—unless one also adds Manhattan, whose skyscrapers, even when decked in European-derived styles, are so conspicuously "American" as a type.

Boston, Chicago, Los Angeles—all are important for the creation of American architecture. Yet the foci of these papers call to mind other major metropolitan centers important for the creation of architecture in the United States. To be comprehensive, one must surely add Philadelphia, also San Francisco, and perhaps Baltimore, New Orleans, and Detroit for sometime episodes of importance to the evolution of American architecture—above all, New York. Certain other metropolitan centers of consequence in the history of American architecture seem traditionally to have been more receivers than creators of significant design. Here opinion will be more varied, but I think of Atlanta, Dallas, Houston, Denver, Miami, Portland (Oregon), Minneapolis, and especially Washington. The list is not meant to be conclusive, and there are episodes in some of these centers (or in others) that might just edge them from lesser into grander status. Moreover, the situation could, in the future, change for any city. Why these centers? Why not other centers?

How curious that the national capital has never had an architect of national (let alone international) importance who is preeminently associated with it. American architects of historical consequence have gone to Washington from other parts of the country for their commissions and withdrawn once their buildings were done. The nation's principal city for architectural export has been its leading commercial and cultural center, while its principal city for architectural import has been its national capital. In this respect, the situation in the United States parallels that of certain one-time colonial countries, like Canada, Australia, or India. There are few parallels in Western Europe (and probably not many outside of Europe). The Netherlands, however, is one. The decision to remove the political center of Brazil to the vast emptiness of its interior is another.

What circumstances account for the occurrence of architectural creativity in relatively few metropolises, and, even more mysterious, the persistent lack of it in others where it might also be expected to occur? As the so-called Sun Belt metropolises swell in size, will some of them become centers of architectural creativity? Surely, not only growing population, wealth, and cultural aspirations suggest that this should happen, but so do environmental conditions. These are sufficiently at variance with comparable conditions in most of the cities of architectural export (Los Angeles excepted) that one could expect architectural invention with regional implications to flourish, even if mechanical equipment tends to make the implications more allusive than actual. Consider two regional features of Houston, for example. Its heat and humidity cause weeds to sprout from every crack in its sidewalks. Its industrial surroundings contain many high-tech refineries. Does the city take either of these features into account in its architecture? Until recently its ideal for the skyscraper plaza was straight-from-New York paving, and hot enough in summer to fry an egg on, had anyone cared to brave these vacant, steamy spaces in July or August to make the experiment. If the New York skyscraper with greenhouse base has finally reached Houston, it has arrived with foliage as timidly circumscribed as that back East. Meanwhile, since New York has yet to create anything like a Centre Pompidou, Houston presumably must wait for inspiration from its refineries, even though any overt expression of mechanical equipment should be especially appropriate in a city that, except for air conditioning, would be uninhabitable. Why is the character of this regional metropolis so unregional? If regional characteristics *are* to be found in such areas, they often depend on the discoveries of the historian of vernacular building poking about in backwater rurality, although reportedly no vernacular of consequence exists in the vicinity of Houston, where, before the city's recent emergence, few chose to live.

Smaller cities, too, have been occasional centers of innovative design of high quality, like Newport, Charleston (South Carolina), Salem, Lowell, Portland (Maine, with Calvin Steven's early work in the Shingle style), or Syracuse (home base for Gustav Stickley and much Arts and Crafts activity, and the almost contemporaneous place of emigration for Joseph Lyman Silsbee and Irving Gill). As with metropolises, so with smaller cities; some are more receivers than creators of fine architecture (although some homegrown creativity may also be present). One thinks of cities and towns as diverse as Natchez, Buffalo, Columbus (Indiana), and the Hamptons on Long Island (unless the last be considered a piece of New York). Some small cities have come to fame simply by virtue of substantially holding onto what they had, like Nantucket, Cape May (New Jersey), Harrisville (New Hampshire), or Galena (Illinois). A few have held onto their place in architectural history as the residues of utopian experiment, as Dolores Hayden has most recently reminded us.[6] Finally—to close this typology of centers of architectural creation and consumption—wherever any particularly creative individual chooses to live, he or she can make that spot loom with the extrageographical luster of a Spring Green (Wisconsin) or Scottsdale (Arizona), Norman or Bartlesville (Oklahoma), Carbondale (Illinois) or Monticello. In such cases, however, we are no longer concerned with a geographical center really, but with the center that any creative individual of consequence carries, as Wright said of his office, under his hat.

But let me focus, as do the papers, on some of the largest metropolises of architectural production and consumption, particularly because to do so may indicate something of the present state of the study of American architecture at this moment when the Buell Center for the Study of American Architecture is getting underway. In thinking about the metropolises and cities I have listed above and speculating on others I might have named, I can call up nothing that may be termed a definitive study of any significant architectural episode or movement that occurred in any one of them. By definitive I mean an account that takes as its theme the total situation in which a significant collective manifestation of building occurs—that is, a study that accounts in a broad way for the interaction of the locale, architect, client, technology, and social and cultural context from which the buildings emerge and take their meaning with respect to the history of architecture. Why this lack? Is the reason for the dearth of such studies that, until recently, they could not easily have been done? Do there now exist, however, circumstances to change this situation?

Consider the basis for any such comprehensive study: simply, knowledge of the relevant buildings to be considered. It is quite astonishing to contemplate the amount of information that has been accumulated on American buildings and architects during the past ten to twenty years thanks to recent scholarship, but also due to the recent growth of governmental commissions charged with the systematic discovery of buildings and areas worthy of the preservationist's consideration, to the significant enlargement of the purview of such organizations as the National Trust, to swelling local conservation groups, and to the steady increase of bus and walking tours that seasonally sweep the country. All this activity has generated a continuous flood of guidebooks and photocopied itineraries to American regions, counties, cities, towns, wards, and districts—many utterly remote, one would have thought, from "architecture." From this base of local enthusiasm and enterprise, information has accumulated to make possible publications of various sorts with grander scholarly intentions.

Suppose, for example, the historian were entering upon a comprehensive investigation of some aspect of the architectural development of one of the three cities at the focus of the papers that follow. If it were Los Angeles, he or she would already have at hand the comprehensive guide by Gebhard and Winter that goes far beyond the casual tourist guide and represents much original (even unconventional) investigation.[7] If we move momentarily outside the purview of these three papers, to nineteenth-century New Orleans, for example, the scholar would have at hand a multivolume compendium, which is no longer a guide at all but a district-by-district scholarly survey of the city by a team of researchers.[8] The survey becomes full-fledged scholarship when, as with Bunting's account of Boston's Back Bay architecture or Brooks's account of the Chicago Prairie school, it is organized within the framework of intellectual analysis rather than by plat maps.[9] A decade and a half ago, this kind of base for further scholarship on these cities would have been almost nonexistent.

But our imaginary scholar venturing a comprehensive study of a city like Boston, Chicago, or Los Angeles (to stay with the themes of the papers) would also have the advantage of scholarship pointing the way and lightening the load in other ways. For Boston, as something of a trial run for the enterprise, there is the catalogue of the Museum of Fine Arts centennial show on Back Bay, which provided a once-over-lightly panorama of its planning, parks, architecture, clients, and collectors and their collections.[10] There is Zaitzevsky's book on Olmsted's creation of the Boston park system[11]—a big chunk of the job done. For Chicago, there are a growing number of reassessments of the so-called Chicago school. One of these, which is especially pertinent, is Landau's demonstration of how much New York's commercial architecture anticipated developments in Chicago.[12] On Los Angeles, aside from Banham's exuberant embrace of its four ecologies, there is Hines's splendid study of Neutra, which does in fact epitomize the architect-in-his-milieu sort of approach; our imaginary scholar would find it directly useful for method as well as for information, were he or she to undertake a larger study of the Los Angeles architecture of the period.[13] These are simply a few examples that come first to mind.

My major point here has been to take off from themes suggested by the papers at hand. I do not mean to suggest that there is some ultimate virtue in the kind of architectural study on which I have chosen to focus here; just that this kind of study requires a density of factual information in combination with a variety of historical approaches, something we may just now be in a position to realize.[14] Hence, a second broad area for exploration: comprehensive case studies of developments in different kinds of architectural centers, and comparative studies of factors across the spectrum of types of centers in which significant architectural history has occurred accounting for these different kinds of developments.

Finally, although these papers deal with individual buildings in urban centers, in all three instances the American preoccupation with nature and with the space of nature obtrudes, and the psychic tug toward the land is both pervasive and insistent. (Only New York seems an exception in this respect.) Recently much architectural history has dealt with man's imprint on the big spaces that are so much a part of American experience, stemming in large part from Jackson's innovative *American Space,* with Stilgoe's *Common Landscape of America* a recent example.[15] Architectural scholarship, to the degree that it has concerned itself with the interrelationship between buildings and larger aspects of the land, has principally concentrated on three kinds of investigation: studies of the traditional vernacular, which have centered on rural buildings scattered in the big spaces between urban areas; studies of the contemporary vernacular, which have emphasized building phenomena like the commercial strip, the builder's subdivision, and the shopping mall on the periphery of urban areas; and studies that emphasize urban buildings in context.[16]

There are also, however, mixes of architecture and planning at a large scale that speak quite as directly as these others about the vastness of American space. They have yet to receive the study they deserve. This year, for example, marks the fiftieth anniversary of the Tennessee Valley Authority, which has so transformed the ecology of its region as to create a chain of man-made lakes with a shoreline more extensive than that of the Great Lakes. It has not been definitively studied. Nor has Henry Ford's River Rouge plant, beyond the very helpful study of the technology of the individual buildings in the complex by Grant Hildebrand;[17] nor restored Colonial Williamsburg under the impact of the automobile. By comparison, the big vertical designs have recently garnered more than their fair share of attention in American architectural scholarship, to the extent that literature on the skyscraper can serve today as a paradigm for the whole spectrum of approaches that may be applied to a single architectural type. The big horizontal designs, which loom equally (even more) importantly in the American architectural scene, have not fared as well. Hence another area for investigation.

These broad territories for further exploration are called up by peripheral musings on the themes of the papers that follow.

NOTES

[1] Talbot Hamlin, *Greek Revival in America* (London and New York: Oxford University Press, 1944).

[2] Irving Gill, "The Home of the Future. The New Architecture of the West: Small Homes for a Great Country, Number Four," *Craftsman,* 30 (May 1916), p. 141.

[3] In the 1890s Montgomery Schuyler was already praising the Chicago commercial style and citing European observers who felt as he did. See especially his "Architecture in Chicago: Adler & Sullivan," *Architectural Record,* 6 (Feb. 1896), pp. 3–48; "D. H. Burnham & Co.," ibid., pp. 49–69; "The Skyscraper Problem," *Scribner's Magazine,* 34 (Aug. 1903), pp. 253–56. Excerpts from all are conveniently available in Montgomery Schuyler, *American Architecture and Other Writings,* eds. William Jordy and Ralph Coe (Cambridge, Mass., 1961), vol. 2, pp. 377–436.

[4] Sigfried Giedion, *Space, Time and Architecture* (Cambridge, Mass.: Harvard Univ. Press, 1941).

[5] Esther McCoy, *Five California Architects* (New York: Reinhold, 1960); Reyner Banham, *Los Angeles: The Architecture of Four Ecologies* (New York: Harper, 1971).

[6] Dolores Hayden, *Seven American Utopias: The Architecture of Communitarian Socialism, 1790–1975* (Cambridge, Mass.: MIT Press, 1976).

[7] David Gebhard and Robert Winter, *A Guide to Architecture in Los Angeles and Southern California* (Santa Barbara: Peregrine Smith, 1977).

[8] Three collaborative volumes under the general title *New Orleans Architecture: The Lower Garden District; The American Sector; The Cemeteries* (Gretna, La.: Pelican, 1971, 1972, 1974).

[9] Bainbridge Bunting, *Houses of Boston's Back Bay: An Architectural History, 1840–1917* (Cambridge, Mass.: Belknap Press, 1967); H. Allen Brooks, *The Prairie School: Frank Lloyd Wright and His Midwest Contemporaries* (Toronto: University of Toronto Press, 1972).

[10] Museum of Fine Arts, *Back Bay Boston: The City as a Work of Art* (Boston, 1969).

[11] Cynthia Zaitzevsky, *Frederick Law Olmsted and the Boston Park System* (Cambridge, Mass.: Belknap Press, 1982).

[12] Sarah Landau, "The Tall Building Artistically Reconsidered: Arcaded Buildings of the New York School, c. 1870–1890," in *In Search of Modern Architecture, A Tribute to Henry-Russell Hitchcock,* ed. Helen Searing (New York and Cambridge, Mass.: MIT Press, 1982). Also to this point is a recent exhibition catalogue, *Chicago and New York: Architectural Interactions* (Chicago: Art Institute of Chicago; New York: The New-York Historical Society, 1984).

[13] Thomas Hines, *Richard Neutra and the Search for Modern Architecture* (New York: Oxford University Press, 1982).

[14] For example, as I write this essay notice arrives of the publication of two volumes illustrative of the kind of studies and dependent on the kind of information to which I refer: Robert A. M. Stern, Gregory Gilmartin, and John Montague Massengale, *New York 1900: Metropolitan Architecture and Urbanism 1890–1915* (New York: Rizzoli, 1983) and Richard Longstreth, *On the Edge of the World: Four Architects in San Francisco at the Turn of the Century* (New York and Cambridge, Mass.: MIT Press, 1983).

[15] John Brinkerhoff Jackson, *American Space: The Centennial Years, 1865–1876* (New York: Norton, 1972); John R. Stilgoe, *Common Landscape of America* (New Haven: Yale University Press, 1982).

[16] Obvious, and key, examples of each type are Henry H. Glassie, *Folk Housing in Middle Virginia: A Structural Analysis of Historic Artifacts* (Knoxville: University of Tennessee Press, ca. 1975); Robert Venturi, Denise Scott Brown, and Steven Izenour, *Learning from Las Vegas* (Cambridge, Mass.: MIT Press, 1972); Colin Rowe and Fred Koetter, *Collage City* (Cambridge, Mass.: MIT Press, 1978).

[17] Grant Hildebrand, *Designing for Industry: The Architecture of Albert Kahn* (Cambridge, Mass.: MIT Press, 1974).

AMERICA AND H. H. RICHARDSON

by James O'Gorman

Contemporaries of H. H. Richardson saw his mature work as standing out from the run-of-the-mill design of post-Civil War America. This they usually attributed to his choice of Romanesque over Victorian Gothic or Second Empire sources, and so they saw his achievement in terms of their own eclectic practice. With the perspective of time we are able to modify that assessment some-what. An analysis of the architect's two most definitive—and dra-matically divergent—buildings demonstrates that Richardson's mature work differed markedly from that of his peers because his intentions differed from theirs. Whereas they sought to compete with European achievements, he sought *in addition* to create an architecture expressive of the environmental and cultural traditions of New England in particular, and the New World in general. The works I will look at here are the Marshall Field Wholesale Store in Chicago of 1885–1887 (fig. 1) and the F. L. Ames Gate Lodge at North Easton, Massachusetts, of 1880–1881 (fig. 2). To understand their American roots is to understand Richardson's particular con-tribution to American architecture.[1]

Below, left:
1 *Marshall Field Wholesale Store*
Chicago, Illinois
H. H. Richardson, 1885–1887.

Below, right:
2 *Ames Gate Lodge*
North Easton, Massachusetts
H. H. Richardson, 1880–1881.

The Field Store is a city building, the gate lodge a rural one, and therein lies our need to approach them by different paths. In 1868, about the time he first met Richardson, the landscape architect Frederick Law Olmsted issued a report on his own work at Riv-erside, Illinois, in which he clearly recognized the major social forces acting to produce the post-Civil War environment, with its densely packed commercial core and its outlying domestic retreats. In his

lecture on public parks two years later at Boston's Lowell Institute, Olmsted demanded that the special needs of each of these distinct social zones be met by distinct architectural forms.[2] His new friend Richardson was to make this environmental vision the framework of his architectural career, a career that culminated in Chicago and North Easton.

For each of Olmsted's social zones Richardson gradually evolved a special image, first by looking for inspiration to the great stone architectures of the European past, and then by turning to New England and eventually to continental American sources. We never learn this from his words, but from his works we may guess that he intended his buildings as an American expression. Let us then concentrate upon American sources for his architectural solutions, leaving for more extended treatment elsewhere the role of European models in his achievement.

The Field Store was the end product of Richardson's search for an appropriate urban commercial form that began in 1867 with the Western Railroad Offices in Springfield, Massachusetts, a work pieced together out of parts published by Letarouilly and Grandjean. By the mid-seventies he had in the Cheney Block at Hartford and, even more importantly, as we shall see, in the Hayden Building in Boston, discovered a home-grown tradition upon which he might build. As Montgomery Schuyler reported, Richardson told him that "there was more character in the plain and solid warehouses that had been destroyed" in the Boston fire of 1872 than in the buildings that had replaced them.[3] Richardson here refers to those mid-century granite wharf buildings for which Boston is famous, and it was to the local tradition of urban commercial design they represent that Richardson eventually turned.

The "Boston Granite Style" begins in the Greek Revival, with the building-block facades of the north and south rows of stores at Alexander Parris's Quincy Market, where uprights and horizontals of local stone make up the image; carries into the early Gothic Revival, where the granite unit forms the module of design; and lends itself to the commercial development of the harbor's edge at mid-century.[4] It is especially in the block-filling warehouses of Gridley J. F. Bryant that Richardson found a native answer to the problem of urban architecture. Here were a series of buildings articulated by repetitive units and constructed of rock-faced granite blocks piled up into either trabeated or arcuated facades. Such mid-century stringent lithic design actually stretched from Paul Schulze's Boylston Hall at Harvard to arcuated public works like Bryant's Suffolk County Prison of 1849, and the Beacon Hill Reservoir of the same year, a work decidedly Richardsonian before Richardson (fig. 3). We not only have Schuyler's word that Richardson took an interest in these buildings; we have the evidence of the Hayden Building as well.

3 Beacon Hill Reservoir
Boston, Massachusetts
Designer unknown, 1849.

The Hayden Building of 1875, a relatively small structure in Boston's notorious "combat zone" of porno flicks and "live shows," can be easily overlooked in an assessment of Richardson's development (fig. 4). It should not be. The slender facade facing Washington Street, especially, is a key composition in granite. The trabeated top floor of monolithic posts and lintels and the two-story arcade just below clearly swing from the Boston Granite style toward the Field facades.

It is its facades of pink Missouri granite and red East Longmeadow sandstone that have made the Field Store the object of admiration for generations of historians, although the scale of the building, which was a blockbuster in the literal sense, was what caught the eyes of Chicagoans in the late 1880s. Field assembled the building site out of a series of real-estate transactions to create a corporate whole, and Richardson responded by adapting the granite block of the Boston waterfront to the needs of the wholesale store. Against the average street front of Chicago in the 1880s, the Field Store appeared, as Louis Sullivan expressed it, to be an oasis "amidst a host of stage-struck wobbling mockeries."[5] This achievement in urban coherence was quickly eclipsed by the rise of the skyscraper, but the Field Store was briefly the model for large-scale urban design. Or so Sullivan thought when he altered his original facades of the Auditorium to conform to those of the Store.

Those famous Field facades do not, however, tell the whole story about the building. They extended down Adams Street, down the intersecting Franklin and Fifth (now Wells) streets, and turned the corners at Quincy Street. But the plan was a square U, and the granite facades reached on narrower Quincy only to the notch containing the loading dock. Here the scale shifted downward, and the walls of the notch were of brick (as far as we can tell from incomplete evidence) and dissolved by broad, segmentally arched

4 Hayden Building,
Boston, Massachusetts
H. H. Richardson, 1875.

5 *Mill Building*
Gloucester, Massachusetts
Designer unknown, ca. 1900.

windows at each level into a grid of piers and spandrels. The origin of this facade is not difficult to find within the New England tradition, for it is a direct reflection of the characteristic facade pattern displayed on mill buildings from Lowell to Lawrence to Manchester and beyond (fig. 5). Richardson used the pattern to reflect the New England origins of part of the structural system within the building.

Writing about "slow-burning construction" in the February 1889 issue of *Century Magazine,* Edward Atkinson, an insurance man who campaigned vigorously for structural reform in mill building, and Richardson's Brookline neighbor, stated bluntly that "the great warehouse built by Richardson and his successors for Marshall Field is but a glorified cotton factory." He based his statement on what he thought was Richardson's use in the Field Store of the slow-burning or heavy timber construction common in New England mills, and he was partially correct. Richardson did employ structural wood, although it appears he combined it with fireproof metallic structure as well. Rear facade and partial structural systems were, then, adapted, like the main facades, from traditional forms found by the architect in his adopted New England environment.

This analysis of the traditions underlying Richardson's culminating urban design purposely overlooks two more common interpretations of the building. It is usually linked to the *palazzi* of the Florentine Renaissance just as its owner is linked to the merchant princes of the same era. And who can deny the connection? Both architect and client did visit the central Italian city in the years prior to the construction of the store, and comparisons to the Strozzi or Pitti palaces do seem just. But to criticize Richardson's mature work *only* in terms of its European sources is to misinterpret badly his search for American solutions to traditional problems. The Field Store, erected in the Loop just at the beginning of the era of the skyscraper development that has come to be called the "Chicago school," was no more a product of the Middle West than the contemporary Monadnock Building, financed by Boston money, was named after a prairie outcropping. The Field Store was physically in Chicago, but as a creative act it formed the culmination of Richardson's search in Boston and New England for precedents for a commercial form suitable to the new urban scale. And these eastern associations were certainly understood if not supported by its owner, a dry goods merchant born in Massachusetts, who frequently visited the mills which produced his merchandise. Chicago in the 1880s had a sizable population of migrated Easterners, and that description fits not only Marshall Field, but the wholesale store Richardson designed for him.

The compacted commercial centers generated by the economic and social forces of the 1880s, and summarized by a building like the Field Store, had their counterparts in outlying satellite towns, bedroom suburbs, and rural retreats. Here urban forms would have been out of place; here Richardson was forced to mine an alternate, actually a non-architectural, tradition in his search for the diversity he, following Olmsted, thought appropriate to this rural zone. His solutions in the realm of residential design are among his most refreshing creations, and this is largely because they are free of the humdrumness of repeated historical forms. In works like the R. T. Paine House in Waltham or the E. W. Gurney House at Pride's Crossing, both in Massachusetts and both of 1884, natural forms often replace expected architectural details, so that glacial boulders or irregular, quarried stones are piled into an overall geological imagery. Nowhere is this more evident than in the Gate Lodge at North Easton (see fig. 2). Only in the occasional work of A. J. Davis, such as the Gate Lodge at Llewellyn Park in New Jersey, do we find precedents for such natural building within American architecture. We must look outside the building industry for the meaning of Richardson's rural work.

Our starting point is the epigraph on the title page of Mrs. Van Rensselaer's fundamental monograph on the architect (1888), a work written by one friend and sponsored by two others: Olmsted and Charles Sprague Sargent. This epigraph echoes the voice of nineteenth-century New England. It is a quotation from the end of Ralph Waldo Emerson's essay "Art" (1841), an essay which ends with this admonition:

> It is in vain that we look for genius to reiterate its miracles in the old arts; it is its instinct to find beauty and holiness in the field and roadside, in the shop and mill.

Here is Emerson's call for new art forms based upon new—American—sources of inspiration. In the Field Store, Richardson seems to have followed the direction toward "shop and mill." In his rural works, he looked to the field, to the land, for his "new and necessary facts."

In "The Young American" (1844) Emerson wrote,

> The land is the appointed remedy for whatever is false
> and fantastic in our culture. The continent we inhabit is
> to be physic and food for our mind, as well as our body.
> The land, with its tranquilizing, sanative influences, is
> to repair the errors of scholarship and traditional edu-
> cation, and brings us into just relations with men and
> things.

Mrs. Van Rensselaer and her sponsors must have thought Emerson's words applied to Richardson. His friend, the painter John
LaFarge, wrote that the architect "was obliged . . . to throw over-
board in dealing with the new problems all his educational recipes
learned in other countries."[6] The message is clear. In seeking an
American architecture, especially a rural American architecture,
Richardson was following the lead of Emerson and those poets and
painters of the previous generation and earlier, like Thomas Cole
or William Cullen Bryant, who had already paralleled or followed
the philosopher's call for a land-based American culture.

America's search for an identity in the years after the revolutionary
period eventually focused upon the land, which was after all the
only strictly American element in the culture. As Norman Foerster
put it so well in the first sentence of his *Nature in American Literature,*
"since the early white settlers of America were Englishmen, who
brought with them and later imported the culture of the Old World,
for a long time the distinction of America, the newness of the New
World, was simply nature."[7] This interest in the land was political
and scientific as well as artistic. It was during these years that the
earth sciences in general, and the study of geology in particular,
reached early maturity. Thomas Cole, often called the father of
American landscape painting, painted *The Ox Bow* fifteen years
after the publication of Charles Lyell's *Principles of Geology* (1830–
1833), the science's first mature synthesis in which the earth-sculpt-
ing dynamics of wind and water were given primacy. The nineteenth-century geologist replaced the eighteenth-century chemist
on the frontiers of science by the 1830s, and by the post-Civil War
era, the western survey geologist had replaced the eastern classroom
geologist.

The discovery of America by Americans reached its climax in the
"era of exploration" following the Civil War, as the railroad bound
West to East and the search for mineral riches became intense.[8]
This era is distinguished by the unrivaled land forms that were
revealed through the work of artists and photographers who
flooded the East with spectacular images. These came as part of
scientific publications or as illustrations for popular literature.
Emerson had foreseen the impact of the new West. Again, in "The
Young American" he sang of this source of inspiration:

> The nervous, rocky West is intruding a new and con-
> tinental element into the national mind, and we shall yet

have an American genius. . . . I think we must regard the *land* [his emphasis] as a commanding and increasing power on the citizen, the sanative and Americanizing influence, which promises to disclose new virtues for ages to come.

These new images took on startlingly architectural forms. Both the scientific and popular literature of the day saw in these products of physical erosion or divine creation parallels to the man-made monuments of the Old World. This was nature's architecture, and it provided provocative sources for someone like H. H. Richardson. I would like to suggest that the architect was indeed taken with these ubiquitous images, that he turned the architectural image in nature into the geological image in architecture.

Richardson would have known about western discoveries merely by being alive in the 1870s and 1880s, or through the circle of New England intellectuals who were his clients, but there are more direct connections as well. It is credible to suggest that a man proud of his descent from Joseph Priestly, the so-called discoverer of oxygen, would have taken at least a passing interest in the sciences at Harvard. He might have on occasion listened to the charismatic Louis Agassiz, father of glacial theory, perhaps even taken some notice of the opening of Agassiz's Museum in 1858. Richardson's friend and future client, Henry Adams, developed a lifelong interest in geology under Agassiz at Harvard in the 1850s.

*6 Ames Monument
Sherman, Wyoming
H. H. Richardson, 1879–1882.*

Later, Richardson's collaborator and, one may say, environmental mentor, Olmsted, acted as a direct link to the West. He had worked at the Mariposa Mine in California and had become involved in the preservation of Yosemite, Yellowstone, and Niagara. The work at Yosemite brought Olmsted into direct contact with Clarence King, a follower of Agassiz and Ruskin, a survey geologist when Olmsted met him, later a leader of the Fortieth Parallel Survey, author of *Mountaineering in the High Sierras,* and first Director of the U.S. Geological Survey. He was also a man who employed photographers on his western surveys and in such vanity gift publications as his *Three Lakes* of 1870, with its frontispiece of Lake Marian by Timothy O'Sullivan.[9] I can find no direct evidence that Richardson knew King, but he must have. The geologist was a warm friend of John LaFarge and, more importantly, a bosom companion of the Henry Adamses and the John Hays. Adams visited King during the Fortieth Parallel Survey, and King responded with occasional visits to the Adamses in Washington during the time Richardson was at work on the Hay and Adams houses.

The Ames Monument in Wyoming of 1879 (fig. 6) is not merely an eastern Mediterranean pyramid, as traditional, Old-World-oriented critics have maintained. Here in the West Richardson created his first essay in geological imagery. The site is a high ridge. The monument is a subtly profiled pyramid of granite ashlar sixty feet

7 *Pilot Knob*
California, 1872–1874.

8 *Detail of Ames Gate Lodge.*

Below:
9 *David Johnson*
Natural Bridge, *1860.*

high embellished only with Saint-Gaudens's portraits of Oakes and Oliver. As it appeared from the proper viewpoint—the railway beneath it—the Ames Monument seemed just another outcropping against the sky. At least Olmsted thought so. Writing to Mrs. Van Rensselaer after the architect's death, he made explicit the impact of the form:

> I never saw a monument so well befitting its situation,
> or a situation so well befitting the special characteristics
> of a particular site. . . . A fellow passenger told me that
> . . . it had caught his eye [but] he had supposed it to be
> a natural object. Within a few miles there are several
> conical horns of the same granite projecting above the
> smooth surface of the hills.[10]

Since Richardson never visited the site, he could have known of such forms only from photographic images or, more likely, from the pages of some popular publication. A suggestive source occurs in William Cullen Bryant's *Picturesque America* (1812–1874), where the view of Pilot Knob in northern California shows a natural form so close in shape and siting to the Ames Monument as to render an accidental similarity incredible (fig. 7). It is no wonder that a view of the monument appears among the geological sights in William Thayer's *Marvels of the New West* (1887).[11]

We could apply the same parallels to other rural Richardson works such as the Gurney and Paine houses, but the Ames Gate Lodge is the paradigm of the geological analogy in the architect's work. The Lodge is a building with little architectural precedent. Here Richardson drew inspiration from natural imagery to embody an American rural style in the way that he drew upon native commercial forms at the Field Store to embody an American urban style. The Lodge combines residence and potting shed, joining the two by a

polychromatic arch over the driveway. The walls are piled glacial boulders punctuated with dressed stone. Characteristically the mature architect relied for effect upon the natural colors and textures of stone, the interplay of organic and shaped forms and textures, solids and voids, and the harmonious integration of building and rural environment (shaped by Olmsted). He also relied upon geological associations.

The detailing of windows, arches, and walls makes little reference to architectural history. The rough stone arch of the wellhead is, for example, primitively composed of natural voussoirs (fig. 8). It is as if Richardson had adapted to the needs of a building with openings and a roof the image of an outcropping, a geological shape such as found in photographs like A. J. Russell's *Skull Rock* (1867–1868). There are in fact a host of suggestive images one might associate with the Gate Lodge (see fig. 2). Among them, David Johnson's painting (1860) of the Natural Bridge in Virginia is a startling parallel (fig. 9), a convincing visual revelation of Richardson's intentions. This is the context within which the Gate Lodge must be interpreted. There is no other, including the architectural, which so enriches our understanding of Richardson's rural building. It is this that Frank Lloyd Wright discovered when he came to study Richardson's work at the beginning of his own career in rural domestic design.

Richardson died at forty-seven, before his work was complete. Against the full sweep of architectural history his achievement in the Field Store must be seen as tentative if measured against the work of Sullivan and the Chicago school, and so his Ames Gate Lodge must be judged as tentative if measured against the fully realized organic architecture of Wright. As unfinished as his work was, however, its impact was clear. As the German Leopold Gmelin wrote as early as 1899, Richardson was "the founder of an independent style of architecture in the New World."[12] Whether he sought to fulfill Olmsted's desire to see appropriate and diverse architectural forms for city or for country, he achieved works in which he reached the stature of that "American genius" Emerson was looking for in "The Young American" essay of 1844.

NOTES

[1] This paper briefly summarizes two chapters of a book now in preparation. It is intended to be suggestive rather than definitive, and to offer an example of cross-disciplinary method for investigation in architectural history. For the section on the Field Store, see my "Marshall Field Wholesale Store: Materials Toward a Monograph," *Journal of the Society of Architectural Historians,* 37 (October 1978), pp. 175–94. For Richardson's buildings mentioned but not illustrated, see Jeffrey Karl Ochsner, *H. H. Richardson: Complete Architectural Works* (Cambridge, Mass.: M.I.T. Press, 1982).

[2] S. B. Sutton, ed., *Civilizing American Cities: A Selection of Frederick Law Olmsted's Writings* (Cambridge, Mass.: MIT Press, 1971), pp. 52–99, 292–305.

[3] Montgomery Schuyler, "Glimpses of Western Architecture: Chicago," *Harper's Monthly Magazine*, 123 (August 1891), pp. 559–70.

[4] Jack Quinan, "H. H. Richardson and the Boston Granite Tradition," *Little Journal, Society of Architectural Historians, Western New York Chapter*, 3 (February 1979), pp. 20–29.

[5] L. H. Sullivan, *Kindergarten Chats and Other Writings* (New York: Wittenborn, 1947), pp. 28ff.

[6] J. LaFarge, *An Artist's Letters from Japan* (New York: The Century Co., 1897), p. 105.

[7] Norman Foerster, *Nature in American Literature* (New York: Macmillan, 1923), p. 1.

[8] W. J. Naef and J. N. Wood, *Era of Exploration* (Boston: New York Graphic Society, 1975), passim.

[9] Joel Snyder, *American Frontiers: The Photographs of Timothy H. O'Sullivan* (Millerton, N.Y.: Aperture, 1981); L. Goldschmidt and W. Naef, *The Truthful Lens: A Survey of the Photographically Illustrated Book* (New York: Grolier Club, 1980).

[10] 6 February 1887, Olmsted Papers, General Correspondence, box 18, Library of Congress, Washington, D.C.

[11] Since the symposium I have augmented my remarks on the Ames Monument in an essay entitled "Man-Made Mountain: 'Gathering and Governing' in H. H. Richardson's Design for the Ames Monument," in Susan Walther and Leo Marx, eds., *The Railroad in the American Landscape* (Cambridge, Mass.: MIT Press, forthcoming 1985).

[12] "American Architecture for a German Point of View," *The Forum*, 27 (August 1899), p. 700.

CHICAGO ARCHITECTURE:
THE OTHER SIDE

Donald Hoffmann

From the beginning, Chicago had its manifest destiny: to be the portal to vast timberlands and to the great prairie, where sometimes the grass grew twelve feet tall, foretelling the most fertile farmland in all the world. Père Marquette and Louis Jolliet understood that much even in 1673. They also could see that Chicago someday would form the essential connection between the Gulf of Mexico and the Great Lakes. Nevertheless, surprisingly little was achieved during the next century and a half. In 1823, a visiting professor from the University of Pennsylvania delivered himself of what is perhaps the first critique of architectural Chicago:

> The village presents no cheering prospect, as, notwith-standing its antiquity, it consists of but few huts, inhabited by a miserable race of men, scarcely equal to the Indians from whom they are descended. Their log or bark-houses are low, filthy, and disgusting, display-ing not the least trace of comfort.[1]

Chicago was only the focus of old Indian trails, a place of portage for taking canoes from the south branch of the river westward to the Des Plaines River, whence the Indians could glide down to the Illinois River and on to the Mississippi. The name of the village came from an Indian word that described its river as a place of wild garlic or wild onions.[2] Apart from missionaries, the first resident non-Indian was J. B. P. DuSable, half French and half black. He married an Indian and hired other Indians to maintain his compound on the north bank of the river as a fur-trading post; his buildings, begun in the 1770s, evidently were much too unimpressive to have inspired Chicago with a tradition related to the architecture of the French West Indies. If the French loved the prairie as the English rarely learned to—indeed, the French named the prairie—their departure nevertheless left few buildings to serve as models. Chicago had no British colonial architecture to be held against it.

In 1832–1833 the federal government improved the Chicago harbor. By 1835 the Indians were gone. It became apparent that the future city would be charted by spectacular leaps in population and corresponding episodes of rampant real estate speculation.[3] Chicago architecture, it was plain, would be an architecture of the bourgeoisie. Toward the end of the century, Henry Blake Fuller made one of his fictional characters describe Chicago as "the only great city in the world to which all its citizens have come for the one common, avowed object of making money."[4]

How, then, is the tradition of Chicago architecture usually defined? Chicago is presumed to suffer from a perpetual state of overbearing adolescence: not merely young, but rowdy, bragging, hustling. Nelson Algren's great prose-poem is titled *Chicago: City on the Make*. One of Ernest Hemingway's last characters is a dying colonel who knowingly tells his chauffeur in Italy, "Chicago is tough North, South, there isn't any East, and West."[5] And of course, Carl Sandburg: "Stormy, husky, brawling,/City of the Big Shoulders:/They tell me you are wicked and I believe them, for I have seen/your painted women under the gas lamps luring the farm boys."[6] Chicago architecture is presumed to find its tradition in buildings that are lean, raw, and largely determined by the structural considerations that serve economic forces. It is also presumed that Chicago architecture attains its masterpieces when it is most intent on confessing structure.

Some questions remain to be asked. Why should the naked ape choose to express himself in naked structure? Why should he be applauded for doing so? In what other walk of life do we much admire the skeleton? Structure, alas, has its advantages. It is the easiest thing to talk about in architecture because it pretends to be objective and measurable, in dimension and in performance. From structural technology we can expect improvements; we cannot be so optimistic about art, or about life itself. Structure stands safely apart from the real issues of life—unless, of course, it collapses. Thus we find Chicago architecture routinely read backward from Mies van der Rohe. Consider the May 1962 issue of the *Architectural Forum*. Myron Goldsmith is identified as the "new structural poet" and is quoted as saying, "It is never possible to go too far in a structural direction." Mies van der Rohe's own Crown Hall is strangely forced into company with Adler & Sullivan's old Auditorium: both are praised as "bold structures of strong materials, dramatically expressed." The dry goods store for Schlesinger & Mayer (later Carson, Pirie, Scott) is hailed as "the frame's purest expression" from the early years. Other early buildings win approval for "frankly displaying their steel frames."[7] One might deduce that architecture properly conceived is a form of exhibitionism. Of all the impoverished progeny of such thinking, a distinguished historian of technology has this to say:

> The formal consequences for the urban skyscraper and lesser breeds have been either naked technology or elemental geometry, without texture, pattern, rhythm, accent, scale, or relation to anything around it, and obviously without symbolic meaning.... A Platonic form, which by definition lies beyond history, must be unhistorical and antihistorical. And what is antihistorical is inevitably antiurban and hence antihuman.[8]

If the city so commonly is seen as harsh and evil, the prairie is revered as loving and good. Here, again, Sandburg: "I was born on the prairie and the milk of its wheat, the red/of its clover, the eyes of its women, gave me a song and/a slogan.... The prairie sings to me in the forenoon and I know in the /night I rest easy in the prairie arms, on the prairie heart."[9] This ancient myth of city versus country encourages the artificial separation of Chicago's commercial architecture from its prairie architecture, the latter of course presumed the more concerned with a wholesome and uplifting environment.

It is time for some radical changes in our thinking. First, the best Chicago buildings, and the best buildings by Chicago architects elsewhere, are not primarily concerned with technological innovation or with structural expression. Second, the ambitions of the best buildings, whether commercial buildings or residential, are about the same. Both types are meant to be safe, healthy, comfortable, and aesthetically enriched. Third, the best Chicago architecture is deeply colored and enhanced by elements of nature, romance, and mystery.

Before 1885, the architecture of Chicago was mostly derivative and second-rate; but that year saw several important commissions. One was a mansion for John J. Glessner (fig. 1). The architect was H. H. Richardson and he was an outsider, as was nearly everyone else in Chicago; those who come to a city from elsewhere sometimes sense its environment and character more keenly than do the native-born. What are we to make of this strange house? Montgomery Schuyler found it much lacking in the social graces, particularly for a dwelling on Prairie Avenue; he wrote that it "ceases to be defensible, except, indeed, in the military sense."[10] Such cleverness hints at the truth but then avoids it. Clearly the house does not depend on European styles, genteel or otherwise. Neither does it express any new technology of structure. In the quality of its masonry walls and even in the shape of the plan it comes surprisingly close to the Field Wholesale Store. Glessner's neighbor, only a block south, was in fact Marshall Field, whose store building, we are told by James O'Gorman, was delayed six months in construction because of labor troubles. Field's delivery wagons had been used as troop carriers in the riots of 1877. George Pullman lived diagonally across the street from Glessner's building site; three months before the Glessner house was commissioned, Pullman was shown what purported to be a letter to the editor of *The Alarm*, one of Chicago's several radical newspapers:

> Dynamite!... Stuff several pounds of this sublime stuff into an inch pipe... plug up both ends, insert a cap with a fuse attached, place this in the immediate neighborhood of a lot of rich men who live by the sweat of other people's brows and light the fuse. A most cheerful and gratifying result will follow....[11]

Strikes occurred at Pullman's company in 1882, 1884, and 1885; early in 1886 a strike at the McCormick Reaper works led to the

1 Glessner House
Chicago, Illinois
H. H. Richardson, 1885–1887.
Photo: Donald Hoffman

2 D. H. Burnham and John Root in the library of their Rookery offices.
Chicago, Illinois 1888.

3 *The Rookery*
Burnham and Root, 1885–1888
Detail of La Salle Street front.
Photo: Donald Hoffman

4 *The Rookery*
Detail at southwest corner.
Photo: Donald Hoffman

5 *The Rookery*
Granite detail at La Salle
Street entrance.
Photo: Donald Hoffman

7 *The Rookery*
Stair tower in light court.
Photo: Donald Hoffman

6 *The Rookery*
Light court.

workingmen's rally of May 4, near Haymarket Square, where a bomb wounded seventy-five policemen, seven of them fatally. Glessner's company was one of the five that later merged to form International Harvester. His very odd and romantic house, I would suggest, was meant to be defensible. That is why it looked so much like an extended log cabin or a frontier fort.[12]

Another important building commissioned in 1885 was the downtown office block called the Rookery. Burnham and Root, its architects, moved into a suite on the top floor. Their library offered a warm environment: window seats and drapes, a statue of Venus, a fireplace handsomely ornamented by carved plant forms (fig. 2). The scale may have been a little larger than residential, but the values were the same. (And why should we ever praise an office building that is not a good place to be?) On the streetfronts at sidewalk level, iron-and-glass bays are tucked within the colossal order of granite columns; they form spaces not unlike those behind the oriel windows of hotels, apartment houses, or single-family residences (fig 3). To think of the Rookery as a transitional building caught between masonry walls and metal framing is to fall far short of the mark, for it in fact proves that both systems have their uses and should not be considered contradictory. Where the two meet head on, as in the alley walls, the result is quite beautiful (fig. 4). Moreover, in this huge, speculative office building the architects cut free their fancy in such details as the carved rooks by the main entrance and the richly ornamented enclosure of the light-court; even the fire escape is turned into a tower of extraordinary romance (figs. 5-7). Between 1884 and 1889 Burnham and Root were at work also on the Monadnock Block, which surely should not continue to be dismissed as merely "protomodern" in stripping itself

8 *Monadnock Block, Chicago*
Burnham and Root, 1889–1892.
Detail of Dearborn Street front
Photo: Donald Hoffman

9 *Bronze doors of Getty Tomb,*
Chicago
Adler and Sullivan, 1890–1891.
Photo: Donald Hoffman

10 *Wainwright Building*
St. Louis, Missouri
Adler and Sullivan, 1890–1892
Detail of Seventh Street front.
Photo: Donald Hoffman

11 *Wainwright Building*
View from attic window.
Photo: Donald Hoffman

of all ornament (fig. 8). No simple-minded negation could have resulted in this great building, or in all its nuances of profiling with specially molded bricks. The Monadnock Block reached beyond the historical styles precisely because its ornamental motif, drawn from the papyrus stem and bud of ancient Egypt, was absorbed into the walls, thus turning the tall building into a metaphor of nature: the plant that springs from the sandy soil.

Now in Louis Sullivan we find an architect who proclaimed himself to be a nature-poet, pledged to practice architecture as the plastic expression and religion of democracy. What could be more absurd than to celebrate Sullivan as the prophet of modern functionalism? He was most at home in his rose gardens, and happiest when drawing ornament. His ornament was the same whether intended for jewelry or for large commercial buildings. Paul Sprague has pointed out that his earliest mature ornament appeared "not in a commercial structure at all, but in his Getty Tomb (fig. 9), a building which has precious little to do with new techniques, structural systems, or modern materials."[13] Sullivan himself told Thomas Tallmadge that the Wainwright Building in St. Louis was the first to incorporate all his architectural principles.[14] In this splendid office building, art exists in spite of the innocuous metal frame, not because of it (fig. 10). The beauty of this building lies not in the hidden steel framework, but in the ripe red color of the brick and terra cotta, the precision with which these materials have been detailed, and the lush organic patterns of the spandrels. Sullivan made his aesthetic decisions almost independently of structure and of any less-than-romantic idea of function. That is why the piers were not differentiated from the mullions, both were narrower than the spandrels were high, the corner piers were exaggerated, the ornament changed from floor to floor although the structure of course did not, and the attic walls were made to flower into a tangled field of plant life. The windows had awnings, just like a Midwestern dwelling, and the top floor was occupied not by austere executive suites but instead by such humble amenities as the men's washrooms, which looked back down to the street through quaint and delightful portholes (fig. 11).

Sullivan's special gift for the emotional use of color appeared again in the trading hall of the Chicago Stock Exchange which has much to say about the enrichment in Chicago's best commercial architecture; and, at the World's Columbian Exposition of 1893, in the Transportation Building, which Henry Van Brunt called "romantic or Barbaric" in the sense that its design lay "outside the pale of classic authority" (figs. 12, 13).[15] The fair could claim the world's largest roof (on the Manufactures and Liberal Arts Building), the world's largest cannon (from the Krupp works), the spectacular Ferris Wheel (two hundred fifty feet in diameter), and even a "monster cheese" from Canada (it weighed twenty-two thousand pounds); but its great value, as nearly everyone reported, was to

14 *World's Columbian Exhibition
    Chicago, Illinois
    D. H. Burnham and others,
    1890–1893
    Court of Honor, looking west.*

12 *Chicago Stock Exchange Building
    Adler and Sullivan, 1892–1894
    View from balcony of trading
    room, as reconstructed in the
    Art Institute of Chicago.
    Photo: Donald Hoffman*

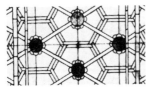

13 *Chicago Stock Exchange Building
    Detail of trading room skylight as
    reconstructed.
    Photo: Donald Hoffman*

15 *Bronze relief above entrance of
    Marquette Building
    Chicago, Illinois
    Holabird and Root, 1893–1894.
    Photo: Donald Hoffman*

be found in the White City itself.[16] This, too, was a grand romantic enterprise, evocative of the highest ideals of order and harmony (fig. 14). Stage-set that it was, the White City offered a devastating critique: it argued that very few cities in America, if approached as works of art, could prove rewarding.

It was also at the fair that the Indian appeared as such an insistent theme in American sculpture.[17] If industry and the profit motive had changed American cities into an ugly matter, so that men and women hungered for some sign of civic care and some slight hint of splendor, now that the poor Indian was vanquished his memory could be courted in a curious way that blended regrets with romantic admiration. D. H. Burnham thought that the White City stood as the first attempt in America, at least since L'Enfant's plan of Washington, to connect landscape with architecture; and he said it led directly to plans for South Shore Drive and to the vast Plan of Chicago.[18] The influence of the Indian was more subtle. A year after the fair, the sculptor Hermon MacNeil encountered on a Chicago street an impoverished Indian called Black Pipe. He was left over from Buffalo Bill's Wild West show. MacNeil hired him as a model. Although the fair was intended to celebrate the discovery of America, it had served better to focus attention on the extraordinary history of Chicago, a story partly told by MacNeil's bronze reliefs above the east doors to the new Marquette Building (fig. 15). More important, the image of Black Pipe, transformed by the sculptor into his "Primitive Chant," appeared in suburban River Forest to preside over the entrance hall and inglenook of W. H. Winslow's house, the first major independent work of the young Frank Lloyd Wright.[19]

Wright's vivid imagination soon blended an early love for nature with the romantic idea of the Indian, his strength and cunning, his unwritten wisdom in the ways of nature. Even thirty years later, at Taliesin, Wright dressed for a Sunday hike in a fantastic gar-

16 *Bradley House*
Kankakee, Illinois
Frank Lloyd Wright, 1900–1901
Detail of living room.
Photo: Donald Hoffman

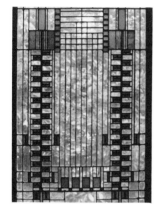

18 *Dana House*
Springfield, Illinois
Frank Lloyd Wright, 1901–1904
Window of studio.
Photo: Donald Hoffman

17 *Robie House*
Chicago, Illinois
Frank Lloyd Wright, 1909–1910
Dining room.
Photo: Donald Hoffman

ment—so Eric Mendelsohn wrote home to his wife in Germany—"more or less without buttons . . . Bark shoes, a long staff, gloves and a tomahawk."[20] That same year, 1924, Wright designed the two Indian memorial sculptures he called "Nakoma" and "Nakomis." The male figure, he wrote, was "teaching his young son to take the bow to the Sun God."[21] With or without bark shoes and tomahawk, Wright preferred the rural; he saw in the prairie all the wonder and mystery that Frederick Law Olmsted could not see.[22] Wright's love of the outdoors, together with his extraordinary intuition, equipped him to express much of the best in the Chicago spirit.

Chicago, to his eyes, was largely an industrial cinderfield. He attacked its environment with all the zeal of a missionary trying, conversely, to bring nature to civilization (fig. 16). Starting around the turn of the century, Wright pursued his vision on a much deeper level than those who would simply retrieve nature in order to tame the city through systems of parks and boulevards encircled by the sylvan scenery of forest preserves. He was convinced that architecture, besides taking its place in the landscape as a quiet foil to nature, might be elevated through intense discipline into an analogue of organic form (fig. 17). If, that is, plan, elevation, and section could be elevated to a level of visual order and invention parallel to that of a natural form, then these two different kinds of organized matter and space might coexist in a mysterious, abiding harmony (fig. 18). The closer he came to this great ideal, the further behind he left Sullivan. How strange that Wright talked so much about nature and so few people have been willing to listen.[23] The habit of tediously tracing all architectural form to previous examples

19 *"Century of Progress"*
paperweight
Coleman Company, 1933–1934.
Photo: Donald Hoffman

of architectural form assumes that broader sources, and indeed the imagination, hardly exist.

The next large fair in Chicago took place in 1933–1934, and was called the Century of Progress. It was nothing like the World's Columbian Exposition, although it inspired such mementos as a cast paperweight with an image of an Indian looming large behind the city of skyscrapers (fig. 19). Which looks the more important, the more enduring? And why are John T. McCutcheon's cartoons of "Injun Summer," which first appeared in 1912, still the most memorable illustrations ever published in the *Chicago Tribune,* (fig. 20)? The old generalizations about Chicago and its architecture cannot serve: neither in history nor through direct experience will they find true support. For the best in Chicago architecture is much more complex, much richer, much more romantic, and much more humane than we have been led to believe.

20 *"Injun Summer" cartoon*
John T. McCutcheon, 1912.

NOTES

1 William H. Keating, *Prairie Days,* ed. Paul M. Angle (Chicago: University of Chicago Press, 1968), pp. 86–87.

2 Virgil J. Vogel, *Indian Place Names in Illinois* (Springfield, Ill.: Illinois State Historical Library, 1963), pp. 24–25.

3 The population reached 4,470 in 1840; 109,260 in 1860; 505,185 in 1880; and, with the help of annexations, 1,099,850 in 1890. In 1833 a plot of land on Lake Street was valued at three hundred dollars at the start of the year and it was sold for six thousand dollars at the end of the year; see Herman Kogan and Rick Kogan, *Yesterday's Chicago* (Miami: E. A. Seaman, 1976), p. 17. A tract bought in 1844 for eight thousand dollars was sold in 1852 for three million dollars.

4 Henry B. Fuller, *With the Procession: A Novel* (New York: Harper and Brothers, 1895), p. 248.

5 Ernest Hemingway, *Across the River and Into the Trees* (New York: Scribners, 1950), p. 36.

6 Carl Sandburg, "Chicago," *Chicago Poems* (New York: Holt, 1916).

7 "Special Issue: Chicago," *Architectural Forum,* May 1962, pp. 90, 127, 134–35, 138.

8 Carl W. Condit, "Technology and Symbol in Architecture," *Humanities in Society,* Vol. 1, No. 3, Summer, 1978, p. 217.

9 Carl Sandburg, "Prairie," *Cornhuskers* (New York: Holt, 1918).

10 Montgomery Schuyler, *American Architecture* (New York: Harper and Brothers, 1892), p. 160.

see Emmett Dedmon, *Fabulous Chicago,* rev. ed. (New York: Atheneum, 1893), pp. 148–62.

12 Burnham and Root's First Regiment Armory of 1889–91 was built only four blocks from Glessner's house as a stronghold against civil disturbances. John Edelmann in 1892 described the Field Store as a "grim fortress of trade"; see James F. O'Gorman, "The Marshall Field Wholesale Store: Materials Toward a Monograph," *Journal of the Society of Architectural Historians,* Vol. XXXVII, No. 3, October 1978, p. 194.

13 See "The Chicago School of Architecture: A Symposium—Part II," *The Prairie School Review,* 2d quarter 1972, p. 27

14 Thomas E. Tallmadge, *The Story of Architecture in America* (New York: W. W. Norton, 1936), p. 223.

15 *Architecture and Society: Selected Essays of Henry Van Brunt,* ed. William A. Coles (Cambridge, Mass., 1969), p. 269.

16 See David F. Burg, *Chicago's White City of 1893* (Lexington, Ky.: University Press of Kentucky, 1976), *passim.*

of the World's Columbian Exposition, Chicago, 1893" (Ph.D. Diss., University of Kansas, Lawrence, 1976), pp. 55–56.

[17] See Wayne Craven, *Sculpture in America* (New York: Crowell, 1968), pp. 514 ff., and Elizabeth Broun, "American Paintings and Sculpture in the Fine Arts Building

[18] Charles Moore, "Lessons of the Chicago World's Fair: An Interview with the Late Daniel H. Burnham," *The Architectural Record*, Vol. XXXIII, January, 1913, p. 44, and Daniel H. Burnham and Edward H. Bennett, *Plan of Chicago* (Chicago: The Commercial Club, 1909), pp. 6–7.

[19] This bronze stands twenty-five inches high. Wright presented it again in a lovely perspective drawing of the gallery in the Susan Lawrence Dana house of 1901–1904, in *Ausegeführte Bauten und Entwurfe von Frank Lloyd Wright* (Berlin: Wasmuth, 1910).

[20] Eric Mendelsohn, *Letters of an Architect* (London: Abelard-Schuman, 1967), p. 73.

[21] *Nakoma-Nakomis: Winnebago Indian Memorials* (Scottsdale, Ariz., 1974), n.p. Strangely enough, the Winnebagos are elsewhere remembered as a savage tribe that periodically sallied forth from a stronghold near Green Bay to rule over most of Wisconsin; see Hjalmar R. Holand, *Old Peninsula Days* (Ephraim, Wis., 1934), p. 22.

[22] Olmsted in 1866 found the environs of Chicago "not merely uninteresting, but, during much of the year, positively dreary." See *Civilizing American Cities,* ed. S. B. Sutton (Cambridge, Mass.: MIT Press, 1971), p. 296. Charles Dickens likewise found the Midwestern prairie "oppressive in its barren monotony." See John Madson, *Where the Sky Began* (Boston: Houghton Mifflin, 1982), p. 17.

[23] In the eight pages of his introduction to *Ausgeführte Bauten und Entwurfe,* Wright uses the word "nature" or "natural" forty-five times and the word "organic" twenty-four times.

LOS ANGELES ARCHITECTURE:
THE ISSUE OF TRADITION IN A TWENTIETH-CENTURY CITY

by Thomas S. Hines

Gertrude Stein once asserted bluntly that America was "the oldest country in the world." It is hard to know what she meant by that, for I still tend to subscribe to the more innocent myth of America as the newest and youngest country in the world. The term "New World" and the adjective "new" as applied to the oldest parts of the country—New England, New York, New Mexico—have helped to shape this image of America. And for most people, the city of Los Angeles, now over two-hundred years old, has epitomized America's eternal newness.

Los Angeles has seemed young and new especially because it has continually encouraged innovation. Its style has celebrated informality, comfort, entertainment, and fun, all enjoyed in a relatively benign climate and a physical landscape that seemingly offers everything. However, at times Los Angeles has pushed its own virtues of healthiness and freshness to excess, making a cult of the new, and exalting a throwaway ethic and aesthetic. By placing a premium on the new, it has frequently turned its back on the values of texture, patina, memory, and tradition, the layering of history, and the need for establishing continuity with the past, and for preserving at least part of the older landscape.

The architecture of Los Angeles both shaped and reflected the images of the city, which in turn shaped and mirrored the physical and cultural landscape. In the architecture of Los Angeles, there has always been an element of self-parody and self-fulfilling prophecy. Two views, in fact, of turn-of-the-century Vienna apply equally well to twentieth-century Los Angeles. "If we live long enough," wrote the Viennese dramatist Arthur Schnitzler, "every lie told about us will someday become true." Equally pertinent to brave, new, decadent Los Angeles is the observation of the critic Karl Kraus that Vienna was "the research station for the end of the world." And, although T. S. Eliot was describing London rather than Los Angeles, these words from *The Wasteland* also capture Los Angeles's perverse fecundity: "Unreal city, under the brown fog of a winter dawn ... that corpse you planted last year in your garden, Has it begun to sprout? Will it bloom this year?" Indeed Los Angeles could have been the model for Brecht and Weill's "Stadt Mahagony," the American "City of No Restraint."[1]

The image of Los Angeles as eternally seeking to be new, young, modern, and contemporary is, of course, true in part. Yet it distorts the reality of a place that, like all places, is also rooted in the past, a city that despite its own fond self-image has often needed, and exploited, tradition. Partially because it is a relatively new city, it has felt so acutely the need for a past that when its own past and traditions have seemed insufficient, it has borrowed unabashedly from those of other places. The failure to understand this important historic fact is the fault not only of professional boosters and professional modernists, but also of historians, who are more interested in change than in continuity largely because it is easier to identify. But even if more elusive, the human need for continuity with the past is as compelling as the need for change and innovation. The poignancy of this truth for all kinds of history is well illustrated in the architecture of twentieth-century Los Angeles—even Los Angeles, the "City of the Future." Los Angeles has embraced at least five major clusters of architectural traditions: first, from its own venerable history, aboriginal Indian and Hispanic forms; second, the craftsman tradition of both native and borrowed sources, which reached its highest expression in the work of Irving Gill and Charles and Henry Greene; third, a spirited, if sometimes naïve embrace of exotic styles and traditions quite remote from Los Angeles, an ambience admittedly fostered by the dream merchants of Hollywood; fourth, the tradition of modernism, and fifth, the new tradition of the postmodern movement of "radical eclecticism," which has embraced most of those other traditions and added a few of its own. This paper will therefore view Los Angeles architecture with a focus on tradition and its attendant anxieties, rather than the usual focus of Brave New World Modernism.

Even the monuments of popular architecture tend to refer not only to a Buck Rogers future, as at the Zep Diner and Happy Landing Service Station, but to a real or mythic past, as in the Sphinx Realty and the Mother Goose Bakery, or at Grauman's Chinese Theater and the Samson Tire Company. Forest Lawn Cemetery features not only reproductions of such historic sculptures as Michelangelo's *David* and Daniel Chester French's *Statue of the Republic* from the 1893 Chicago World's Fair, but the Wee Kirk o' the Heather from Bonnie Scotland and, inevitably, Boston's Old North Church. Disneyland reproduces Ludwig's Neuschwanstein, Old West villages, a nineteenth-century train station, and an "authentic" American main street. Pacific Savings pays tribute to the founding couple, George and Martha Washington; only the palm trees give it away. The Getty Museum is a Pompeian villa built atop the inevitable Los Angeles parking garage.

Hollywood, of course, has been blamed for much of this foolishness, with the one-dimensional false fronts of its fabled back lots, from D. W. Griffith's Babylonian temples, built for the movie *Intolerance,* to old New York, built for the *Hello Dolly* street, at Twentieth Century Fox. Occasionally, even local traditions have been invoked, the bells of the Franciscan missions returning in the bells of a ubiquitous chain of restaurants. While there are only three surviving Spanish churches in Los Angeles County, the most notable being San Gabriel Mission, the Taco Bells are virtually uncountable, spreading from the mother city to fast-food missions around the country.

Los Angeles was founded in 1781, but for almost a hundred years, it was a sleepy outpost of the Spanish colonial empire. It was not until the late nineteenth century, with the completion of the transcontinental railroads, that it began to look like a city. The first great urban architectural style that left its mark on Los Angeles was the Queen Anne and its numerous kindred Victorian modes. Transplanted rather literally from the Middle West, the East Coast, and Europe, this architecture made Victorian Los Angeles look something like Victorian St. Louis or Cleveland or Buffalo, though the tropical flora suggested the ambience of the far-flung British Empire of the same era.

Almost everywhere in the late nineteenth century these dominant modes at their richest and most flamboyant epitomized Thorstein Veblen's description of "conspicuous consumption"—spending, acquiring, accumulating, in order to advertise oneself socially, to keep up, as the Chicago novelist Henry Fuller put it, "with the procession." This was the Gilded Age, as historians have labeled it, the Age of Excess, the Age of Opulence, the Great Barbeque: an age of increasing wealth, before the income tax, and of the increasing division between rich and poor, progress and poverty.

1 Bradbury Building, Los Angeles, California
George Wyman, 1893.

Surely the greatest Victorian structure in Los Angeles was (and still is) the Bradbury Building (fig. 1), in the downtown business district, designed by George Wyman in 1893 for Louis Bradbury, the mining baron, whose mansion by the Newsom brothers rose two blocks to the east on Los Angeles's Bunker Hill—named, of course, for the original in Boston. Bradbury originally gave the commission to the prominent local architect Sumner Hunt, but he was not pleased with Hunt's proposals and turned to Wyman, a young draftsman in Hunt's office, whom he had met while dealing with Hunt and whose ideas were obviously closer to his own. At first Wyman hesitated to take on his boss's client, but in good Los Angeles fashion, a mysterious voice from the planchette board, a forerunner of the Ouija board, told him to "take it," and he did.[2]

Born in Dayton, Ohio, in 1860, Wyman had no formal training in architecture, but developed his talent as an apprentice in several offices. Debilitated by pneumonia and tired of the cold weather, Wyman moved to Los Angeles in 1891, where, restored by the climate, he entered the Hunt office. In its steel-frame construction, its Romanesque accents, and its central light court, the Bradbury Building recalled certain works of the early Chicago school, but in its central court, it broke resoundingly with street facade architecture, opening the building to an interior landscape of iron balconies and exposed elevators—machine architecture indeed, a resolutely nineteenth-century machine. Yet, whatever his debts, conscious and unconscious, to the Chicago school and the Industrial Revolution, Wyman claimed that his real inspiration came from the descriptions of Boston in the year 2000 in Edward Bellamy's utopian novel, *Looking Backward,* written in 1887. One of Bellamy's typical commercial buildings was indeed "a vast hall full of light received not alone from the windows on all sides, but from the dome, the point of which was a hundred feet above. The walls were frescoed in mellow tints to soften without absorbing the light which flooded the interior."[3]

Wyman produced virtually nothing of importance either before or after his brilliant Bradbury Building. But, there he merged the tradition of industrial, commercial architecture with another one that would come to be important in Los Angeles, that of utopian architecture, the tradition of the future. This latter tradition, of course, was applauded by the promoters of the modern movement, at the same time as they overlooked Wyman's use of neoclassical detailing, Romanesque fenestration, and ornament recalling Victorian bric-a-brac.

Though the work of Charles and Henry Greene derived in part from the woodsy Queen Anne, the Stick and Shingle styles, and their European antecedents, it was a cluster of other traditions that made it possible for a later generation to classify the Greenes as Pevsnerian pioneers of the modern movement. These included classical Japanese design, the one grand tradition to which all modernists were sympathetic, and the almost equally acceptable legacy of William Morris and the Arts and Crafts movement. Thus, after decades of neglect, the Greenes' work of the early twentieth century was rediscovered in the 1950s, an A. I. A. citation of 1952 honoring them as "formulators of a new and native architecture ... who reflected with grace and craftsmanship emerging values in modern living...." And in 1958, Henry-Russell Hitchcock confirmed their status as "modern pioneers" in his famous chapter "Frank Lloyd Wright and His California Contemporaries." The Greenes' work, he observed, "offers a more coherent corpus than that of any modern architect of their generation except Wright."[4]

Like Wright, the Greenes downplayed their debts to history and cultivated their identity as American originals. "I am an American," Charles Greene wrote as early as 1907.

> I want to know the American people of today and the things of today.... I seek till I find what is truly useful and then I try to make it beautiful.... I believe this cannot be done by copying old works, no matter how beautiful they may seem to us now.... The old things are good, they are noble in their place; [but] let our perverted fingers leave them alone. Let us begin all over again.[5]

Yet the biographical and architectural evidence suggests just how much the Greenes did learn from history and tradition. Born fifteen months apart, in 1868 and 1870, in Cincinnati, they were descended from the great Mather family of Puritan New England. They spent boyhood summers at the family home on Nantucket and the Mather farm in Virginia, but they grew up in St. Louis where they attended Woodward's Manual Training High School. After studying architecture at M.I.T., both brothers apprenticed in Boston offices, Henry significantly with Shepley, Rutan, and Coolidge, the successor firm of H. H. Richardson. In those early years and later, they absorbed the growing interest in the "colonial homes of our ancestors," built in the "olden" manner, as Gustav Stickley later phrased it in *The Craftsman* magazine. In 1893, they crossed the country to visit their parents, who for reasons of health had retired to Pasadena, one of the oldest and grandest Los Angeles suburbs. The brothers like it so much they decided to stay.[6]

On their way west in 1893, they had stopped to see the Chicago World's Fair and had found there an architectural example that moved them enormously—the Japanese pavilion, the fabled Ho-o-den that had also moved their contemporary, Wright. This discovery of Japan and its relation to their own Craftsman background took them the next year to the Mid-Winter Exposition in San Francisco to study the Japanese gardens, and steadily over the years they cultivated this interest through books and pictures of Japanese design and craftsmanship. They must have encountered the great wood architecture of Switzerland and south Germany in the same way, as they never personally visited any of these places, but in their mature work, the Swiss tradition was almost as pervasive as the Japanese. A group of their houses along Pasadena's Aroyo Seco is still known as "Little Switzerland." Their education and natural leanings toward those various Craftsman traditions was reinforced in the early twentieth century by the theory and example of Gustav Stickley, whose own Craftsman bungalows both shaped and reflected the Greenes' achievement. Like Stickley, the Greenes honored William Morris's axiom to "have nothing in your home that you do not know to be useful or believe to be beautiful."[7]

The greatest example of the Greenes' eclectic genius is the Gamble House, 1908, built in Pasadena as the winter home of the David Gamble family of the Procter and Gamble empire from Cincinnati (fig. 2). It is itself a village or cluster of bungalows, Stick and Shingle style, Stick and Stickley. The joinery, the ornament, and much of the landscaping is Japanese, but the great wooden masses, the hovering, harboring roofs, and the eaves suggest Europe just as strongly. The glass is Tiffany, designed by the Greenes, assembled in Los Angeles. The furniture is a mixture of Greene and Stickley. The lamps and other objects by Van Erp and Rookwood form a veritable museum of the Arts and Crafts. And such richness led to a parody of William Morris's line: "Have nothing in your house

that you do not believe to be rare or know to be expensive."[8]
However, it was just this synthetic chemistry in the Greenes' work
that Ralph Adams Cram particularly admired. "Where it comes
from, Heaven alone knows," he wrote in 1913. "There are things
in it Japanese; things that are Scandinavian, things that hint at Sik-
kim, Bhutan, and the fastness of Tibet, and yet it hangs together;
it is beautiful, it is contemporary, and for some reason or another,
it seems to fit California."[9]

Of Wright's other California contemporaries, Irving Gill was an
even more obvious choice for Hitchcock to enshrine in his modernist pantheon, though Gill acknowledged his historical debts
more openly than the Greenes. Born in 1870 in Syracuse, New
York, another early center of the Arts and Crafts movement, Gill
worked briefly in the early 1890s in the Chicago office of Louis
Sullivan before going to California in 1893, again for reasons of
health. He settled and began his practice in San Diego but by 1910
his work had spread northward up the coast to Los Angeles. Gill
loved the old architecture of southern California. He found the
missions in particular an "expressive medium of retaining tradition,
history, and romance, with their long, low lines, graceful arcades,
tile roofs, bell towers, arched doorways and walled gardens." But
Hispanic architecture was not to be copied slavishly and was to
furnish the theme only for a new California architecture. "The West
has an opportunity unparalleled in the history of the world," he
wrote in *The Craftsman,* "for it is the newest white page yet turned
for registration ... great wide plains, noble mountains, lovely little
hills and canyons waiting to hold the record of this generation's
history, ideals, imagination, sense of romance and honesty." [10]

It was Gill's definition of architectural "honesty" that would tend to pull him from the Hispanic orbit and qualify him as a proto-modernist. His clean, unornamented surfaces and crisp, cubistic volumes recalled the older forms, but in ways so abstract and astringently minimalist that they truly had more in common with the International Style than with the missions or the pre-Spanish pueblos of the Southwest. This modernist sensibility was heightened by Gill's explicit use of industrial hardware and labor-saving devices—vacuum cleaner outlets in each room, for example, taking dust to the furnace. Indeed Gill had perhaps learned more from Sullivan's words than from his work. "Gill's interiors are very fine and quite like Loos," Hitchcock noted. "Very different from the rich orientalizing rooms designed by the Greenes, they are in fact more similar to real Japanese interiors in their severe elegance."[11]

After Gill's great houses for the Dodge, Banning, and Miltimore families, the Los Angeles work that best typifies this transition in his work is the Horatio West Court (fig. 3), consisting of four connected houses built near the beach in Santa Monica (1919). The stepped flat roofs and clusters of building units suggest the pueblos; the arched entrance porches recall the missions. But the bands of casement windows and the pueblo-like, cubistic masses look forward to the twenties and thirties. Probably the first, though certainly not the last European modernist to discover Gill and identify him with Adolf Loos was Richard Neutra, who arrived in Los Angeles in 1925. Neutra included his own early snapshots of Horatio West in his book on American architecture, published in the German series *Neues Bauen in der Welt* in 1930.[12]

Intrinsically Gill's achievement was a brilliant synthesis of regional tradition and innovative abstraction. Its only negative legacy—through no fault of Gill's—was the sentiment it inspired from the

*3 Horatio West Court
Santa Monica, California
Irving Gill, 1919.*

teens through the sixties, that his stark interpretation of the early Southwest legacy was the only proper one—and far superior, in modernist eyes, to the more spirited and ornamented derivations from the Spanish Baroque and Churrigueresque. If Gill was unjustly excluded from Bertram Goodhue's San Diego Exposition of 1915, which emphasized those modes, many of the great purveyors of the more literally historicist Spanish architecture were eclipsed in the high modernist era as Gill's star began to rise. Those included, among others, A. C. Martin, George Washington Smith, Reginald Johnson, Roland Coate, Wallace Neff, and Gordon Kaufmann, architects who also built in other traditional modes, from Tudor to Norman to a southern European–southern Californian blend of styles labeled "Mediterranean" by Los Angeles realtors. Gordon Kaufmann's Eisner House of 1925 illustrates this "Mediterranean" mode, both its intrinsic excellence and its importance as a model for such later and larger work as Kaufmann's Scripps College, Claremont, of the late 1920s.

Kaufmann was born in London in 1888 to parents of middle-class Scottish and German origins. He attended both the London Polytechnic and the Royal College of Art, after which he was apprenticed to the London architect A. W. S. Cross, known for both his technical skill and his interest in history. The greatest source of inspiration for Kaufmann was Sir Edwin Lutyens's contemporary architecture of grand Edwardian mannerism, an influence that would pervade most of Kaufmann's later work. In 1910, Kaufmann migrated to Canada, where he married and had a son, but his wife's fragile health called for a milder climate, and in 1914 they moved to Los Angeles. Arriving there virtually penniless, without contacts or commissions, Kaufmann worked for a while as a gardener, but by 1916 he had become a draftsman in the established firm of the eclectic traditionalist Reginald Johnson, and by 1922 he became a partner in a three-man arrangement with Johnson and Roland Coate. Together in the early twenties they built such monuments as All Saints' Episcopal Church, Pasadena, and St. Paul's Episcopal Cathedral, Los Angeles; but Kaufmann wanted more independence, and opened his own office in the middle twenties.[13]

One of his first independent commissions was the Eisner House of 1925, built in Hancock Park, one of Los Angeles's grandest and most exclusive residential areas, a section never friendly to modern architecture and hence not well known in the history of the city's architecture. Built for a rich businessman who went broke and committed suicide during the Depression, the house has a typically urban main entrance off an alley-like driveway on the west. It is organized around three courtyards, the main central courtyard harboring the pool and leading to the hallway, living room, library, dining room, and banquet room, the last especially imposing with original frescoes and a musicians' balcony. A service court on the north leads to kitchens and garages, and a garden court opens the house to the south. The grandest of stairways leads to the second-floor bedrooms.

As Kaufmann's work increased, he took on more draftsmen, and in 1925, one of these was Richard Neutra, who had just arrived in Los Angeles, ostensibly to work with Rudolph Schindler, but who needed a steady income while awaiting his own commissions. "My new boss is an Englishman and very decent," Neutra wrote his wife's parents. "He treats me excellently and his commissions are executed in Florentine early Renaissance style. The marvelous large illustrated publications that form the source material awake my longing for Italy.... The central part [of the house] reminds me of New York's Fifth Avenue." Neutra initialed as his own the working drawings of elevations and floor plans. He may have had some initial design input as well. The elevations, porches, steps, and garden walls of the east side of the house leading from the banquet hall and central courtyard suggests, in their massing and subtle details, a Neutra still heady from his recent sojourn at Taliesin with Frank Lloyd Wright.

Indeed the Los Angeles of Wright and of Neutra would loom much larger as the century wore on than the more "traditional" Los Angeles of Gordon Kaufmann's Hancock Park.[14] By 1910 Frank Lloyd Wright, then in his early forties, had established himself nationally and internationally as a leading practitioner and prophet of modernism. His "Prairie Style" epitomized what he called "organic" architecture. It, of course, drew from a number of sources, including the Craftsman movement of Morris and Stickley, the East Coast Shingle style, and the timeless elegance of Japanese design. Between 1910 and 1920, however, Wright's life and architecture underwent dramatic changes as he seemed to tire of the formulas and patterns of the Prairie school image and began searching for new intellectual stimulus. Wright had always been pulled toward a certain cultural nationalism, drawn like his heroes Emerson and Whitman to find and create an "American" culture. His search for the roots of a distinctly American architecture led him to the buildings of the first Americans, the Indians. Later, he would use the tepee as a reference, but in the teens and early twenties, he seemed drawn to the pueblos of the American Southwest, as at Taos, and to their even grander Mayan cousins of pre-Columbian Mexico. He never explicitly acknowledged the pre-Columbian sources though he used them throughout the twenties, as he had even earlier in certain Prairie fragments. They are visible in Unity Temple (1906), the A. D. German Warehouse, Richland Center, Wisconsin (1915), and the Imperial Hotel, Tokyo, of the late teens, but never appear as strongly appropriate as in the complex of buildings he completed in Los Angeles for the oil heiress Aline Barnsdall.

Wright's Los Angeles buildings also reflected the restlessness and the series of tragedies in his personal life, including the dissolution of his first marriage and his elopement to Europe with one of his clients, Mamah Cheney; their subsequent retreat to his ancestral farm in Wisconsin, where in 1912 he built Taliesin; and the break-up in 1914 of his life with Mamah as she and three of her visiting children were brutally murdered by a deranged servant, who also burned the house. For a time, then, Wisconsin and the Middle West held too many painful memories, and Wright yielded to the impulse to get away to the sunnier climes of Japan and California. But the personal travail could not help but have an effect on the work. In the Los Angeles houses more than ever before, Wright built aloof and impregnable bastions to protect himself vicariously—through his extended family of clients—from the intrusions of a critical and hostile world, buildings which, with their guarded access routes, seemed to place a greater premium on privacy than ever before. It was a significant historical intersection of culture and personality.[15]

Even in the grandest of his Prairie School buildings, Wright had maintained a relative simplicity and modernist sobriety, but in Los Angeles he yielded to the temptation to escape such restraints and to indulge in the California ethos. He was abetted in this by his clients. "A complex creature," Wright wrote of Aline Barnsdall, "neither neo, quasi, nor pseudo ... as near American *as any Indian,* as developed and traveled in appreciation of the beautiful as any European. As domestic as a shooting star." "A socialite socialist," a "rich parlour communist," her detractors called her, as she built her grand shelter for plotting the revolution, not only in the arts but in politics as well. Wright called the Barnsdall house a "California Romanza" (fig. 4). He admitted he was "on vacation" in Los Angeles.[16] Indeed, the house suggested a Maxfield Parrish painting of a voluptuous Mayan shrine. It was designed around an open garden court, with outside stairways leading to roof terraces, bridges spanning integral lily pools, battered walls, and cornice ornament of abstract hollyhocks, the client's favorite flower. Yet somehow the geometry of its heavy masonry wall masses evoked

*4 Barnsdall "Hollyhock" House
Los Angeles, California
Frank Lloyd Wright, 1920.*

certain effects of the *Wagnerschule* as well. It is tempting to ascribe these to none other than Rudolph Schindler, Wright's intimately involved associate, who moved to Los Angeles to supervise the work on the house and ended up designing numerous crucial details.

Through the Barnsdall connection, Wright met other clients in search of modernity and of California romance. He built four more great houses in the spirit of "Hollyhock," as the house was named, all recalling pre-Columbian references, all constructed of beautifully molded, steel-reinforced concrete blocks. His own favorite was "La Miniatura" in Pasadena (1923), built, Wright insisted, "as the cactus grows," for another strong-willed, single woman, Alice Millard, who had been a client in the Prairie days back in Illinois. She typified, as Wright observed, "the folk from the Middle Western Prairies," who when "prosperous came loose and rolled down there into that far corner [of the country] to bask in eternal sunshine." The Millard house sat in its lush ravine, erect and tall, as did the Storer, Freeman, and Ennis houses, all perched grandly on their Hollywood hilltops. Never before or after those Los Angeles houses did Wright yield so unabashedly to the romance of history and regional tradition.[17]

There were similar qualities in the simultaneous achievement of Wright's oldest son, Lloyd, who had migrated west to apprentice with Irving Gill, and whose work of the twenties strongly echoed his father's. His Taggert House of 1923 was a miniature Ennis House. His own house and studio of 1927, built of concrete blocks, reflected much of the aesthetic of his father's whole Los Angeles period. His Sowden House (1927) was a great cyclopean, expressionist rock, with a slightly more relaxed interior courtyard. His house of the same year for the silent-screen star Ramon Navarro had, like his father's Los Angeles work, many of the qualities of the burgeoning Art Deco style, as the style was labeled after its prominent use in the 1925 Paris Exposition of Industrial and Decorative Arts.

In its abstract, stylized gestures to modernity, Art Deco drew from a number of historic sources: from the pre-Columbian forms the elder Wright had used, from the vivid geometry of Southwest Indian design from various Egyptian motifs popularized in the early 1920s after the excavation of King Tut's tomb, and finally from the more rectilinear phases of Art Nouveau.[18] The greatest Art Deco monument in Los Angeles is Bullock's Wilshire Department Store, designed in 1928 by Parkinson and Parkinson (fig. 5), its air-age porte-cochère ceiling mural by Herman Sachs. In fact, the building's social significance in Los Angeles history is indicated by the placement of its main entrance not on a street side, but at the rear facing the parking lot. Also important in the galaxy of Art Deco architects working in Los Angeles—surely, along with those in New York and Miami, the greatest in the world—were Morgan,

Walls, and Clements, with their black and gold Richfield Building
(1926) and their green terra-cotta Pellisier Building (1930). Bertram
Goodhue's Los Angeles Public Library (1925), has obvious Art
Deco elements, although it also contains other equally dominant
references. Like the more sophisticated architecture of Frank Lloyd
Wright, Art Deco blended modernity with history and romance,
but for the average person it epitomized the modern age.

Of all the major figures and movements in twentieth-century Los
Angeles architecture, the ones least consciously touched by tradition, local or otherwise, were probably Richard Neutra and his
fellow purveyors of the International Style. Though most modernists admitted to a fascination with Japan, with the simple structures of certain primitive cultures, and with the stark—by this time
white—ruins of classical antiquity, their stated goal was usually a
forgetting of things past. Their great acknowledged stylistic reference was, of course, the machine, as adapted to the needs and
demands of modern life. This commitment was obvious in Neutra's
major works in Los Angeles, from large villas such as the Lovell
House of 1929 (fig. 6) to small prototype workers' cottages such
as the Mosk House of 1933. Yet even Neutra and other practitioners
of the International Style were touched by tradition, perhaps more
than they knew.[19]

When Neutra first arrived in America in 1923, his favorite buildings
were not the New York skyscrapers, but rather the model of the

Taos pueblo in the New York Museum of Natural History (fig. 7). "Whole villages were built in one block," he wrote to his wife. "These cubes with hardly any windows are more than one story, have terraces in front of the set back of the upper stories. It is impossible to fathom the complexity of these agglomerations of building cubes." When he reached Los Angeles in 1925, he was delighted to see vestiges of the early Hispanic variants of those forms as well as the more modern renditions of the same tradition in Irving Gill's Horatio West apartments.[20]

Consciously and unconsciously, he combined both vernaculars—the stacked apartments of the pueblos and the garden court tradition of Los Angeles—in his 1935 design for the Strathmore Apartments (fig. 8). Here Neutra was his own client, as he and a friend who owned the land split the cost and the ownership of the new apartment court. The eight connected units each opened onto the central, terraced garden and to rear kitchen stairs that led back to the street. The white stucco, the silver-gray trim, the skinny detailing, the great walls of glass, and the "industrial" ambience reflected the building's modernist sources as its layout and form looked back to older references.

The blend of tradition and modernity appealed to and attracted an interesting group of early tenants, including such Hollywood figures as Orson Welles, Dolores Del Rio, Luise Rainer, Clifford Odets, and Lilly Latte, the companion of Fritz Lang, who rented an apartment in the quiet hills of Westwood as a retreat from Lang and the demanding Hollywood life. John Entenza, editor of *Arts and Architecture*, lived at Strathmore, as did Charles and Ray Eames, who used their apartment as an early laboratory for their shaped-

Above, left:
9 *Coca-Cola Bottling Company*
Los Angeles, California
Robert Derrah, 1936.

Above, right:
10 *Pan-Pacific Auditorium*
Los Angeles, California
Wurdeman and Beckett, 1936.

wood chair experiments. In some ways, Strathmore was a middle-class prototype for such later, larger developments as Neutra's Channel Heights Housing for shipyard defense workers.

Indeed the work of Neutra and Schindler and that first generation of international modernists inspired a variety of derivative and cognate modes, thereby fostering the Los Angeles "tradition" of modernism. One of these—the Moderne, or Modernistic—was viewed by the high modernists with generally bemused contempt. The Streamline Moderne drew its inspiration from the more curvilinear elements of the International Style and from the same machines that inspired the high modernists—the automobile, the train, the ocean liner, the airplane, the blimp, the space ship, all of these strongly suggesting the spirit of flight, of movement, of "getting away," if not on a spaceship at least on the *Super Chief.* The best examples in Los Angeles are certainly Robert V. Derrah's Coca-Cola Bottling Company of 1936 (fig. 9), a nautical remodeling of an older building, and Wurdeman and Beckett's Pan Pacific Auditorium of 1935 (fig. 10), with its green and white pylons suggesting great engines pulling the rest of the huge building forward. Less open, more massive than the style of the high modern movement, more concerned with color, mass, and packaging than with the definition of space, Streamline Moderne is significant, along with its cousin Art Deco, in the social history of architecture as representing the popular image of modernism. It was indeed a cunning compromise with modernity.

The more "legitimate" development of the modernist tradition in Los Angeles occurred in the work of Gregory Ain and Raphael Soriano, whose Edwards House and Ross House revealed them to be disciples of Neutra. Likewise, Harwell Harris acknowledged his debts to Neutra in a house for John Entenza of 1935, but he departed from his modernist mentor with the Wyle House in Ojai, of 1947, which looked back to the Greenes and the early William Wurster. Charles and Ray Eames had lived in Neutra's Strathmore, but their

11 Eames House
Santa Monica, California
Charles Eames and Eero
Saarinen, 1949.

1949 house in Santa Monica Canyon (fig. 11) reminds one more of Mies, and of Mondrian as well. It was one of dozens of important modernist houses sponsored in the postwar forties and fifties in the Case Study program of John Entenza's Los Angeles-based magazine *Arts and Architecture,* a program which featured distinguished modern work by such other Los Angeles architects as J. R. Davidson, Pierre Koenig, and Craig Ellwood.

But in the fifties and sixties the modernist tradition in Los Angeles and elsewhere began to lose its way and its nerve with work that seemed to grow more tired and bland with every year. This decline was nowhere better—or more sadly-illustrated—than in some of the late work of Richard Neutra: the Garden Grove Community Church of the mid-1960s, for example, the predecessor of Philip Johnson's Crystal Cathedral of the 1980s. Neutra once told a client that in his own work he tried to "imagine out" the verticals, but at Garden Grove he turned the horizontal flagstone unnaturally on end, suggesting his own confusion as well as that of his aging modernist generation.

But in the late sixties and seventies Los Angeles architecture was to take on new life with the work of such architects as Frank Gehry and Charles Moore, who responded to the problems of late modernism in a number of significantly heterogeneous ways, and whose work began to have an impact on the entire American scene. The first responded with a variety of solutions drawn from that rather neglected branch of modernism called "constructivist"—the branch largely ignored in the Giedion Bible and somewhat forgotten or dismissed as a result.

12 Gehry House
Santa Monica, California
Frank Gehry, 1979.

Frank Gehry was born in Toronto in 1929, but migrated with his family to Los Angeles as a teenager, in deference once again to the health of his father. Gehry's U.C.L.A. Placement Center of the early 1970s consciously mirrored certain regional expressions of the International Style, though his Malibu house for the painter Ron Davis (1974), his studio-gallery for Gemini GEL, and his own house in Santa Monica (1979), encircling and modifying an older Craftsman cottage, were essentially restatements of high expressionist themes, with corrugated metals and chain-link screens suggesting Brutalist and Punk imagery. In his own house (fig. 12), certain walls and partitions are progressively stripped away, nostalgically evoking the old house being built. The poignantly crumpled group of connected artist studios on Indiana Street in Venice is carefully designed and constructed to look poorly constructed and hastily thrown up, melding convincingly with its poor and run-down neighborhood. The name of a movie starring these buildings might be something like "Gehry Meets Caligari." But in more recent work, Gehry has turned to traditions beyond the modernist and expressionist movements. His Loyola Law School library complex echoes the architecture of Renaissance and Baroque Italy in its color, its deep reveals, and its abstractly flamboyant outside stairways. The courtyard is filled with classical templets. Still, notwithstanding these historic references, Gehry has responded to the problems of modernism with a personal neo-expressionist, modernist sensibility.

That is not the case with Gehry's fellow transplanted Californian, Charles Moore, who of all twentieth-century Los Angeles architects has made, in words and buildings, the deepest break with the modernist tradition. With Robert Venturi, his Philadelphia contemporary, Moore became one of the two seminal figures in the postmodernist critique. He condemned the modern movement's overly stark sobriety and called for more wit, color, and irony in architecture. Most importantly he called for the unabashed use of historic allusion, or as he himself put it, for "architecture with a memory." The century-long Los Angeles anxiety over the issue of tradition had at last come full-circle.

Moore's grandparents had amassed a considerable fortune, and his parents lived comfortably, spending long winter holidays in California. Moore was born in Benton Harbor, Michigan, on Halloween, 1925. The senior Moores' closest friends in Hollywood were Fibber McGee and Molly. Charles's own favorite playmates were the precocious child stars of *Our Gang*. So it was fitting that Moore, after several decades in the architecture schools of Princeton, Berkeley, and Yale, should return in the mid-1970s to teach and practice in a city full of his childhood memories. He said once that he had come back for two reasons: one was the Gamble House; the other was Disneyland. At the time, he happened to be standing on a porch of the Gamble House. No doubt his reasons for returning vary with the "location" he is in, to use that Hollywood word—something which is hardly surprising, for despite its image as "the nowhere city" and "the city of the future," there are perhaps more different locations, more different moods, different kinds of buildings, and different sources of ideas in Los Angeles to appeal to Charles Moore than in any other city in the world. And he has managed, in his inclusivist memory, to include a great many of them in his buildings. Ironically, the one great historic style he has not yet been able to remember and "include" is the modern; but perhaps someday he will rediscover this one too.[21]

Moore's recent winning competition design for the Beverly Hills Civic Center and his St. Matthews Episcopal Church in Pacific Palisades challenge the early criticism that he was, like other important Los Angeles architects, unable to translate to a larger urban scale the brilliance of his smaller designs. Indeed, of the finished work, it is his smaller buildings that constitute his greatest contribution to the Los Angeles tradition of tradition-touched architecture. The Santa Barbara Faculty Club of 1969 (fig. 13) brought to southern California a sunny, stucco version of the shack, shed, and

13 *Faculty Club*
University of California,
Santa Barbara
Charles Moore, 1969.

lean-to mien of the Sea Ranch condominium of 1965. But in Los Angeles proper, Moore's most representative work remains the house for Leland Burns of 1974 (figs. 14, 15). Painted in a warm, multicolored Mexican palette, the house looks across Santa Monica Canyon to the ocean, but is approached from the rear by a narrow, urban alley. A *Ramona*-like entrance court and authentically ancient Mexican doors lead to the music room, which has a German pipe organ and Mexican Baroque trumpet gallery. The book-lined stairway leads to Burns's second-floor bedroom and third-floor study, and is "stolen," Moore insists, from the stairs at Wells Cathedral. A sitting room nestles by the fire beneath the stairs and opens out to the terrace and obligatory swimming pool, designed, in deference to Los Angeles car culture, in the shape of the Chevrolet logo. Its cardboardlike thinness suggests the Hollywood back lot. Indeed, like so much of Los Angeles architecture, it reminds us, piece by piece, of something borrowed from somewhere else. Yet as Cram said in his assessment of the Greenes, "for some reason or another, it seems to fit California."

"If architects are to continue to do useful work on this planet," Charles Moore has written, "then surely their proper concern must be the creation of place—the ordered imposition of man's self on specific locations across the face of the earth. To make a place is to make a domain that helps people know where they are and by extension who they are."[22] This concern has characterized other generations as well, other architects, builders, clients, and users of the Los Angeles environment—not only in terms of the well-known and significant innovations, but also the use of tradition. During the course of its history, Los Angeles has recognized its own traditions, from the Spanish missions to the Hollywood back lot. It has also borrowed, in the best Hollywood manner, from the traditions of other times and places. And even in its "revolt" against tradition in the work of its "modernist pioneers," Los Angeles has cultivated a tradition of modernism.

It seems that we have been so beguiled by modern movement orthodoxy and the "American" myth of progress that in order to legitimize our own newness and innocence, we have trumpeted Los Angeles's—and America's—innovations and repressed our strong need also to remember the past. It should be a mark of that city's—and this nation's—increasingly secure sense of identity that we can now acknowledge the necessary role of tradition in our lives and architecture.[23]

NOTES

[1] Arthur Schnitzler, quoted in Adolf Opel, "Introduction: The Legacies of Dissolution," in Nicholas Powell, *The Sacred Spring: The Arts in Vienna, 1898–1918* (Greenwich, Conn.: New York Graphic Society, 1974), p. 19; Karl Kraus, quoted in Erwin Mitsch, *The Art of Egon Schiele* (London: Phaidon, 1975), p. 18; T. S. Eliot, "The Wasteland," *Collected Poems, 1909–1962* (New York: Harcourt, Brace and World, 1963), p. 55.

[2] Esther McCoy, " 'A Vast Hall Full of Light,' The Bradbury Building, 1893," *Arts and Architecture,* vol. 120 (April 1953), pp. 21, 42–43.

[3] Ibid.; William Jordy, *American Buildings and Their Architects: The Impact of European Modernism in the Mid-Twentieth Century* (Garden City, New York: Doubleday, 1973), pp. 190–91.

[4] Henry-Russell Hitchcock, *Architecture, Nineteenth and Twentieth Centuries* (Baltimore: Penguin Books, 1963), pp. 333–34.

[5] Charles Greene, quoted in Randell L. Mackinson, *Greene and Greene: Architecture as a Fine Art* (Salt Lake City and Santa Barbara: Peregrine-Smith, 1977), p. 160.

[6] Mackinson, *Greene and Greene,* pp. 26–34; William Jordy, *American Buildings and Their Architects: Progressive and Academic Ideals at the Turn of the Twentieth Century* (Garden City, New York: Doubleday, 1972), pp. 217–45.

[7] Quoted in Reyner Banham, Introduction to Mackinson, *Greene and Greene.*

[8] Ibid.

[9] Cram, quoted in Randell Mackinson, "Greene and Greene," in Esther McCoy, *Five California Architects* (New York: Reinhold Book Corporation, 1960), p. 146.

[10] McCoy, *Five California Architects,* pp. 59–100; Jordy, *Progressive and Academic Ideals,* pp. 246–74.

[11] Hitchcock, *Architecture, Nineteenth and Twentieth Centuries,* pp. 334–35.

[12] Richard Neutra, *Amerika: Die Stilbildung des Neuen Bauens in den Vereinigten Staaten* (Vienna: Schroll Verlag, 1930).

[13] Alson Clark, "The 'California' Architecture of Gordon B. Kaufmann," *Society of Architectural Historians, Southern California Chapter Review,* I (Summer 1982), pp. 2–8.

[14] Neutra to Alfred and Lilly Niedermann, 21 February 1925; Neutra to Lilly Niedermann, 19 and 21 August 1925, and n.d. [1926]; Dione Neutra Papers, Los Angeles.

[15] Cf. Robert C. Twombley, *Frank Lloyd Wright: An Interpretive Biography* (New York: Harper and Row, 1973).

[16] Frank Lloyd Wright, *An Autobiography* (New York: Horizon Press, 1977), pp. 248–77.

[17] Ibid.

[18] Cf. Bevis Hillier, *Art Deco* (New York: Sutton, 1968).

[19] Cf. Thomas S. Hines, *Richard Neutra and the Search for Modern Architecture: A Biography and History* (New York: Oxford University Press, 1982).

[20] Richard to Dione Neutra, December 1923, Dione Neutra Papers.

[21] Thomas S. Hines, conversations with Charles Moore, Pasadena, 30 January 1976, and Los Angeles, August 1980.

[22] Charles Moore and Gerald Allen, *Dimensions: Space, Shape, and Scale in Architecture* (New York: Architectural Record Books, 1976), p. 51.

[23] In addition to the works cited above, I am generally indebted to David Gebhard and Robert Winter, *A Guide to the Architecture of Los Angeles and Southern California* (Salt Lake City and Santa Barbara, Peregrine-Smith, 1977); Reyner Banham, *Los Angeles: The Architecture of Four Ecologies* (New York: Harper and Row, 1972); Paul Gleye, *The Architecture of Los Angeles* (Los Angeles: Rosebud Books, 1981): and Richard Oliver, "Like Someplace Else: The Architecture of Los Angeles," unpublished manuscript.

R E S P O N S E

by Rosemarie Bletter

The directing of our attention away from the technocratic, progressivist view of modernism to the full intentions of the late nineteenth century is most welcome. Thus, in Donald Hoffmann's "Chicago Architecture: The Other Side" the depiction of the Chicago school as much more than the expression of structure rings true. The emphasis laid by both Sigfried Giedion and Carl Condit on the engineering aspect of Chicago skyscrapers was extreme, to be sure. Hoffmann's contention that technological innovation is a preferred point of view for the historian because it *appears* "objective and measurable" in this regard is to the point. Writing about commercial and residential buildings, he says that both types were above all " ... meant to be safe, healthy, comfortable, and aesthetically enriched ... the best Chicago architecture is deeply colored and enhanced by elements of nature, romance, and mystery." The only shortcoming of Hoffmann's description is its great generality: it could apply to almost all nineteenth-century architecture.

This approach is indeed useful when we try to show that Chicago architecture was not provincial, but corresponded to larger trends. If we cannot fully agree with Giedion's and Condit's engineering-oriented view of the Chicago school, we must still inquire how architecture in Chicago differed from that of other urban centers. At any rate, in planning the "Building" section of this symposium the authors seem to have had in mind such a regional differentiation (Hoffmann, of course, may or may not agree with this organization). When we try to distinguish Chicago's contribution from that of other important centers, a consideration of its skyscraper development is crucial. Existing studies on the origin of the skyscraper tend to focus narrowly either on engineering (Giedion, Condit) or on the skyscraper's aesthetic definition (Henry-Russell Hitchcock, Winston Weisman).[1] While both factions are preoccupied with identifying the "first" skyscraper, their conclusions differ because their criteria for what constitutes a skyscraper are not the same. Those historians interested in technology have tended to see Chicago as the birthplace of the skyscraper, while those more intent on a stylistic definition believe that this building type originated in New York.

In fact, because skyscraper construction depended on a large set of variable preconditions, finding the "first" skyscraper is a bit like chasing windmills. Even in earlier periods with far simpler technology and less complex economies it is impossible to determine the first example of a given building type. There is no general agreement on which building is the first temple or the first cathedral. That would require total agreement about the constituent characteristics of each type. It might for this reason be more fruitful to explore further the rapid acceptance of the skyscraper. The technophile historians have explained its quick spread in Chicago in terms of material conditions: the earlier invention of the elevator and cast-iron architecture, high land values, the availability of steel, and engineering know-how. While these may all have been important factors in the rise of the skyscraper, psychological and "soft" economic issues such as competition for status, advertising, and public relations have hardly been dealt with.[2]

Further, even if we regard Giedion's and Condit's approach to the history of the skyscraper as one-sided, as historians we cannot ignore their interpretation. For whether we regard their methodology as satisfactory or not, it represents a perception of Chicago architecture that affected not only the historiography of architecture, but also the practice of architecture. Colin Rowe in his article "Chicago Frame," first published in the *Architectural Review* in 1956,[3] writes that the European modernists, who had no direct experience with the construction of skyscrapers, adopted the steel skeleton as an ideal proportional system. European architects in the early twentieth century interpreted it as a neutral grid that could be used to establish a common ratio. For them the skeleton frame became the contemporary equivalent of the Classical vocabulary, a modern language. Thus, a manner of building, which in the Chicago context had been a response to very practical situations that often led to hybrid solutions containing both steel and masonry structures, became for the Europeans the paradigm for a theoretical ideal.

Despite the Europeans' different interpretation of the skeleton frame, it is clear from this particular example that neither American nor European architecture should be studied in isolation. For instance, it is wrong to see the last phase of the International Style in America after World War II exclusively as a European import, as some critics have done. There were from the start a number of American ingredients in the International Style. Moreover, during the Depression, before the arrival of Mies van der Rohe and Walter Gropius in this country, American architecture had begun to meet European Modernism halfway: it underwent a gradual change away from the Beaux-Arts ideals of the earlier twentieth century toward a plainer and more severe expression.[4] As buildings became bigger and budgets were tighter, all that often remained of the Classical ideal was a three-part division of the building, a composition which by itself did not keep these stripped structures from being any less anonymous than our blander American instances of the later International Style.

To come to another important point made in Hoffmann's presentation, the use of nature as a referent in American architecture, Hoffmann states that few historians have paid enough attention to Frank Lloyd Wright's allusion to nature in his buildings. He believes that academics prefer to discuss architectural precedents " ... as though there were no primary sources." I would suggest instead that in the case of Wright his great fascination with nature has been well documented, if only because Wright himself continually pointed it out as one of his inspirations, and that architecture and nature can both be regarded as primary sources. It is generally known that Wright minimized the influence of living architects on his work. For someone of his self-centered genius, it was rather more convenient to claim nature as a prime model. As historians we are surely under the obligation to sort out what Wright claimed he did and what he actually did. Nevertheless, Hoffmann's complaint is well taken. Unless an architect chooses to write about his direct experiences, they are more difficult for the historian to document than references to established architectural monuments. This dilemma holds true for the study of Le Corbusier as much as for Wright; we know more about Le Corbusier's relationship to Palladio than about his deep interest in the vernacular traditions so important for his country houses of the thirties in southeastern France. Only recently, with the publication of his extant sketchbooks, has this aspect of Le Corbusier's source material been somewhat clarified.[5]

The issue of landscape and regional setting brings me to another symposium paper, James O'Gorman's "America and H. H. Richardson." O'Gorman is extremely careful to establish references to an American tradition in Richardson's work, without rejecting at the same time his better-known European sources. They are not mutually exclusive: he shows that New England factories and Italian *palazzi* could be invoked simultaneously. I wonder, however, whether it is not too restrictive to claim, as O'Gorman does, that "the land ... was the only strictly American element in our culture." To the extent that we are ever able to distinguish between various national contributions—between the cultures of Germany and France, for example—by the nineteenth century, American literature and painting, among other cultural expressions, had surely developed their own identities.

Richardson's references to the American landscape and to its geology in particular are indeed impressive, but this is not unique to nineteenth-century America. John Ruskin, correctly referred to by O'Gorman as a possible paradigm for Richardson, had been preoccupied with geology since childhood. He later studied it at Oxford along with literature, and this interest was crucial in his definition of beauty in his widely read *Seven Lamps of Architecture* (1849) and in his call for ingrained ornament in *The Stones of Venice* (1851–1853). When we try to sort out what is American in American allusions to nature, we must keep in mind that Ruskin had set up an unequivocal ideal of nature when he wrote that ". . . most lovely forms . . . are directly taken from natural objects . . ." and conversely ". . . forms which are *not* taken from natural objects *must* be ugly."[6] Richardson then developed this characteristic nineteenth-century concern for nature in a unique and perhaps American fashion. His Ames Monument may even be "a true American beginning," as O'Gorman states. But what does that make of Thomas Jefferson's complete reinterpretation of European Classicism at Monticello and the University of Virginia? How many beginnings may we have?

It is necessary to say something further about the regional character of American architecture. Possibly as an answer to our late modern disorientation, and as an antidote to sameness and placelessness, the use of regionally distinct forms is being advocated today by such ideologically different critics as Kenneth Frampton and Robert Stern. Their assumption appears to be based on the conviction that our older architecture was in fact regionally distinct. This is true to a degree. There were regional adaptations to extreme climates, as in the houses of New Orleans, for instance, or to the absence or presence of building materials, and some purely stylistic conventions developed in certain areas as well. But there were also many trends in the nineteenth century that mitigated against regional identity. The most obvious of these was, of course, the development of the railroad, which made possible a speedy importation and exportation of materials and services. The unassembled parts of the balloon-frame house and later of cast-iron architectural elements were shipped from centers of production to distant new frontier towns. Further, the increasing popularity of pattern books by the middle of the nineteenth century also worked against regional differentiation. The rapid expansion of many American cities as well as the constant influx of new immigrants was not conducive to architectural stability. Donald Hoffmann refers to H. H. Richardson in Chicago as an "outsider," although he immediately acknowledges that this lack of belonging was the case for nearly everyone else as well. And James O'Gorman makes poignantly clear that Richardson was alluding to New England factories in his Marshall Field Store in Chicago, and in his Ames Monument in Wyoming (the site of which Richardson never saw) he may have been inspired by an illustration of a rock formation in northern California. Thus, even in the nineteenth century regionalism is not a clear-cut matter.

In this context Thomas Hines's "Los Angeles Architecture: The Issue of Tradition in a Twentieth-Century City" is most significant. Cross-cultural and cross-regional influences only multiply in the twentieth century, as Hines demonstrates in his display of a vast catalogue of styles in use at the same time in a single region. The Mission style, references to Spanish Baroque, and Frank Lloyd

Wright's pre-Columbian motives were used to invoke slightly different regional identities. The Craftsman cottage, historicizing buildings, and modernist ones all flourished at the same time. Kenneth Frampton has singled out the architecture of Greene and Greene as a particularly fine example of California regionalism. That theirs was an especially good response to the local setting is no doubt true. But if we look at the current housing subdivisions from Los Angeles to San Diego, the experimentation present in the earlier twentieth century seems to have disappeared. We see the same Tudor and French Provincial styles as we would in Houston or Chicago. Perhaps this is to be expected in a place where still today the majority are from somewhere else.

Even in the early twentieth century Los Angeles was a crazy-quilt of many imagined places. The contemporary desire to create a sense of place is well founded, but, as history shows, regionalism may be just another mirage.

NOTES

[1] Winston Weisman, "A New View of Skyscraper History," *The Rise of American Architecture*, Edgar Kaufmann, jr., ed. (New York: Praeger, 1970), pp. 115–60. Henry-Russell Hitchcock, *Architecture: Nineteenth and Twentieth Centuries* (Harmondsworth: Penguin, 4th ed., 1977), p. 335.

[2] Rosemarie Haag Bletter, "La possibile storia del grattacielo," *Casabella*, no. 457/458 (April-May 1980), pp. 57–60.

[3] Colin Rowe, "Chicago Frame," *The Mathematics of the Ideal Villa and Other Essays* (Cambridge, Mass.: MIT Press, 1977), pp. 91–117.

[4] Rosemarie Haag Bletter, "Modernism Rears Its Head—The Twenties and Thirties," *The Making of an Architect*, Richard Oliver, ed. (New York: Rizzoli, 1981), pp. 103–118.

[5] *Le Corbusier Sketchbooks*, preface by André Wogenscky, introduction by Maurice Besset, noted by Françoise de Franclieu (New York and Cambridge, Mass.: The Architectural History Foundation with the MIT Press in collaboration with the Fondation Le Corbusier, 1981–1982), 4 vols.

[6] John Ruskin, *The Seven Lamps of Architecture* (New York: Noonday Press, 1969), p. 101.

RESPONSE

by Kenneth Frampton

It goes without saying that owing to the demise of what Jürgen Habermas has referred to as the "liberative modern project" we are living through a revisionist period. One would have to be insensitive not to detect in the structure, the leading participants and content of this symposium, an effort to initiate a debate or in some cases to formulate a position whose underlying aim is to buffer or misrepresent the cultural consequences of modernization. These consequences persist despite the critical and sometimes *retardataire* concerns of scholars, critics, designers, and architects. One of the greatest paradoxes of the current debate as to an appropriate form for postmodern culture is the prevailing consensus that two of the most seminal figures of twentieth-century American architecture are somehow to be set aside and left out of any serious reevaluation of our present predicament. I have in mind Frank Lloyd Wright and Louis Kahn. Although the work of Wright has been alluded to during this symposium, no one has had the temerity to make a reassessment of his work as a whole and hence to affirm his necessary relevance to the future of a significant American architecture.

As a brief aside before going on to address the papers themselves, I would like to suggest that the last deeply felt, practical and democratic attempt to render the ubiquitous suburb the place of *poesis* and cultivation was made by Frank Lloyd Wright. I am referring to the projection and extensive realization of Wright's Usonian house during the thirties and forties, and by way of rebuke I would also like to remind you that the only scholar who has fully recognized the stature and significance of this particular achievement happens to be an Englishman—the architect John Sergeant, in his book on the Usonian house.[1]

Louis Kahn's stature has been recognized in the past by many of the distinguished participants attending this conference, scholars such as William Jordy and Vincent Scully, and by a number of extraordinarily sensitive but relatively unknown Italian critics. Each has variously illustrated the subtlety, stoicism, and relevance of Kahn's poetic contribution. Kahn's reputation today has nonetheless fallen on hard times, so much so that almost no one now turns to mention his name. These outriding polemical remarks serve, I suppose, much the same function as Edgar Kaufmann's hands-on exhibition of a forgotten bibliography, a kind of sharp reminder of what we have lost.

I am struck by the theme of regionalism running through all of these papers, although with the single exception of James O'Gorman's polished gem of Richardsonian scholarship, this theme seems never to have been directly confronted or handled with sufficient conviction. It is not that critical analysis has been absent, for surely nothing could be more acute than Donald Hoffmann's sensitive appraisal of the poetic dialectic between masonry and steel-frame construction as this appears in Burnham and Root's Rookery Building, Chicago, of which Hoffmann rightly says, "where the two meet head on, as in the alley walls, the result is quite beautiful." However, what I find disappointing in his presentation is his refusal to arrive at any general conclusions from such incidental observations. Instead, he seems to have chosen to confine himself to a gentle and, in the case of the Glessner House, to a not so gentle, polemic, assuming a revisionist stance without sufficient regard for the strong presence of decorative and romantic motives in the Chicago tradition as a whole. Moreover, Hoffmann regrettably uses this position to misread the heroic force and pathos of Louis Sullivan's achievement.

It was, of course, as Hoffmann insists, the delirious tattoo on the Wainwright and Guaranty buildings which was to be the acme of Sullivan's effort to transform the tertiary industrial instruments of the department store and the high-rise office building into objects of culture, comparable to the highest achievements of Assyrian or Islamic civilization. But why should the prime role played by vitalist ornament in these works be taken as a denial of the fact that Sullivan's efforts were synthetic? That is to say, the ornament is indicative of his desire to mediate between industrial civilization and culture, as his own words indicate in "The Tall Office Building Artistically Considered" of 1896. It seems to me that Sullivan's project was ultimately defeated by universal civilization, in other words by Daniel Burnham's City Beautiful movement. At this juncture I wish to acknowledge the work of Leonardo Benevolo, who has so perceptively reminded us that the socio-cultural demands of a booming industrial civilization could not be met by the idiosyncrasies of the so-called Prairie school, however poetic and authentic it may have been. Architects had to be trained in large numbers in order to design and build the institutions of a booming country: in order to build the state capitols, the merchandise marts, the post offices, the railroad stations becoming necessary to the "sleeping giant" which had suddenly awakened. Sullivan's awareness of this is surely evident in *The Autobiography of an Idea* wherein, after stating how the steel frame was handled differently in the East and the West and how the architects of the West mastered it, he writes, "The flag was in the breeze. Yet a small white cloud no bigger than a man's hand was soon to appear above the horizon. The name of this cloud was eighteen hundred and ninety three. Following the little white cloud was a dark dim cloud, more like a fog. The name of the second cloud was Baring Brothers."[2] Sul-

livan reveals, then and there, how he was aware of the part played
by international monopoly capital in reducing the capacity of the
United States to evolve a culture of its own.

While reading James O'Gorman's paper I could not help being
reminded of Lewis Mumford's interpretation of Richardson as a
conscious regionalist.[3] I was also reminded of the conflict and debate, now forgotten, which took place with great ferocity in the
late forties in the Museum of Modern Art. Mumford, on one side,
asserted the crucial cultural relevance of what he had recognized as
the Bay Area school, which Sigfried Giedion, Alfred Barr, and
other members of the East Coast élite dismissed as nothing but
sentimentalism and above all as soft, anti-intellectual, and antimodern.[4] I mention this because in my view it is nothing short of
demagogic to pretend that the current effort to mediate between
culture and the impact of modernization is brand new. It is not
new; it is a struggle that has been going on for a long time.

Equally reactionary is the refusal to admit that this struggle has not
taken place many times over throughout the entire modern movement, or at least from the critical years of the early thirties onward.
I would like to recall the position taken by Harwell Hamilton Harris
when he spoke of restrictive versus liberative regionalism, in an
address given to the Northwestern Chapter of the A.I.A. in Eugene,
Oregon, in 1954.[5] In this address, Harris argued with great lucidity
that a region may both generate and accept ideas. In the American
West in the twenties, he continued, European modernism met a
still evolving regionalism, which allowed it to develop itself to a
higher and more specific cultural level. Harris was, of course, referring here to the work of Gill, Neutra, Schindler, Soriano, Ain,
and finally his own work. He went on to state that in the East of
the American continent, European modernism met a petrified and
restricted regionalism of frozen rules which first resisted and then
capitulated wholesale; a regionalism which accepted European
modernism without any kind of critical mediation. It became, in a
word, formalism because its own regionalism was no longer fluid
and alive, but had been reduced to a system of élitist rules.

Whether one fully accepts Harris's analysis or not, I submit that
such a distinction between liberative and restrictive regionalism is
useful today since it enables us to analyze the historical past criti-
cally. The subtlety of Harris's argument is borne out by his observation that Pasadena was made for Greene and Greene, just as
San Francisco was made for Maybeck. In both instances he states
that they built in local materials, but the fact that they did so "is
not what makes their work important." Indeed, as Thomas Hines
has brilliantly shown in his paper for this symposium, what was
important in the new cultural synthesis of the Greene brothers was
that while it was appropriate to Californian topography and light
and even craftsmanship, it was also a subtle synthesis of Swiss,

Anglo-Saxon, Japanese, and American craft traditions. At its best this synthesis cannot, in my view (with apologies to Thomas Hines), be classified simply as eclectic. It is something of a much higher order. A similarly non-eclectic synthesis, I feel, can also be detected in the work of Gill, again as Hines has demonstrated, with Gill's remarkable capacity to subtly transform elements drawn from Pueblo culture.

I would like to think that Richardson was an architect committed to the project of a liberative regionalism in the sense that Harris uses this term. Harris's provocative assertion that Greene and Greene built in local materials is not of primary import to the cultural richness and significance of their work. I maintain, as James O'Gorman has demonstrated, that it is this question of cultural density and complexity which determines whether a regionalism is nothing more than some form of solipsism, a sentimental veering toward kitsch, or whether it is in fact a new work achieving what I will call a level of synthetic contradiction such as we find in Richardson's Marshall Field Store. This work enriches the model of the Florentine *palazzo* with syntactic structural details drawn from New England mill construction. O'Gorman demonstrates equally convincingly how Richardson's country houses were a kind of speculation about their mythical roots in an autochthonous geology. He refers to America's search for cultural identity after the Civil War. An implicit issue needs to be emphasized here, namely that an authentic cultural identity must ultimately be land-based in some way, although at the same time it must avoid falling into a kind of sentimental isolationism. Land, geology, and utilitarian building practice constitute the range of semantic, non-stylistic references which Richardson applied to both rural and urban situations. When he did so these elements were always resynthesized; they were combined with reinterpreted historical styles such as the Romanesque, the Florentine Renaissance, or even the English Arts and Crafts tradition.

I was struck forcibly by O'Gorman's phrase "escape from history, a true American beginning," when he characterized the Ames Monument in Wyoming as Richardson's attempt to escape from history and propose a new level of interaction between nature and culture—a form of interaction which would later be followed by Sullivan and Wright. A great gulf clearly separates Richardson's Marshall Field Store and Sullivan's tall office buildings from either the John Hancock Tower or the recent Sears megalith erected in Chicago, works which reflect above all else the technical genius of the late Fazlur Kahn. Of the formal consequences of such Chicago megaworks, Hoffmann appropriately cites Carl Condit to the effect that the urban skyscraper and its lesser breeds have been either naked technology or elemental geometry. Bereft of texture, pattern, rhythm, accent, scale, or relation to anything around them, they are without symbolic meaning—Platonic forms which by definition lie beyond history. Certainly I agree with this judgment that what is antihistorical is inevitably antiurban and antihuman.

Hoffmann goes on to juxtapose, appropriately, the city of Chicago with Carl Sandburg's and Frank Lloyd Wright's beloved "prairie." This polarity brings me back to the necessity of thinking about our historical situation in terms of civilization versus culture. With regard to this issue I would like to draw your attention to the existence of different states of mind, to the state of mind, for example, of the man who commissioned the Glessner house. His spiritual cultivation is touchingly revealed in a letter to his children which records the way in which the family brought the so-called living fire from their old home to the new building that had been designed for them by Richardson.[6] When I first read that letter I was absolutely astonished that an executive of a major agricultural machinery company would actually go to the bother in the mid-1880s of taking the fire from his old house to his new one.

Richardson's idea of place creation, whether unduly defensive or not, seems to me to have always been committed to the idea of boundary, topography, and enclosure. Surely Glessner's ritualistic transfer of the household fire represents, together with the house itself, a state of mind which is totally removed from the high-tech architecture of Skidmore, Owings and Merrill. Furthermore, I would also submit that such an attitude is equally distant from Charles Moore's tendency to interpret place as something which varies with location, like a commodity, with no more commitment to one place than any other.

Here we would finally have to discuss the origins of our true sense of place, ultimately dependent on, perhaps even conditioned by, tectonic density. It is certainly not something which can be schematically evoked by pure scenography and historicist illusion. Thomas Hines's strange remark about the tendency of historians, like modern architects, to be more interested in change than in continuity reminds me of a sharp aphorism made by the Dutch architect Aldo Van Eyck, namely that what antiquarians and technocrats have in common is a sentimental attitude toward time. Where the technocrats are sentimental about the future, antiquarians are sentimental about the past. From this aphorism we may conclude that direct borrowing from history is not the crucial issue, nor is it even relevant. The issue, I would submit, is twofold—first, to reinterpret history, as I believe the more sensitive practitioners of the modern movement have always done, and second, to mediate advanced technology and set some limits on the domain of universal civilization.

I would like to add as a final gloss to this rich, rewarding, and interesting conference, that today, when we speculate about our architectural past in the Americas, by implication we speculate about its future. We should realize that if we are serious about contributing to the future of architecture in any profound sense, we must understand that what we are involved in is a kind of rearguard action, and that we can no longer see our task as the optimization of modernity. Rather, what we have to do is to regulate the processes of a universal civilization which finally cannot be renounced or denied. Whether regionalism is a mirage or not, as Rosemarie Bletter has suggested, I think it forms a basis on which to construct a viable cultural strategy for the future of American architecture.

NOTES

[1] John Sergeant, *Frank Lloyd Wright's Usonian Houses: The Case for Organic Architecture* (New York: Whitney Library of Design, 1976).

[2] Louis Sullivan, *The Autobiography of an Idea* (New York: Peter Smith, 1949), p. 314.

[3] Lewis Mumford, *Sticks and Stones: A Study of American Architecture and Civilization* (New York: Dover Press, 1955), pp. 99–114.

[4] "What Is Happening in Modern Architecture?" symposium at the Museum of Modern Art, New York, 1948. See also Anthony Alofsin, Liane Lefaivre, Alexander Tzonis, *"Die Frage des Regionalismus,"* in M. Andritzky, L. Burkhardt, and D. Hoffmann, eds., *Für eine andere Architektur,* vol. I. (Frankfurt am Main: Fischer Taschenbuch Verlag, 1980), pp. 121–34.

[5] Harwell H. Harris, "Regionalism and Nationalism," *Student Publication of the School of Design,* North Carolina State College of the University of North Carolina at Raleigh, vol. 14, no. 5.

[6] John J. Glessner, *The House at 1800 Prairie Avenue, Chicago 1886, H. H. Richardson, Architect* (Chicago: Chicago Architecture Foundation, 1978), p. 2.

KEYNOTE ADDRESS:

VERNACULAR

by J. B. Jackson

VERNACULAR

by J. B. Jackson

The inauguration of a nationwide program devoted to the study of the traditions of American architecture is, I hope, an occasion when an examination of the vernacular and its role in American design will not be out of place.

There has never been a time when the concept of the vernacular has enjoyed so much interest as now. Whether clearly defined or not, it is seen as a vital element in our architectural past and an even more important element in the architecture of the years to come. To many Americans an infusion of vernacular architectural design promises to invigorate the style we are presumably evolving at present and lead us to a more human scale, and to a simpler and more democratic built environment. An ambitious program, devoted to the study of "American domestic vernacular architecture" scheduled for Los Angeles in October of this year, refers to the vernacular as an element in the American Dream, and as a key to a revived sense of place. Architects in particular, it is said, will rediscover the neglected roots of our culture. I hope this proves to be the case, yet I cannot help wondering why there is no mention of the contemporary vernacular architecture, particularly domestic vernacular architecture flourishing throughout America and producing a wealth of new forms.

Perhaps there is need for updating the current definition, for the emphasis in the various conferences and exhibitions listed, if I understand it correctly, will be less on the task of defining the American vernacular than on examining various examples from the past: the bungalow, the Californian ranch house, the French Creole cottage, the homestead architecture in Colorado, and the dog-trot house of Appalachia. Generally speaking, the exhibitions seem to endorse a widely held belief that vernacular architecture consists of traditional rural or small-town or pioneer dwellings, using local resources and adjusting to the local environment. Stylistic innovation is excluded.

What might be called the official definition is one quoted from the English architectural historian R. W. Brunskill in his book *A Handbook of Vernacular Architecture,* published in 1973 and widely read in this country. The definition is too long to quote. Briefly, Brunskill says that a vernacular architectural style is the creation of local building traditions, using forms and materials and techniques long familiar in the region. The design of a vernacular dwelling is usually the product of a local craftsman or of the prospective occupant. The basic forms are domestic in origin, and while additions and modifications may occur, the style emphasizes timeless, unchanging elements, and maintains a strict regard for function—though what that function is is not mentioned. A vernacular style does not welcome radically new techniques, or materials imported from elsewhere. Brunskill's book concentrates for the benefit of his English readers almost exclusively on existing vernacular specimens in rural England, dating from between the sixteenth and the first half of the nineteenth century—at which time he believes that vernacular architecture ceased to be produced.

There are several aspects to this definition that from the American point of view are worth examining. In the first place, it is clear that the definition could never have been formulated by a geographer or an anthropologist. Its emphasis on design and form and material, and on the absence of the professional architect, marks it as the work of architectural historians. It must be said that vernacular architecture, as currently defined, was in fact the discovery of the architect and antiquarian and only later of the geographer.

Secondly, we might note that the environment which presumably determines the vernacular structure is the *natural* environment—soil, topography, climate; not the social environment of community and law. Thirdly, the definition implies no evolution or historical change. In its reluctance to take on new ideas and new techniques, and in its loyalty to ancient prototypes, the vernacular stands *outside* of history.

I suggest that these characteristics, however appropriate to the discussion of a certain type of pretechnological rural dwelling, are *not* appropriate to a discussion of vernacular architecture in this country, and that if we are to include contemporary dwellings, or even the dwellings of nineteenth-century America, we must modify the definition.

The origin and subsequent uses of the word *vernacular* give us some guidance. It derives from the Latin *verna,* meaning a slave born in the house of his or her master. By extension, the adjective *vernacular* in Classical times came to mean association with the place of birth. or (as a noun) a native, usually a peasant or dependent. The significance of the word was identification with a local or village society, rather than with the *natural* environment, and implied a way of life devoted to work—usually farm work—and to family.

The word first became common in English in the late Middle Ages, characterizing the language or dialect of a particular country or district. Vernacular was distinguished from Latin, an international, unchanging language used in the church, in law courts, in diplomacy, scholarship, and polite literature. It was the language of written contracts and even the language of prayer. It was a work of art. On the other hand, vernacular was the everyday language spoken by people in England or France or Germany or Italy or Spain. A vernacular language at that time was still in the process of evolving. Its syntax was confused, its vocabulary, spelling, and pronunciation were capricious, and it was less a work of art than a tool, a rough-and-ready instrument for workaday relationships and communication.

It was only in the early nineteenth century that the word was used in an architectural sense. This was when archaeologists and students of rural culture began exploring what survived of tradition in the countryside. Their interest was perhaps focused less on the function and operation of old buildings than on the identification of old forms or of forms unaffected by modern urban or industrial existence. Much of the architecture they examined was abandoned or in ruins. The great variety of housetypes thus brought to light were interpreted as reflecting the old relationships with the environment: the use of local materials, the influence of the local natural setting. *Vernacular* seemed an appropriate word to describe the vestiges of a culture which was rural, traditional, and on the verge of extinction. The evolution of these forms and the impact of social, technological, and political change were no part of the investigation.

One consequence of this concentration on environmental factors in the early days of the study was that while no one had any precise idea of what vernacular architecture was (aside from being rooted in tradition) a great many regional and national styles were discovered—in this country a New England style, an Appalachian style, a Texan, a Southwestern, and a California style. The proliferation of vernacular styles in Europe was of course much greater, all of them coming under the head of an ineffable concept variously called *Volksbaukunst, architecture rurale,* or *spontaneous* or *anonymous* or *popular* architecture. The later injection of theories as to the nature of the dwelling deriving from Heidegger, Eliade, Bachelard, or Jung, none of whom was concerned with the prosaic economic or technological aspects of the subject, has not helped matters.

But what has made a great difference and brought us much nearer a workable definition of the vernacular is the new archaeology in Europe focused on the Middle Ages, and the work of such Americans as James Deetz and Henry Glassie. Over the past generation new archaeological techniques—aerial photography, paleobotany, soil analysis, and dendrochronology—as well as a closer cooperation with historians have combined to give the study of vernacular architecture what it had previously lacked: a historical dimension. In his recent book entitled *Le Village et la maison au Moyen Age,* Robert Fossier mentions the recent discovery, as it were, of the medieval village and the medieval dwelling:

Between the tenth and the twelfth centuries there occurred a break in the history of the rural habitat which
had, generally speaking (at least in Western Europe) been
identified with the Bronze Age or the beginning of the
Neolithic. Chronologically the birth of the village is
closely tied to the establishment of the 'feudal system';
taking place over a long period of demographic growth,
the birth of the village is certainly a fundamental trait
in subsequent rural history and probably one of the most
characteristic traits in European history until the Industrial Revolution.

The picture of vernacular culture now taking form suggests that
beginning in the eleventh century vernacular building underwent
constant change. The development of carpentry techniques allowed
for more solidity and more storage space for crops under the roof
of the dwelling, and created larger uninterrupted interior spaces.
Sturdier exterior walls and new roof coverings were introduced.
The chimney was developed, a separate structure for livestock became common, brick and stone were used. The dwelling was thus
transformed and improved, and specialized craftsmen became more
essential. Eventually in the late Middle Ages distinct regional house
types started to emerge, and dependence on strictly local materials
decreased.

Technical innovations were not, however, the only influences at
work. Such developments as the use of horses instead of oxen, the
introduction of new crops and new agricultural implements, and
at a later date the shortage of wood for construction, the advent of
specialized farming for the urban market, and finally the shift from
the farm village to the independent self-sufficient commercial farm,
all made for many changes in the construction, layout, and function
of the dwelling, and in its relationship to the village and to the
fields.

Thus even in pretechnological times, the vernacular dwelling
proves to have been anything but "timeless" and blindly loyal to
traditional forms and methods. On the contrary, recent investigations show it to have been extraordinarily flexible and adaptable.
To use an old-fashioned term, the vernacular dwelling was and is
"existential," defining itself as it evolves and without a recognizable
prototype. Fifty years ago the French geographer Albert Deman-
geon defined the rural dwelling as an "agricultural implement," an
implement for processing and storing crops, for planting, culti-
vating, and harvesting, for sheltering animals and people. He downplayed the importance of environmental factors in the design and
location and construction of the dwelling, and likewise downplayed
those ornamental architectural features which the architectural historian finds significant. To him they were merely uncouth imita-
tions of the local manor or chateau. Perhaps he was right: the
masonry farm house, common throughout Western Europe since
the Renaissance, was and is a monolithic structure, modified only

slowly and at great expense. For one feature of medieval vernacular architecture—the use of wood—has all but vanished from Western Europe and is now an American characteristic; hence the remarkable flexibility and inventiveness of American vernacular.

But the identification of the vernacular solely with the rural scene is a notion which we must abandon, and no definition of the idiom can be adequate for the nineteenth and twentieth centuries which omits the dwellings of the urban worker, the craftsman, and the small merchant.

Shifts in form in the urban environment are less easy to observe, but one particular shift, one historic modification of the vernacular dwelling both urban and rural, was the gradual separation between those spaces identified with work and those identified with private domestic existence. I have already mentioned another long-term modification: the increase in the size of uninterrupted spaces. A third change should be added: greater speed in construction.

Our present concern, of course, is with American vernacular, but it is by understanding the Renaissance European background that I think we can eventually see how the American vernacular dwelling resembled in certain respects its Old World contemporary and how in other respects it had a distinct identity of its own.

What were some of the building traditions which the first settlers in New England and Virginia brought with them? We should bear in mind that those settlers were for the most part young, blue-collar men and women of rural or small-town background, part of the prevailing vernacular English culture. The most widely accepted architectural tradition they had was the still vital one of building out of wood, and of adapting new materials and new methods as the supply of wood diminished. The second tradition was the tendency to separate the dwelling from the barn and stable and to emphasize its strictly domestic function. Third, there was the tendency to move out of the farm village with its collective rules and procedures and to establish an independent, relatively self-sufficient farmstead in the open country. Finally, there was a growing sentiment among these settlers for the nuclear family, centered on the child. Philippe Aries has written about this new kind of home in his book *The Centuries of Childhood*.

At the same time we should ask what conditions here in America influenced the development of a specifically American vernacular architecture. The most obvious was the inexhaustible supply of wood; the second was the inexhaustible supply of land; the third was the inexhaustible demand for labor. There are other political, economic, and social factors to be taken into account, but I suggest that if we are to undertake a chronological and typological study of the American vernacular dwelling from the seventeenth century to the present, we start by considering the topic under the following heads: the various forms of construction, including the use of different techniques and materials; the various kinds of layout; the notion of the lifespan of the dwelling; the relation of the dwelling to the community; how the family interprets the function of the dwelling; and finally the introduction of utilities and amenities and their relation to the occupants. Two other topics—the regional stylistic or aesthetic character of the dwelling, and its relation to the wider natural environment—ought also to be considered, and (simply by way of contrast) the nature of formal, institutional architecture in America. But those are matters which many architectural historians and local historians have already dealt with.

In terms of construction and use of materials it is clear that almost from the beginning there was experimentation in building methods—as, for example, in the slab house of Virginia and the clapboard and the modified braced frame of New England—and also experimentation with materials. There seems to have been an early tendency to use many nails instead of relying on traditional carpentry joining techniques. The log cabin may well have had a Scandinavian origin, but it developed its American form in construction and kind of wood; and it rejected traditional craftsmanship. The balloon frame is a spectacular instance of a new use of wood and nails and new kinds of construction, rejecting not only orthodox methods but the traditional village cooperation. Building a frame house became a family affair, and what was needed from the community was not help but the presence of a utility: a saw mill.

The nineteenth-century box house, largely confined to the South, the West, and California, was a further development of the slab house, and a further rejection of the craftsman—even of craftsmanship. Although many architectural historians still believe that vernacular architecture in America came to an end with the development of the "ready-cut" or mail-order house of the mid-nineteenth century, it is my belief that these houses, shipped in bundles of boards and hardware by rail all over the West, merely represent an extension of the self-built wooden house, and so for that matter does the prefabricated house. The trailer qualifies, if only on the score that it uses unorthodox materials—materials, that is to say, not used in formal architecture—and completely bypasses the carpenter craftsman and community cooperation.

A similar change can be noted in the evolution of the layout of spaces in the American vernacular dwelling. In the earliest beginnings the one-room and two-room dwelling, often with some storage either under the roof or in a cellar, seems to have been common, but as one reads accounts of pioneer housing one becomes aware of an attempt, often purely temporary, to produce more rooms not only for greater privacy but for a greater specialization of domestic functions. Even the standard workers' dwelling in American mill towns achieved three rooms by the 1850s—at a time when *one* room for a similar family was still the rule on the Continent. A less easily chronicled change in layout is the gradual appearance of a dining room separate from the kitchen, of bedrooms in the attic, and (beginning some time in the early twentieth century) the disappearance of spaces for storage: the attic and cellar become less important, and the parlor as a repository for family heirlooms is eliminated along with the guestroom and the pantry and with the appearance of the bathroom. It might be said that spaces once identified with preserving the heritage of the past and providing for the family future vanish from the vernacular home. The trailer is a good example: the mini-storage or self-storage facility and the ad hoc garage are contemporary substitutes for those spaces identified with family continuity.

On the other hand, ever since the first settlement, the American dwelling has evolved a variety of what the English call "outshots"—converted attics, new partitions, stairways, verandas, roofed-in outdoor spaces, and many sheds and shelters for domestic purposes; in the South one even finds the separate kitchen and separate milkshed. This ingenious kind of remodeling and adding, only possible on a frequent basis in a wooden house, this search for more space, is still one of the hallmarks of the American vernacular home, though since it is largely interior, it often goes unnoticed. It contributes, of course, to the flexibility of the house, its exterior complexity, and its use for many different functions; and, again, we are often confronted by unorthodox construction methods—the use of power tools and prefabricated materials, with instructions coming from popular magazines and handbooks.

The problem of the projected lifespan of the American dwelling is not easy to isolate from construction factors. Let me merely mention the notorious short-term use of houses in Colonial Virginia, the practice, even in Colonial New England, of moving houses and barns and using them for other purposes, and the built-in mobility of many ready-cut houses in mill towns and company towns. The mobility of the medieval wooden dwelling is something I have discussed elsewhere; but whereas that earlier mobility represented a shift of location and a renewal of the old dwelling, mobility in the American context often means a discarding of the old and an improvement in the standard of living. The log cabin is abandoned in favor of the tract house, the tract house is abandoned in favor of the personalized, architect-designed suburban house. The formal mansion, on the contrary, the plantation house or ranch house, and the rich estate all remain as originally conceived: monuments to position and family permanence. It is this lighthearted moving on the part of the wage-earning American family from one type of house to another, or from one region to another in search of a job, that gives the American landscape its peculiarly impermanent quality. Thus, few Americans are likely to interpret every abandoned house as a symbol of tragedy. It is simply a symbol of mobility and of a concept of the dwelling as a temporary convenience.

The apparent isolation of many American dwellings, particularly farm dwellings, is another feature of our landscape that foreigners find difficult to understand, though it is one of the oldest features, even in New England. Yet I doubt if any American dwelling, except during brief periods of pioneering, was ever totally independent of a community; if no man is an island, no dwelling, certainly no vernacular dwelling, is ever entirely solitary: each of them, even in the open spaces of the West, is dependent on a church, a school, a post office, a gas station, a general store. This too is a vernacular characteristic. The medieval and Renaissance dwelling was dependent on the village for services and amenities and for law and order. Only the feudal estate and the nineteenth-century dream of an ideal homestead attached to the ancestral land were without ties to the community. I would say, however, that the community we need has changed in quality: it is now the source of utilities and services rather than a social or political center, and I believe that many vernacular dwellings are identified with what one could call a non-political community. I am thinking of such places as company towns, resort areas, construction sites, trailer courts, communes, and restricted residential areas once protected by covenants. As with the medieval village, these groups of dwellings are ruled by custom, by convention, and often do not own their land outright. In such communities—again, as with the vernacular village of medieval Europe—there are restrictions on membership and definite community obligations and privileges.

I have roughly defined the American vernacular dwelling in terms either of characteristics inherited from the vernacular dwelling of Western Europe (before the shortage of wood for building) or of uniquely American characteristics appearing early in our history. I have said that our typical vernacular dwelling is rarely designed to conform to a traditional prototype or built with the permanent needs and tastes of the occupants in mind. Insofar as it is not a farmstead it is seen as a temporary structure, to be enlarged and improved as time and money become available, or to be abandoned in favor of a better dwelling—or moved and used elsewhere. Second, I have suggested that the average working-class vernacular dwelling is a *minimal* dwelling, with little space for storage, and dependent on the community for many services and amenities. Third, it is often the product of new techniques and new or unorthodox materials, built with some haste in order to be of immediate use as an implement in the business of making a living or the providing of shelter. Finally, the American vernacular dwelling, divorced from the land, divorced from the past and from the political community, is thought of as a private environment, a place for relaxation, for privacy, and for bringing up children.

As I have said elsewhere, the dwelling is a transformer, transforming the energy of the outside world into a form suited to domestic life. It is an instrument to establish relationships with the wider environment and other people. It is not a monument to the family. It is not a work of art; in many important respects its identity is the direct opposite of that of the specimen of formal architecture, domestic or institutional. It is, in short, the expression of adjustment and adaptation and compromise with social, economic, and environmental forces constantly impinging upon it, but never under final control.

THE PLACE:
URBANISM AND SUBURBANISM

INTRODUCTION

by J. B. Jackson

We have come together this morning to hear three talks on the elusive subject of space, particularly public space, and then to hear responses to these talks. Afterward everyone present will be invited to participate in the discussion. Each speaker has been allotted forty minutes, and each respondent will have ten minutes. In order to allow as much time as possible for the public to express their views, I will keep my introductory remarks as brief as possible.

The first speaker is Denise Scott Brown of the architectural firm of Venturi, Rauch and Scott Brown. She is not only an architect, but a teacher, lecturer, and writer. Her field of interest, I think it can be said, is not utopias or model communities, but towns and places that are "almost all right." That is her expression for the type of space or place that she will discuss: everyday aspects of everyday American communities that somehow manage to function satisfactorily and even beautifully, regardless of their occasional disorder and lack of conscious design. She will discuss contemporary American urban spaces in terms of the colonial experience and the colonialists' initial uncertainty when confronted with the spaciousness of the New World, and then she will suggest how Americans have learned over the course of time to produce new kinds of public spaces that hold promise for our future. These spaces, not always recognized and rarely designed, will, when properly studied, lead us to reassess and reinterpret our European architectural legacy, and encourage us to accept ornament and symbolism in our public design. As we will see, Denise's talk contains much that is stimulating, new, and controversial.

The second speaker is John Coolidge, Professor of Fine Arts at Harvard, and author of perhaps the first scholarly study of an artificial industrial community in the United States. *Mill and Mansion,* a description of the planning and organization of Lowell, Massachusetts, has been for more than a generation the inspiration and model for countless similar studies of industrial towns. Today Mr. Coolidge will discuss public space in terms of three historic designs: that of L'Enfant for Washington, D.C., that of Olmsted for Riverside, Illinois, and that of Frank Lloyd Wright for the campus of Florida Southern College. Though very different in form—L'Enfant's Washington being classical in inspiration, Riverside being Victorian-Romantic, and the little-known Florida campus being deliberately innovative—all three designs represent an attempt to produce by means of public spaces a sense of community, identity, and pride among the inhabitants and users.

The third speaker is Dolores Hayden, Professor of Urban Planning at the University of California at Los Angeles, and author of two important books: *Seven Utopias* and *The Grand Domestic Revolution*. Both of them express her interest in the design of socially effective communities and public spaces. She will recall the once powerful vernacular tradition of three pre-technological societies in America: the Pueblo Indians, the early nineteenth-century communities identified with the Greek Revival in architecture, and finally the communities of the Shakers and other religious groups. In all of these the public spaces set aside and designed for common use and enjoyment were successful because they were defined not as commodities for sale, but as instruments for the fostering of a just social order. They were in fact early expressions of social order and of socially conscious architecture. Dolores Hayden suggests that we can learn once again to design effective public spaces by recalling such early examples. It is for teachers and practitioners of environmental design to lead the way.

Our two commentators or respondents are particularly well qualified to discuss these several points of view. Max Bond is not only a practicing architect—the designer of the Martin Luther King Memorial among other public spaces—but also Chairman of the Department of Architecture here at Columbia. Christine Boyer, Assistant Professor in the same department, is an authority on historic preservation and a long-time student of the American urban tradition. Her book *Dreaming the American City* is scheduled to appear next month.

The topic is a very ambitious one, and yet it is one that we can all discuss from experience and with something like authority. Not all of us are craftsmen or designers or architects, but each of us is incessantly engaged, either as a solitary individual or as a member of a group, in the process of transforming ill-defined and impersonal spaces into unique places of interaction and self-identification and ultimately into places of beauty and symbolism. It follows that we can all contribute to the discussion, and I think that those responses that express a personal point of view may be even more valuable than those that merely comment on the remarks of the various speakers.

Let me offer you a little guidance as to how this subject can be thought about. This is from Yi Fu Tuan's book called *Space and Place*:

> The discourse of planners and designers must be enlarged to include questions such as these: what connection is there between space awareness and the idea of future time and goal? What are the links between body

postures and personal relationship on the one hand and spatial values and distance relationships on the other? How do we describe 'familiarity', that quality of 'at-homeness' we feel toward a person or place? What kinds of intimate places can be planned, and what cannot—at least, no more than we can plan for deeply human encounters? Are space and place the environmental equivalents of the human need for adventure and safety, openness and definition? How long does it take to form a lasting attachment to place? Is the sense of place a quality of awareness poised between being rooted in place, which is unconscious, and being alienated, which goes with exacerbated consciousness—and exacerbated because it is only or largely mental? How do we promote the visibility of rooted communities that lack striking visual symbols? What is the loss and gain in such promotion?

These are some of the topics that these speakers will invite us to consider.

INVENTION AND TRADITION IN THE MAKING OF AMERICAN PLACE

by Denise Scott Brown

Some Paradoxes of Colonial Cultural Landscapes

I once overheard the following conversation on a bus:
First woman: "I can tell from your accent that you're from Home."
Second: "Yes, I left Home thirty years ago."
Third: "I've never been Home but one day I hope to go."

This exchange, in Johannesburg, South Africa, was not an expression of sentimental nostalgia, it was the affirmation of an alliance among members of a caste. By tracing their origins directly or at one remove to England, these women reassured each other of their social status in the South Africa of the 1940s. Their jingoism induced my xenophobia. As a child, I wriggled uncomfortably when English visitors likened views of the low veld to "a little piece of Surrey," and I pondered the incongruity of black children in French West Africa reciting lessons about *"nos ancêtres les gaulois."* As a teenager, I joined an art class where we were exhorted to paint from what was around us, to see the landscape of veld and sun and the life of Africans in the city as our most important inspiration—if we were to produce vital art, if our art was to be "African."

I have long since realized that my art teacher's formulation was too simple. After all, we spoke English. More than a few hundred years before, and in my case less than a hundred years before, the roots of our culture were in Europe. European, and particularly English, culture pervaded our intellectual lives, conditioning our perception and appreciation of our African world. As artists, our attempts to understand our own landscape were inevitably made in the context of the mother culture. This orientation toward outside influences limited our ability to use local experience as material for our art.

The South African writer Dan Jacobson defined this colonial artistic condition in his introduction to *The Story of an African Farm* by Olive Schreiner.[1] He observed that Schreiner's un-English, African setting, "her snow-less, wood-less, lawn-less Karroo," seemed implausible, even in South Africa, as a background for fiction, because it had never been depicted in literature before. When Jacobson first read the novel, he had to struggle with his own incredulity "that the kopjes, kraals and cactus plants she mentions were of the same kind as those I was familiar with; so little experience had I had of encountering them within the pages of a book."

"This is not to deny," he added, "that *The Story of an African Farm* is . . . a very 'literary' piece of work; the fruit in places more of reading than of life." This literary quality Jacobson found damaging to the novel; however, it may have played an important part in the unlocking of colonial artistry. Perhaps Schreiner's conversion of African sources to "literature" was key to making them artistically available. Her tale of the veld was told, not in voortrekker prose, but in the style of the author's literary contemporaries in England. By making the work comprehensible in London, Schreiner may have rendered the African landscape visible for the first time to her audiences in South Africa and England. If so, then, in an artistic sense, she invented the African landscape.

When, in the late 1960s, Robert Venturi and I tried to do something similar in Las Vegas, it was relatively easy to transfer my African xenophobia to America, and to suggest that American architects, for the sake of cultural relevance and artistic vitality, look at the landscape around them and learn. Yet our analyses of the American suburban landscape were based, in large part, on European modes of scholarly inquiry; we defined the Las Vegas Strip by comparing it with historical European architecture, using categories set up for the study of traditional, European urban space.

These paradoxes beset societies and cultures whose origins are in another place. As problems, they are surely no worse than the problems of more settled societies, but they are different, and they persist as tensions between artistic dependence and independence long after political freedom has been won.[2] In America the paradox is fourfold:

—The United States is a diverse nation, differentiated regionally and ethnically, stratified socially, and pluralistic culturally; yet it is also a mass society that shares symbols and systems to such an extent that Americans are accused by outsiders of being a nation of conformists.

—Many if not most Americans left their lands of origin because they were different from those around them. They were poorer, more oppressed, different racially or religiously; they were adventurers or mavericks. The cultures they took away with them were not the same as those of the people they left behind, and in the ensuing years they diverged even further. America is far more different from Europe than most visiting Europeans realize. This is in part due to the emigrants' search for a new world, which they defined as the counterform to the unsatisfactory old world. American morality, polity, governance, social structure and culture, and a physical container expressive of American aspirations had all to be invented. Inventing America was a great experiment and high adventure. Nevertheless, most immigrants brought their old world to the new, carrying landscapes and mores in memory and reasserting them, *mutatis mutandis,* in city or farm. Some Elizabethan English and nineteenth-century Italian customs that were lost in their countries of origin are preserved in Kentucky and South Philadelphia. Landscapes transported from England to New England settle again uncomfortably in Arizona.

—We Americans, like other former colonials, are xenophobes, yet in some areas of life, we clutch the apron strings of our mother cultures. We are proud of our indigenous styles, yet at times we still require European endorsement to validate them in our own eyes.

—The United States is artistically both precursor and follower, and the pendulum swings quite rapidly. But in architecture, discovery by latter-day European "colonizers"—a Reyner Banham for Los Angeles, an American-born Charles Jencks for Postmodernism—is still needed to dignify, for Americans, those artistic forms that originate in America.

Is the American architectural experience a colonial experience? Can it be termed colonial after 1776? Assuredly not in all spheres. I have used the terms "colonial" and "colonizer" to discuss attitudes toward artistic sources and artistic identity in American architecture. I have not attempted here a general analysis of relations between colonialism and architecture; nor have I investigated the expression of colonial power through architecture—either in colonial America or by America today. Where I describe colonial architecture, it is settlers' rather than rulers' architecture; and I have seamed settlers and immigrants together, viewing the colonists, architecturally, as early ethnic groups with problems of adjustment not wholly different from the problems of those who came later.

Inventing America and Inventing the Landscape

What are the effects of immigration on the artist? If earliest stimuli, the sights and scents experienced when the infant first comes to awareness, are in some way linked to future creativity, what is the artistic prognosis for immigrants or refugees removed, probably forever, from the environment they knew when two feet above ground? What of the immigrant group and its group artistic culture?

In most group migrations to America the first generation was lost, in an artistic sense and indeed in most senses. They heaved their young above their heads and saw their reward as the success of the second generation. "Culture," when there was time for it, was internal to the group. It lay in Little Italy or in the Yiddish press and theater. Subsequent generations turned to "face America."[3] Yiddish poetry began to read like Walt Whitman, house decorations in Italian neighborhoods included the American eagle. Yet later, immigrant descendants, speaking and writing in English, have shared in the artistic life of the dominant cultures and have added to the vitality of what is called "American." They play a leading part today in the inventing and reinventing of America. Perhaps their off-center starting point lends intensity to their art.[4]

How does this generational sequence of adaptation, invention, and reinvention tie in with American architecture and the making of place? Only fitfully perhaps, in a literal sense—most architecture is not designed or developed by actual or metaphorical immigrants—but perhaps rather well in the artistic and cultural sense of "inventing."

European colonists took their architecture with them and adapted it to conditions they found in the colonies. Dutch farm houses in the Cape Colony developed porches and pergolas. To English houses in the United States were added porches and jalousies in the South and clapboard in the North. The two major colonial heritages in the United States were the English and the Spanish, with the Anglo predominating and forming the basic matrix of architecture in this country. The English heritage was itself bifurcated, encompassing, on the one hand, a rural cottage and Romantic landscape tradition and, on the other, a Classical tradition derived from English Palladianism.

High culture grafted other strands to this matrix.[5] Classical influences from antiquity and republican France accompanied the birth of the new republic, symbolizing republican virtue in furniture, architecture, and urbanism. A later Classical influence from Haussmann's Paris gave expression to civic pride and served commercial boosterism in the turn-of-the-century American city. European borrowings included nineteenth-century Eclecticism, the International Style, and Art Deco Moderne. There were also reactions against European influences and toward non-European ones, by Frank Lloyd Wright and others, in the name of Americanism.

Ethnic groups, facing the basically English character of the everyday realm, sought to express identity through a melding of ethnic and dominant group symbols, but ethnic symbolism receded as subsequent generations allied themselves to taste cultures related more to their socio-economic than their ethnic status. The social movements of the 1960s and the interest in roots in the 1970s brought renewed expressions of group identity, both ethnic and racial, although usually at the level of home decoration.

House styles, whether "French Provincial," "Cape Cod," or "Contempo," are assigned greater importance in the American suburban environment than in equivalent European housing areas. Styling represents perhaps one final resting place of American pluralism— although during the Sun Belt migrations of the 1960s and 1970s, a further layer of complexity was added to house styling, as new residents in Houston, for example, sought highly decorated, eclectic, townhouse precincts to serve as stage sets and symbols for a new way of life in a new city.

In sum, social and migratory movements to the United States and within it have been paralleled by a process of architectural invention and reinvention that started with the inception of the nation and continues today. Has this process educed space and place that are different from anywhere else?

What's American about American Place?

Such a question is typical of the colonist's search for identity. Given the paradoxes, the multiple influences, and the newness of the culture, the answer is hard to find and will be found, if at all, in slivers of evidence that lie between borrowings and inventions, as insinuations rather than firm statements.

A literature has grown up around the question. John A. Kouwenhoven,[6] in search of "what's American," observes that one characteristic landscape is "the 'interminable and stately prairies', as Walt Whitman called them, ruled off by roads and fences into a mathematical grid. They have become, as Whitman thought they would become, the home of 'America's distinctive ideas and distinctive realities'." Among a dozen such landscapes that Kouwenhoven lists, the first three are the Manhattan skyline, the gridiron town plan, and the skyscraper. Their particularly American quality, for him, is their "fluid and ever changing unity" and their state of being "always complete but never finished." Vincent Scully perceives "a kind of uneasiness, a distrust of the place, a restlessness," that emanates from the American experience of "a vast landscape, a more or less scarifying contact with the Indian population, certain racial crimes, colonialism, a sense of distance from centers of high civilization, a feeling at once of liberation and of loss."[7]

Ronald Lewcock, writing of nineteenth-century colonial architecture in general, claims that its character derives from limitations of the conditions in which it was built; "amateur designs, semi-skilled or unskilled labour, and restricted building materials transformed the intricacies of fashion into fortuitously subtle and restrained statements . . . enforcing by simplicity the impact of the lines and forms of the styles."[8] Scully describes American colonial architecture in the same terms, seeing architecture of both Spanish and English origin as "simplified, clarified, and primitivized. These qualities . . . become positive ones, like the beginning of something which— though deriving or degenerating from a more developed style— had worked its way back to first principles, from which a new kind of growth may well be possible." In America the English or Spanish original was "distilled into a more rigid order, less compromised by variety, less rich in modulation . . . the virtues sought were now the elemental ones of strong obvious shapes and plain surfaces."[9] Lewcock adds, "Excessive copying may have produced stereotyping, but it also ensured a familiarity with the true meaning of 'style' which is one of the strongest attributes of the best colonial work."

George L. Hersey suggests that there is a particularly American way, different from the European, of borrowing from artistic sources.[10] He defines "replication" as the copying or adaptation of "some principal work of art" in various ways for different places and times. The work of art, for example the Roman Pantheon, becomes "an artistic signal that is picked up by lesser transmitters, which extend and modify the original signal." Replication was the rule rather than the exception during the nineteenth century. In Europe, Hersey claims, architectural borrowing followed the original in respect of siting, relation between inside and outside, and relation between scale and building type. For example, the European pantheons all contain large, "impressively scaled" single spaces that house chapels or civic uses, and they are sited as in Rome. But in America, a shift accompanied the borrowings, the rules broke down and improper adaptations occurred: Jefferson's Rotunda is pantheonic on the outside only; a Romanesque style is used by Richardson for other than religious architecture; public buildings have Second Empire outsides and High Gothic insides; Eero Saarinen builds village hillside architecture on the flat, urban Yale campus; and whereas the English architects of the new Caius College, in following Le Corbusier's monastery, "properly" relate college idiom to monastic tradition, a Boston firm replicates La Tourette untraditionally as the Boston City Hall. In the same way, type and use collide at the roadside, as in the names "Dog City" or "Frank Palace."

The "not necessarily undesirable" effects of such free replication are, in Hersey's words, "jarring stylistic dissonances, the impermanent look of having been transferred from some other site, and weird scale." This is an illuminating interpretation of an essential yet difficult-to-define difference between American and European architecture.[11] Although Hersey does not mention shifts in symbolic meaning directly, it is clear that such shifts cause the collisions in several of his examples—an ecclesiastical style is used for commercial architecture, royalty is associated with hot dogs.

I have culled these writings of the late 1950s and the 1960s from a larger body of assessment of American urbanism, because they highlight the importance of invention and tradition in the making of place. A second, related theme carries through a broad range of disciplines at about this period. The writings of Melvin Webber, J. B. Jackson, and Herbert Gans suggest that what we perceive as chaos in the urban and suburban landscape may be an order that we do not understand; that simple nostrums to complex problems may make the problems worse; and that the concept of "organized complexity" should be understood by architects and planners working in the social and physical realms. During this period, Tom Wolfe responded to the same notions in the arts with an apotheosis of Las Vegas and the Pop Art movement, and Robert Venturi in *Complexity and Contradiction in Architecture,* called into question some simple nostrums of Modern architecture. In delineating the anatomy of complexity in architecture, Venturi grounded his analysis in historic precedent seen in a new light.

Something in the air caused these parallel inquiries by separate individuals to be undertaken and brought to fruition at the same time. In my opinion, the common influence was social change. Shifts in American society spelled a shift in sensibility among perceptive scientists and artists. Changes in sensibility induced changes in perception. These in turn called for a reassessment of tenets and philosophies, particularly in disciplines concerned with urban life. The social turmoil of the 1960s demanded the reinvention of American architecture.

The Process of Reinvention

In the arts, change in sensibility signals impending changes in aesthetic perception and preference, which are in turn, a precondition for innovation and invention. When the time is ripe for aesthetic change, a chance perception, even a side glance at the familiar, can set the process in motion. At first sight, the new and meaningful may not appear beautiful. It may appear ugly. But we feel it is important.

That feeling often, perhaps usually, precedes rational reassessment, and may lead to it. To take a personal example, although my move to the West Coast in 1965 was part of an intellectual migration, and although I had for more than ten years joined in reasoned reassessments of architecture and the environment, nevertheless my first response to the landscape of Las Vegas and Los Angeles was not an analytical appraisal; it was an aesthetic shiver. The shiver was composed of hate and love; the environment was as ugly as it was beautiful. It shrieked of chaos, yet it challenged one to find the whispered order within it—because this order seemed to hint at a new architecture for changed times.

"Towards a new architecture" had been the slogan of an earlier process of architectural reinvention, based on social change. In the first decades of this century, a liberating aesthetic shiver induced by industrial architecture and engineering goaded and guided the development of Modern architecture. "Eyes which do not see," Le Corbusier cried in 1923 against architects who could not perceive the beauty-in-ugliness of grain elevators, steamships, and airplanes.[12] Forty years later, when some cities were literally in flames, and when a hundred voices railed against architects who could not see, the Modern rhetoric of industrial process and the old vision of glass towers seemed irrelevant to the social problems at hand. There was also no shock value left to factory architecture; it could produce no galvanizing aesthetic shiver. What horrified in the 1960s was the urban chaos the urbanists were studying: the deteriorated inner city and the signs, strips, and tracts of suburban sprawl.

Facing America through Learning from Las Vegas

Robert Venturi, Steven Izenour, and I selected Las Vegas and Levittown for study because they were archetypes of the landscape of suburban sprawl that surrounds all American cities. Analysis of the extreme forms would be easier than analysis of more typical ones, which were usually overlaid upon earlier patterns. However, the intention was to throw light on the everyday. We aimed to document the characteristics of American place that were alluded to by the writers of the 1960s and also to teach ourselves, as artists, to be receptive to the mandates of our time.

So we faced the desert Strip of Las Vegas, the winding roads and curving greens of Levittown, and later, the traditional nineteenth- and early twentieth-century American city. The forms we chose for analysis were new and undeniably American. Although scorned by architects as vulgar distortions and malformations of urbanism, they were the quotidian of the landscape; we sensed that they contained important lessons for architecture in the latter part of the twentieth century.

We tried to define the components of strip and sprawl carefully, and considered the factors that caused them to be as they were— primarily the automobile, the geometry induced by its motion, and the ability of the human brain to react to communication from the environment while the body is traveling at approximately thirty-five miles per hour. We described the nature of the communication conveyed and the methods used for conveying it. We compared the constituents of American suburban architecture with those of traditional European urban architecture, matching the vast space of the A&P parking lot with the expanses of Versailles, and the pace of movement on the medieval market street with that on the Las Vegas Strip. We evolved a taxonomy of the forms of the everyday landscape and endeavored to set these within a broader taxonomy of the traditional elements of architecture and urbanism. The following excerpts from our writings of the 1960s and 1970s give the flavor and some of the substance of our inquiry:[13]

> The English cathedral sits upon a close, the Greek temple upon an acropolis, the medieval castle against the medieval town wall, and the town hall on the main

square. . . . In American cities, the only establishment whose location is predestined is the corner store.

Suburban sprawl eludes our concepts of urban form. It isn't enclosed or directed like the space of traditional cities—it is open and indeterminate.

[In Levittown,] the lawn is a stage, the facade a backdrop, and the roofline a romantic silhouette.

The image of the commercial strip is chaos. The order in this landscape is not obvious.

The commercial persuasion of roadside eclecticism provokes bold impact in the vast and complex setting of a new landscape of big spaces, high speeds, and complex programs.

The sign for the Motel Monticello, a silhouette of an enormous Chippendale highboy, is visible on the highway before the motel itself.

Symbol dominates space. Architecture is not enough. . . . The big sign and the little building is the rule of Route 66.

The message is basely commercial; the context is basically new.

What Did You Learn?

Our aim in studying suburban sprawl had been to push the growing body of thought on American urbanism in directions interesting and useful to us as practicing architects and theoreticians. We sought a new open-mindedness that would both enable us to act sensitively and receptively on social questions in architecture and lead us to a new aesthetic: a formal language or languages less restrictive than that of late Modern architecture and tuned to the social and creative needs of our time.

When asked, "What did you learn from Las Vegas?" we were at first at a loss for an answer. An early reply was, "What did *you* learn from the Parthenon?" By this we meant that aesthetic ideas that engage the minds of architects are not always, or in their most important aspects, definable in words. Later we suggested that what we learned would show in our subsequent work, and indubitably it has. However, more than ten years away from these studies, it is perhaps possible to discern some areas of learning more clearly than we could at the time.

The Forgotten Symbolism of Architectural Form

The primary lessons that we learned, as architects, from Las Vegas and Levittown were about symbolism. We started our study with investigations of the character of the symbols that could best communicate over the vast space of the American strip; we continued with analyses of the buildings behind the signs and what they could communicate symbolically at different scales. Finally, we turned to symbolism at the traditional scale of architecture for pedestrians. Here, ornament and decoration became a major interest.

In the succession from strip to buildings our methods of analysis completed a full circle. In 1968 we suggested that "we look backward at history and tradition to go forward." In 1975 we recommended that "we architects who went to Las Vegas and Levittown to reacquaint ourselves with historical symbolism should now return to Rome; it is time for a new interpretation of our architectural legacy, and particularly for a reassessment of the uses of ornament and symbolism in architecture."[14] Our initial analyses comparing strip phenomena with historic European architecture—the A&P parking lot with Versailles—we defined as going "from Rome to Las Vegas." We said we went "from Las Vegas back again to Rome," when we applied categories learned from the Strip to the study of conventional and traditional buildings—seeing the front of Chartres Cathedral, for example, as a type of billboard. The journey from Las Vegas back to Rome allowed us to learn again from historical architecture through a reappraisal of its symbolism and decoration. Although these had been there in the first place, we had ignored or forgotten them. Under the influence of Modern architecture, we had interpreted them as texture and pattern alone, not as symbolic communication.

Las Vegas therefore helped us to reinterpret traditional architecture and, by redirecting us to Rome, set us to mending the rupture Modern architecture had made with its tradition. In so doing we were able, as well, to incorporate portions of the American suburban landscape into the fold of architecture, where they had not been included before.

The Oscillation between Innovation and Tradition in the Process of Reinvention

Our analyses of the American everyday environment were part of a continuous process of reinvention, whereby tradition and innovation, the historical and the new, are matched and rematched with changing times. We face America, then we face Europe, struggling to resolve the paradoxes of different cultural origins, in order to become creative artists in the flux of history.

In studying Las Vegas and Levittown our intention was not to promote particular commercial idioms for architecture, nor did we turn to Rome to find good sources for historical borrowing. In my opinion, the lessons learned from Las Vegas by architects to date have been superficial ones. Stylish Postmodernism has picked up the image but not the substance of our quest. And the professions of urban design and landscape architecture, although involved along with architecture in the making of place, seem to have been affected even less than has architecture, by changing times and sensibilities. The built results indicate that social and cultural change has brought about little reassessment by design practitioners of either the emerging American landscape or the traditional roles of the professions.

Lacking this reassessment, some efforts of the design professions tend to make environmental chaos worse. If you see an awkward strip, where wirescape overwhelms imagery and the whole purveys neither communication nor order, look again; if the signs are all twelve feet high, you can be sure an aesthetic ordinance is at work, promulgated by the design professions and intended to produce order in the environment. A more successful approach might be to encourage the erection of taller signs that dominate the rest of the clutter. The fact that this suggestion would be dismissed by most design review boards in the United States suggests that urban designers still lack means to describe and define the strip landscape; therefore they cannot see it; therefore they cannot handle it aesthetically.

As designers, we have not yet developed a profound sense of history. "A colonial culture," says Jacobson, "is one which has no memory." A colonial heritage makes it "extremely difficult for any section of the population to develop a vital, effective belief in the past as a present concern, and in the present as a consequence of the past's concerns." Yet absence of memory may not inhibit the perpetuation of prejudice. Indeed, "precisely because the sense of history is so deficient, these enmities tend to be regarded as so many given, unalterable facts of life . . . as little open to human change or question as the growth of leaves in spring . . . ."[15] Because we designers lack a sturdy grasp on our historical heritage, we lack the confidence to tolerate architectural change. An understanding of the role of invention in historical architecture and of the way the past affects present preferences would help designers and design controllers to conquer their own aesthetic prejudices and therefore to deal more effectively than they do now with the everyday American landscape and the making of American place.

Conclusion: Work in Progress

In this thesis on colonies and mother cultures, innovation and tradition in the invention of American place, I have tried to suggest that the colonial paradoxes are as much opportunities as problems and that they add intensity and uniqueness to American architecture. Two "colonial" heritages, one American and the other African, both set in a European mold, have helped define my argument. Its edge probably derives from the marginal nature of my relation to dominant cultures.

The colonial frame of reference is, of course, not the only applicable one. Indeed, American architects are not alone in looking beyond the border. They are part of an international profession whose philosophy has been avowedly and idealistically internationalist and whose practitioners, in most nations, are eager for outside influences. However, I have chosen to focus on the colonial aspect here because it is rarely considered, and because it opens up a host of questions that should be understood as part of our artistic heritage. This is particularly so as the architectural pendulum swings now toward regionalism, and as America assumes the leadership in architectural ideas. In addition, relating American architecture to a worldwide diaspora of colonial architectures can broaden our understanding of American architecture, and may bring new insights in the future as the field of colonial studies widens in Europe and the Third World.[16]

In discussing our own research on American place, I have emphasized the process of invention rather than the nature of our findings, because such a focus seemed suitable to a symposium opening a Center for the Study of American Architecture. In this inaugural venture, we are at the port of entry to a new territory that is paradoxically familiar but unknown. It must be explored and reexplored, and there is a long distance to be traveled. Artistically, we American architects are cultural immigrants who must face the American hinterland yet make our roads return to Rome.

NOTES

[1] Dan Jacobson, Introduction to Olive Schreiner, *The Story of an African Farm* (Harmondsworth: Penguin Books, 1971), pp. 18–19.

[2] The paradox may persist although there is a new colonial power: *vide*, "We do not need the Graves, the Sterns and the Jahns to tell us how to design in Africa. We also do not need to be chauvinistic in our approach." Bannie Britz, "Is a South African Architecture Possible?" in *Towards Appropriate Architecture for Southern Africa: Architecture SA*, ed. Ivor Prinsloo, Nov.-Dec. 1982, p. 68.

[3] *Mitn ponem tsu America*. The experience was common enough to have given rise to a Yiddish saying. I first heard it in English. I am grateful to Mr. Max Rosenfeld of the Sholem Aleichem Club in Philadelphia for clarifying its derivation.

[4] Each group plays its part in its own way. The sequence described in this passage refers largely to late nineteenth- and early twentieth-century migrations from Europe. It is not immediately applicable to black groups, owing to the unwilled circumstances of their immigration and to the destruction of their heritage which ensued. However, the black artistic contribution has paralleled that of other groups from the start and, since their second migration, northward, their role in the reinventing of America, north and south, can be discussed in the same terms as those used for other immigrant groups. Hispanic and Asian immigrants today seem to be in early stages of the same sequence.

[5] The terms "high culture" and "taste culture" are borrowed from Herbert J. Gans, *Popular Culture and High Culture* (New York: Basic Books, 1974).

[6] John A. Kouwenhoven, "Preliminary Glance at an American Landscape" and "What's 'American' about America," *The Beer Can by the Highway, Essays on What's American about America* (Garden City, New York: Doubleday, 1961), pp. 19, 42, 44, 49.

[7] Vincent Scully, *American Architecture and Urbanism* (New York: Frederick A. Praeger, 1969), p. 12.

[8] Ronald Lewcock, *Early Nineteenth Century Architecture in South Africa, A Study of the Interaction of Two Cultures, 1795–1837* (Cape Town: A. A. Balkema, 1963), pp. 420, 421.

[9] Scully, *American Architecture and Urbanism,* pp. 27, 37.

[10] G. L. Hersey, "Replication Replicated, or Notes on American Bastardy," *Perspecta,* 9/10 (1965), pp. 211–248.

[11] This difference is found in other colonial situations where similar encounters "between local cultures and international systems of exchange" produce "a population of hybrid architectural languages that are full of promise." "Hybrid Architecture," *Lotus International,* 26 (1980), p. 3. One such hybrid is the Bengali temple with imitation church towers. George Michell describes the Hindu Temple of Sonarang as "genuinely hybrid architecture combining, in a unique manner, elements from different traditions to create completely original forms." See his "Neo-classical Hindu Temples in Bengal. European Influences in the Bengal Temples," *Lotus,* 26, p. 99. They sound like the architecture of the Strip; especially as Michell writes, "Bewildering to the architectural historian, the genius of Bengali designers is undeniable, though their inventions still await an appropriate terminology by which they might be effectively described"—and without which, we may add, like the Karroo and Las Vegas, they will not be effectively seen.

[12] Le Corbusier, *Vers Une Architecture* (Paris, 1923); English transl., *Towards a New Architecture* (London, 1927).

[13] These are taken from *Learning from Las Vegas: The Forgotten Symbolism of Architectural Form* (Cambridge, Mass.: MIT Press, rev. ed. 1977), pp. 8, 9, 13, 20, as well as from the unpublished text "Signs of Life, Symbols in the American City," an exhibition for the Smithsonian Institution, Washington, D.C., 1976. Both are by Robert Venturi, Denise Scott Brown, and Steven Izenour.

[14] *Learning from Las Vegas,* p. 3, and "Signs of Life," n.p. (exhibition text).

[15] Jacobson, Introduction to *The Story of an African Farm,* p. 7.

[16] For example, *Lotus International,* 26, is devoted to colonial architecture considered as a worldwide phenomenon.

AMERICAN ARCHITECTURE:
THE SEARCH FOR TRADITION

by John Coolidge

Three American Places

I propose to discuss, in chronological order, three American places: Pierre Charles L'Enfant's Washington, Frederick Law Olmsted's Riverside, and Frank Lloyd Wright's Florida Southern College. I shall consider them as interpretations of architectural themes which have long preoccupied the Western world and have received distinguished expression in several countries.

Today, much of the study of American visual arts is parochial. There is antiquarianism, whose results are of little but local interest. A monographic treatment of a major American artist—the recent Eakins show, for example—is likely to suggest a genius who existed in a vacuum. All this implies that certainly until the Prairie House, perhaps until Jackson Pollock, artists working in this country made only peripheral contributions to the progress of Western visual culture. Intensely researched achievements like the skyscraper or even the Prairie House were, to be sure, remarkable, but they were not central.

That implication is just not true. Americans have made contributions at the level of high art, contributions which ultimately have been central, if not always immediately influential.

L'Enfant's Washington

I have chosen to discuss L'Enfant's plan of Washington as my first "place" for a simple reason (fig. 1). It was the first work of Western art of international importance that was produced in or for America. Consider first the fundamental concept, for which George Washington and L'Enfant were jointly responsible. The city was to be a metropolis, the American London. L'Enfant believed this metropolis involved the creation of a port, a civic center, and an array of buildings for the national government. As in London, these three areas were to be separate. In London there has always been tension between "the city" and Westminster; a long no-man's-land lies between them. In Washington the three basic areas were to be adjacent but in balance.

Most people do not realize that the idea of creating a brand new metropolis was both novel and archaic. Admiration for a metropolis was a seventeenth-century phenomenon—witness Wren's replan-

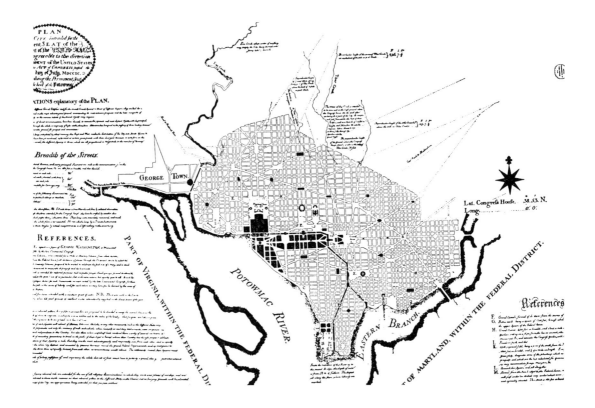

The map contains the following textual elements:

GEORGE TOWN

POTOWMAC RIVER.

EASTERN BRANCH.

PART OF VIRGINIA WITHIN THE FEDERAL DIS

OF MARYLAND, WITHIN THE FEDERAL DISTRICT.

Lat. Congress House. 38.53. N.
Long. ... 0° 0'.

References

1 *Projected plan for Washington,
D.C.*
Pierre Charles L'Enfant, 1791.

ning of London or Peter the Great's creation of Leningrad. Broadly, the eighteenth century was opposed to big cities, explicitly so. As one French social theorist of the period observed, "A country should not have one city that is much larger than all the others."[1] The characteristic eighteenth-century phenomenon was the small city, say Bath or Nancy. To be sure, during the course of the eighteenth century large cities began to regain their importance. But this did not involve grand planning, rather remodeling or extension. Almost exactly contemporary with L'Enfant's plan was the desire of the Directory to improve Paris. For this purpose they set up a Commission of Artists. The random tinkering they proposed contrasts sharply with L'Enfant's grand design.

A second factor, well known but often passed over, is L'Enfant's background. He had studied at the Royal Academy of Painting in Paris. In America he was commissioned to paint portraits; unfortunately, none of them have been identified. He certainly could reproduce landscapes, as an admirable drawing of West Point demonstrates (fig. 2). He approached the creation of Washington with a landscape painter's sense of topography. What makes the result remarkable is, first, the concept of national institutions: the presidency, Congress, a national church, a national university, and so forth. There were precedents for each of these, but they had been little developed. The initial clarity of function of our national institutions and their success in performance were amazing. Secondly, each of these national institutions was to have a building of its own.

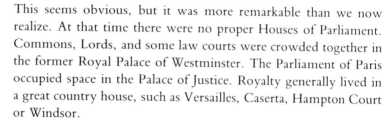

2 Drawing of West Point Pierre Charles L'Enfant.

This seems obvious, but it was more remarkable than we now realize. At that time there were no proper Houses of Parliament. Commons, Lords, and some law courts were crowded together in the former Royal Palace of Westminster. The Parliament of Paris occupied space in the Palace of Justice. Royalty generally lived in a great country house, such as Versailles, Caserta, Hampton Court or Windsor.

3 Aerial view of Pantheon Paris, 1757.

L'Enfant's architectural concept of these national institutions was completely up-to-date. They were to be crystal-like buildings set in open urban spaces. That neoclassical concept was exemplified by the Panthéon in Paris, but by few other public buildings (fig. 3). In contrast, private buildings would line the streets or frame the squares of Washington. East Capitol Street was to be devoted to shops, and arcaded. L'Enfant proposed to unite these national buildings by great diagonal boulevards. This visual unification would reduce the sense of distance between buildings. But the boulevards, lined with trees, would also serve as processional ways. This concept seems wholly new. Elsewhere a processional way might terminate in a major building, as the Nevsky Prospect terminates at the Admiralty, but it did not originate in the desire to lead from one building to another. Moreover, some of L'Enfant's boulevards continued beyond the city as national roads. Again, contrast Paris, where most boulevards, intended for exercising horses of the aristocracy, led nowhere, while the route to London, for example, was merely a sequence of narrow streets. Although in principle L'Enfant used a large square module to define the location of the major streets, in practice he envisioned the distance between one ordinary street and the next as varying, depending upon the function of the buildings defining each.

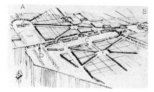

4 Washington D.C. boulevards and malls as envisioned by Pierre Charles L'Enfant.

Remarkable, too, was the attention given to transportation by canal, and the careful integration of this system with the pattern of roads and the location of buildings. Just as the boulevards were for beauty as well as use, L'Enfant related his canal system to five great fountains and a splendid cascade.

Finally, there is the awareness of the aesthetic value of landscape. Views are created from the Capital to the Virginia Hills, and from the White House down the Potomac to Alexandria (fig. 4). The major buildings are identified with these views. Symbolically these views unite the national monuments to the nation. They suggested the major roads which were to link every part of the country to the Capitol. The distances from Washington to every important city in the country were to be measured from a column on a hill east of the Capitol.

The tragedy of L'Enfant's Washington was that it did not work. The port depended on the Eastern Branch, which the cautious Jefferson estimated was thirty-five feet deep. It had nothing like that depth, and soon silted up so that it became commercially unusable. Nor did government evolve with the rapidity the founding fathers expected. For decades Washington was a miserable quasi-village, appallingly spread out. Hence L'Enfant's plan did not achieve the familiarity or the influence it deserved.

Riverside

The Riverside Improvement Company was chartered in April 1868. It bought a sixteen-hundred-acre stud farm nine miles from downtown Chicago, centered about the point where the Burlington and Quincy Railroad crossed the Des Plaines river. In August the company asked Olmsted and Vaux to plan a suburb. The architects submitted a preliminary report in September and produced a plan dated 1869 (fig. 5). Both reflect Olmsted's conviction that "there are to be found among suburbs the most soundly whole-

5 *Proposed plan for Riverside, Illinois*
Frederick Law Olmstead, 1869.

some forms of domestic life, and the best application of the arts of civilization which mankind has yet attained."[2]

In 1850, on his first trip to Europe, Olmsted had been greatly impressed by the twenty-five-year-old city of Birkenhead, just across the Mersey from Liverpool. A rather dreary shipbuilding town, it contained a remarkable park designed by Paxton created between 1843 and 1847. It was the first park in England to be paid for by municipal funds. A polygon of roads defined an area of 226 acres. One hundred of these, along the inner side of the roads, were given over to houses whose gardens adjoined the park. Income from the sales of these expensive properties enabled the city to maintain the park exceptionally well. Olmsted's considered reactions were twofold: "In democratic America there is nothing to be compared to this people's garden,"[3] but equally he was impressed by "the vast increase in value of eligible sites for dwellings near public parks."[4]

In 1859 he visited Paris. "He was in touch with Adolph Alphand, director of the Department of Roads and Bridges, under which the suburban improvements of Paris were being carried on."[5] It seems likely that he saw something of the settlements along the Seine, especially as the plan of the new model town Le Vesinet had been prepared and publicized with imperial encouragement only the year before. One feature which distinguished these settlements west of Paris was their double function—as residential communities, but also as weekend resorts for the citizens of the metropolis, as we know so well from paintings of the late nineteenth century.

"The essential qualification of a suburb is domesticity," wrote Olmsted in the preliminary report, "each family being well provided for in regard to its private life."[6] "The chief advantages which a suburb can possess are those which favor open-air recreation." The atmosphere Olmsted desired to create was "secluded peacefulness," or "leisure, contemplativeness and happy tranquility."[7] In contrast to such earlier American suburbs as Llewelyn Park, which had fifty houses, Riverside could accommodate up to ten thousand people and was designed for families of comparatively moderate means. To be sure, most normal lots were 100 feet by 200 feet and all houses were to have cost at least $3,000. In contrast to Birkenhead, Riverside was to be a dormitory suburb. Aside from family and residential services, the only opportunity for local employment would be provided by the Riverside Female University, which the company proposed to establish in 1869.

The principal advantages of the site were the railroad and the river. Riverside would have the first out-of-town station on the Burlington; every train would be obliged to stop, and the company guaranteed twelve trains a day each way. In addition, Olmsted proposed the building of a parkway, 150 to 200 feet wide, with separate lanes for pedestrians, carriages, horseback riders, and heavy wagons. Alas, this parkway was never built.

Much of the land was marshy and the river had to be adapted to provide drainage. Heightened, the existing mill dam could, as the report said, "enlarge the area of the public water suitable for boating and skating ... and there should be pretty boat landings, terraces, balconies overhanging the water, and pavilions ... mainly of rustic character, and to be half overgrown with vines."[8] Seven hundred of the sixteen hundred acres were set aside for roads and parks. The main parks were to line the western edge of the property and enclose the river on both sides. In addition there were seventy small parks or playgrounds. To populate the parks and adorn the roads Olmsted acquired thirty-two thousand deciduous trees, seven thousand conifers, and forty-seven thousand shrubs—roughly four trees and five shrubs for each of the maximum number of inhabitants.

Burlington Street and Quincy Street parallel the ruthlessly straight line of the railroad one block away on either side. They were lined with smaller lots for shops and inexpensive housing. Elsewhere all the roads are narrow and curving, "the only curving roads in the Middle West," a shocked Frenchman recently declared.[9] This was partly to slow down traffic in the interests of safety, partly because, in Olmsted's opinion, "men of taste always use winding roads."[10] Today, according to the same Frenchman, automobiles are "condemned to drive with a slowness that is majestic and urbane."[11] The original houses are set at least thirty feet back from the roads, and each was intended to have at least two trees on its front lawn; there were to be no walls or fences separating these lawns.

Olmsted was so entirely concerned with domesticity and outdoor recreation that he gave almost no thought to anything else. Only utilitarian buildings appear on the plan—no public library or town hall. There are stations for freight and passengers, a single open square beside the latter. The water tower is fed by an artesian well 739 feet deep (fig. 6). Nearby is an ice house and a business building. The single church is located in the woods not far away—one little

6 *Early view of main square, Riverside, showing (left to right) the refectory, the back of the business block, the railroad station, and the water tower.*

church for ten thousand people. Of greater interest was what the developers described as "the most complete and comfortable hotel in the United States," as well as a large refectory or restaurant and a playhouse offering card games and billiards (fig. 7). A pamphlet entitled *Riverside in 1871* includes an illustration showing families seated on the porch of the refectory overlooking the boating on the river (fig. 8). The resemblance to Renoir's *Déjeuner des Canotiers* of 1881 is astonishing, as Walter Creese has pointed out (fig. 9).[12]

7 Hotel in Riverside, Illinois
William Le Baron Jenney, 1871.

Three well-known architects practiced in Riverside at the start. Olmsted's partner, Calvert Vaux, designed a few houses. Frederick Clark Withers, an architect Olmsted admired, designed the church and the business building, a muted Victorian Gothic structure. William Le Baron Jenney lived in Riverside and was responsible for the picturesque water tower and the refectory and the rambling hotel, the latter complete with an octagonal "music pagoda" two stories high, alias a bandstand. Of the hotel, Jenney wrote, "the Swiss style was selected . . . as best adapted to a rural hotel, giving opportunities for most desirable features; extensive broad verandas, overhanging roofs, shaded balconies and many pleasing though inexpensive details."[13] Jenney also executed several houses, wooden chalets with elaborate jigsaw work.

Riverside did not prosper. Rival developers suggested the river fostered malaria. The Improvement Company went bankrupt during the depression of 1873. The community had only 450 inhabitants by 1880, 2,500 by 1920, the hoped-for 10,000 today. West of the river Olmsted's plan was abandoned, although the community benefits from the nearby presence of the zoo. Yet much remains of the original plan, and much that was built is in the intended spirit. And this settlement, which translated the park of Birkenhead and the resort suburbs of Paris into American terms, in turn engendered European offspring. Ebenezer Howard lived in Chicago from 1872 to 1878 and, in the words of his biographer, "it is likely that the pattern of his lifelong interest was set during those four years."[14] Surely the model suburb, Riverside, must have exerted some influence upon the Garden City movement Howard launched.

Florida Southern College

As my third place I have selected Frank Lloyd Wright's campus at Florida Southern College. We are perhaps insufficiently conscious of how much building for higher education has taken place since World War I. Along with art museums, these academic buildings are the only public structures which have engaged the attention of all leading Western architects—be it Gropius in his Bauhaus and Harvard Graduate School buildings, Le Corbusier in his Parisian pavilions, Mies at IIT, Aalto at Otaniemi, or Wright at Florida Southern.

Most continental European universities have been built by the state, often in one major continuing effort—the Sorbonne or the University of Munich come to mind. Most American colleges or universities, on the other hand, have had to be created one building at a time, as state legislatures have had outbursts of generosity or as college presidents have found patrons. Most American campuses are now, in effect, unplanned; if there ever was an overall plan it has usually been modified into chaos. Wright was fully aware of this problem and at Florida Southern proposed a plan so flexible he must have hoped it would prove unwreckable.

Florida Southern, in Lakeland, Florida, is a co-educational Methodist college, founded in 1885. It occupies eighty-seven acres on Lake Hollingsworth. An official pamphlet declares that they have

10 Plan of Florida Southern College
Lakeland, Florida
Frank Lloyd Wright, ca. 1938.

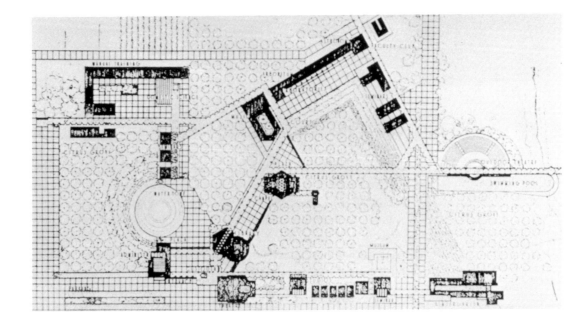

11 Esplanade and Annie Pfeiffer Chapel
Florida Southern College,
1938–1941.

"the world's most beautiful campus, designed by the greatest architect of all time."[15] How this came about is best told in their own words.

"Dr. Ludd M. Spivey became president of Florida Southern in 1925. In 1936 he was in Geneva. Looking over the beautiful buildings of that city from his hotel room, the idea came to him that he should return to America and build a modern college campus—a campus that would have architecture which would match the beauty of Florida Southern's orange-grove acres sparkling under the blue and white of a semitropical sky. Dr. Spivey immediately canceled the remainder of his vacation in Europe and returned to Lakeland. There was only one man to tell of his vision. His name was Frank Lloyd Wright. Dr. Spivey flew to Taliesin East and told him of the idea that had come to him in Switzerland. The college president said frankly that his school was without funds for such a tremendous undertaking. But Dr. Spivey quickly added that if Mr. Wright would design the buildings, he in turn would find the means to bring the idea to fulfillment. To his drawing board went the great architect. And to tiny villages and great cities in the United States and in many foreign lands went Dr. Spivey to tell men and women of this wonderful vision and to seek their interest and assistance. There were those who believed, and by 1938 Wright's overall plans were drawn" (fig. 10).[16]

The total college property is a rectangle, oriented east to west, with one long side along the lake. The property slopes gently but distinctly toward the lake, and is split roughly in half. The eastern portion contains a few pleasant conventional brick neo-Georgian buildings, now used for dormitories. The empty lower half contained a citrus grove. For this location Wright was asked to design teaching and administrative buildings. Aesthetically the two halves were to be quite unrelated.

In the middle of the citrus grove Wright created an irregular open polygon, defined by covered "esplanades" (fig. 11). "Occasionally the esplanade becomes a building," he declared.[17] Thus those surrounding the polygon "become" in succession an administrative building, a library, and a chapel. This last, the most prominent building, is near the center of the citrus grove. One esplanade was to link the chapel with a small peninsula on the lake shore. Near the end of this esplanade Wright planned a large open-air theater, a swimming pool, and a long wharf. Opposite the chapel, inland, was to be a water dome—a circular pool surrounded by jets of water directed inward.

On the northern portion of his campus Wright intended two complexes, one for industrial arts, one for science and research. The southern portion was likewise to have two complexes, one for theater and music, the other for the visual arts, that is, studios and

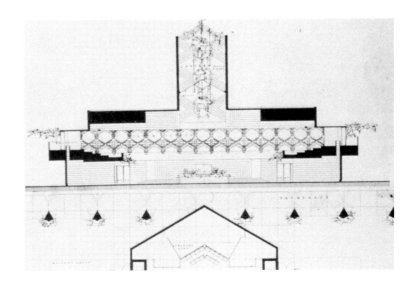

*12 Annie Pfeiffer Chapel
Plans and cross-section.*

a museum. In contrast to all these, conventional classrooms were few and modest. Wright called them "seminars."

Behind this proposal are three basic concepts. In Wright's words, "the entire scheme is given an outdoor garden character, fit for Florida."[18] Everywhere there were to be flowers, rising from the ground or hanging from the buildings. Second, Wright visualized college life as pedestrian movement: from dormitory to chapel, from chapel to class, from one class to another, from class to cafeteria, from cafeteria to library, from library to dormitory. Thus the esplanades are basic (fig. 12). Because of the Florida heat they have to be covered, and they consist of markedly sculptural piers which support continuous flat roofs. The pier is the dominant architectural form on the campus. With a sheet of glass connecting two or three such piers you have the side of a building. Wright expressed the third principle vividly: "For five hundred years buildings have tended to make people feel inferior ... buildings not built for human scale." At Florida Southern he sought "buildings for human people, that give joy to the occupants, simplicity in their own right."[19] "The scale is small, one can touch the roof slab." That is fair enough, but as one college official observed, "it's tough on the basketball players."

The esplanades lead into the vestibules of the principal buildings. The major interior spaces face away from these vestibules, so that to examine the most interesting aspects of the exteriors you must leave the central polygon and look at the structure from the surrounding outer spaces. But most buildings hardly exist as exterior entities, only as bits of exteriors, a pavilion here, a curving wall there. To these generalizations the chapel forms an exception (see figs. 12, 13). It alone is a powerful, complex sculptural form. There are two conspicuous roofed porches opening from the galleries inside. The central tower is glazed at the top and along its two

13 Interior, Annie Pfeiffer Chapel, ca. 1948.

14 Emile E. Watson Administration Building
Florida Southern College, 1948.

ends. Finally there are roof terraces. Yet the building is also fortress-like. The solid surfaces of the chapel tower are paneled, embossed, as it were, and of course separated. Seen at an angle their form and proportions at once suggest a great lectern Bible standing upright and opened, not a bad symbol for a Methodist college chapel. The interior of the chapel is a hexagon (fig. 13). It seats one thousand people on the floor and in the four galleries. But everybody is within fifty feet of the pulpit. The tower pours light down upon the minister.

More important perhaps are the dozens of less conspicuous spaces, beautifully proportioned classrooms, cheerful offices, or a grand interior which Wright intended for a cafeteria, but which is at present unused. Wright's concern with pedestrian motion, and his recognition that stopping places are a series of incidents in the students' life, make Florida Southern campus reminiscent of an elaborate eighteenth-century garden, with its wealth of contrasting features, each viewed briefly. The buildings which relate most strikingly to their immediate environment are devoted to administration (fig. 14). These have been placed adjacent to the water dome. Monumental in style, they are enchantingly domestic in scale and especially bedecked with greenery.

Wright has not been the favorite professional of everybody at Florida Southern. For example, he made little provision for plumbing; one small ladies' room in the basement is all he provided in the administration buildings. There is no plumbing in the chapel, which adds appreciably to the rigors of choir practice or preparing a sermon. He had such strong feelings about reading only by daylight that he installed no electric lights in the reading room of the library. To help students, the librarians supplied the cheapest little desk lamps. Whenever Wright came to visit, the president's secretary would call up so that the librarians could unplug the lamps and hide them. Nonetheless, Wright's campus has been spectacularly and unexpectedly successful. Since it was inaugurated, the student population has quintupled.

Wright's plans for Florida Southern have already been seriously altered for a variety of reasons. The esplanade to the lake, the open-air theater, the swimming pool, and the wharf have not been built. The fountains around the water dome were never installed, and recently the circular pool has been filled in. The chapel has been wrecked twice by hurricanes and the tower has had to be modified. Wright's library became too small and a new one has been built.

Two other unpardonable things have happened since Wright's death. First, the college has erected a number of large buildings all designed by the same architect, who shall be nameless. These completely violate Wright's human scale. Thus, the upper focus, Wright's water dome, has been utterly destroyed by the creation of the monstrous new library. Second, maintenance and minor alterations have been carried out with ruthless insensitivity. Much elsewhere also has been needlessly damaged. But much survives, and as at the University of Virginia, much could be successfully restored. The essence remains intact. Florida Southern College still makes a deliberate and drastic commentary on the International Style.

Conclusion

"American Architecture: Innovation and Tradition" is a good post-modern title, but for historians, surely better is "Tradition and Innovation." For in the seventeenth century Anglo-Saxons on this continent were building vernacular Gothic in the age of Bernini, and today we are one of the small group of countries capable of occasionally producing architectural inventions and forms which better adapt buildings to the ideals of our society.

There are many ways of commenting upon this American evolution. I have chosen to view it in terms of three individual responses to challenges America presented: L'Enfant, the eccentric foreign quasi-professional who planned a capital on a scale possible nowhere else at that time; Olmsted, the native evangelist, superbly self-educated, wholly international in outlook, eclectically adapting and integrating whatever he found appropriate at home or abroad, and capable of profoundly influencing what many Anglo-Saxons have considered the most suitable kind of domestic "place"; Wright, the rebel, who in his twenties refused an all-expenses-paid scholarship to study abroad, and who to the last, fully cognizant of what was happening elsewhere, determinedly sought what he thought to be American solutions.

I justify this great-man approach to our architectural history in two ways. First, I believe that each of these three responses to American opportunities is still possible today, and will continue to be possible as far into the future as we can reasonably reckon, and second, because this symposium symbolizes the inauguration of an educational venture. The three approaches I have discussed differ from one another most fundamentally in the professional education these three men obtained, and in their attitudes toward their education.

NOTES

[1] Germain Brice, *Nouvelle description de la ville de Paris ... 1725,* vol. 1, pp. 364-65, cited in Louis Hautecour, *Histoire de l'architecture classique en France* (Paris: Editions A. et J. Picard, 1950), vol. 3, p. 47.

[2] S. B. Sutton, ed., *Civilizing American Cities: A Selection of Frederick Law Olmsted's Writings* (Cambridge, Mass.: MIT Press, 1971), p. 295. A reprint of Olmsted, Vaux & Co.'s *Preliminary Report.*

[3] F. L. Olmsted, *Walks and Talks of an American Farmer in England* (Ann Arbor, 1967), p. 52.

[4] Sutton, *Civilizing American Cities,* p. 293.

[5] L. W. Roper, *FLO: A Biography of Frederick Law Olmsted* (Baltimore: Johns Hopkins University Press, 1973), p. 147.

[6] Sutton, *Civilizing American Cities,* p. 303.

[7] Ibid., pp. 268, 299, 300.

[8] Ibid., p. 304.

[9] Gerald Bauer, Gildas Baudez, Jean-Michel Roux, *Banlieus de Charme* (Aix-en-Provence: Pandora, 1980), p. 18.

[10] Albert Fein, ed., *Landscape into Cityscape, Frederick Law Olmsted's Plans for a Greater New York City* (Ithaca, N.Y.: Cornell University Press, 1967), p. 368.

[11] Bauer, et. al., *Banlieus de Charme,* p. 19.

[12] Walter Creese, *The Search for Environment* (New Haven: Yale University Press, 1966), p. 156.

[13] *Riverside in 1871,* n.p.

[14] F. J. Osborn, "Sir Ebenezer Howard, The Evolution of his Ideas," *Town Planning Review,* vol. 21, no. 3 (October 1950), p. 226.

[15] *Florida Southern College, Lakeland: The Frank Lloyd Wright Campus,* a picture booklet published by the College, n.d.

[16] Ibid. Published sources give slightly differing dates for Wright's buildings. The following are approximately correct: Annie Pfeiffer Chapel, ground-breaking May 24, 1938, dedicated March 9, 1941; Carter Wallbridge Hawkins Seminar Building, completed 1941; E. T. Roux (original) Library, ground-breaking 1942, dedicated 1945; Emile E. Watson Administration Building, dedicated 1948; J. Edgar Wall Water Dome, dedicated 1948; Lucius Pond Ordway Arts Building, dedicated 1953; William H. Danforth Chapel, completed 1955; Polk County Science Building, 1958.

[17] "Frank Lloyd Wright," *Architectural Forum,* 94 (January 1951), p. 103.

[18] "Special Issue: Frank Lloyd Wright," *Architectural Forum,* 88 (January 1948), p. 129.

[19] Frank Lloyd Wright, *Speech at Chapel Service, Florida Southern College,* 25 October, 1951, College Mimeograph, p. 1.

THE AMERICAN SENSE OF PLACE AND THE POLITICS OF SPACE

by Dolores Hayden

> Every force evolves a form.
>
> Shaker proverb

> . . . seek to isolate an American strain in this country's architecture, and in so doing establish and examine the cultural and environmental conditions that have determined the course of American building.
>
> Helen Searing, David DeLong, Robert Stern, directions for contributors to "American Architecture: Innovation and Tradition"

There exists a unique American sense of place rooted in preindustrial vernacular building and settlement design that can be celebrated in many different parts of this country. There also exists a passionate sense of neighborhood territory, of turf identified by class, race, gender, and ethnicity, that generates connectedness and belonging in many localities in this immigrant nation. Yet Americans frequently complain of placelessness, of what novelist Alison Lurie calls "nowhere cities," what historians Blaine Brownell and David Goldfield call a progression in American urban history "from downtown to no-town."[1] In her song "Big Science," performance artist Laurie Anderson asks, "Hey, pal, how do I get to town from here?" The answer in New Wave lyrics: "Well, just take a right where they're going to build that new shopping mall, go straight past where they're going to put in the freeway, take a left at what's going to be the new sports center, and keep going until you hit the place where they're thinking of building that drive-in bank. You can't miss it." Across the United States, in clubs and at private parties, young people are dancing to this, nodding agreement, and driving home past sites where the American commercial vernacular is being constructed: shopping malls, sports centers, and drive-in banks (fig. 1). Despair about placelessness is as much a part of the American experience as pleasure in the sense of place.

1 *Los Angeles from the air, 1982*

To understand the possibilities and limits of American architecture more fully, it is necessary to study place and placelessness together, as cultural and economic products. There are a few theoretical approaches and historical methods that might help, and a few that might hinder the process of understanding American building this way. Placelessness has implications not only for the study of architecture but also for the organization of curricula in schools of design and planning, and for the practice of architecture, urban design, planning, preservation, and community organizing.

Place and the Preindustrial Vernacular

The strongest, most positive sense of place in America comes from the preindustrial vernacular. Its most striking quality is coherence: the fusion of object, building, settlement, and natural landscape that characterizes these traditions and that defies analysis according to conventional divisions. To take an example, in the pueblos of the Southwest, where housing and kivas surround dancing grounds, such sculptural elements as fireplaces, kilns, handsome pots, beautifully woven blankets, and rugs contribute to the whole. Pueblos are but one of many hundreds of native American traditions of settlement making. The tepees of the nomadic Kiowa also represent an indigenous architecture. Made of fourteen buffalo hides, they are painted with brilliant designs representing weather, heavens, animals, and battles. The Kiowa sun dance circle arrayed several hundred tepees around a medicine lodge.[2] At the opposite extreme in terms of size and permanence are the sculptural earthworks of the Mound Builders. At Cahokia, Illinois (fig. 2), and Marietta, Ohio, at Greenup, Kentucky, and Poverty Point, Louisiana, or at Peebles, Ohio, their scale, as William Morgan has shown, can be compared to the Piazza San Marco or other massive works of urban design.[3] These traditions of building are unfortunately rather marginal to American architectural culture today. Very few contemporary historians of "American" architecture ever deal with native American material (Vincent Scully is a notable exception); very few designers focus on them as precedents for their work, even in the Southwest.

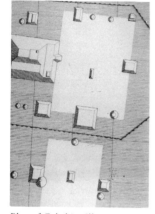

2 Plan of Cahokia, Illinois, 800–1500 A.D.

Such cultural neglect is a product of architectural fashion as well as racial bias. The Greek Revival is surely our strongest, most consistent national architectural language, used by white Anglo-Saxon Protestants in the antebellum era from Maine to the Midwest and the South. But ordinary Greek Revival buildings are not well understood as a part of American architectural culture, although John Stilgoe's new book, *Common Landscape of America, 1580–1845,* is making many early rural settlement plans and building types better known,[4] and Ronald Fleming and Laurie Halderman's book, *On Common Ground,* shows how to protect the traditional village greens of New England covenant communities that are often surrounded by fine Greek Revival structures.[5]

The fusion of object, building, landscape, and settlement, still typical of the early nineteenth-century Greek Revival towns, seems to me particularly effective in the northwestern hills of Connecticut, an area of small covenant communities amid woods and the rolling meadows of dairy farms. Granite foundations connect these buildings to the rocky soil, while clapboards shaped to the most perfect proportions suggest a Yankee improvement on all imported styles. Local builders began to develop wonderfully personal approaches to ornament in wood and metal. These consistent settlements included not only churches, but schoolhouses, farmhouses, ingenious

3 Hancock Shaker Village
Hancock, Massachusetts
Trustees office, main dwelling,
1830.

barns, and covered bridges.[6] Completing the environment is the
long tradition of gravestone carvings, as well as painted wooden
furniture, painted signs for inns, wooden farm implements, and
the quilts that women made reflecting the tools, the buildings, the
changing seasons, and the landscape around them,[7] with such patterns as Sawtooth, Schoolhouse, Rail Fence, and Tree Everlasting.

A related type of settlement, the Shaker village, is contemporary
with some of the best Greek Revival towns (fig. 3). Nineteen of
these communistic settlements existed from Maine to Ohio, and
today their remains are also in need of attention and protection.
The Shakers were part of a national movement of building model
towns linked to communitarian socialism. Although every designer
knows of Shaker furniture, relatively few understand the Millenial
Laws that equated the planning of towns with the development of
a "living building."[8] Few designers have studied the "spirit drawings" used to orient Shaker villages to sacred mountains and systems
of religious belief.

Whether or not historians of American architecture choose to celebrate the powerful sense of place many native American settlements, Greek Revival towns, and Shaker villages possess, these are
part of a great national preindustrial tradition of place-making.
Scholars in American studies often discuss their symbolic importance, and the works of great American writers who have celebrated
these places will endure: Willa Cather's admiration of the pueblos
in *Death Comes to the Archbishop*, Edith Wharton's evocation of
a New England town in *Summer*, Walt Whitman's praise of the
Yankee builders and their tools in his "Song of the Broad-Axe,"
William Dean Howells's *Three Villages*, a sketch of the Shaker village at Shirley, Massachusetts.

Placelessness and the Commercial Vernacular

This glance at the quality of American preindustrial vernacular building indicates that these settlements were shaped of local materials, in response to site and climate, by builders creating space for use rather than for sale. Everyone in the preindustrial cultures that produced such buildings shared some common acceptance of the principles of construction, proportion, and decoration applied by the builders. While land speculation has always existed, the change to massive speculative building in mid-nineteenth-century America began to destroy the preindustrial building process. A commercial building process appeared that stressed the creation of spaces by speculators for sale or rental, not for use.[9] Building workers' skills decreased; the range of manufactured products available to builders increased. Architects organized a professional guild, but real estate developers got and held most of the power to make decisions about American space for commercial reasons. Their desire to eliminate risk made the commercial vernacular one of interchangeable, salable spaces leading to inherent placelessness. Built space became a commodity.

4 Decentralization and the automobile.

This distinction between the preindustrial vernacular and the commercial vernacular is often entirely missing in contemporary architectural debates. As Mary Alice Hinson has shown in her excellent essay, "The Last Frontier: Post-Modernism and the Meaning of American Vernacular Architecture," many American postmodern designers have not analyzed the concept of "vernacular" but romanticized it.[10] Many architects, students, and critics have approached the "vernacular" of America in a spirit of deference to speculative tracts and commercial strips. This is one kind of romance that exalts Las Vegas and Levittown, but ignores the fusion of Mafia and Mormon financial clout in Las Vegas, or the absorption of merchant builders into multinational corporations. Describing such places as products of American working-class taste is simply a mistake. The tastemakers are Bugsy Siegal and Bill Levitt.

Another kind of romance is to admire the "vernacular" from Europe—defined as primitive huts, Italian hill towns, or Scandinavian carved wooden houses. The editors of *Progressive Architecture* defined the qualities of its design award winners in 1983 in just such a misleading way. There were three subcategories of postmodernism: "Classical," "vernacular," and "historical ornament." The term "Classical" had no reference to the American preindustrial Greek Revival, and the term "vernacular" was for them neither American nor Classical but characterized by "peaked roofs, picturesque massing, and irregular fenestration"[11]—possibly German or Scandinavian?

When architects draw on a muddle of American and European, preindustrial and commercial traditions, as well as high-culture traditions, they compound the placelessness that is the economic tendency of the speculative builders. These designers may claim to speak a universal architectural "language," but it is *not* a language that most local residents comprehend, so long as the project ignores the American context in, say, New Orleans, Louisiana, or Fargo, North Dakota. For speculators and architects alike, if "place" has become not a logical result of settlement making but a possible "feature" to be added to identify an architectural and economic product, a feature derived by evoking some *other* place and time, often this feature is not convincing. "Contextualism" may solve the problem if one is adding a new building to a preindustrial vernacular environment, but it does not work if the context is the commercial vernacular world of placelessness and eclecticism.

The Writing of History and the Problem of Placelessness

For the most part, architects and architectural historians have not focused much scholarly attention on the production of the speculators' commercial vernacular, which characterizes much American building history. Yet this commercial vernacular becomes the context for much architectural design, and if we want to ask how to be "contextual" designers in a country where placelessness often wins over place, it needs attention. The task of defining placelessness has been left to writers such as Gertrude Stein whose comment "there's no there, there" still resounds beyond Oakland, California, her target at the time. In contrast, American architectural history is largely concerned with the exceptions, the small number of designers who defied their circumstances to create convincing places. However, it is just as important to ask why so many good designers have been defeated in their attempts to create uniquely American architectural styles and uniquely American places.

Refining the theory and methods used to study the production of American space could improve the situation. From the 1920s on, Lewis Mumford was always interested in the economic pressures on commercial space in cities; in the 1950s J. B. Jackson pioneered in the area of studying ordinary American rural spaces and their social context, while John Coolidge was one of the first to look at institutional contexts in factory towns. During the last fifteen years there have been great changes in American history and European urban sociology that can offer additional insights into how to write a more convincing, more accurate history of American building, a history that can offer more compelling ideas to educators and designers about how to situate themselves and their work in the context of several hundred years of American economic and architectural development.

First of all, American social history, under the leadership of Herbert Gutman and others, has moved toward the study of the everyday lives of ordinary people. This trend still has to be explored fully in terms of the everyday built environments people inhabit, but some

fascinating work has been done in this area by Elizabeth Blackmar, Gwendolyn Wright, Thomas Bender, and Christine Stansell, to name a few.[12] Second, urban economic history and economic geography have moved toward the analysis of large-scale economic forces on the spatial form of the city, as seen in the work of Sam B. Warner, David Harvey, Richard Walker, Ann Markusen, David Gordon, and Christine Boyer, among others.[13] These scholars have periodized urban development following economic history. They have distinguished between the mercantile city, based on a mixture of commercial, artisanal, and residential uses, and the industrial capitalist city, marked by the separation of areas for industrial production and residence and the development of specialized office districts. They have shown how urban densities increased and then decreased as the advanced capitalist city dedicated large areas to single-family residences and to the consumption of mass-produced goods (including shopping centers and automobiles) and to mass-produced entertainment (spectator sports, movies, theme parks) (figs. 5, 6).

One can see the possibilities of reducing the rather broad sweep of this kind of urban history to the spatial scale of American commercial vernacular building, by situating familiar building types (urban parks, apartment houses, single-family houses, skyscrapers) within this broad social and economic framework.[14] Between urban history and architectural history, there needs to be a history of the built environment that reconnects planning and architecture and illuminates the production of built space. At the same time, one can identify social movements that have resisted the production of commercial space and offered other approaches, from public parks to public housing, from the communitarian socialists' model towns to the material feminists' neighborhood renewal plans.

To analyze the full implications of these counterproposals to the commercial vernacular, one must turn to recent advances in sociology and political theory. In the last decade, urban planning and urban sociology have been influenced by the work of Manuel Castells, who has stressed the importance of analyzing social movements in relation to urban space.[15] The recent theoretical work of the French urban sociologist Henri Lefebvre is even more suggestive. While his best ideas are often embedded in a thicket of academic prose, in a major book, *The Production of Space* (1976), Lefebvre argued brilliantly that every economic mode of production involved the production of a distinctive type of urban space. He suggested provocatively, "The history of space will periodize the productive process in a way which won't precisely coincide with the periodization now taken for granted."[16] He further proposed that a new scholarly, scientific understanding of the production of social space could lead to new fields of social action, as well as improve urban planning as a discipline.

In many ways Lefebvre's work offers a more optimistic framework for the study of American buildings than the traditional class analysis applied by some European art historians and architectural historians (such as the Frankfurt school or the Venice group).[17] Lefebvre stressed the importance of built space as both a cultural product and an economic product. He distinguished between what he called the "code of space" (stylistic expression, or superstructure) and space as a material factor (its production and use as part of the economic base of society). Looking at the material side, he defined space as a commodity (tract houses, office buildings) whose production and financing are increasingly important to the economy in advanced capitalist societies. At the same time, he defined space as a material force in the reproduction of society—he hinted this analysis might be appropriate at the spatial scale of the body, the room, the building, the neighborhood, the city, the region, and the nation. To understand all socially created space as a continuum from private to public—including the personal space described in environmental psychology, the architectural space that is the subject of much architectural history and criticism, the public space that is the subject of urban design history and criticism, the urban and regional space that is the subject of much economic analysis—is to restore a wholeness to the subject long lost to the Environmental Design Research Association, the Society of Architectural Historians, and the American Planning Association.[18]

To extend Lefebvre's work one can begin to think about the microscale and the macro-scale of space simultaneously. In making the following analytical diagram, I found it was particularly helpful to read the American environmental psychologist Nancy Henley, author of *Body Politics*,[19] whose work on micro-space complements that of Lefebvre. I now connect these diverse theoretical insights into a spatial continuum:

Discipline	Spatial Scale	Social Scale
environmental psychology	*body*	*biological reproduction*
architecture and urban design	*dwelling, neighborhood*	*reproduction of daily life*
urban planning	*city*	*reproduction of social relations*
policy analysis	*nation*	*reproduction of the national economy*

To continue this diagram, one might list the specific design issues or political battles that correspond to each scale of space.

The linking of built space and reproduction provides a sharper political focus for social analysis than much quantitative, normative American environmental psychology has ever offered. It also improves on the concept of "popular culture." A theory of reproduction makes it possible to analyze working-class environments without falling into the trap of defending all of them as the product of working-class hopes and desires, a flaw common to Herbert Gans's scholarly *The Levittowners,* Denise Scott Brown, Robert Venturi, and Steven Izenour's provocative *Learning from Las Vegas,* and Tom Wolfe's impressionistic *From Bauhaus to Our House.*[20] A careful study of the role of built space in the reproduction of society can also make the variables of gender, race, and ethnicity clear, so that the concept of class is *not* mistakenly defined around white male skilled workers, and the consequences of racial segregation and gender isolation, so crucial to American experiences, can be better understood.

Most important of all, this kind of broad analytic framework promotes a dynamic aesthetic, social, and economic history of the production of space, using the American landscape as the stage for a drama involving developers, planners, architects, contractors, construction workers, and citizens. "Architecture," says Lefebvre, "takes a place from nature and appropriates it for politics."[21] In discussing different levels of political power used to manipulate built space, different economic interests, and different social, aesthetic, and personal goals, I would use the term developed by anthropologist Hilda Kuper, regional planner John Friedmann, and geographer Edward Soja, "the politics of space."[22]

Let me give an example of how this framework could be used to relate issues about housing design to political campaigns for changing private and public life, the domestic economy, and the market economy in the nineteenth century and the twentieth century. These spatial and social issues were focused in the context of the movement for women's rights, satirized by Currier and Ives just after the Civil War as women's unthinkable, mad desire to step out into the city and leave men with the child care and laundry tasks. In fact, women did not plan for such role reversals until very recently.

But they did not accept a simple progression from farm homestead to suburb either.

In *The Grand Domestic Revolution,* I showed how the nineteenth century "material feminists" pushed for the transformation of the patriarchal family and the traditional home. They wanted new kinds of housing linked to neighborhood centers for housework, cooking, and child care, places that they believed it was possible to create in an urbanizing nation.[23] They saw themselves as arguing against an artificial split between public and private life, and wanted to locate their economic activities in social reproduction downtown. They saw the potential for industrial capitalism to bring people and activities together in new ways in the workplace, and in an urbanizing America, they wanted the benefits of new residential densities for women's work too. In this endeavor material feminist activists like Melusina Peirce, who favored cooperative neighborhoods, cooperative apartment hotels, and neighborhood kitchens and child-care centers, were supported by such well-known figures as Frederick Law Olmsted, whose place-making created new urban park systems, and Jane Addams, whose place-making generated new social settlement houses, formed around community organizing, as well as the construction of housing for working class and professional women and men, and of public playgrounds and day-care centers for children.[24] Central Park, Hull House, and Peirce's schemes shared an activist approach to creating collective space to suit new forms of social reproduction with an emphasis on enhancing equality. When Peirce's followers failed to distinguish her non-profit approach from commercial hotels, restaurants, and child care, they lost their unique approach to economic and social change. When the mass production of suburban space occurred, women's issues seemed to vanish.

The opposing tradition of conceptualizing housing as exclusively private space divorced from community services is the one we know best in American life, but it tends to create speculative housing as a way of defending the ideal of an allegedly "classless" society. While this second tradition may be said to begin with Jefferson's dream of "each farmer on his own farm," expressed in his National Survey, and to continue in Catherine Beecher's model of *The American Woman's Home* where rich and poor women alike could be model wives, this second tradition is heavily promoted in the 1920s by housing experts who argue that *Good Homes Make Contented Workers,* and is supported by corporations who believe in *Selling Mrs. Consumer.* The automobile, developed for mass production by Henry Ford, is one spatial invention crucial to the success of mass-produced suburbia. The national highway systems promoted by Robert Moses also play a role, and so do federal mortgage programs. The spatial program of Levittown, and all the post–World War II suburbs, is an expression of national public policy, where race and gender identity are subordinated to an ideal of white male

7 A typical main street, U.S.A.

8 Main Street U.S.A., Set
Disneyland, California.

"middle class" homeownership, stylistically expressed as tract house, Colonial or Tudor (see fig. 6).[25]

By the time that women tackled the problem of housing, child care, and housework once again, in the 1960s, seeking to recover a lost political and social movement, housing space was a crucial issue for women's rights; but while the social and economic issues women faced were much the same, the urbanized world had changed. Miles of placeless suburbs served by commercial strips and shopping malls provided the stage for everyday life for the majority of white families in metropolitan areas, dividing the society by race, class, and gender experiences. Amid the tracts, Disneyland, sports centers, and Las Vegas looked like interesting public places to be, although they were also commercial spaces, and the first simply recreated a right-wing version of United States history on a fake Main Street that was really a shopping mall, while the second and third carried commercialism to new flamboyance, and a new level of city support (figs. 7, 8).

The politics of space in the United States since the mid-nineteenth century, as far as housing goes, can be understood in terms of these two distinctly American spatial traditions (fig. 9). The dominant,

The Politics of Space and Social Reproduction

Discipline	Spatial Scale	Social Scale	Women's Movement 1848–1930	Women's Movement 1960–1983
environmental psychology	body	biological reproduction	"domestic feminism"	reproductive rights
architecture	dwelling and residential neighborhood	reproduction of daily life	"material feminism"	"room of one's own," or male housework, or wages for housework
urban planning	city	reproduction of social relations	"social feminism"	"take back the night"
policy analysis	nation	reproduction of national political economy	suffrage	ERA

9 The Politics of Space and Social
Reproduction.

commercial vernacular American tradition emphasizes a policy of using private space to promote the development of a society of male homeowners; the spatial and social inventions of Jefferson, Beecher, Ford, Moses, Levitt, and Disney support the fiction that this will be a society free of *traditional* European working-class consciousness, because gender identity is more important than class, and racial segregation is ignored. Commercial space replaces public space because mass consumption is crucial to this fiction. It is a placeless tradition because the house itself becomes the utopia, not the society.

The other minor American tradition of housing design, prefigured by the communitarians, developed by Peirce, supported by Olmsted and Addams, and continued in the twentieth century by projects like Stein's Baldwin Hills Village and the World War II defense workers' housing at Kaiserville, Oregon, stressed the creation of new kinds of spaces for social reproduction. In its emphasis on neighborhood and city life, it was a place-*making* tradition, rather than a tradition of placelessness. This approach to social reproduction has always been at odds with the speculative context, the economic power of those banks, builders, and speculators involved with the production of built space in the commercial vernacular as a major part of the American economy.

What are the implications of this analysis of the politics of space for American architecture? Many designers believe that design is an artistic, creative activity that has nothing to do with politics. They argue that the great error of the architects of the modern movement was to attempt what Robert Stern has rightly criticized as "built sociology," and certainly we all know Le Corbusier oversimplified the problem when he said, "The choice for the twentieth century is architecture or revolution. Revolution is unnecessary."[26] Yet the experience of the United States can be illuminated by this famous Corbusian remark. Beginning with Herbert Hoover, and with Better Homes for America and other such groups in the 1920s, and continuing with FHA, VA financing, national highways, and tax breaks for homeowners, the United States became a country ruled by just this kind of strong architectural determinism. It was architecture with a small *a,* the commercial vernacular, or just plain badly built, historically eclectic, nostalgic tract houses that won out, now owned by two-thirds of American households—green, quiet, private spaces at best, but private spaces that create placeless urban regions where the aesthetic whole is far less than the sum of the parts.

What can the designer who wants to be identifiably American, to relate to the vernacular, to be contextual, ever do? Certainly not return to the Greek Revival village, join the Shakers, or live in a tepee again. Historic preservationists have a better chance than most in the design fields to strengthen and enhance the preindustrial vernacular traditions. But for the designer of new buildings and the urban designer and planner, the problem is to find a critical stance that is not trivial or paralyzing but constructive.

In 1972 Denise Scott Brown and Robert Venturi made the bold step by taking their Yale students west, and in the book that resulted they argued:

> To find our symbolism we must go to the suburban edges of the existing city that are symbolically rather than formalistically attractive and represent the aspirations of almost all Americans, including most low-income dwellers and most of the silent white majority. Then the archetypal Los Angeles will be our Rome and Las Vegas our Florence, and, like the archetypal grain elevator some generations ago, the Flamingo sign will be the model to shock our sensibilities towards a new architecture.[27]

10 *Las Vegas, Nevada, at night.*

They applied the shock treatment. I would suggest a new history of American building must go beyond symbolic attractiveness and seek the underlying social and economic forces that have shaped American space. If Los Angeles and Las Vegas sent the Venturis back to Rome as a model, I suggest that the American commercial vernacular should also send us back to the grain elevators and the barns, to Taos, Poverty Point, and Hancock (fig. 10). And, as Richard Longstreth has reminded us, the grain elevator was not simply an interesting object on the prairie: it was a symbol of the farmers' resistance to the railroad trusts. Without a better underlying social and economic analysis, without a better grounding in the aesthetic excellence of the American preindustrial vernacular, postmodernism will reach a dead end as an *American* stylistic experiment, and the hopes expressed in Currier and Ives's "Westward the Course of Empire" will find their best expression in the Cadillac Ranch at Amarillo, Texas, ten years of shapely fins on automotive dinosaurs (fig. 11).

11 *Ant Farm*
Cadillac Ranch
Amarillo, Texas, 1975.

In addition to reinterpreting the ideology of the male homeowner culture so linked to the placeless commercial vernacular, American designers need to rediscover the other, activist place-making tradition that forms a strong minor theme in this country's history, as an alternative to the speculators' commercial vernacular. The client groups most likely to support this kind of endeavor are urban planners, community organizers, and citizens, especially those racial and ethnic minorities that have been excluded from the white homeowner culture. Here one will find the human struggle to make meaningful places has gone on heroically. In Los Angeles alone the Chicano mural movement has created a thousand political murals in public places, enlivening dreary subsidized housing with a powerful imagery connecting the landscape, preindustrial vernacular architecture, and the commercial vernacular (fig. 12). In other cities and in the rural South, black folk-art traditions, as Bill Ferris has

12 *Mural by Chicano artists*
at the Estrada Courts
Los Angeles, California
Note the high-rise city floating
on a cloud [left] wrapped by a
monorail.

shown in a recent book on black folk art and the sense of place, are strong. The resources of professional schools and a center for the study of American architecture can be used to support such groups and to encourage young designers and planners to learn from *East* Los Angeles, as well as from the rest.

Ultimately, however much American historians and architects see themselves as afflicted by a colonial mentality, constantly borrowing ideas and forms from Europe, it must be understood that the United States no longer imports most of its spatial forms. The speculative builders of America have been exporting the car, the tract house, the highway, the theme park, and the skyscraper (with no calculation of their real social and economic costs). The American spatial tradition established by Ford, Levitt, Moses, and Disney is reshaping parts of the rest of the world, but it is not too late for the United States to export some well-reasoned social concern as well. This will require a better fusion of history, theory, and practice, and better connections between architecture, urban design, urban planning, and preservation.

NOTES

[1] David Goldfield and Blaine Brownell, *Urban America: From Downtown to No Town* (Boston: Houghton Mifflin, 1979).

[2] John C. Ewers, *Murals in the Round: Painted Tipis of the Kiowa and Kiowa-Apache Indians* (Washington, D.C.: Smithsonian Institution Press, 1978).

[3] William N. Morgan, *Prehistoric Architecture in the Eastern United States* (Cambridge, Mass.: MIT Press, 1980).

[4] John Stilgoe, *Common Landscape of America, 1580–1845* (New Haven: Yale University Press, 1982).

[5] Ronald Fleming and Laurie Halderman, *On Common Ground* (Boston: Harvard Common Press, 1982).

[6] Eric Sloane has published many charming drawings of these buildings.

[7] Dolores Hayden and Peter Marris, "The Quiltmaker's Landscape," *Landscape, 25* (Winter 1981), pp. 39–47.

[8] Dolores Hayden, "Heavenly and Earthly Space," *Seven American Utopias* (Cambridge, Mass.: MIT Press, 1976), pp. 64–103. I call this an "intentional vernacular."

[9] This process is discussed in many works on the vernacular around the world. For a brief summary see Amos Rapoport, *House Form and Culture* (Englewood Cliffs, N.J.: Prentice-Hall, 1969).

[10] Mary Alice Dixon Hinson, "The Last Frontier: Post-Modernism and the Meaning of American Vernacular Architecture," *L'hotel d'Architecture,* Proceedings of 1982 ACSA Conference, Montreal (Washington, D.C., ACSA, 1983), pp. 39–47.

[11] John Morris Dixon, "Design Score Card," *Progressive Architecture, 64* (Jan. 1983), p. 7.

[12] Betsy Blackmar, "Re-Walking the 'Walking City': Housing and Property Relations in New York City, 1780–1840," *Radical History Review* 21 (special issue on space in history. Winter 1979–80); Gwendolyn Wright, *Moralism and the Model Home* (Chicago: University of Chicago Press, 1980), and *Building the Dream* (New York: Pantheon, 1981); Thomas Bender, *Toward an Urban Vision* (Louisville, Ky.: University of Kentucky Press, 1974); Christine Stansell, "Women and Children on the Streets of New York," unpublished paper.

[13] Sam B. Warner, Jr., *The Urban Wilderness* (New York: Harper and Row, 1972); David Gordon, "Capitalist Development and the History of American Cities," in W. K. Tabb and L. Sawyers, eds., *Marxism and the Metropolis* (New York: Oxford University Press, 1978), pp. 25–63; David Harvey, "The Urban Process under Capitalism: A Framework for Analysis," and Richard Walker, "A Theory of Sub-

urbanization: Capitalism and the Construction of Urban Space in the United States," both in M. Dear and A. Scott, eds., *Urbanization and Urban Planning in Capitalist Society* (New York: Methuen, 1981), pp. 91–122, 383–430; Ann R. Markusen, "City Spatial Structure, Women's Household Work, and National Urban Policy," *Signs: Journal of Women in Culture and Society* 5 (Spring 1980 supplement), pp. S23–S44; Christine Boyer, *Dreaming the Rational City* (Cambridge, Mass.: MIT Press, 1984).

[14] Dolores Hayden, "Capitalism, Socialism, and the Built Environment," in S. Shalom, ed., *Socialist Visions* (Boston: South End Press, 1983); Dolores Hayden, "Skyscraper Seduction, Skyscraper Rape," *Heresies*, 2 (1977), pp. 108–115.

[15] Manuel Castells, *The Urban Question* (Cambridge, Mass.: MIT Press, 1977).

[16] Henri Lefebvre, *La production de l'espace* (Paris: Anthropos, 1976), ms. translation by A. Kravitz, p. 89.

[17] Manfredo Tafuri, *Architecture and Utopia: Design and Capitalist Development* (Cambridge, Mass.: MIT Press, 1976); Giorgio Ciucci, Francesco Dal Co, Manfredo Tafuri, *The American City* (Cambridge, Mass.: MIT Press, 1977).

[18] Dolores Hayden, "Social Space, Women's Labor, and Socialist Feminism," paper delivered at the 1981 Berkshire Conference on the History of Women, Vassar College.

[19] Nancy M. Henley, *Body Politics* (Englewood Cliffs, N.J.: Prentice-Hall, 1977).

[20] Herbert Gans, *The Levittowners,* rev. ed., (New York: Columbia, 1983); Robert Venturi, Denise Scott Brown, and Steven Izenour, *Learning from Las Vegas,* rev. ed., (Cambridge, Mass.: MIT Press, 1977); Tom Wolfe, *From Bauhaus To Our House* (New York: Farrar, Strauss, and Giroux, 1981).

[21] Henri Lefebvre, *La production de l'espace,* p. 90.

[22] Hilda Kuper, "The Language of Sites and the Politics of Space," *American Anthropologist* 74 (June 1972), pp. 411–25; Edward W. Soja, "The Socio-Spatial Dialectic," *Annals of the Association of American Geographers* 70 (June 1980), pp. 207–25; John Friedmann, "Life Space and Economic Space: Contradictions in Regional Development," Discussion Paper 158, U.C.L.A. School of Architecture and Urban Planning, 1981.

[23] Dolores Hayden, *The Grand Domestic Revolution* (Cambridge, Mass.: MIT Press, 1981).

[24] Dolores Hayden, "Dream House or Ideal City?" Annual Frederick Law Olmsted Lecture, Harvard Graduate School of Design, 1982.

[25] Dolores Hayden, *Redesigning the American Dream: The Future of Housing, Work, and Family Life* (New York: W. W. Norton, 1984).

[26] Le Corbusier, *Towards a New Architecture* (London, The Architectural Press, 1952).

[27] Scott Brown, Venturi, Izenour, *Learning from Las Vegas,* p. 161.

RESPONSE

by Max Bond

It is my view that architects and architectural historians have not been as effective as novelists, essayists, and writers in other fields in discussing modern culture. Nadine Gordimer in her novels and Ralph Ellison in *The Invisible Man* have written well about the complex interaction between racial groups and about people caught in a situation in which they perhaps know better but play the role expected of them. I too will play my role, perhaps knowing better. I am charged with responding to the other speakers but, as the token black voice in this assembly, have inevitably to respond to other expectations. Given that, I will comment not solely on today's discussions but to some extent on the whole conference and exhibition.

I have been struck in everything that I have seen and heard so far— with the exception of Dolores Hayden's presentation—by a sense of all the issues that are being ignored in this conference. In the exhibition there are precious few buildings that have any social content. There are many private houses, hardly any public housing. There is virtually only one native American building. There are some university buildings but few, if any, public schools.

Earlier Bob Stern said to me something to the effect of, "Well, why does that matter? Anyway, there hasn't been very much well-designed public housing." I think that this misses the point, because if we are to study American architecture, we cannot ignore the products of our own building activity. We should also look at that which in conventional terms may not be "good architecture."

I read with interest the little red folder that accompanies the exhibition. In it, Gerald Allen comments about the South and its genteel tradition. To me his text reads more like the atmospherics for a cheap remake of *Gone With the Wind* than a true analysis of the Southern tradition. In fact, the pre-Civil War Southern tradition was only superficially genteel. We need to look beyond the forms of the South's "genteel" architecture to understand what those buildings and town plans symbolized. Though it may have used traditional forms, the Southern slave plantation represented a new type of agrarian organization. In its adaptation of Classical order and hierarchy it represents a unique phenomenon that has reverberated through later American architecture and town planning, an abhorrent system whose significance cannot be glossed over. To fall for the disguise of "genteel tradition" is to miss the complexity inherent in this and other manifestations of American culture.

I feel that the exhibition and discussion devote too little attention to public spaces and their problems. The parks of New York City— Central Park and Morningside Park, for example—are areas of contention. Some preservationists feel that they should be preserved as built, but the argument they offer is not always about preserving the parks; it is often an argument about class, race, and culture. Who will the parks serve? Does Olmsted's plan for Morningside Park serve the people who live next to the park now? How might it possibly serve them? The same questions apply to parts of Central Park. How can it be made to respond more adequately to current uses and to the increasing number of people who go there? That the exhibition does not suggest such issues, let alone alternative points of view, is why it seems to me bound to an elite view of architecture—a view that does not address America's evolving popular culture. One should make a distinction between popular culture and the vernacular. Certainly, the vernacular is easy to accept, but modern industrial mass culture seems to be much harder to accept and respond to in a profession geared toward representing the culture of the powerful.

The colonial mother-culture argument that was raised by Denise Scott Brown is, I think, quite an interesting one. However, it seems almost to turn reality on its head. That is because it ignores a good deal of writing by Third World analysts. For example, Franz Fanon in *The Wretched of the Earth,* Amilcar Cabral in his many speeches, and Nathan Huggins in *The Harlem Renaissance* describe the colonial mentality very thoroughly, offering some real insight into why the people who colonize a country seek to recall the forms of "home." Obviously that recall has to do with power. The reason that "Schreiner may have rendered the African landscape visible for the first time to her audiences in South Africa and England" (see Denise Scott Brown's essay) does not represent an authentic invention to me, but rather an appropriation. That appropriation was really an assertion of power. When one conquers another country, one brings one's culture, religion, and language and imposes them on the indigenous inhabitants. It is thus natural that what is rendered afterward is rendered in the language of the colonizers. The colonizers use their own culture—their "civilizing mission"—to express their power and to strip and destroy the traditional culture. Wherever Europeans have colonized there has been a constant reference to Europe as the "ancestral home," and thus European culture has become in the American context a symbol used by the powerful.

In America there is a great deal of contention over culture. The fact that there is a Lincoln Center in New York but no equivalent for jazz is not just about a symptom of cultural preference. It is a symbol of the continuing struggle over culture as an expression of authority. The analyses of Fanon and others who have written eloquently about the interaction between the colonized and colonizers help us to understand why the "establishment" promotes only a small spectrum of America's cultural productions.

One cannot talk about American architecture today without being aware of the limitations that have up till now characterized the analysis of American culture. To pursue a hermetic discussion of architecture and its precedents in a traditionally elite context runs the risk of ignoring the social, political, and cultural dynamic that has shaped American art and the choices implicit in its representations. I would hope that the Buell Center would transcend past racial and cultural biases.

RESPONSE

by M. Christine Boyer

In reviewing the diverse set of papers occasioned by this symposium, two questions continually come to mind. How have we used, and do we continue to use, "history" in creating our sense of American place? And why do we want to study the history of this American place? What does it tell us about ourselves, about the present, about current practices, tactics, and strategies in architecture, city planning, and historic preservation?[1]

Let me start with how we use history. First, we use history as a repository of reminiscences, as a grab bag of illustrative models that help us recognize ourselves in this strange foreign land. As Denise Scott Brown has pointed out, we most often borrow European models, gathering "cultural legitimacy" from these established aesthetic forms. American examples are numerous: the imposition of the concepts of Haussmann's Paris across the plains of Chicago, as illustrated in Jules Guerin's renderings of the 1909 Chicago Plan; or the utilization of the garden city and regionalist theories of Sir Patrick Geddes and Raymond Unwin in the development of new suburban towns in the 1920s. But we have also used history in a commemorative mode, as parody, for example, when we borrowed the monuments of Imperial Rome to disguise the uncouthness of our American cities in the City Beautiful movement of the late nineteenth century. No doubt these were false props, meant to evoke the glory and dignity which once were Rome's. Or, to take another example, when our aristocratic *chateaux* along Fifth Avenue in the 1880s were more sumptuous than those provided for European royalty, these were monuments to our merchant princes and captains of industry. At times we must have had a sense of humor, as we endowed the city with qualities reminiscent of a festival or a carnival.

We use history to give ourselves a sense of continuity, gathering representative artifacts from cultural traditions that carry with them the roots of our identity. Thus, Denise Scott Brown reminds us, the customs carried over by immigrant groups have made ethnic neighborhoods such as Astoria, Queens, more Greek than Greece. But there has also been the attempt by many historic preservation purists to carve out of our urban spaces whole districts set aside as memory banks for future generations. History, we begin to see, in the context of historic preservation, has a sellable, commercial quality: we have only to look from Boston to San Antonio, from Savannah to Los Angeles, to see this "packaged" sense of place.

History as Dolores Hayden uses the word provides us with a standard by which we can negatively criticize the formlessness and placelessness of our present American cities. When the commodity logic of capitalism invaded the production of space in the nineteenth century, the totality that enveloped our preindustrial vernacular space broke apart the unique fusion which held together the sense of place, the building, and the object. Still another use of history relative to the sense of American place has been suggested by John Coolidge: a history of monumental events. In this case we study the major challenges the American context offered, at different times and for different reasons, to American designers: to Pierre Charles L'Enfant, the creation of a great eighteenth-century metropolis in the plan for Washington, D.C.; to Frederick Law Olmsted, the development of an autonomous garden city in Riverside, Illinois; and to Frank Lloyd Wright, the plan for an entire campus in Florida Southern College.

In all of these approaches there is an underlying assumption that our past animates our present, that an unbroken continuity exists between our historical origins and our current destiny. This assumption enables us to trace the evolution of our American sense of place from its traditional form to its industrial type, and beyond to its postindustrial variation. Do we now hope that a return to past collective values will erase the placelessness of our fragmented modern American cities? Do we still hope for a golden age of American cities? Let me propose an alternative reason for studying the history of American place. That would be the desire to interpret analytically the aesthetic principles that have been used at different times in the representation of place, and the hope for an awareness of how these aesthetic models influence the categories and concepts we select to examine reality in order to turn this understanding back upon ourselves in the historical present.

Suppose we take the three different periods on which these papers have focused: the traditional, the industrial, and the postindustrial. We can posit three different artistic models to characterize the sense of American place in these different periods: the City as a Work of Art, the City as Panorama, and the City as Deconstructed Reality. Next we can ask how each of these models directs our expectations about tradition and innovation within its own perspective. Let me turn to the City as a Work of Art.

The typical model of representation in this first city is that of the picture as a window on the world; the artist in this case is one who reconstructs the world on the surface of his canvas. Vincent Scully has used this analogy with respect to the Hudson River school and the view of the American suburban streetscape seen through the frame of the front porch. This traditional urban order, as seen through the example of the painter's art, offers us an enclosed and framed space; a regular harmony of solids and voids is established through the American grid plan and the rectangular block and lot subdivisions. Individual buildings tend to relate to each other: no matter how eclectic their style, their heights and streetscapes are uniform; only a few monuments are permitted to stand out, such as church spires, city halls, commemorative monuments. This representational space, however, makes us look for the presence of an individual artisan, a craftsman whose labor and knowledge of materials and production techniques were sufficient to complete the work of art in a limited period of time, a work, moreover, whose conceptual organization grew out of an ideal and image held in the mind of the artist.

In this manner Montgomery Schuyler, a nineteenth-century architectural critic, spoke of the early nineteenth-century small city-house as the most respectable and artistic pattern of habitation ever to have adorned New York streets, a style that had vanished by the mid-nineteenth century. These small houses, Schuyler wrote, were "gay and positively attractive, by reason of the architectural tradition that had grown up among their mechanics . . . The houses were more than decent; they were 'elegant' . . . The New York small house owed its elegance to the ornament which was applied to it, very modestly and very sparingly, but none the less effectively."[2] As Schuyler noted, the idea for these houses was arrived at by general consent, and was essential in the creation of a sense of place, a streetscape, and a total experience of the city.

Turning to the City as Panorama—the city of soaring skyscrapers and metropolitan extension, a city, moreover, seen from above, a spatial representation demanding to be deciphered and reordered— we can use another representational model, the camera obscura. Here an image of the world is cast upon a screen, a world more or less unbounded and unframed, a world that absorbs the viewer in its expanse. Gone is the individual artist: there is no one subject that produces this scene, there is no knowledge of craft processes that can account for all of the images which simultaneously display themselves. Nor is this city produced in finite time sequences, for many of the materials and processes that make up this city of steel and glass are themselves products of other processes. Their origins have been erased.

In this urban place, space itself becomes an object of investigation, a focus of social concern, dominated by administrative controls. The panoramic model tends to draw the entire urban context into critical awareness: the analysis of legal controls, technical processes, political forces, cultural pressures that prefigure it. Urban chaos becomes the cornerstone for the modern architect and planner. The sense of enclosed space is broken, the center of the city displaced, the ceremonial realm voided. Free-standing buildings of increasingly mammoth proportions begin to float about in this city; assemblages of lots and the centralization of capital enable larger and taller buildings to be built, which begin to dominate the homogeneous grid pattern. The multiplication of so many spaces that belong to no one—bridges, subways, highways, airports—destroys the image still further. The response evoked by this model is a reaching out to order the sense of this American place; hence the great strategies of the twentieth century were born in the City Beautiful movement, comprehensive physical planning, zoning, and urban renewal.

So many examples could be cited, but just think of the proposals by Ernest Flagg for the improvement of New York City in the early years of 1900. Perhaps it is Flagg who was the real inventor of our modern-day transfer of development rights, because shortly after designing his famous Singer Tower building, he proposed that New York should become a city of isolated towers, with adequate light and air surrounding each structure. This could be done, he said, if towers were only allowed to rise on a quarter of their plot, the rest of the bulk not to exceed in height one-and-one-half times the width of the street. However, he further proposed that allowable building heights be purchased and sold between owners of adjoining buildings.[3] One of his more controversial suggestions was to do away with Central Park, for, in his view, a naturalistic park was out of place in a modern metropolis. In its place he planned a long and narrow park between Sixth and Seventh avenues, stretching from Fourteenth Street to the Harlem River. He believed that "if the city was to be laid out *de nouveau* no one with a modicum of sense would think of so placing a park as to block the two central avenues or to cut off the east to the west sides of the city from convenient access to each other for a distance of two and a half miles." With his new park, however, the city would obtain a grandiose parkway twelve hundred feet wide and nine miles long running right through its heart.[4]

Of course, within this same time period, there were borrowings from our first representative model. Frederick Law Olmsted is a good example. In writing about Central Park in the 1870s, Olmsted stated:

> The study of [park design] must begin with the consideration that the Park is to be surrounded by an artificial wall, twice as high as the Great Wall of China, composed of urban buildings. Wherever this should appear across the meadow-view, the imagination would be checked abruptly, at short range. Natural objects were thus required to be interposed which while excluding the buildings as much as possible from view, would leave an uncertainty as to the occupation of the space beyond, and establish a horizon line, composed, as much as possible, of verdure.[5]

In 1893 Olmsted retrospectively claimed that although he had held professional responsibility for more than a hundred public grounds, he would call only twenty of these "parks," reserving the term for "places with breadth and space enough, and with all other needed qualities to justify the application to what you find in them of the word scenery, or of the word landscape in its older and more radical sense, which is much the same as that of scenery."[6]

There were, as well, those who closed their eyes in order to escape from the mechanical maws, the giant hoppers of the twentieth-century cities. So Lewis Mumford and his friends proposed autonomous garden cities, planted in regional, cultural, ecological, and technological balance in the hinterlands. But these nostalgic retreats and escapes could not stem the dominant desire to create an efficient, utilitarian, productive, and well-ordered city.

It is Denise Scott Brown who leads me to think that perhaps a different representational space has evolved in the post-World War II period: the City of Deconstructed Reality. What did we learn from Las Vegas? We see a new American landscape of vast spaces, whose architecture is to be seen as one whizzes by in an automobile, a space in which the commercial symbol establishes the main spatial reference points, information which does not survive beyond a moment, to be replaced by serial additions and a fusion of different sensory modes of writing, of flashing neon, of whirling tectonics. To escape this, in her view, and to reestablish a connotative, expressive architecture, we have to return to Rome. I, for one, would rather return to Athens as a source for urban imagery. But that is a separate argument for this deconstructed reality is basically American.

Perhaps the closest representational model for this new sense of space is the modern cinema, with its jump cuts, its close-ups, its slow motion, its shock tactics, its montage effects: for this is the reaction against order, the attempt to break apart the dominant unity which prevailed for so many years in the city as panorama. But what limits does this model place upon our sense of change and innovation? And how does this city of deconstructed images separate art from society, and reinforce a compliant and affirmative culture? Just think of how many "decomposed" words apply to our current-day cities: displacement, dispersal, decentering (of the individual from the center of the focus, gentrification of neighborhoods); devitalize, destroy, devalue, throw away whole sections of the city such as the South Bronx; deregulation of controls: on busing, on abortion, on private enterprise, leading to affluence for the few and austerity for the many: disassemble; disassociate; disappoint. . . . You complete the list, the point has been made. Some of these conditions we simply accept as reality. But most importantly, the City of Deconstructed Reality reveals a resistance to historical interpretation. Perhaps this is because a certain amnesia set in during the 1950s; was it due, as some claim, to World War II, or the Cold War, or the International Style of architecture? A history of isolated moments, however, offers no possibility of synthesis.

We cannot ask, what is this part doing here? Why is downtown Los Angeles there, where it never was before? What is Madison Avenue doing there in midtown with its super-tower development; couldn't it be relocated to the western side of Manhattan? Why are suburban homes being built on Charlotte Street in the South Bronx? Aren't these questions we are asking based on our old ordering principles of the panoramic city? Do they make sense in the deconstructed reality of the 1980s?

Instead of such questions, we are getting used to the manipulation of codes by new spatial artists who define city spaces by using well-ordered grammars, a kind of combinatorial logic which does not aid our memory. I have alluded to the preservationists, who are busy carving away at our cities, setting aside vast historic districts to be dominated by regulatory controls specifically designed for their isolated architectural context. I have also noted the serial replication of similar-looking revitalization projects, such as waterfront renewal schemes in city after city: The Rouse Company and their architect Benjamin Thompson's appearance in Quincy Market in Boston, the Baltimore Harborplace, and now South Street Seaport in New York. In like fashion, new contextual zoning on Madison Avenue attempts to recreate the sculpted set-back skyscrapers of the 1920s, although in fact these regulations may create nothing more than wrap-around step-down facades embracing the remaining nineteenth-century streetscapes.

Our current inability to "think history" in spite of a return to history may be covering over a failure of creative spirit, an inability to envision a new sense of place. Thus we place a too heavy reliance upon past achievements. But then this is the purpose of studying the above representational models: we may search for the small resistances by which to hold out against the strong pressures drawing us all toward an affirmative culture.

NOTES

[1] There are many sources which have inspired these comments, among which the following were especially important: Svetlana Alpers, "Interpretation without Representation, or, the Viewing of *Las Meninas*," *Representation* 1, no. 1 (February 1983), pp. 31–42; Michel Foucault, "Nietzsche, Genealogy, History," in Donald F. Bouchard, ed., *Language, Counter-Memory, Practice* (Ithaca: Cornell University Press, 1977), pp. 139–64.

[2] Montgomery Schuyler, "The Small City House in New York," *The Architectural Record*, Vol. 8, No. 4, April–June 1899, pp. 277–388.

[3] Ernest Flagg, "Public Buildings," *The Third Conference on City Planning* (1911), pp. 42–52.

[4] Ernest Flagg, "The Plan of New York and How to Improve It," *Scribner's Monthly*, Vol. 36, August 1904, pp. 253–56.

[5] Frederick Law Olmsted, in F. L. Olmsted, Jr., and T. Kimball, eds., *Forty Years of Landscape Architecture: Central Park, Frederick Law Olmsted, Sr.* (Cambridge, Mass.: MIT Press, 1977), pp. 46–47.

[6] Ibid., p. 212.

THE PROFESSION:
CONTEMPORARY PRACTICE

INTRODUCTION

by Arthur Drexler

The general subject of this section of the symposium is the profession: architecture as it is practiced.

When you finish architecture school and go out into the world, your first task is to get a commission. Having gotten it, your second task is to think of something to do whereby you will distinguish yourself from your competition. This gets harder as you go along. The second commission is even more nerve-racking, and pretty soon you discover that you either have to improve on someone else's perfection or reject it entirely. The combinations and permutations of these personal traumas constitute a large part of architectural history—architecture as it is practiced, that is, which is a different kind of history from that which we usually hear about in assemblies of this kind.

Charles Gwathmey first became known to me in 1966. I was spending the summer in Amagansett, and I drove past a house that I thought was nifty. I climbed up onto the porch—just in time for the owners to arrive home, Charles's parents. I thus got to know his parents before I got to know him. The house was quite a skillful, accomplished, sparkling kind of statement. It sat well in the landscape, and it seemed to me to demonstrate that it was entirely possible to practice Modern architecture: Modern architecture was alive and well, at least in 1966. Charles Gwathmey has gone on to design his form of Modern architecture extremely successfully. He tells me that he has done forty houses in seventeen years. That is not bad.

Allan Greenberg represents a different position altogether. He came to this country from South Africa and graduated from Yale in 1965. He worked with the Redevelopment Agency in New Haven and began an independent practice in 1971. What fascinates me about Allan is that his work is neither Premodern nor Postmodern; it is Antimodern. He rejects Modernism in its entirety and has moved on to something else. Others will say he has moved backward to something else. Whatever Allan's architecture is, however, it is not engaged in witty reworkings of history. It is his own notion of what Classical form can be now.

Kevin Roche is an equally fascinating but again quite different figure. He came to the United States from Ireland in 1948 to do graduate work at I.I.T. After working at the United Nations Head-quarters office, he went into the office of Eero Saarinen in 1950 and, after Saarinen's death, took over the successor office in 1961. I think it is fair to say that since then he has done some of the most distinguished, technically proficient buildings in the history of Modern architecture. His accomplishment was recognized last year when he received the Pritzker architecture prize.

I have always particularly admired Kevin Roche's work because I like technology. I am one of those people who like shiny glass buildings. I even like mirrors. The bad period of Modern architecture, for me, was when everything was made of concrete. Concrete is a rotten building material—it decays rapidly and always looks nasty. The so-called heroic style of *béton brut* was launched on a helpless world by Le Corbusier, and was taken up with a mad passion by the English. But during and after that convulsion of the sixties there was a rethinking of the technical, machine-art possibilities of Modern architecture. No one has surpassed Kevin Roche in managing the development of those possibilities. At the same time he is by no means unresponsive to what has been happening in architecture—to the changes in attitude we have been hearing about these last two days. His use of historical allusions, for instance, is almost as startling as his technical innovations.

Let me now begin this section by asking Charles Gwathmey to tell us how to continue to make a successful practice out of respectable Modern architecture.

STATEMENT

by Allan Greenberg

I would like to make an amendment to Arthur Drexler's introduction. I do not see myself as Antimodern. You cannot tear out leaves from the book of history. The Modern movement tried to do that and failed, and I would not like to be accused of the same sin. The change of sensibility that has taken place in the United States since 1950, and in Europe since 1920, simply cannot be erased. I see myself as standing not only on the shoulders of the ancients, but also on those of the Modernist architects of the past sixty years.

*1 State Library and Supreme
Court Building addition
Hartford, Connecticut
Allan Greenberg, 1969–1976.*

You can see this in the first building I designed—the addition to Donn Barber's State Library and Supreme Court building in Hartford of 1910 (fig. 1). The new annex is for the Supreme Court and was designed in 1969 and completed in 1976. The instructions from the Chief Justice were very explicit: to design an office that would be completely secondary to the older building, which contains the Supreme Courtroom. There is an earlier addition to the State Library behind the wing I designed, which is not visible in the illustration. My addition forms an arc of a circle and curves away from the old building. It suggests that the proper form for an addition would be a full hemicycle. The detailing contrasts with that of the older building. There is no sense of depth at the window reveal; structure is marked by recessed panels in the curved wall rather than by heavy pilasters and columns as in the 1910 building, and there is no plinth or cornice. For me, despite pride of authorship, the design fails in the detailing. The dialogue between new and old does not reach the level of intensity to which I aspired. Part of this failure stems from the elements with which the building was composed. They simply do not speak the same language as the older building.

*2 Addition to Dushkin House
Guilford, Connecticut
Allan Greenberg, 1975.*

I was trained in Classical architecture and have always loved architectural history. Because of my love for the Classical tradition, I decided that my next project, an addition to an eighteenth-century saltbox house in Connecticut, should be designed as an extension of the older building (fig. 2). Therefore, in raising the attic for a sculpture studio and building a new wing along the rear of the building, I made reference to both colonial precedent and to the Colonial Revival, including the Shingle style and the work of McKim, Mead & White.

*3 Facade of proposed courthouse
and office building
Alexandria, Virginia
Allan Greenberg, 1975–1976.
Plaques above each of the three
archways represent the three
courts housed in the building.
The bronze screen over the center
arch depicts the seal of Alexandria. The archways lead to a
plaza, which provides a formal
setting for the courthouse.*

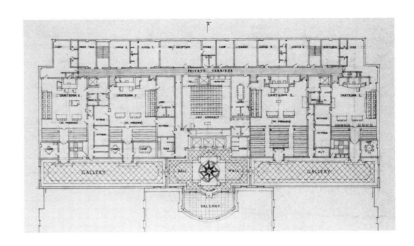

Right:

4 Plan of proposed courthouse and office building
The parcel of land was part of an urban renewal project and lay vacant for several years. In order to take advantage of the depth, retail and office space was allotted along the main street frontage and sides. The courthouse was planned to occupy the deepest part of the site.

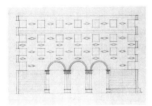

5 Interior courtyard of proposed courthouse and office building
The interior courtyard facade is white glazed brick with a diamond pattern of red brick. The superstructure is set on a limestone plinth.

Below, left:
6 Supermarket
Manchester, Connecticut
Prior to its conversion into a state courthouse.

Below, right:
7 State courthouse after conversion.

The next project is a rather large commercial development and courthouse in downtown Alexandria, Virginia, in the center of the historic district (fig. 3). A new U-shaped office building occupies the front of the site (fig. 4). The new courthouse is entered through a public courtyard. The project was completed some years ago. I show the drawing because I was not involved in the detailing of the realized project, and it was developed differently (fig. 5). In the design I looked not only to the Colonial and Federal styles of Virginia, but to their root in England and north Italy. In this case, I was inspired by the gateways to Verona by Sanmicheli.

In another project, for Manchester, Connecticut, I was commissioned to transform a supermarket speedily and cheaply into a courthouse (fig. 6). The budget was forty-four dollars per square foot. The remnants of the supermarket can be seen on either side of the new brick and limestone facade, which is superimposed on the old glass front (fig. 7). In designing the facade, I looked at the civic and religious buildings of colonial Manchester, which are white clapboard with restricted quoins, at twentieth-century American Renaissance and Colonial Revival buildings of brick and limestone, and at the Italian and English-Georgian roots of American archi-

8 *Interior of courthouse*
The salle des pas perdu *serves as the major organizing space of the new courthouse.*

9 *Aerial view of proposed mid-block park between Sixth and Seventh avenues and 49th and 50th streets New York Allan Greenberg, 1979 This view shows the square portion of the site planned as a hemicycle with niches and spaces cut from it. This frames a monumental fountain which is contained within an elaborate structure of walls and columns so as to provide a variety of sitting spaces.*

11 *Rectangular portion of proposed mid-block park.*

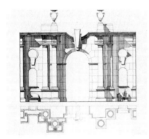

12 *Gateway at 49th Street, mid-block park.*

tecture. The entrance in the center is defined by a pediment and framed by large windows on either side. The limestone rustication is bold and overscaled to counter the rather low setting of the building. The shopping center parking lot remained but was re-landscaped in a more formal manner. The lobby, the *salle des pas perdu,* is the core of the building (fig. 8). It gives access to every major public destination in the building, the courtrooms on one side through the double doors, and the offices on the other through the single doors. A frieze with an inscription, columns, and a barrel vault combine to produce a cohesive interior space that is the noblest aspect of the building. While it is simply a public waiting space used prior to entering the courtroom, it also represents the dignity and importance of the law in our lives. The wainscot of marble tiles, the wood moldings, and the columns are all available out of a catalogue.

The next project is a park designed for a corner of Rockefeller Center between Sixth and Seventh avenues on the west side of the Exxon building. It is an odd-shaped site, an *L* divided into two parts, one square and one rectangle (fig. 9). In the square part I designed a hemicycle with an elaborate fountain in the middle. The water falls into an octagonal space defined by a wall with openings cut into it (fig. 10). The space is surrounded by a tree hedge. For the second part, the rectangle, I made an *allée* lined with columns (fig. 11). An existing cafeteria serves the aisle spaces. The "roof" is like a baroque ceiling with gilded beams and frames; instead of paintings by Tiepolo of gods and their entourage in the sky, you have the real sky. The gateway to the *allée* is derived from Roman and Renaissance gates, and its decorative elements evoke nature—garlands, rams, etc. (fig. 12).

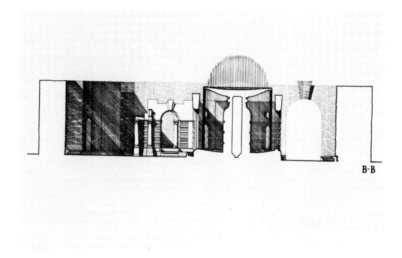

B-B

10 *Section through the fountain and park shows the fountain structure as a twenty-foot-high basin with jets forming a water dome. Water flowing over the edge of the basin is contained by an octagonal structure.*

14 *Facade of indoor swimming-pool room, Horse Farm.*

13 *Horse Farm, Connecticut. Allan Greenberg, 1979–1983. The entrance elevation plays on the asymmetry of the facade at Mt. Vernon and the Pope House in Farmington, Connecticut.*

15 *Entrance door to Horse Farm. The door has a split pediment and Ionic pilasters.*

16 *Entrance door, Horse Farm.*

17 *Side door, Horse Farm.*

Charles Gwathmey and I decided that we would coordinate our presentations by each emphasizing a single building—a house (fig. 13). The house I wish to show you is under construction. Its design models were specified as part of the commission: Mount Vernon in Virginia and the Pope House in Farmington by Stanford White and Theodate Pope. The material is wood, actually redwood siding dressed like stone, as was used in many very large Colonial and Federal wood buildings. The large size of the rusticated elements helps articulate and control the scale of the complex. The indoor swimming-pool room has triple-sash windows that open up completely to the exterior in the summer (fig. 14). Arcades connect the two buildings ancillary to the main house. The entrance door has carved capitals; the consoles which are four-feet-six-inches high, carry the pediment and transfer the load down to the wall (figs. 15, 16). All of the millwork you see in this building has been done by sophisticated shaping machines. They fabricate in a matter of minutes what it would have taken an eighteenth-century carpenter weeks of hand labor to produce. There are many themes that I could emphasize in taking you through the house. I have chosen to concentrate on doorways. All of these are based on Colonial or Roman models. It is the articulation of the moldings, the actual curves of the profiles, and the rhythm of the sequences of forms that display, I think, the late twentieth-century sensibility I talked about at the beginning. The kitchen door does not have a proper entasis and is based on themes related to "country" architecture (fig. 17). The garden entrance is very slightly overscaled, as may be seen in the moldings around the entablature (fig. 18). Inside the house, the pediments over the doors become increasingly complex as you move from room to room. The living room doors have a reeded frieze that picks up the theme of the reeded columns around the fireplace mantle (fig. 19). The dining room door has a split pediment and is framed by pilasters. A similar door in the library has a pedestal in the pediment and a very rich, handcarved deco-

Above, left:
18 *Doors leading to garden, Horse Farm.*

Above, center:
19 *Living room doors, Horse Farm.*

Above, right:
20 *Library door, Horse Farm.*

ration (figs. 20, 21). The master bedroom has a doorhead composed of the same elements, at a different scale, that you see in the fireplace mantle; the moldings here are interesting as a number of the small fillets and other transitional elements have been left out. (fig. 22).

The staircase has balusters consisting of columns sitting on urns, and the elaborate articulation of the side of the risers and treads occupies four planes. The stairhall is dominated by a large window at the landing. This window is seen over the front door at the foot of the stair; the rail swings around on itself as it rests on a large newel post. This columnar element grows to become a miniature building. All of the windows in the house have window seats with deep reveals that modulate the light. Viewed from inside the house, both the surrounding landscape and other parts of the complex, like the roof, chimney, keystones, and windows, become decorative elements in themselves. The keystones, architraves, and round windows are especially important as devices to articulate light and shade and control the scale of the different buildings (fig. 23).

21 *Library door, Horse Farm.*

22 *Door to master bedroom, Horse Farm.*

23 *View from house to wing, Horse Farm.*

Above, left:
24 *Detail of decorative niche.*

Above, center:
25 *Cornice study.*

Above, right:
26 *Detail of decorative pediment.*

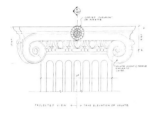

27 *Drawing of Ionic capital.*

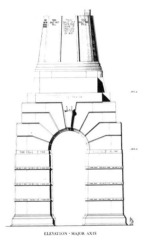

ELEVATION · MAJOR AXIS

28 *Proposed Holocaust Memorial for Battery Park, New York.*

The cabinet in the dining room is for the display of glassware. The split pediment picks up all the themes of the dining room door and has a radiating shell pattern with a mini-shell articulating the niche. The baseboard and chair rail are incorporated in the design so that the architecture of the room becomes part of the architecture of the object. In an issue of *Spazio* published almost thirty years ago, Luigi Moretti, the great Italian architect, noted that moldings are a purely abstract element of architecture, and he wondered why, with our love of abstract art, we ignore the abstract quality of moldings since they are, after all, pure form and light and shade. In designing these moldings I use graph paper (fig. 24).

This drawing is one of a series of studies for a cornice on the exterior of the building (fig. 25). I have taken as a model cornices used in similar situations by great architects of the past. The sketch study indicates the relationship of my cornice design to one by William Buckland on a house in Maryland. On the right is a sketch of one of the decorative "propellers" of rotating vine leaves with grapes which occurs at the front door (fig. 26). Note the center of the rondel, where the same design exists in miniature and rotates in the opposite direction. The drawing of an Ionic capital for the front door shows the craftman what to do; such drawings require a level of draftsmanship that is no longer readily available (fig. 27).

The last project I am going to discuss is for a memorial to the Holocaust. The proposed site is Battery Park. The memorial is a quadrifrons arch, a four-sided arch like that which the Romans used to articulate the crossroads of a city (fig. 28). The keystone of the arch is the Torah—the Scrolls of the Law, which include the first five books of the Bible and are the fundamental and basic foundation of Judaism. The two axes of the arch are different, and their intersection has projecting piers, on top of which there are to be carved lions of Judah with a major inscription located over the arch dedicating the monument. The three horizontal bands on the piers, 1200 feet in length, would have carved into them the words "In Blessed Memory" followed by the number of dead at all 144 concentration and death camps as well as the number of dead at the sites where Einsatzgruppen slaughtered two-and-a-half million Jews in Russia and Eastern Europe. There is an oculus in the roof

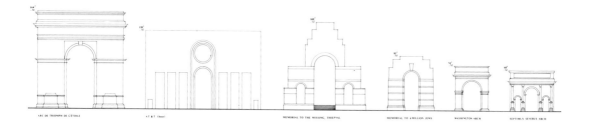

30 Comparative drawing showing triumphal arches drawn to the same scale.

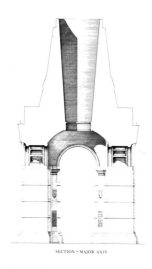

SECTION · MAJOR AXIS

29 Section through the Holocaust Memorial.

of the interior crossing (fig. 29). This space is octagonal and has a dome intersected by four archways cutting through it, as at St. Peter's. The diagonal sides of the octagon are articulated with pilasters. On each of these pilasters is a six-inch candelabrum—a candelabrum of mourning—to burn in perpetuity. Carved into the lower part of each pilaster will be the Kaddish, the Jewish prayer for the dead. The interior space is a sanctuary. The forms are derived from the Roman memorial arch. But one can also trace them back to the Middle East, to the great gates of the Biblical cities of Mesopotamia, where the ruler of the city would sit and receive the tribute of his conquered and vassal states. In my project, this sanctuary would be a place where we, the living, pay tribute to the memory of the six million dead. The comparative drawing (fig. 30) shows the Arc de Triomphe, in Paris, the base of the AT&T building by Philip Johnson, Lutyens's Memorial arch at Thiepval, the Washington Square arch, and that of Septimus Severus.

All the buildings I have shown are composed of elements of the Classical language of architecture. The elements are combined to form doors, porticos, domes, colonnades, arcades, all of which are imbued with meanings—meanings that have come to us down the ages. These buildings in turn stand in cities. Our notion of the city is Classical. For me, the great challenge of architecture today is to reestablish our links with the past by extending this tradition into the future.

STATEMENT

by Charles Gwathmey

When I was asked to participate in this symposium, I took its title, "American Architecture: Innovation and Tradition," seriously, and wondered, when does innovation become traditional and when does tradition become innovational? I also realized that I was being given an opportunity to encapsulate seventeen years of my own practice, which have largely been spent investigating one particular building type, the residence. This investigation has culminated in a very large house, our most complete design to date. It summarizes my seventeen years of research and brings it, through a spiraling cycle, to closure. In this exhaustive period of designing houses, I have used the house as the primary means for analyzing a process. Now I find myself at a juncture, at a point from which I hope to extend myself and go on to investigate new, and perhaps old, horizons.

A question that has always interested me is the relationship of, or opposition between, abstraction and representation: when does abstraction become non-representational, and when does abstraction become representational. This is the line of interpretation and invention that I have followed and that is now enabling me to cross back from the purely abstract to potentially more representational references. The houses I am going to discuss, a sequence beginning with my first and ending with our most recent project, represent this investigation. Although the sequence has, of course, included some failures, each failure was also a lesson learned, reevaluated, and then recycled and reconstituted in the next effort. Reviewing the course of this development, I can distinguish three major types. The first is the clearly autonomous object, self-defining and without contextual reference. The second is the object in a frame, sometimes making a contextual reference. The third is the sliver house, either urban or suburban, with a strongly defined front and back, which establishes very clearly public and private domains.

My first house, built for my parents in Amagansett in 1966, was initially conceived as an isolated form (figs. 1, 2). Its stance as a single object in space is more readily understood if we look at the house alone, unaccompanied by the later addition of a studio (fig. 3). With the addition of the studio, the concept was transformed into two objects in dialogue and tension. Furthermore, a simple site plan was initiated, creating an arena in which the buildings referred to each other and to the spaces between them. A third

1 *Gwathmey House
Amagansett, New York
Gwathmey and Henderson, 1966.*

2 *Gwathmey House
Living room.*

3 *Gwathmey Studio
Amagansett, New York
Gwathmey and Henderson, 1967.*

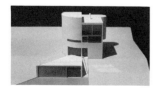

building was constructed on the lot adjacent to the studio and my parents' house, and the wall that separates them and defines a tennis court establishes the transition between what are now three objects. The wall became the site reference, and its large surface plane guides one's perception of the three objects while also establishing a datum for the overall site (figs. 4, 5). Each stage in the development of this site represents a different interpretation of the object, its relationship to other objects, and their relationship to communal space and vista.

The next project, a house in Connecticut, was our first exploration of a "containing" object, an object within a distinct volumetric frame. The house becomes a double frame, and the notion of layering is introduced through the element of the sunscreen (fig. 6). All the elements interlock through a formal manipulation of frame, void, and object. This project, as well as others, is a composition of interpenetrating volume, transparency, and extension. It also exploits the sense of a simultaneous presence of exterior and interior. As we continued this line of inquiry, the programs we were given became more complex, and consequently the buildings took on different qualities. The constituent concept remained, however, an existing volume into which a building or object intrudes. This process became even more varied with the introduction of denser and richer materials, as well as the imposition of color.

The third type of house I have worked with is the townhouse or sliver house. The distinguishing characteristic of this type is that it consists predominantly of a front and a back, a public and a private side, and at times these are joined by a central court. Projects of this type have been of many sorts, ranging from single dwellings to apartments to renovations, and each has its own idiosyncrasies. For example, a house in New Jersey was designed with a greenhouse as an integral component of the building (fig. 7). Another is strongly influenced by its site on a steep slope (fig. 8). A third project, a sliver house in North Carolina, stands out because of its interesting

parti: in essence it is a front building and a rear building, with a court occupying the space between (fig. 9). In another project, a renovation of a Neutra house in Santa Monica, we left the exterior intact, doing only a minimal amount of refurbishing (figs. 10, 11). It was the redesign of the interior, designed within the framework of given constraints, that was the central issue here. The inside became a reinterpretation of Neutra's plan and section. As you can see, this house type can assume many guises and incorporate a multitude of elements unique to a given program. However, our preoccupation has consistently been the thorough analysis of the townhouse type itself.

Each of these studies made its contributions to the final project I will discuss, and justifies my characterization of this latest house as a summation of the past seventeen years; every lesson learned from working on these building types finds an expression or a conscious elimination in this house. It is the first time that we were given the opportunity to design all aspects of a site and to develop a complete dialogue that informs and unifies the whole. The house is located on seven acres in East Hampton and faces the ocean across a half mile of dune. There is a turn at the entry, which brings the visitor around a man-made pond covering a half acre. There follows a second turn in the opposite direction, bringing one to a gate, to a driveway on axis with the house. This driveway is lined on one side by thirty-five linden trees and takes one past a sunken tennis court and a guesthouse/garage structure (fig. 12). The last part of the entry route is one's arrival in the auto court (fig. 13), at which point one confronts the north facade of the house sitting at the end of the site, parallel to the ocean (fig. 14).

Our intention was to develop a strategy that was in scale with the site, the house itself, and the ocean. The difficulty of this lay in the vastly differing dimensions of these three components. Our solution was to provide a system that could create and articulate interconnections between elements on every scale, from the grounds down to the furnishings.

One illustration of this is the circulation system for the house and the site. Circulation for the site is north to south, perpendicular to

Above, left:
15 De Menil House
 Brise soleil.

Above, center:
16 De Menil House
 *View looking north from second
 level of outside stair.*

Above, right:
17 De Menil House
 West facade.

18 *De Menil House
 Entry.*

19 *De Menil House
 Entry hall.*

the ocean, whereas circulation for the house is east to west, parallel to the ocean. What is important is that these circulation systems cross at critical places. A bridge connects the house to the pool and is also a major gateway from the house to the ocean (figs. 15, 16). Pedestrian paths intersect vehicular roadways. The two circulation systems are articulated by single objects that float in space: a wall rises from the pond and establishes itself as marker, and it is in turn echoed by a satellite receiver floating on the pond. The systems are unified throughout by the interconnections between these autonomous forms.

Materials and colors have been designed to parallel the circulation systems. Walls—of the gate, the guesthouse, the garage, the arbor, and the swimming pool—not only define the site but also refer to each other by virtue of the fact that they are all made of colored stucco. This creates an effect of layering. The entry sequence formed by the stucco walls continues inside the house, so that the walls become memory devices when one looks out from the house toward the grounds.

With other elements, changes of material clearly articulate distinct uses. Terrace spaces on the ground level are paved in green Vermont slate, whereas the driveway is in cobblestone (fig. 17). Inside, on the ground level, the floor material is a highly polished black granite, contrasting with the exterior grass, cobblestone, and slate surfaces (figs. 18, 19). On the second level, the black granite changes to solid mahogany, a material that was first introduced in the cabinetry of the lower level, but there finished with a dark stain. Upstairs, the wood floor is left its natural color, and thus a gradation of color and material marks one's progression through the house. These subtle shifts in coloration play against the natural colors and light of the outside, variously seen through oculi, skylights, and the greenhouse roof.

As is evident, layering, stratification, and multiplicity are integral to the structure of the house, and refer back to the experiments I have already described with objects in dialogue and objects within

20 *De Menil House*
Game room.

Right:
21 *De Menil House*
Aerial view from north.

22 *De Menil House*
East facade.

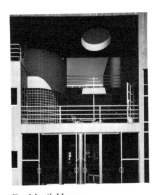

23 *De Menil House*
South facade.

24 *De Menil House*
Roof.

frames (fig. 20). Vertical and horizontal layering, as well as the polar effects of recognition and surprise, are achieved through an interplay of spaces and planes. For example, the guesthouse/garage consciously blocks the major facade of the house, developing a sense of expectation and of the unknown (fig. 21). Its scale mediates between that of the house and that of the site, while its stucco walls recall other uses of the same material on the site. The layering of outdoor planes echoes the layering of outdoor spaces: the volume of the guesthouse/garage building straddles the spaces of the pedestrian and vehicular roads, and the space of the outdoor garden is continued by the interior greenhouse, both an outdoor and an indoor space, followed by the terraces, and capped by the sunscreened deck (figs. 22–24).

In plan, the spatial layering is carried out by the division of the building into four zones: entry, circulation, living, and sun deck, and this *parti* is continued in the roof plan. Exclusive of the study, which "floats" in the greenhouse, the disposition of these zones is essentially traditional. What is unusual, within the evolution of my work, is that the house is defined and closed by four walls rather than two; but what might have resulted in an extremely dense facade is relieved by the glazing of these walls. Thus, the facade is layered by its transparency and echoes the stratification of the plan, articulating places and spaces, providing them with both cohesiveness and identity.

The section of the house is likewise layered. The vertical cuts are complex as a result of the manipulation of various vertical elements. The roof, however, rather than leaving the house cut off at the top, provides a resolution of the section (see fig. 24). It is a major outdoor space within which objects such as a gate and *brise-soleil*

25 *De Menil House*
View of south facade.

26 *De Menil House*
Dining room.

27 *De Menil House*
Living room.

extend the building by a fifth elevation, which is both virtual and real. This roof space is almost another building, a cage or frame, which grows out of the building and intrudes into it (fig. 25). Variations of volume relate to changing ceiling heights and are articulated by strong edges, cornices, materials, and transparent planes.

The final two components of the house, the furnishings and the greenhouse, illustrate further how this project is both a compendium of my work over the past seventeen years as well as a return to the beginning of my practice. They reflect my investigation into the properties of objects and frames superimposed on objects, and my attempt to use this investigation to knit together a composite of plan, section, and facade. The furniture includes a major collection of Austrian Secession pieces, all objects designed by architects (figs. 26, 27). It expresses ideas about its own weight, about the relationship of one piece to another, and about self-definition and a sense of "objectness." Moreover, it engages in a dialogue with the building that frames it. Our use of mahogany in the house intensifies this dialogue, not only by enriching the interiors but by echoing the wood tradition of furniture and cabinetry.

The greenhouse contains the most explicit expression of both horizontal and vertical layering (figs. 28–30). In it, the study is an object that belongs equally to the greenhouse and to the living room. It is also an extension of the major circulation system of the building. The study is an object within another object, the greenhouse; but the greenhouse, though defined by its facades, is glazed. Therefore, the greenhouse as object is also the greenhouse as frame,

223

28 De Menil House
    Greenhouse.

Right:
31 De Menil House
    Southeast facade.

29 De Menil House
    Study.

30 De Menil House
    View of study in greenhouse.

as void. A single space, it is at once interior and exterior, solid and void, object and frame, independent but also incomplete.

My parents' house of 1966 explored ideas about the solid, the void, the rectilinear frame, the object, and the object within the object, and successfully wove these ideas into a coherent composition (fig. 31). Our most recent project explores the same ideas, but with more complexity and with seventeen years of work to refer back to. I hope it will prove to be an equally rich repository of compositional ideas seventeen years hence.

STATEMENT

by Kevin Roche

One of the objectives of the Buell Center, being inaugurated at this celebration, is to provide architects in mid-career an opportunity to pause and review their development. Now that sounds like inviting a downhill skier to pause in mid-flight and consider his exact position. Nevertheless, I will try to address the theme of where I am in my architectural career and to present a review of my work.

Of the sixty buildings I have designed in the last twenty-two years, about half defy categorization—there seems to be no convenient pigeonhole to accommodate them. Of the identifiable buildings, half again seem to be more or less in the framework of the Modern movement; the remainder appear to have been very strongly influenced by the Beaux-Arts tradition. Now that choice of style is not unusual because my education was in the Beaux-Arts. I fled from that education to study in Chicago with Mies van der Rohe, only to discover that Mies's school was an update of the Beaux-Arts tradition; instead of drawing acanthus leaves, we drew bricks, which essentially was the same. So I fled from that too and joined Eero Saarinen. Having worked with Eero, as well as with Charles and Ray Eames, I discovered my definition of Modern architecture, which is (as Charles Eames might have defined it) a total immersion in the substance of the problem in order to arrive at a solution that is based on the specific circumstances. Eames would have put it much more eloquently, I am sure, but his formulation would not have included any formalist overlay at all. What distinguishes Beaux-Arts architecture from Modernist is just this overlay of formalism. Sometimes, of course, there is nothing more than empty formalism in the evolution of a building.

The first group of buildings I will discuss falls more or less into the Modernist tradition, having emerged from a very serious study of nature of the problem and omitting the formalist overlay as much as possible. These buildings show that with a common Modernist point of origin there are many ways, many places to end up. This is not true of their detail or decoration necessarily, but of their generating ideas.

My first example is a suburban office building, the Union Carbide headquarters (fig. 1). The point of office buildings is to house people, people who work in offices. So we begin with the question, "what is an office?" in order to define what an office building is.

*1 Aerial view of Union Carbide
Headquarters
Danbury, Connecticut
Roche, Dinkeloo and Associates,
1976.*

Offices presented a relatively simple problem until the arrival of
the module and movable partition; with these came the notion of
changing partitions overnight, making a small office into a larger
one and vice versa. With this flexibility corporations realized that
they could reward people by changing the size of their office. The
diagram for such an office shows a series of spaces ranging from
ten by ten feet to fifteen by twenty feet, the latter with an attached
toilet, which is a further reward. When you finally reach the top
of the company, you have an office of fifteen by twenty-five feet,
also with an attached toilet. That is the hierarchical system employed in corporations today.

My argument against this was that the chairman of the board and
the mailboy were essentially the same size. If they weren't, then
why didn't the chairman of the board wear an outsized suit and
the mailboy a very small-sized suit? You wear a suit that is appropriate to your physical size, and since physical size is more or less
the same, offices should be more or less the same. The premise is
that a lower executive, a senior executive, and the chairman of the
board, all office workers, are doing the same thing. They are all
shuffling papers, answering telephones, making decisions, and
looking out the window. Thus, I argued in favor of making all the
offices the same size. If we did so, we could eliminate all of the
movable partitions, which tend to be costly anyway. We could also
have simple mechanical systems and simple structural elements.
Furthermore, we would be removing what is, in fact, a rather sore
point with many people who work in offices, making the office
space a good deal more utilitarian.

Much to my surprise, the chairman agreed, and we developed what
we considered an optimal office size and shape. In this optimal
office you can sit at a table, turn around and have a desk behind
you, and conveniently arrange the furniture; this is because the

room is thirteen-and-a-half feet square. It can accommodate three to four people and still serve all office functions. Each office was also provided with windows in this particular plan. We applied all this to the program at hand which specified a low building with a central corridor giving access to the offices. We ended up with a building that was a little over two-and-a-half miles long. Clearly, more work needed to be done.

2 Union Carbide Headquarters

Let us look at another aspect of the organization of the office interior. The ratio of secretarial help to professional help was 1:3. In order not to isolate secretaries from human communication, we grouped two secretaries together, and carried through this pattern in L-shaped units; we also grouped the professional offices, square in shape, together. In the middle we located all those elements necessary to the support of the operation: elevators, stairs, toilets, interior conference rooms, communications center, resource center, and copy machine. It was a building designed essentially for office purposes, but there was too much core and too little office space. We needed additional office space, so we altered the design to incorporate more; we included offices of identical size but different shapes, wrapping around the perimeter and surrounding the central common-use spaces. We pushed this idea a little further and came up with a series of modules lining the perimeter of the building, with access from two major corridors (fig. 2).

3 Union Carbide Headquarters

Another major component of the suburban office building we considered was the automobile. Of course, the American office worker would like very much to be able to drive into his or her office and operate from the automobile. Unfortunately, that simple an approach cannot work, but in this project we did put the parking on the same level as the offices. You could then park within a hundred feet of your office and walk right in.

The building was also made accessible from the ten roadways coming in from the north and ten roadways coming from the south. There are two large parking structures; access to them is achieved by means of two thirty-foot-wide roadways that run right through the building in two locations, separating the parking structure from the office building (fig. 3). The center building houses the front door, lobby, loading docks, cafeteria, medical services, recreational facilities, and so on. This is an entire building uncontaminated by any kind of formal idea, at least as far as possible. The building design grew entirely out of the initial seed of the office arrangement. In a sense, it designed itself.

4, 5 Plans for gate, Central Park Zoo, New York, Kevin Roche, 1982.

In developing the design, we presented thirty different designs for carpets, chairs, tables, work surfaces, light fixtures, artwork, pen and pencil sets—everything. Although it was agreed that the offices would be the same in size, indeed there was no reason that they should be the same in character. Thus, the 3,500 to 4,000 employees

Above, left:
6 E.F. Hutton Building
New York, New York
Roche, Dinkeloo and
Associates, 1980.

Above, right:
7 Model of E. F. Hutton Building.

8 Conoco Inc. Petroleum
Headquarters
Houston, Texas
Roche, Dinkeloo and
Associates, 1972.

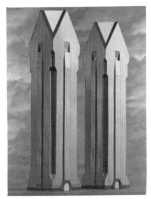

9 Two high-rise buildings
Denver, Colorado
Roche, Dinkeloo and Associates.

who were going to work in this building were each asked to select their own furniture based on the different variations available. In this way they could feel that the design was not being imposed on them.

The outside of the building has awnings over the windows and is sided with large aluminum panels. The site is wooded and slightly sloped and, rather than disrupt the ground water table, we allowed the building to extend out at the highest grade, supported by columns as it projects into the woods. There are no cars on the site except for those in the parking structure. The woods have been restored where they were cut down, and the building nestles into them. The building represents my version of what Modern architecture is about.

I would next like to present a series of studies involving various applications of a particular column design. The first is for a small ceremonial gate at the Central Park Zoo. I was trying to find a simple, inexpensive way to make a column that had a base with a single cut, a brick shaft, and a capital with two simple cuts. The goal was to use a limestone block with a simple chamfer in it as an implied capital, and the same element for a base. I used a collar, located a little further down, to suggest a molding. On top of this collar is a network of cantilevered beams (figs. 4, 5).

In another study of the same element, I wondered, could we, should we, or even dare we, try to make a building out of the form of a column? Well, maybe not. But we could try grouping columns together. I reasoned that since high-rise buildings essentially have nothing to dictate their form and their structure is very straightforward, they can take on almost any image. For the E. F. Hutton building, we took columns and grouped them together to form a sixty-eight-foot-high arcade (figs. 6, 7). Then, for a fifty-five-story Houston high-rise we made the column into the entire building (fig. 8). We also employed the column in two high-rise buildings in Denver (fig. 9); there, instead of being chamfered, it has a setback at the corner, and at the top it peaks to a campanile. It seems that one can start almost anywhere with a column and end up somewhere else.

Above, left:
10 *Private residence.*

Above, right:
11 *General Foods Corporation Headquarters*
Rye, New York
Roche, Dinkeloo and Associates, 1977.

The next set of buildings I will discuss exhibits the Beaux-Arts influences to which I have been subject. These buildings fall into the Beaux-Arts category by virtue of their planning, the formalist approach to their design. In this group, no effort was made to transform Beaux-Arts elements—they were simply incorporated. In one house, designed but never built, I borrowed a Roman plan and a colonnade with a trellised arcade. Doric columns emerge from the cubic forms of a modern architecture to define the shape and cruciform plan of the house. Thus a formalist set of ideas has been overlaid on a very functionalist program.

Another house, built in 1982, has a similarly formalist conception (fig. 10). Entirely symmetrical, it has a moon gate in the center, a traditional symbol of prosperity. The other side of the house also has a very formal elevation. However, I was not able to make this elevation extend the entire length of the house; on the right side a piece of the house peeps out behind the elevation, revealing the architecture behind to be a series of layered walls with trellises between, which describe the surface as the sun moves around.

The final project I would like to describe is an office building completed for General Foods. The lower tier of rectangles in the diagram (fig. 11) represents parking; the upper tier, the office building itself. Since the parking area required more ground space than the office building, we designed a built-in podium. As with the Union Carbide building, the parking lot here was too long, so we made it accordian-shaped.

The axial approach road is for visitors. Contrary to Beaux-Arts tradition, it intersects the center of the building. In a Beaux-Arts building, you would never enter through the middle of the rotunda, but would use the other way instead. The employees enter on the other side of the building. Since the office spaces are atop three levels of parking and there must be some communication with the

ground, stairs run from the center of the main lobby and parking level up to the office concourse. There are four levels of offices above the parking, and a fifth level in the center. To provide the necessary formal sense of entry and departure from the building, visitors drive under the stairs.

This building too is covered with aluminum siding, the kind you can buy in a hardware store. It is a product that is commonly available and in this application was intended not to act as decoration. The panels of the siding cover the columns.

From the inside of the building you can see past the stairs to the entrance roadway across the lake. In the central space, which is also the dining room, you can look down on the mirrored surface of a cafeteria table and see the reflection of the space up above (fig. 12). When you approach from the visitors's entrance, you enter the lobby (fig. 13). In front of you is the receptionist and directly overhead, a distraction: you can see right through the garage, about fifty feet up, to the great central space. And just as you are grappling with this image the receptionist says, "May I help you please?"

EXHIBITION

EXHIBITION
AMERICAN ARCHITECTURE:
INNOVATION AND TRADITION
Co-directors
David G. De Long

Helen Searing

Robert A. M. Stern

James Stewart Polshek
*Dean, The Graduate School of
Architecture and Planning,
Columbia University*

Executive Director
Ann Kaufman

*General Curator
of the Exhibition*
John Zukowsky

Editorial Consultant
Suzanne Stephens

Assistant Editor
Sylvia Lavin

Designer
Heidi Humphrey/H+, New York

The exhibition was made possible by
generous contributions from:
Charter Sponsor
A. Alfred Taubman and the Taubman Co., Inc.

AIA Foundation, College of Fellows Fund
Charrette Corporation
Formica Corporation
Graham Foundation for Advanced Studies
in the Fine Arts

Additional support was provided by the
United States Information Agency.

INTRODUCTION

by Suzanne Stephens

"American Architecture: Innovation and Tradition" is one of the first efforts of Columbia University's Buell Center for the Study of American Architecture to assess the relationship between our architecture and our culture. The purpose of the exhibit is to initiate an investigation of the political, social, and economic determinants of forms as they pertain to geographical regions. Material has been gathered from six different areas of the country—the Northeast, Midwest, South, Southwest, Plains States, and West Coast. This material concentrates on the architectural expression found in vernacular forms, indigenous building methods, and consciously-adopted styles over the last three hundred years or so. The exploration was undertaken to determine the effects of local historical, social, and climatic factors—as well as more perceptible trends worldwide—on American architecture.

In the twentieth century, standardized production, building materials and methods have increasingly created a uniformity in architectural expression. New forms and techniques have been adopted without regard to local circumstance, climate, or culture. They have generated a simplified and homogenized environment in which tradition, place, and regional expression have no role.

Yet, as numerous instances in this show demonstrate, a sense of place and a sense of region has survived or become manifest over time. Since the United States was first founded, architectural expression has never been completely indigenous. It has always represented some form of hybrid between what exists and what is imported and modified according to specific desires, needs, and constraints. Thus while similarities exist across the regions, differences can still be discerned. Those similarities and differences are telling. They need to be investigated by architects who are attempting to create a new architectural expression that takes into account attributes of time and place otherwise lost through the homogenizing forces of marketing and production.

The exhibit in no way attempts a comprehensive history of American architecture, or a survey of all "regional" responses. Each of the curators for the six geographical regions has assembled examples of building types, styles, and settlements that support a particular argument through the medium of the black-and-white photographic essay. * The curators, who represent both the academic and professional communities, were asked to analyze the architectural expression peculiar to their regions according to three scales of environmental expression—the country, the town, and the metropolis. A seventh section, "America as a Region," is also included to address some of those characteristics identifiable to the nation as a whole.

---

*A limited number of the original exhibition photographs appear in this book. Complete lists of illustrations accompany each section.

THE EAST

by Deborah Nevins

The architectural heritage of the Northeast has been shaped by close cultural connections to Europe, the density of its cities, and the length of its seacoast. The land is fertile and natural resources are plentiful. From the earliest days the region's access to inland and coastal water routes spurred manufacture and trading. Adoption of new transportation modes as they evolved—the steam railroad, the elevated urban railroad, the subway, and the airplane—also fostered greater growth. In the twentieth century corporations have been drawn to the Northeast along with banking, advertising, and communications enterprises.

While the region attracted businesses and population swelled as a result of immigration, the density and complexity of northeastern cities have inspired architects and designers to find new solutions to urban problems, such as housing, transportation and work spaces. Working with building technology as it developed, architects evolved new building types to serve the city: the apartment house, the skyscraper, multi-level commercial developments.

The Northeast has consistently been one of the most architecturally influential regions in the U.S.: many of the most prominent figures of American architecture and design have lived and worked here, among them Benjamin Latrobe, Charles Bulfinch, Frank Furness, Henry Hobson Richardson, Stanford White, Frederick Law Olmsted, Eero Saarinen, and Louis Kahn. These architects, supported by sophisticated and wealthy patrons, were quick to incorporate in their work new European developments such as the Palladian mode, the Adam style, the various revival styles of the nineteenth century and the International Style. Americans always transformed these architectural vocabularies into an idiom acceptable to this country's needs, and in the process developed forms uniquely their own.

The region's national influence on architecture owes as much to its architectural schools and periodicals as to its talented architects. The first schools of architecture were established here after the Civil War. The leading architectural periodicals have always been published in New York and Boston, where architectural clubs and societies have also served as forums for the exchange of ideas among practitioners. Even the first museum in the country to have its own department of architecture, the Museum of Modern Art, is located in New York.

From the "saltbox" to the Shingle style house, from the brick mill to the 1920s Art Deco skyscraper, forms have evolved out of particular circumstances, the influence of European examples, and the personal vision of the region's architects, builders and car-penters, inspired by the energy generated in this most densely populated region. From the Baltimore rowhouse to the Manhattan apartment building, from multi-leveled train stations to multi-leveled parks, the East Coast has promoted the evolution of certain types of buildings and urban forms.

THE COUNTRY

Tall mountains, farmland, coastal beaches and islands distinguish the countryside of this region. The rural landscape is marked as much by small groupings of buildings as by isolated houses strung across open country. A village with dwellings grouped around a meetinghouse and farmland beyond was the most common type of settlement in the late eighteenth and early nineteenth centuries. Because of minimal development of rural and agricultural lands in the Northeast after World War II, the countryside retains much of its nineteenth-century character. Only the incursion of highways and commercial architecture rivals the dominance of the older landscape.

The independent congregational churches built by Puritans who settled in New England in the seventeenth century constituted a unique building type. Original to the New World, the type became known as a meetinghouse, fulfilling religious and communal needs for the small town or village in which it was erected. The first meetinghouses were rectangular or square and domestic in scale. They were initially painted in earth tones, but by the eighteenth century, when they were used increasingly for worship, they were usually painted white, and sometimes adorned with a tower to properly announce their religious function.

The term "continuous architecture" describes well the construction of houses and farm buildings as a single entity. Common in farmstead architecture north of New York City, it represents a vernacular tradition developed in response to the cold climate. The typical rectangular barn of the Northeast—the Crook farmstead in Vermont, for example—was of heavy timber frame construction with wood siding. Since barn frames were constructed or "raised" with the help of one's neighbors, a standard method of building was needed and we see little innovation in the designs of these buildings.

Seventeenth-century settlers in the northeastern region came from Sweden and Holland as well as England, although by the 1660s the English were the most numerous. Each group evolved distinct architectural responses to their new circumstances, depending on the materials and techniques available.

The Jethro Coffin House represents the archetypal New England "saltbox" cottage, with an asym-

*Jethro Coffin House, Nantucket, Massachusetts, ca. 1686.
Photo: Jack E. Boucher, courtesy The Library of Congress.*

metrical gable and a long sloping roof line that resembled salt containers of the period. Its wood frame construction, wood shingles, and central chimney also repeated the building patterns of the counties in the eastern part of England from which Puritans had come.

The Dutch colonized the Hudson Valley, Long Island, and the shores of the Delaware, where they evolved two types of buildings—a tall brick house for town, of which only a few original examples survive, and the long one-and-a-half story farmhouse. The Germans, who had settled in Pennsylvania, were also to build with fieldstone in a manner that became identified with the region. The Miller House is typical of Pennsylvania German traditions.

Since the mid-1960s architects have been returning to the forms and materials of northeastern traditional architecture in order to design buildings more suitable to the natural and man-made environment than most Modern movement examples. In particular, the coastline has provided the occasion for their explorations, due both to the scenic value that still remains far from urban growth, and to the growing popularity of second "vacation" homes. Venturi, Rauch and Scott Brown's houses have been innovative in their adaptation of the cottage and Shingle style vocabularies of nearby older structures.

Yet even "modern" architecture can seem to belong to a vernacular idiom, as the house that Gwathmey and Henderson designed in 1967 in Amagansett well illustrates. The architects took the simple closed geometrical forms of the Modern movement, such as the cylinder and the cube, and adapted these configurations to the design of the house. By their use of wood siding and single-pitched roofs they were able to make direct links to traditional barns and houses of the area.

In 1982, Caroline Northcote Sidnam designed a house on the Massachusetts coast that makes even more explicit references in its massing to farmhouses located nearby, as well as to the one-story fishing shacks often seen along the coast.

THE TOWN

The Puritan ideal of grouping public and domestic buildings around an open space or green proved to be a constant force in the development of northern towns. Thoughtfully planned small communities in suburbs and cities of the twentieth century often retain this open space concept, although new suburban development usually ignores its benefits.

A plan of New Haven engraved in 1748 offers a clear example of a northeastern town designed according to prevailing traditions of the seventeenth century. The original plan was drawn up in 1638, and was composed of nine equal squares with farmland adjacent to the town divided into regular plots. At the center of the grid was the open Green. In the earliest phases of the Green's development, meetinghouses, a courthouse, prison, burial ground, and Yale College stood in or on its perimeter. By the end of the century the Green had assumed the character it has today: it was split down the middle, and planted with elms. The three churches that now border the Green were added during the early nineteenth century.

Like so much eighteenth- and nineteenth-century American architecture, the First Congregational Church built in 1812–1815 on the Green was based on an English model. In this case the model—James Gibbs's St. Martin-in-the-Fields in London of 1726— was an especially popular one. Construction of the New Haven church was supervised by Ithiel Town, who became one of the leading American architects of his time and who would design the imposing Greek

First Congregational Church, New Haven, Connecticut. Asher Benjamin, 1815. Photo: Courtesy New Haven Colony Historical Society.

Revival State Capitol on the Green in 1827. The Greek Revival style was favored for public buildings. In the style's association with the democracy of ancient Greece and the nineteenth-century Greek wars for independence, Americans found a model for their aspirations.

Nevertheless, by the time New Haven's City Hall was built across the Green from the Capitol in 1861, High Victorian Gothic architecture had become the popular style. Designed by Henry Austin, the city hall building is striking, with its dark brownstone polychromed surfaces and powerful massing. Later, in 1908, Cass Gilbert designed the Beaux-Arts Public Library on the Green. The Green's assortment of different historical styles offers a splendid statement about the constantly shifting taste in the design of buildings with symbolic weight. Fortunately, twentieth-century redevelopment of New Haven did not tamper with this extraordinary space.

Near the Green is Yale University, an exemplary model of town planning and architecture applied to the educational institution. Instead of organizing its buildings around one large green, the university has used smaller greens, courts, and mews, creating a dense and variegated tissue connecting the small-scale buildings to each other. This fabric was largely the work of James Gamble Rogers, whose collegiate Gothic vocabulary suited the planning ideal reminiscent of Oxford and Cambridge.

The style and configuration of the buildings was further enhanced by the landscape design of Beatrix Farrand, who was well-known for similar work on other campuses. She planted the spaces with sprays of green vines and climbing plants to accent rather than obscure buildings. Trees and shrubs were chosen that would have visual interest during all phases of the year.

Avon Old Farms School near Hartford, by architect Theodate Pope Riddle, was inspired by planning concepts similar to those used at Yale. The architectural vocabulary is drawn from medieval vernacular prototypes. Influenced by the Arts and Crafts movement, Riddle employed late medieval tools and traditional building techniques in the construction.

The growth of industrialization in the Northeast before the Civil War was concentrated particularly in New England, where a thriving textile industry was the first to make use of the advanced techniques of mass production. The buildings housing the manufacturing were often constructed of brick, although the Durfee Mill of 1872 was built of granite local to the Fall River site. Here window trim painted white further distinguishes the building from its more somber brick counterparts.

The expansion of manufacturing and shipping that fostered the growth of towns and small cities also promoted the construction of residential townhouses and rowhouses to accommodate the burgeoning middle classes. Architects and their clients looked to the London townhouse as the model, but soon evolved local variations. In Baltimore, a distinctive type of housing developed for the middle and lower-middle classes—a very simple brick rowhouse of two to three stories in height, with marble steps. One variation is larger in size and includes a marble stoop of four or five steps.

Our legacy of eighteenth- and early nineteenth-century domestic architecture in the Northeast is visually stunning. Much of this building fabric still exists in towns from Maryland to Maine. Its presence has provided inspiration to architects in periods before and after the reign of Modern movement architecture in the 1940s and 1950s. This heritage of forms has been transposed to American suburbs to imply solidity, tradition, and elegance.

By the eighteenth century English culture and tradition dominated the Northeast. Designers looked to English pattern books for models for the elevations, plans, and details for their buildings. The standard motifs used in these books were themselves inspired by the architecture of the English Palladian movement. Yet within this stylistic homogeneity many local variations became apparent. These evolved from regional differences in materials, cultural influences, and seventeenth-century building traditions. The projecting central entrance bay at Cliveden and the flattening of this entrance motif in McKinstry Manor recall Palladio, as does the second-story window over the front door in the Vermont house. Nonetheless, both houses are constructed in materials of their areas: stone for Pennsylvania and wood for New England.

The wood-carved ornament of the mantle in the Hawkes House is also inspired by Classical motifs. The delicacy and slenderness of the decorative details is indicative of the Adam style drawn from English precedents, which became important here at the turn of the nineteenth century. The mantle illustrates the sensitive approach often taken in the American adaptation of architectural elements.

Architects of the nineteenth century received stimuli from vernacular idioms of particular regions. While the Church of the Redeemer is not one of Frank Furness's better-known works, it does illustrate the interest in local building traditions that prevails in some of his more individualistic work. In this building, designed in 1879, one sees the sharp juxtaposition of heavy masses and polychromed surfaces executed within the framework of the Victorian Ruskinian architecture characteristic of his other buildings. The Church of the Redeemer is particularly "regional" in its use of the fieldstone found in Pennsylvania German architecture of the seventeenth and eighteenth centuries.

The relationship of architecture to its natural setting has been a major preoccupation of northeastern architects, particularly in settled but still bucolic areas. An experiential concern combined with a platonic attitude towards architecture underlies the design of Philip Johnson's Glass House in Connecticut. The connection to nature is achieved by the unobstructed view offered through the transparent glass wall. The house and its siting on a hill overlooking a pond are reminiscent of historic descriptions of the ideal classical villa where the elevated view, water, temple and grove are all brought (sublimely) together. Perhaps Johnson is making an intellectual gesture towards Jeffersonian Neoclassicism as well.

As polemical—if not more so—in its influence was the Modernist wood house that Walter Gropius and Marcel Breuer designed in 1937 in Lincoln, Massachusetts. Gropius, the former head of the Bauhaus, had emigrated to the States in 1937 to take over the architecture department at Harvard's Graduate School of Design. In partnership with Breuer, another Bauhaus-trained architect and teacher, he designed this house which embodied the transparency, light, and rational construction typical of Bauhaus ideas. Quite unlike a Shingle style predecessor in its simple tight plan, the house nevertheless responded to its site by facing south toward light and view, and to local construction techniques by the architects's insistence on using only material easily available to the building industry. A projecting canopy of louvers and a screen porch shield inhabitants from too much sun, and a fieldstone base ties the rectilinear wood house more closely to the ground.

Louis Kahn was always considered a "modern" architect who believed in the articulation of a building's function and the clear expression of materials and structure. In this work, however, he also demonstrates his respect for archetypal forms of vernacular building and Classical models. The open air Trenton Bath House he designed in 1956 is one of his least expensive projects but a very clear-cut example of his attitude toward architecture and the direction his thinking was to take. Based on cross-axial planning and topped by symmetrically arranged hipped roofs resting on hollow concrete block piers enclosing mechanical equipment, the Bath House is a striking example of Kahn's ability to create a sense of grandeur, monumentality, and timelessness through simple materials and open spaces.

Many architects today receive commissions for new houses in quite settled and sometimes quite dense residential areas in the Northeast. Residents of those areas greatly value privacy and natural vegetation. In order to accommodate these considerations architects often incorporate elements of more traditional domestic architecture into their new designs. Painted wood lattice, a common but distinctive element used in nineteenth- and early twentieth-century houses to screen off back pantries or permit privacy on front porches, has been exploited by contemporary architects for various purposes. Susana Torre, for example, explored the formal and functional possibilities of latticework, which she uses to echo the outline of a gabled house as well as to afford privacy to the inhabitants. Lattice, treated as an overlay to a box-like modern house, becomes a metaphor for rusticity and domesticity in the house Joel Levinson de-signed in 1972 in a suburb of Philadelphia.

The 1876 Exposition in Philadelphia, commemorating the 100th year of American independence, inspired an interest in America's Colonial past. Both the seventeenth and eighteenth centuries served as architectural inspiration to practitioners. Not surprisingly, the influence was greatest in New England, which contained the largest number of extant Colonial-style buildings. A number of architects, including the firm of McKim, Mead & White, looked closely at the seventeenth-century examples to develop their approach to domestic building. The style they developed, now known as the "Shingle style," was characterized by seemingly informally arranged spaces of different sizes, irregular roof lines, and large porches. As their Isaac Bell House of 1883 shows, the composition was held tightly together by a continuous skin composed of wood shingles wrapping around a wood frame.

The influence of the Exposition often led to fairly explicit expressions of vocabulary of the Colonial and Federal period, as seen in the projecting entrance bay ornamented with dentils and scrolled pediments of the Cary house of 1882 by Sturgis and Brigham. The general characteristics of the Shingle style—the flow of spaces and the manipulation of forms to respond to view and characteristics of the site—marked a departure in American architecture.

A cottage in Rhinebeck, New York, with its gable roof, capacious porch and Gothic tracery, is typical of A. J. Davis's designs, which drew on the picturesque style. The picturesque had a widespread influence during the mid-nineteenth century, due not just to Davis, but also to his friend, landscape architect and critic A. J. Downing. Downing's book *The Architecture of Country Houses,* advocating a clear expression of wood structure and asymmetrical planning, was illustrated in part by Davis.

The library was a distinct building type that the Northeast developed into a particular architectural response suited to its towns and suburbs. It was required to be both monumental and domestic in scale to seem "important" while still fitting in with the small scale of the residential setting. As the Crane Memorial Library in Quincy, Massachusetts, illustrates, Henry Hobson Richardson was a master at achieving this sort of balance, using a Romanesque-inspired vocabulary of forms as elements and emphasizing the massive qualities of stone. The influence of this style, known as "Richardsonian Romanesque," was enormous in the Northeast and soon appeared in domestic as well as public buildings. Even early skyscrapers were often designed in the Richardsonian Romanesque style.

THE METROPOLIS
The region's several metropolises—Philadelphia, Washington, and Boston among them—each have their own special character. But the one city that comes to mind when one thinks of a "metropolis"

is, of course, New York. As a response to the density dictated by New York's island location, innovative urban forms have reached their apotheosis here: the apartment house, the multi-level skyscraper, the naturalistic urban park.

Historians have come to recognize New York as the birthplace of the skyscraper—that is, the tall building with passenger elevators and steel frame construction—even though Chicago was equally important in the development of this type. The New York skyscraper achieved distinction in the early part of the century by its emphasis on the pedestrian entry level and lobby and an ornamented top, which frequently took the shape of a campanile spire or stepped-back ziggurat. This configuration was reinforced by the 1917 zoning law that legislated a setback massing derived from a complex formula related to the width of the street. The goal to allow sunlight and air to reach lower-level buildings and the street would foster the development of the tower as a distinct form with a base, a middle, and a top "scraping" the sky. Before the International Style's rectangular box with flat top took hold, several quintessential New York buildings came to symbolize the skyscraper in full flower: William Van Alen's Chrysler Building of 1930 and Shreve, Lamb and Harmon's Empire State Building of 1931. Today architects such as Philip Johnson and John Burgee are returning to buildings with distinctive tops and bases to recapture that past glory, as can be seen in their A.T. & T. Headquarters.

In Philadelphia the firm of Howe and Lescaze was to create a different kind of skyscraper, expressing the International Style vocabulary of planar rectilinear forms and taut materials without ornamental effects. Their P.S.F.S. Building of 1932 soon became a landmark and influenced succeeding skyscraper construction in that city and elsewhere. The building's shifting scale of elements and the variety of materials used, combine to create a kind of ornament, but a new and more abstracted one.

More than forty years later, in 1975, Philadelphia architects Mitchell/Giurgola developed this theme in a different manner. The architects built a new high-rise in the modern idiom behind the nineteenth-century Egyptian Revival facade of an earlier building, using it as a false front. The conjunction of elements and the articulation of parts breaks down the overall massing of the building and ties it to adjacent buildings.

The American Beaux-Arts period produced imposing public spaces in the Northeast, such as Boston Public Library, the Metropolitan Museum and Grand Central Station, among others. These places allowed all sectors of society to experience the grandeur of architecture. New York's now demolished Pennsylvania Station by McKim, Mead & White still ranks in memory as one of the most inspiring of these spaces. The proportions and coffered vaults of the station's ceiling recalled the Baths of Caracalla: these eminently functional great public rooms provided the

Empire State Building, New York. Shreve, Lamb and Harmon, 1931. Photo: Dorothy Alexander, courtesy Skyline.

visitor with an awe-inspiring first experience of New York City.

The density and narrowness of Manhattan Island inspired a great deal of creative effort on the part of architects and engineers who had to work with the needs of traffic and pedestrian circulation and the functional requirements of a complex society. At Grand Central Terminal, the architects placed hotels and office buildings over the tracks, the terminal itself, and the city's subway system. They developed underground passageways connecting transit lines with stores, restaurants and commercial space in this multi-level interior city within a city.

Planners of Rockefeller Center in the 1930s, led by Raymond Hood, took their cue from Grand Central. A grouping of freestanding typically modern skyscrapers surrounding open space form a coherent urban ensemble at street level. Beneath is a multi-level base, connecting the buildings, containing interior streets lined with shops and restaurants and providing access to the subway system.

Activity at many levels was the hallmark of another great urban space—Central Park. The naturalistic look of the park was intended to offer relief from the urban environment for city dwellers. The designers, Frederick Law Olmsted and Calvert Vaux, addressed the problem of transportation by providing separate paths for horses, carriages, and strollers. Whenever two modes of transportation crossed, one route was placed a level above the other.

The density of New York City and the diverse needs of its inhabitants have prompted the development of certain specialized building types. The Alwyn Court, with its interior organization around a central sky-lit court, recalls the Parisian residential prototype, but here executed with a more compact *parti*. The Alwyn Court's exterior was particularly of its place and time. Terracotta became a common material for architectural ornament after 1880. In Alwyn Court it is used to extravagantly clothe the building in a dense fabric of heraldic, Gothic, and Renaissance motifs, frequently used in New York apartment houses.

Most cities in the Northeast have managed to keep nineteenth- and early twentieth-century townhouses intact. New York has furthered the development of the townhouse type with outstanding updated examples. One of the first was William Lescaze's own house designed in the International Style in 1934. Its scale and vertical linear quality helped it to fit in with the surrounding environs.

The grid-like opaque curtain wall facade of Paul Rudolph's dark brown steel and glass townhouse in Manhattan articulates its actual structure. Because of its coloration and subtle detailing, the building is an extremely elegant and unobtrusive object in the midst of turn-of-the-century landmark townhouses.

In the 1970s Stern and Hagmann renovated a Park Avenue townhouse in the "postmodern" style. The house follows the traditional townhouse *parti* with an office at the ground floor and a living room above. The facade's flattened columns recall the classically-inspired ornament of the adjacent apartment building, while the alignment of the "capitals" of the columns with the similarly flattened quoins next door relates this building to the traditional idiom in an appropriately referential but individual manner.

THE EAST

Introduction
1. Cable Screw Wire, trade card, c. 1875. Photo: courtesy The New-York Historical Society.

2. Mariners Cove clam chowder, 1983. Photo: Steven Lewis.

3. East Corinth, Vermont. Photo: courtesy VT Travel Division.

4. View of New Haven Green in 1800, oil on canvas. William Giles Munson, c. 1830. Photo: courtesy New Haven Colony Historical Society.

5. Aerial view of Manhattan, 1948. Photo: Ch. Miller, courtesy The New-York Historical Society.

Country
1. Rockingham Meetinghouse, Rockingham, Vermont. General Fuller, master builder, 1801. Photo: courtesy Vermont Division for Historic Preservation.

2. Thomas Crook House, Corinth, Vermont, c. 1800, barn and wings, c. 1855. Photo: courtesy Vermont Division for Historic Preservation.

3. Jethro Coffin House, Nantucket, Massachusetts, c. 1686. Photo: Jack E. Boucher, courtesy The Library of Congress.

4. Miller House, Millbach, Pennsylvania, 1752. Photo: Cervin Robinson, courtesy The Library of Congress.

5. Trubek and Wislocki Houses, Nantucket, Massachusetts. Venturi and Rauch, 1973. Photo: courtesy Venturi, Rauch and Scott Brown.

6. Gwathmey Residence and Studio, Amagansett, New York. Gwathmey-Henderson, 1967. Photo: David Hirsch.

7. Plan, Gwathmey Residence and Studio, Amagansett, New York. Gwathmey-Henderson, 1967. Photo: courtesy Gwathmey/Siegel.

8. Summer Residence, West Harbor, Massachusetts. Caroline Northcote Sidnam, 1982. Photo: Robert Levin.

Town
1. A Plan of the Town of New Haven in 1748. William Lyon publisher, T. Kensett, engraver, 1896. Photo: courtesy The New-York Historical Society.

2. First Congregational Church, New Haven, Connecticut. Asher Benjamin, 1815. Photo: courtesy New Haven Colony Historical Society.

3. Connecticut State Capitol, New Haven, Connecticut. Ithiel Town, 1827 (demolished 1889). Photo: courtesy New Haven Colony Historical Society.

4. City Hall, New Haven, Connecticut. Henry Austin, 1861. Photo: George Bradley, courtesy New Haven Colony Historical Society.

5. New Haven Public Library, New Haven, Connecticut. Cass Gilbert, 1908. Photo: courtesy New Haven Colony Historical Society.

6. Branford Court, Yale University, New Haven, Connecticut. James Gamble Rogers, 1917, landscaping, Beatrix Farrand, 1923–1946. Photo: courtesy Yale University.

7. Avon Old Farms School, near Hartford, Connecticut. Theodate Pope Riddle, 1909. Photo: ©Laura Rosen.

8. Durfee Mills, Fall River, Massachusetts, c. 1872. Photo: Jack E. Boucher, courtesy The Library of Congress.

9. Rowhouses, Baltimore, Maryland, 19th century. Photo: courtesy Baltimore Department of Housing and Community Development.

10. Cliveden, Germantown, Pennsylvania. Chief Justice Benjamin Chew, designer, 1767. Photo: Wayne Andrews, courtesy Avery Library, Columbia University.

11. McKinstry Manor, Bethel, Vermont. Joseph Emerson, builder, c. 1805. Photo: Eric Gilbertson, courtesy Vermont Division for Historic Preservation.

12. Fireplace detail, General Benjamin Hawkes House, Salem, Massachusetts, early 19th century. Photo: courtesy The Library of Congress.

13. Church of the Redeemer, Philadelphia, Pennsylvania. Frank Furness, 1879. Photo: courtesy The Library of Congress.

14. Crane Memorial Library, Quincy, Massachusetts. Henry Hobson Richardson, 1882. Photo: Wayne Andrews, courtesy Avery Library, Columbia University.

15. Jewish Community Center Bath House, Trenton, New Jersey. Louis I. Kahn, 1956. Photo: John Ebstel.

16. Plan, Jewish Community Center Bath House, Trenton, New Jersey. Louis I. Kahn, 1956. Drawing: courtesy Ann Kaufman.

17. Isaac Bell Jr. Residence, Newport, Rhode Island. McKim, Mead & White, 1883. Photo: Wayne Andrews, courtesy Avery Library, Columbia University.

18. Plan, Isaac Bell Jr. Residence, Newport, Rhode Island. McKim, Mead & White, 1883. Drawing: courtesy Ann Kaufman.

19. Cary Residence, Cambridge, Massachusetts. Sturgis and Brigham, 1882. Photo: Soule Art Photo Co., c. 1893, courtesy The Society for the Preservation of New England Antiquities.

20. Henry Delamater Residence, Rhinebeck, New York. Alexander Jackson Davis, 1844. Photo: Wayne Andrews, courtesy Avery Library, Columbia University.

21. Gropius House, Lincoln, Massachusetts. Walter Gropius and Marcel Breuer, 1937. Photo: Robert Damora.

22. Lattice detail, Clark House, Southampton, New York. Susana Torre, 1981. Photo: courtesy Susana Torre.

23. Glass House, New Canaan, Connecticut. Philip Johnson, 1949. Photo: courtesy Philip Johnson.

24. Arbor House, Philadelphia. Joel Levinson, 1972. Photo: Lawrence Williams.

Metropolis

1. Aerial view of Manhattan, 1930s. Photo: Richard Wurts, courtesy Municipal Art Society.

2. Chrysler Building, New York. William Van Alen, 1930. Photo: ©Laura Rosen.

3. Empire State Building, New York. Shreve, Lamb and Harmon, 1931. Photo: Dorothy Alexander, courtesy *Skyline*.

4. AT&T Headquarters, New York. Johnson and Burgee, 1983. Photo: courtesy Cervin Robinson.

5. The Philadelphia Saving Fund Society Building, Philadelphia. Howe and Lescaze, 1932. Photo: courtesy the Philadelphia Saving Fund Society.

6. Penn Mutual Building, Philadelphia. Mitchell/Giurgola Architects, 1975. Photo: Rollin LaFrance.

7. Elevation detail, Penn Mutual Building, Philadelphia. Mitchell/Giurgola Architects, 1975. Photo: Rollin LaFrance.

8. Pennsylvania Station, New York. McKim, Mead & White, 1910 (demolished 1963). Photo: L.H. Dreyer, courtesy Avery Library, Columbia University.

9. Grand Central Terminal, New York. Warren and Wetmore, Reed and Stem, 1912. Photo: Municipal Archives.

10. Aerial view of Rockefeller Center, New York. Reinhard and Hofmeister, Corbett, Harrison and MacMurray, Hood, Godley and Fouilhoux, 1933. Photo: courtesy Rockefeller Center.

11. Central Park, New York. Frederick Law Olmsted and Calvert Vaux, c. 1898. Photo: Deborah Nevins.

12. Alwyn Court, New York, Harde and Short, 1909. Photo: Peter Maus.

13. William Lescaze House, New York. William Lescaze, 1934. Photo: Mary Bachman.

14. Townhouse, New York. Paul Rudolph, 1970. Photo: courtesy ESTO.

15. Townhouse, New York. Stern and Hagmann, 1975. Photo: Ed Stoecklein.

THE SOUTH

by Gerald Allen

The South is not in the south at all. Relative to the configuration of the rest of the United States, the only thing to which it lies truly south is what southerners still call "the North"—New England and the mid-Atlantic states. For many southerners this has been a sufficient definition of their region: the South is the place unlike "the North."

In actual fact, the South's cultural lineage has a much broader frame of reference. It extends back and spreads over five different sources—the original Indian culture, the culture of the Africans imported as slaves, and the cultures of the Spanish, French, and English settlers. In the sixteenth century, Florida was settled by the Spanish and the lower Mississippi Valley by the French; the rest of the region was settled by the English, beginning very early in the seventeenth century. All of these peoples have shaped the South, but none more so than the English. Indeed most of the South's character results from that culture being gradually imprinted onto all of the others.

The original English colonies were Virginia, North Carolina, South Carolina, and Georgia. West Virginia and Tennessee were formed out of Virginia and North Carolina, Alabama and Mississippi from Georgia. Louisiana was acquired from France in 1803, and Florida from Spain in 1810–1819. In this process, the predominant "Englishness" was bent, enriched, and reshaped as it came to terms with the ideals and customs of other cultures. It was reshaped, too, by the climate and the economy of the region.

Out of all these influences developed that complex of qualities called "southernness." During the nineteenth and twentieth centuries this was thought of by most southerners—with a mixture of pride and defensiveness—as something to be understood, even prized, in comparison to the presumed national norm. Until well into the twentieth century, that norm was set largely by the image of the northeastern United States.

Unlike most northern states, the South remained an essentially agrarian society for three hundred years after European colonization. Also unlike the North, much of the South possesses a temperate climate, benign at best, hot and soporific at worst. Finally, the South is imbued with a mood and a feeling at once elegant and somber. Its people have a demeanor as genteel as the climate is gentle and as urbane as its finest urban creations, Charleston and Savannah.

What kind of architecture did the southern character produce? Using materials and forms available elsewhere, it produced, first of all, an urbane architecture. The South is a region of notably fine towns, but even in rural buildings southern architects have seemed determined to produce an architecture that is ordered, mannerly and—in the case of large plantations like Stratford Hall and institutions like the University of Virginia—actually urban on a small scale. Southern architecture also makes use of a host of memorable strategies to adapt itself to the climate of the region—the front porch being one splendid example. Such strategies for dealing practically with the weather also incorporate a cultural vision of a proper lifestyle: the front porch is as much a social as a climatological invention.

One realizes that southern architecture, like the culture it reflects, is the product not just of necessity but also of preference. It is a mixture of the determined and the maintained. Climate, terrain and, indeed, history *determine* part of its character. Other elements of the character are *maintained* by the will of the region's people.

And so the architecture of the South has sequentially reflected every major development of the nation at large, but in its own peculiarly polished mirror. As a result the area has produced an architecture unique for two things—its affability and openness towards the climate and the land, and its genuine urbanity, a communal acceptance of what is given, tempered, toughened, and maintained out of veneration and desire.

THE COUNTRY

The genius of southern architects, builders, and planners in making towns spilled over into the country, producing a rural architecture that is often urbane in character and urban in form.

From the side facing the Potomac River, Mount Vernon, designed by an anonymous architect in the late eighteenth century, appears to be one single, stately

The Riverfront of Mount Vernon, Fairfax County, Virginia, 1785. Photo: Gerald Allen.

structure. But the site plan reveals what Mount Vernon really is: an urbane little working community that is like a small town, with kitchens, gardens, storehouses, shops, stables, and slaves' quarters, all arranged around a sward of lawn that serves as a village green for the plantation.

Originally outside the town of Charlottesville, the University of Virginia is a town in itself. In his design for the University, Thomas Jefferson, America's most famous anti-urbanist, showed himself to be a true southerner, easily capable of creating an urban fabric of distinction. Through his scholarly interpretation of Roman buildings—shown in the Rotunda, which he adapted in 1826 from the Pantheon—Jefferson singlehandedly transcended *and* helped to further the Greek Revival in America. The site plan is similar to that of Mount Vernon, although it was doubtless based on the rational eighteenth century plans Jefferson had seen while he was ambassador to France.

Oak Alley in Louisiana illustrates the Southern talent for borrowing a style used elsewhere and transforming it into something especially local. With its high colonnade, the house assumes the Greek Revival style that was popular throughout the United States in the early and mid-nineteenth century. The colonnade is also, however, the familiar Southern front porch—made up of two floors in this case. And the building itself, opening onto a long alley vaulted over with Live Oak trees dripping with Spanish moss, is the very essence of the Mississippi plantation house.

Simpler and smaller than the great eighteenth-century plantation houses of Virginia and South Carolina, and also much more common, were farmhouses like Rock Castle in Tennessee. Made of precisely fitted but rough-hewn stone, it reflects, in its double-hung windows, classically inspired details and symmetrical facade centered on a pedimented portico, the ideals of Georgian English architecture.

Even humble farmhouses like the John Ross House in north Georgia show, by their overall massing and composition, a common ancestry with Colonial architecture in New England. The long, characteristically Southern front porch and the absence of most architectural detail link this house to thousands still existing today in the rural South.

Longwood, near Natchez, was designed by the Philadelphia architect and pattern-book writer Samuel Sloan in an "Oriental" mode, one of the succession of revivals that swept through American architecture in the middle of the nineteenth century. Longwood indicates the shift away from traditional plantation-style houses at the time that the economic and ethical bases for plantation life were being challenged in the Civil War. Construction of Longwood was interrupted by the war, and the house was never completed.

Biltmore, the South's grandest country house, also by far the biggest single-family house in America, was designed in 1888 by two leading figures of the day—the architect Richard Morris Hunt and the landscape architect Frederick Law Olmsted. Built for George Washington Vanderbilt, the house adapts motifs of the French Renaissance to recall the chateaux of the Loire Valley. The plan shows that the house is also based on a freer version of academic French axial planning. In the tradition of previous southern plantation houses, this was a working estate, but only nominally: the resources for building it came from industrial wealth accumulated elsewhere.

In the twentieth century, the process of dissociating fine estates from actual farming operations, as seen at Biltmore House, became almost complete. Houses like Ca'd'Zan, built in 1925–1926, and the Deering House, built in 1962 in Florida, were intended as tranquil retreats from work and other public activities. Ca'd'Zan, which was the home of the circus entrepreneur John Ringling, is designed in an exotic and free Venetian Gothic mode. The Deering House, with its pure planar surfaces and walls of transparent glass, exemplifies the sort of modern architecture popularized in the middle of the twentieth century.

Also modern in spirit is Frank Lloyd Wright's asymmetrical plan for Florida Southern College of 1938, which, like the University of Virginia, is conceived as a small village. Covered walkways for protection from the sun connect the buildings and lead to a lake on the right and a fountain on the left.

The South has always been reasonably open to new architectural developments, and thus contains as complete a catalogue of American architectural history as any other region. But what the South has always welcomed even more warmly are restatements of tried-and-true architectural themes, as in the extremely simple but elegant and richly detailed stable for thoroughbred horses at Gainesway Farm, in Lexington. The buildings were erected in 1981, but like the John Ross House in Georgia, they seem almost undatable.

THE TOWN

Crops produced on plantations and farms initially were traded in places like Norfolk, Wilmington, Savannah, Charleston, Mobile, and New Orleans—small urban centers that had sprung up at the mouths of navigable rivers. As the South developed, these were joined by other market centers further inland. Inland and coastal waterways were the lifespring of all early southern towns, permitting farm products to be taken to market and traded for goods manufactured elsewhere. The photograph of Savannah in 1864 shows its wharfs. In the background is the Savannah River, which forms the border between Georgia and South Carolina. Savannah's version of the gridded city plan is unique in the United States: a series of squares intersect some but not all of the main streets. The plan is thought to have been designed by James Oglethorpe, the Englishman who founded the town in 1733.

Southern architects, planners, and builders knew how to make livable towns as well as, if not better than, their counterparts throughout America. For all its rural and agricultural characteristics, the South was and in many places still is a region of fine towns. Charlestonians are fond of recalling the comments of French essayist Jean de Crèvecoeur, who wrote in 1782 that Charleston was the "center of the beau monde," and that Europeans were "surprised" at the "elegance" of its houses. Settings like the stair hall of the Nathaniel Russell House, graced by its beautiful stairway, help substantiate such opinions.

The illustrations of two houses in Charleston show the characteristically local type known as the "single" house. Set sideways on deep lots, these houses have long porches facing private lawns that separate them from adjacent houses. The front doorways lead not to the inside, but to long porches or "piazzas" usually with two and sometimes three levels.

In the second quarter of the nineteenth century, the Greek Revival style began to manifest itself in southern towns. A very early example embodying this style in a stark and almost abstract way is Charleston architect Robert Mills' Fireproof Building of 1827. The North Carolina State Capitol designed by Ithiel Town, A.J. Davis, and David Paton, a team of architects who worked mainly in New York and New England, is of a slightly later date and more somber and weighty in feeling.

Another version of Greek Revival architecture is St. Paul's Church in Richmond, designed in 1844–1845 by Thomas S. Stewart. In this case the exterior is elegantly slender while the interior is in a latter-day version of English Baroque. The Episcopal Church in the United States is said to consist of a "high" church, a "low" church, and a "Virginia" church. This church, which originally had a pulpit as its focus, thus had something in common with traditional New England meeting houses. The austerity of the design was subsequently modified in late nineteenth-century renovations by Louis Comfort Tiffany, who provided an altar.

A refined Egyptian Revival style was chosen for the First Presbyterian Church in Nashville by William Strickland—an architect more famous for his classical designs for the Treasury Building in Washington and the Tennessee State Capitol. Strickland's Egyptian motifs of 1851 were elaborated in subsequent renovations to the church later in the nineteenth century. The second and third rows of Egyptian columns are painted on the wall in false perspective.

The photograph of Charleston in ruins in 1864 shows how the South's physical fabric, like its pride, was deeply wounded by its defeat in the "War for Southern Independence." This event had two interesting consequences for southern architecture. Newer, inland towns with ongoing economic viability—like Richmond and Atlanta—were rebuilt and thus contain rich collections of late nineteenth and early twentieth-century buildings. Older towns along the coast,

Elm Street, Lumberton, North Carolina, early 20th century. Photo: Gerald Allen.

like Charleston and Savannah, slipped into an economic and social slumber. Ironically, it was this process, as much as recent preservation and restoration efforts, that allowed them to remain splendid examples of antebellum urbanity.

Elm Street in the small North Carolina community of Lumberton is an example of the South's early twentieth-century version of the livable town. It effectively incorporates the quality Frederick Law Olmsted deemed essential to satisfactory places of residence: "good outgoings." Part of its coherence and beauty comes from a gradual transition from tree-shaded public spaces to private domestic realms. The street and sidewalk are public; the front lawns are private, but just barely so. The porches are more private still, but provide the inhabitants of the houses with a view of the passing scene. These distinctions are delicately drawn, and doubtless require or, equally, reflect a society with a similarly delicate sense of decorum.

Modern architecture, which first proposed radical new principles of town planning, has more recently begun to turn once again to regional traditions and regional vernacular architecture. A small dental office in a transitional neighborhood of Spanish Revival houses in West Palm Beach, Florida, shows how old-fashioned forms are now being recaptured in new buildings, albeit in a pared-down and abstracted way.

THE METROPOLIS

When railroads were built in the nineteenth century, commerce shifted to cities like Richmond, Charlotte, Columbia, Atlanta, Nashville, and Birmingham. It was mainly in the areas around these towns that manufacturing began to develop as an important alternative to farming. In the twentieth century, several such places, including Atlanta and more recently Miami, have developed into true metropolises of near total economic diversity.

Jefferson Hotel, Richmond, Virginia, Carrere and Hastings, 1895, and Peebles & Ferguson, 1901. Photo: Richard Cheek.

The Jefferson Hotel in Richmond, a splendid, rambunctious building designed by well-known New York architects Carrere and Hastings in 1895, is a fine example of the commercial tone of the post-Civil War southern city. The stairway in the background is said to be the model for the one that Rhett threw Scarlett down in the film *Gone With the Wind*. Whether or not this is true, the crassness and sentimentality of the room would certainly suit the occasion.

Main Street Station in Richmond was designed in a Romanesque style by Wilson, Harris, and Richardson in 1901. It is a straightforward example of a type of monumental architecture common throughout the United States in the late nineteenth century. Like the Jefferson Hotel, it provides a clear sense of the tone of a reviving, post-Civil War southern city.

Myers Park and the surrounding streets in Charlotte are based on prototypes like Frederick Law Olmsted's plan for Riverside, Illinois, executed more than half a century before. The district consists of broad curving double avenues, vaulted over with trees, from which smaller two-lane streets branch out. Almost completely intact, and graced by a particularly fine and flourishing stand of trees, this is one of the finest extant examples of the classic suburban plan in the United States.

The Academy of Medicine in Atlanta that Philip Trammell Shutze designed in 1940 is a late example of the perfectly correct, perfectly academic Classical building. During the twentieth century, traditional (as opposed to modern) architecture seems to have survived longer in the south than in the rest of the United States. Indeed it still flourishes in many southern cities today, where some builders can still turn out a good "Colonial" church or house on request.

The Callaway House in LaGrange, a twentieth-century southern mansion built on a site that originally contained a nineteenth-century formal garden, demonstrates the re-revival of classical themes. The

house, designed by Hal Hentz and Neel Reid in 1916, was inspired by the work of the well-known New York architect Charles Platt.

The State Fair Arena in Raleigh erected in 1950 was intended to be a particularly pure and daring instance of modern architecture's fascination with structure and its expression. The Arena is made up of two interlocking concrete parabolas held up by the weight of the roof slung between them, with outside walls hanging from the parabolas and a functioning exhibition area nestled inside. Practicality compromised purity, however, and the outside walls actually do carry some weight.

The North Carolina National Bank branch in Charlotte addresses the problem of drive-in banking with a design inspired, like much of the architecture of the 1960s, by the 45-degree angle. In the crystal clarity of its concept and its consistently elegant execution, though, it matches the work of slightly earlier southern architects like Neel Reid and Philip Trammell Shutze.

The Atlantis, a dazzling new 20-story condominium, shows that postmodernism, like other styles in American architectural history, has arrived in the South—in this case Miami, which in recent decades has transformed itself from mainly a resort town into an international city. The Atlantis faces out onto Biscayne Bay and stands next to a restored 1910 bungalow that serves as a meeting center for the condominiums. The new building features mirrored glass walls, which are overlaid on one side with an enlarged blue stucco grid. Halfway up its facade, a 37-foot square opening is punched clear through from one side of the building to the other, and contains a skycourt with a hot tub.

THE SOUTH

4. Site plan of the University of Virginia, Charlottesville. Thomas Jefferson, 1826. Drawing: William Hersey.

5. Oak Alley, Vacherie, Louisiana, c. 1836. Photo: Wayne Andrews, courtesy Avery Library, Columbia University.

6. Rock Castle, Sumner County, Tennessee, late 18th century. Photo: Jack E. Boucher, courtesy *Architecture of Middle Tennessee.*

7. The John Ross House, between Chattanooga and Atlanta, Georgia, early 19th century. Photo: George N. Barnard, courtesy *Photographic Views of Sherman's Campaign.*

8. Longwood ("Nutt's Folly"), Natchez, Mississippi. Samuel Sloan, 1860. Photo: Wayne Andrews, courtesy Avery Library, Columbia University.

9. Biltmore, near Asheville, North Carolina. Richard Morris Hunt and Frederick Law Olmsted, c. 1888. Photo: Gerald Allen.

10. Plan of Biltmore, near Asheville, North Carolina. Richard Morris Hunt, c. 1888. Drawing: Troy Caperton.

11. The Great Hall of the Ca'd'Zan, near Sarasota, Florida. Thomas R. Martin and Dwight James Baum, 1926. Photo: Joseph J. Steinmetz.

11A. Plan of Savannah. James Oglethorpe, 1733. Drawing: William Hersey.

12. Deering House, Casey Key, Florida. Paul Rudolph, 1962. Photo: © Ezra Stoller, ESTO.

13. Florida Southern College, Lakeland, Florida. Frank Lloyd Wright, 1938. Photo: courtesy Henry-Russell Hitchcock, *In The Nature of Materials.*

14. Stables for Gainesway Farm, Lexington, Kentucky. Theodore M. Ceraldi, 1981. Photo: A. E. Bye.

Town

1. The wharfs in Savannah, mid-19th century. Photo: George N. Barnard, courtesy *Photographic Views of Sherman's Campaign.*

2. Staircase, Nathaniel Russell House, Charleston, South Carolina, 1809. Photo: Louis Schwartz, courtesy Historic Charleston Foundation.

3. Pringle House, Charleston, South Carolina, 1774. Drawing: William Turnbull.

3A. Entryway, typical Charleston single house, mid-19th century. Photo: Gerald Allen.

4. The Fireproof Building, Charleston, South Carolina. Robert Mills, 1827. Photo: South Carolina Historical Society.

5. North Carolina State Capitol, Raleigh, Ithiel Town. Alexander Jackson Davis and David Paton, 1833. Photo: Wayne Andrews, courtesy Avery Library, Columbia University.

6. St. Paul's Episcopal Church, Richmond, Virginia. Thomas S. Stewart, 1845; apse, altar, and stained glass windows by Louis Comfort Tiffany, late 19th century. Photo: Jack E. Boucher, courtesy *Architecture of Middle Tennessee.*

7. First Presbyterian Church, Nashville, Tennessee. William Strickland, 1851. Photo: Jack E. Boucher, courtesy *Architecture of Middle Tennessee.*

8. Interior, First Presbyterian Church, Nashville, Tennessee, renovated late 19th century. Photo: Jack E. Boucher, courtesy *Architecture of Middle Tennessee.*

9. Charleston, South Carolina, in ruins, 1864, showing St. Michael's Church spire, 1761. Photo: George N. Barnard, courtesy *Photographic Views of Sherman's Campaign.*

10. Elm Street, Lumberton, North Carolina, early 20th century. Photo: Gerald Allen.

11. Dental Office, West Palm Beach, Florida. Aragon Associated Architects, 1981. Photo: courtesy Aragon Associated Architects.

Metropolis

1. Jefferson Hotel, Richmond, Virginia. Carrere and Hastings, 1895, and Peebles & Ferguson, 1901. Photo: Richard Cheek.

2. Main Street Station, Richmond, Virginia. Wilson, Harris and Richardson, 1901. Photo: Richard Cheek.

3. Beverly Drive, Charlotte, North Carolina, 1920s. Photo: Gerald Allen.

4. Academy of Medicine, Atlanta, Georgia. Philip Trammell Shutze, 1940. Photo: H. H. Reed.

5. Callaway House, LaGrange, Georgia. Hal Hentz and Neel Reid, 1916. Photo: Tommy Morgan, courtesy *Architecture of Neel Reid in Georgia.*

6. State Fair Arena, Raleigh, North Carolina. Matthew Nowicki and William Henry Dietrick, 1950. Photo: courtesy State Fair Arena.

7. North Carolina National Bank, Park Road Branch, Charlotte, North Carolina. Wolf Associates, 1972. Photo: Gordon Schenck, courtesy Wolf Associates.

8. The Atlantis, Miami, Florida. Arquitectonica, 1982. Photo: Norman McGrath.

9. The Atlantis, Miami, Florida. Arquitectonica, 1982. Photo: Norman McGrath.

THE MIDWEST

by John Zukowsky

Many of the architectural forms in the Midwest can be considered either responses to or impositions on the region's landscape. It is this link with the land itself that characterizes the architectural innovations of the Midwest. This is a region whose topography varies only slightly from gently rolling, wooded areas, to flat farmlands, to the Great Lakes themselves—enormous inland seas whose broad sweeping flatness is akin to that of the prairies. Architectural forms that were imported and, therefore, imposed upon rather than responsive to the region date back to European, particularly French, colonization in the early 1700s and widespread American agrarian expansion after the Congressional Land Ordinance of 1785. The Ordinance provided a functional approach to subdividing large masses of relatively flat land west of Ohio into quadrangular plots. It proved to be an easy way to organize the Midwest since there were no drastic variations in this relatively flat topography.

The practicality of this rectilinear grid set the tone for functional solutions in planning, designing, and building that were to emerge as American architectural innovations: the balloon frame of the 1830s; the Chicago school of commercial architecture and the technological innovations of fireproofed steel high-rises during the 1880s and 1890s; the Prairie school of residential design popularized by Frank Lloyd Wright and his followers in the early twentieth century; and the so-called Second Chicago school of architecture characterized by the sleekly proportioned International Style buildings of Ludwig Mies van der Rohe in the 1950s and 1960s. The works of contemporary architects, consciously or unconsciously, frequently recall those earlier midwestern innovations which can now be considered regional architectural traditions.

Many midwestern cities such as St. Louis, Cleveland, Detroit, Milwaukee, and Minneapolis began as fortified trading posts connected via rivers such as the Mississippi to the Great Lakes. Subsequent growth came from the immigration into the area of Polish, German, Irish, Norwegian, Swedish and other laborers, which influenced the region's architectural character. The region, however, is best represented by Chicago. The birthplace of many of those regional innovations and the largest architectural and commercial metropolis in the Midwest, Chicago has been the crossroads of our nation from its days as a railroad center in the second half of the nineteenth century to its current status as a major air transport hub. Carl Sandburg's famous characterization of Chicago as the "hog butcher for the world" is, at best, an understatement when one considers the history of the Union Stockyards, established in the 1860s and finally closed in 1971 following their decline. At the

stockyards's peak operation around 1910 the annual figure of livestock transported into the city jumped to 3 million cattle and 6 million hogs! The early growth of the stockyards was furthered by the introduction of the refrigerated railroad car in 1869—a boon that made Gustavus Swift and Philip Armour names known throughout American homes.

Chicago celebrated its 150th anniversary in 1983. Its tough, positive, pioneer attitude toward progress in architecture is reflected in clichés that relate to its practical, functionalist architectural innovations. Its official city slogan is "I will." It is a city whose architects since Sullivan and Mies have always said "form follows function" and "build, don't talk." Few contemporary architects disregard the midwestern tradition in their work: fairly restrained and visually uncomplicated in comparison to eastern counterparts, it is nonetheless technologically sophisticated.

THE COUNTRY

France was the dominant colonial power in the Great Lakes and Mississippi Valley during the eighteenth century. Current placenames such as Joliet and LaSalle in Illinois, Terre Haute and Vincennes in Indiana, Cadillac, Detroit, and Marquette in Michigan, and Des Moines in Iowa all testify to the impact of eighteenth-century explorers, missionaries, trappers and traders on the Midwest. Tangible expressions of France's colonization can be found in large-scale projects—such as the reconstructed star-shaped fortifications of Illinois's Fort de Chartres—as well as in small construction details. The *poteaux* walls of vertical timbers and mortar seen in the Cahokia Courthouse are typical of French colonial building in this region, as are the broad overhangs of the roof planes, reminiscent of French colonial architecture further down the Mississippi Valley.

Galena began as a French lead mining outpost in the late eighteenth century, and in the 1830s became a boomtown as the price of lead increased. Before that time, Galena's houses were built either of rough-hewn logs or undressed limestone. After full-scale production of bricks began here in 1837, wood and stone were replaced as the principal building materials. The Hoge House is a good example of one of these brick homes. A Baltimore contractor who moved his business here in 1837 built the house in 1842 and replicated it for himself two years later in the same town. The house is a hybrid, typical of other midwestern homes in the first half of the nineteenth century. It combines Greek Revival details, such as the Tuscan-columned entrance portico and frieze on the Park Avenue facade, with double-chimneyed end

Tri-State Office Buildings, Northbrook, Illinois.

walls typical of earlier Georgian and Federal houses common throughout the East Coast some forty or fifty years earlier. This is especially so in the James M. Roberts House near Galena that looks like an eastern Federal-style house from the early nineteenth century. This combination of outmoded styles in one building is usually, and with some truth, interpreted as the late development of a primitive era. It could also be indicative of the region's indifference toward accurate replication of eastern fashion, and greater interest in the practicalities of building—shelter, housing, and just enough ornament to suggest affluence.

In contrast to those midwestern architects who imitated the European-influenced designs and details of their eastern counterparts, Prairie school architects such as William Drummond, Barry Byrne and Walter Burley Griffin, led by Frank Lloyd Wright, attempted to design open-planned houses whose clean, simple forms, horizontally massed spaces, and correspondingly designed interior furnishings reflected the natural simplicity of the midwestern prairie. Wright's concrete Unity Temple in Oak Park, which shows the influence of oriental design, also expresses well the Prairie school use of interpenetrating planes, masses, and spaces. This style is most dramatically represented in the cantilevered roofs of his slightly later Robie House, more appropriate in design to a rural site than to urbanized Chicago. George Mann Niedecken's chair and table design for the Babsons is also indicative of Japanese influence in the presentation drawing style itself, but the simple rectilinear furniture forms relate to Prairie school designs Niedecken worked on when he executed furniture for Wright and Sullivan. Thus, by turning to mostly non-Western and sometimes native American sources, Prairie school architects attempted to develop an American architecture that responded to the typical midwestern American landscape.

In addition to promulgating Prairie school principles, Wright also developed two other residential types that he felt were appropriate to American society: The Usonian House or inexpensive suburban home for the automobile-oriented family, and the passive solar hemicycle. The earliest examples of both were built in Wisconsin for Herbert and Katherine Jacobs in 1937 and 1948. In the first Jacobs House, intended to be the model for his ideal Usonian House, he cast the utilities in a concrete slab foundation, constructed the house with prefabricated plywood, and incorporated a carport within his design. The second Jacobs House was built on a berm reminiscent of countless Indian mounds throughout the Midwest. The circular stone walls of the house evoke images of midwestern round barns and rough-laid boundary walls. The concave glass wall faces south to the warming sun, whereas the convex north wall is half buried in the earth to conserve energy. Wright's greatest impact immediately occured with his first Jacobs House. The development of the American suburban house after the Second World War followed Wright's model, as did suburban town planning subsequent to Wright's Broadacre City project of 1934.

With the Johnson Wax Building in Racine, Wisconsin, Frank Lloyd Wright had also taken the rounded earth forms of local vernacular building and created a large low-rise office space and research tower out of brick and glass tubing. Tree-like columns dramatically punctuate the main workspace. Wright's accommodation of the automobile through the long curved carport integrated into the design also provided a formal solution that would be imitated in commercial facilities serving the suburbs proliferating after World War II.

Some contemporary Chicago architects have responded to Wright's example as well as to the midwestern landscape. Harry Weese and Associates's First Baptist Church in Columbus, Indiana, employs Wrightian simple geometric massing to make this building very much a part of the rural Midwest. Cynthia Weese's references to Wright and the Midwest are more specific; her Kuntz House is clearly a product of the Prairie school tradition in its horizontal planes and use of light brick and large roof overhangs.

Responding to the flat landscape and the ever-present Interstate, Hammond, Beeby and Babka built in 1979, a speculative office building in Northbrook, Illinois of precast concrete whose entrance facade is horizontally massed starkly detailed and classically proportioned with wings flanking a central *porte cochère*. These characteristics have caused writers to compare this project to Chicago school industrial buildings of the early 1900s.

THE TOWN

Although a number of midwestern towns and cities grew out of fortified trading posts established by the French in the 1700s, still more emerged along the paths of canals and railroads, such as the Illinois-Michigan Canal and Illinois Central Gulf Railroad. It was those very same canals and railroads and their connections to the Great Lakes that made cities such as Cleveland, Detroit and especially Chicago prosper.

Small and large towns were rapidly built through the invention of the balloon frame, a construction technique developed in 1832 by Chicagoan George Snow. With this technique lightweight timbers were quickly nailed together rather than morticed and tenoned, causing observers to make comparisons between the process used for these rapidly constructed buildings and blowing up balloons. Rows of wooden cottages throughout Chicago's neighborhoods indicate the pervasiveness of the balloon frame, and the expediency of the technique itself is similar in ease to the grid system used in planning the Midwest.

If the French were the most influential ethnic group in the eighteenth century, the Germans must be considered as equals after their mass immigration from Europe following the unsuccessful revolution of 1848. Towns such as Chicago, Milwaukee, Indianapolis and Cincinnati became cities via their designs and the designs of their descendants. In Chicago German immigrants included architects Dankmar Adler, Augustus Bauer, Frederick Baumann, Fritz Foltz, Otto Matz, and Richard Schmidt. Edwin May and his Swiss-born and Austrian-trained draftsman Adolf Scherrer completed the Indiana State Capitol in 1888. The building's elaborate surface decoration, correct classicism and blocky massing has been attributed partially to Scherrer's Germanic background and education. Its details are similar to those executed by other German-American architects. Alexander Eschweiler's elaborate Jacobean mansion for beer baron Robert Nunnemacher fits within this tradition of ornately decorated buildings for German clients. Beyond the superficiality of elaborate ornamentation, these Germans brought a hard-headed professionalism that was well-accepted in the Midwest long before the next major wave of architect-immigrants came to the New Bauhaus in Chicago in the late 1930s and 1940s. They also brought precise technology in the mass production of drafting instruments and the introduction of the blueprinting process to the Midwest after Eugene Dietzgen established his factory in 1891.

In recent years the craftsmanship of the German heritage is being harnessed once more; James Nagle, well-known for his interest in vernacular housing, found skilled German craftsmen to execute masonry work for his mid-Quad dormitories at Northwestern University. The new buildings are designed to blend into the 1930s collegiate Gothic style buildings at Northwestern designed by James Gamble Rogers.

The Chicago Fire of 1871 catalyzed an important midwestern innovation—the Chicago school tall office buildings, called "skyscrapers" in 1889 publications on Chicago buildings. The Chicago "skyscraper" was developed by a number of easterners who moved there soon after the great fire, among them Louis Sullivan, John Wellborn Root and William Holabird. They joined others who were already in Chicago during the 1850s and 1860s, namely Dankmar Adler, Daniel Burnham and William Le Baron Jenney. Their first post-fire commercial build-

Indiana State Capitol, Indianapolis. Edwin May and Adolf Scherrer, 1888. Photo: Bass Photo Company, courtesy The Burnham Library of Architecture, The Art Institute of Chicago.

ings looked like their pre-fire predecessors: they were four-story walkups with a sunken first floor for retail space. The 1880s brought what have been termed the first "skyscrapers," multi-storied elevator buildings that were constructed of iron and steel, fireproofed with terra cotta, and covered with terra cotta facades. In general, they were inexpensively constructed speculative office buildings built by eastern investors, particularly from Boston and New York. Their function as marketable investment property is partly responsible for their stripped detailing and skeletal appearance. Especially striking examples are the Reliance Building of 1894 and the demolished Stock Exchange from 1893.

The elaborate trading room of the Exchange has recently been reconstructed at The Art Institute of Chicago. Its ornament, primarily interior decoration of stenciled-canvas surfaces, gilt plaster and scagliola columns imitative of marble, illustrates Sullivan's ability to use inexpensive materials for an opulent effect.

The stripped Chicago school buildings, with their horizontal, tripartite "Chicago Windows," reflective of the midwestern grid and responsive to the flat prairie, were built at so-called "skyscraper" height of twenty stories, as well as in lower-scaled commercial buildings. As with the balloon frame, the stripped commercial buildings in the Chicago school and Prairie school mode spread from Chicago to all the small towns on the railroads, sometimes in a diminutive scale in jewel-box-like banks by Sullivan and his followers Parker Noble Berry, Homer Grant Sailor and Purcell and Elmslie. These prairie gems often have a flowering of Sullivanesque ornament— an abstract floral ornament that Sullivan felt should be based on the underlying geometry of natural forms. The Wainwright Building in St. Louis well-illustrates an integration of organic expression of structure and ornament in handling the skyscraper form. Mitchell/Giurgola's addition of 1981 attempts to maintain the scale and linear quality of the original in a minimal manner.

Banks and small commercial buildings in places such as Cedar Rapids, Clinton and Mason City, all in

Iowa, Owatonna and Mankato in Minnesota, and Manlius, Illinois, brought the Prairie school philosophy of open horizontal spaces to the townscape. Many of these small structures are major public buildings in their respective locales and blend perfectly into the diminutive scale of small towns, while also expressing the rambling horizontality of design appropriate to the Midwest.

THE METROPOLIS

The 1893 World's Columbian Exposition, with its whitewashed, classically detailed buildings, catalyzed the spread of Beaux-Arts classicism throughout America. It was the training ground in master planning for Daniel Burnham, who was coordinator of construction, and it showed midwesterners that they too could have a "white city," a Paris or Rome on the Prairie. The fair also combined picturesque elements of Olmsted's planning in the so-called wooded island in the lagoon.

After the 1893 Fair, Burnham executed a plan in 1909 that further supplied the ingredients for making Chicago a European City on the Prairie. Burnham's assistant, Edward H. Bennett, implemented a number of Burnham's ideas in Chicago, notably the Classical bridges over the Chicago River and the equally detailed embankments on the river, based on similar bridges and embankments on the Seine and the Thames. Architects such as Sullivan and Wright considered these bridges to be impositions on Chicago's cityscape and on the midwestern landscape when compared with Chicago's earlier architectural innovations. But Bennett continued to design these popular forms for Minneapolis, St. Paul, Cedar Rapids and Joliet, among other cities.

In contrast to the Classical symmetry of the 1893 Fair, the asymmetrically planned 1933 Fair, the Century of Progress Exposition, reinforced Burnham's lakefront as a public playground and the stageset of Chicago. The *"moderne"* buildings of the 1913 Fair corroborated the theme of progress in the arts and sciences over the past century and, in cases such as the model homes of George Fred Keck demonstrated Chicago's sympathy for functionalism and the Modern movement before the establishment of the New Bauhaus here by Ludwig Mies van der Rohe.

> Do you know what I'd like to see . . . ? Not an armory, not a museum, not any structure built by man. Instead, the blue waters of Lake Michigan, the blue sky, the sweep of sandy shore. Between us the beach, green grass and flowers . . .
>
> —A. Montgomery Ward

Thanks to Dan Burnham, Chicago seems to be the only great city in our States to have discovered its own waterfront.

> —Frank Lloyd Wright

Montgomery Ward successfully spearheaded a campaign at the turn of the century to clean up the lakefront park and prevent the incursion of numerous permanent structures on this waterfront. But with the electrification of the rail lines in the early twentieth century, a number of proposals were suggested to build on the air rights of the Illinois Central's lines, which already cut through the park and ended in massive rail yards.

Finnish architect Eliel Saarinen, who later relocated to Bloomfield Hills in Michigan to establish Cranbrook Academy, was among the first to submit a proposal for a hotel, automobile thoroughfare and extensive parking. His hotel design bears similar details and massing to his renowned second-place entry in the 1922 Chicago Tribune Tower competition. Saarinen's project set the tone for Terminal Park, the Illinois Central air rights project of the 1920s. Construction of its densely packed setback skyscrapers was stopped by the depression of 1929, and development on this site was not renewed until the office of Mies van der Rohe planned and built Illinois Center I and II in the mid-1960s. Presently, this complex of office towers, hotel, and apartment building, all interconnected by underground passages, has been criticized for its sterility and blandness. Yet it functions fairly well as a "city within a city," and several new hotel, office and residential buildings are still slated for construction. Its location near Chicago's parkland and lakefront make it a prime development area, but its continued realization inhibits completion of Burnham's link between Grant Park to the south and the near north-side beaches.

The Chicago school buildings of the 1880s and 1890s, thought to be innovative in their time (and afterward by 1940s writers such as Siegfried Giedeon and Carl Condit), were perceived as obsolete by writers in the 1910s and 1920s.

The Beaux-Arts 1893 Fair had a serious stylistic impact. By the 1920s midwestern and Chicago buildings were designed in accordance with the new Classicism, with schemes that Chicago school and Prairie style architects would have considered too traditionally based. Yet Classically inspired buildings of the early 1920s and their *"moderne"* counterparts of the late '20s and early '30s frequently incorporate wide, triple-bayed Chicago Windows at least in their lower levels. These are an obvious extension of an architectural conceit associated with this region. Chicago moderne buildings by architects such as Holabird and Root and Graham, Anderson, Probst and White are also akin to their earlier Chicago school ancestors: their massing is sparse when compared with more ornate New York Art Deco buildings, which are closer to French sources. In these post-Chicago school buildings, certain aspects of earlier midwestern simplicity are joined with the boldness of Chicago design, hinting at an underlying functionalist design philosophy for the region.

The Depression and Second World War stopped large-scale building developments throughout

America for some fifteen years. In the post-war construction boom, Chicago witnessed the widespread acceptance of the visual structuralism of the finely proportioned International Style modernism championed by Ludwig Mies van der Rohe and his followers, many of them his students at the Illinois Institute of Technology (IIT). The structural basis of this so-called "Second Chicago School" of architecture was said to derive from similar values expressed in the late nineteenth-century buildings of the Chicago school. Even more importantly, postwar research here in structural systems, catalyzed in studies at IIT, led to innovative building support systems designed by architects and engineers at Skidmore, Owings and Merrill.

Two of the most significant systems are in the John Hancock Tower, with its diagonally braced steel structure, and in the Sears Tower, where nine structurally independent shafts were bundled together for stability in the "bundled tube" system. It is the world's tallest building, 109 stories and 1,450 feet in height. SOM's Bruce Graham continues to experiment with new structural forms to design skyscrapers more than twice the height of the Sears Tower in the tradition of Frank Lloyd Wright's 1956 proposal for a "Mile High Skyscraper" on Chicago's lakefront. This fascination with structural solutions is related to the region's tradition of comparable technological achievements, including the fireproofed iron and steel frame of the 1880s and the 1830s development of balloon frame construction. The urge to build better and bigger in Chicago than anywhere else in the country expresses architecturally the region's confidence in technological progress, and Chicago's ease with the tall office tower. Chicagoans even nickname their buildings in a direct, friendly way. The John Hancock Tower, all 1,105 feet of it, is frequently called "Big John" and Edward Durell Stone's Standard Oil Building from 1974, eighty stories high, is called "Big Stan."

The 1970s and early 1980s witnessed a shift toward contextualism in architecture across the nation, inspired in part perhaps by the 1976 Bicentennial. Current Chicago projects draw on the area's rich architectural heritage, consciously continuing a Chicago tradition. With Three First National Plaza Bruce Graham of SOM draws on the bay-window imagery of the first Chicago school buildings. Stanley Tigerman's Pensacola Place II Apartment Building (1978–1981) makes several allusions to that essence. Typical of Tigerman's wit and interest in intellectual polarities, Pensacola Place has a curtain-walled facade facing east toward Tigerman's similarly detailed Boardwalk Apartments and the prime real estate of upper-middle-class Lake Shore Drive, where Mies van der Rohe's apartment buildings stand. Pensacola's west facade, symbolically on axis with the graves of Mies and Sullivan in Graceland Cemetery and the working class neighborhoods, bears a giant Ionic order of balconies serving as pilasters.

Laurence Booth's cast-in-place concrete apartment building at 320 North Michigan Avenue gives its tenants picture-window views of the avenue through Chicago Windows; the facade uses innovative concrete technology while its moldings and terraced setbacks at the top recall 1920s urban structures.

Helmut Jahn's recent work in various tones of reflective glass, such as the office building at One South Wacker Drive and, particularly, the setback addition to the Board of Trade originally designed by Holabird and Root from 1927–1930, reflect his interest in the excitement of American cities of the 1920s. His materials and use of glass and steel structuralism, however, are also evidence of his training at Illinois Institute of Technology and his experience with so-called "Second Chicago school" buildings like McCormick Place from 1969. The massing and materials in the Board of Trade Addition, as in Jahn's other work, are reminiscent of earlier clean, severe massing in the 1920s work of Holabird and Root. Like their architectural predecessors, current Chicago architects have not completely lost their fascination with structure and techology.

Addition to the Board of Trade with the original Board of Trade building behind, Chicago. Helmut Jahn of Murphy/Jahn with Shaw. Photo: Keith Palmer and James Steinkamp.

THE MIDWEST

Introduction

1. Armour and Company poster, color lithograph, France, 1891. Photo: courtesy Chicago Historical Society.

2. Early Wrigley brands, 1905–1914. Photo: courtesy Wm. Wrigley Jr. Company.

3. Union Stockyards, Chicago, before 1916. Photo: courtesy The Burnham Library of Architecture, The Art Institute of Chicago.

4. Stand for Japanese print and vase. Frank Lloyd Wright, 1908. Photo: Quiriconi-Tropea, courtesy Kelmscott Gallery, Chicago.

5. St. Louis Gateway Arch, Missouri. Eero Saarinen, 1966. Photo: American Society of Civil Engineers.

6. Terra cotta model for the iron ornament of the National Farmer's Bank, Owatonna, Minnesota. Louis H. Sullivan, 1907. Photo: courtesy The Burnham Library of Architecture, The Art Institute of Chicago.

Country

1. Courthouse, Cahokia, Illinois, 1763. Photo: courtesy Historic American Buildings Survey.

2. Courthouse, Cahokia, Illinois, reconstructed 1939. Drawing: Courtesy Historic American Buildings Survey.

3. The Joseph Hoge House, Galena, Illinois. Henry J. Stouffer, 1842. Photo: courtesy Historic American Buildings Survey.

4. James M. Roberts House, near Galena, Illinois, 1847. Drawing: courtesy Historic American Buildings Survey.

5. Unity Temple, Oak Park, Illinois. Frank Lloyd Wright, 1908. Photo: J. W. Taylor, courtesy The Burnham Library of Architecture, The Art Institute of Chicago.

6. Robie House, Chicago. Frank Lloyd Wright, 1909. Photo: Richard Nickel, courtesy The Burnham Library of Architecture, The Art Institute of Chicago.

7. Library table and side chair for the Babson House, Riverside, Illinois. Niedecken-Waldgridge, c. 1912. Drawing: Ink and watercolor on windowshade cloth, courtesy Prairie Archives Collection, Milwaukee Art Museum.

8. The First Jacob House, Madison, Wisconsin. Frank Lloyd Wright, 1937. Photo: courtesy The Jacobs Collection, The Burnham Library of Architecture, The Art Institute of Chicago.

9. The Second Jacobs House, Middleton, Wisconsin. Frank Lloyd Wright, 1948. Photo: courtesy The Jacobs Collection, The Burnham Library of Architecture, The Art Institute of Chicago.

10. S. C. Johnson Administration Building, Racine, Wisconsin. Frank Lloyd Wright, 1939. Photo: Torkel Korling, courtesy The Burnham Library of Architecture, The Art Institute of Chicago.

11. Interior, S. C. Johnson Administration Building, Racine, Wisconsin. Frank Lloyd Wright, 1939. Photo: Torkel Korling, courtesy The Burnham Library of Architecture, The Art Institute of Chicago.

12. Desk designed for the S. C. Johnson Administration Building, Racine, Wisconsin. Frank Lloyd Wright, 1939. Photo: courtesy The Burnham Library of Architecture, The Art Institute of Chicago.

13. First Baptist Church, Columbus, Indiana. Harry Weese and Associates, 1965. Photo: Balthazar Korab, courtesy Harry Weese & Associates.

14. Kuntz House, St. Charles, Illinois. Cynthia Weese of Weese, Hickey, Seegers, Weese and Margaret McCurry of Tigerman, Fugman and McCurry, 1980. Photo: © Howard N. Kaplan, HNK Architectural Photography.

15. Tri-State Office Buildings, Northbrook, Illinois, 1979. Photo: © Howard N. Kaplan, HNK Architectural Photography.

Town

1. Tri-State Office Building, Northbrook, Illinois. Hammond, Beeby and Babka, 1979. Photo: © Howard N. Kaplan, HNK Architectural Photography, courtesy Hammond, Beeby and Babka.

2. Map of Chicago streets and sub-divisions, 1834. Photo: courtesy Chicago Historical Society, I Chi-05614.

3. Advertisement for worker's cottage, from S. E. Gross 10th Annual Catalog (1891). Photo: courtesy Chicago Historical Society, I Chi-03649.

4. Indiana State Capitol, Indianapolis. Edwin May and Adolf Scherrer, 1888. Photo: Bass Photo Company, courtesy The Burnham Library of Architecture, The Art Institute of Chicago.

5. Robert Nunnemacher House, Milwaukee, Wisconsin. Alexander Eschweiler, 1906. Detail of an ink on linen drawing, courtesy The Wisconsin Architectural Archive, Milwaukee.

6. Mid-Quad Dormitories, Northwestern University, Evanston, Illinois. Nagle and Hartray, 1982. Photo: David Clifton.

7. The Gage Building, Chicago. Holabird and Root, and Louis H. Sullivan, 1899. Photo: J. W. Taylor, courtesy The Burnham Library of Architecture, The Art Institute of Chicago.

8. The Reliance Building, Chicago. Charles Atwood of D. H. Burnham and Co., 1984. Photo: J. W. Taylor, courtesy The Burnham Library of Architecture, The Art Institute of Chicago.

9. Chicago Stock Exchange Building. Adler and Sullivan, 1984 (demolished). Photo: J. W. Taylor, courtesy The Burnham Library of Architecture, The Art Institute of Chicago.

10. Chicago Stock Exchange Trading Room, reconstruction, Vinci-Kenny, at The Art Institute of Chicago. Photo: courtesy The Burnham Library of Architecture. The Art Institute of Chicago.

11. Model Factory for Marshall Field Company, Chicago. D. H. Burnham and Co., 1905 (unexecuted). Drawing: ink on linen, courtesy Department of Architecture, The Art Institute of Chicago.

12. Wainwright Building and State Office Complex, St. Louis, Missouri. Adler and Sullivan with Charles Ramsey, 1981, renovation and addition, Mitchell/Giurgola Architects in association with Hastings and Chivetta, 1981. Photo: courtesy Mitchell/Giurgola Architects.

13. The Peoples Savings Bank, Cedar Rapids, Iowa. Louis H. Sullivan, 1910. Drawing: ink on linen, courtesy Department of Architecture, The Art Institute of Chicago.

14. First National Bank of Mankato, Minnesota. Purcell and Elmslie, 1911. Rendering: Ink on linen, courtesy Collection of Northwest Architectural Archives, University of Minnesota.

Metropolis

1. Water Gate and Peristyle, World's Columbian Exposition, Chicago. D. H. Burnham and Company, 1893. Inscriptions by Charles Williams Eliot. Photo: courtesy The Burnham Library of Architecture, The Art Institute of Chicago.

2. Proposed Civic Center Plaza, Chicago. Daniel H. Burnham and Edward H. Bennett, 1907. Rendering: ink and watercolor on paper for The Plan of Chicago (1909), courtesy Department of Architecture, The Art Institute of Chicago.

3. "New Gateway of the Greater Chicago," Edward H. Bennett, (Michigan Avenue Bridge) 1920; Graham, Anderson, Probst and White (Wrigley Building), 1921. Drawing: courtesy The Burnham Library of Architecture, The Art Institute of Chicago.

4. Home of Tomorrow at the Century of Progress Exposition, Chicago, George Fred Keck, 1933. Photo: Kaufmann and Fabry, courtesy The Burnham Library of Architecture, The Art Institute of Chicago.

5. Aerial view of Chicago, 1929, showing Grant Park and Buckingham Fountain. Edward H. Bennett, 1925. Photo: courtesy The Burnham Library of Architecture, The Art Institute of Chicago.

6. Proposed Grant Hotel and Central Plaza. Eliel Saarinen, 1923. From *American Architect* (December, 1923).

7. Chicago Daily News Building (now Riverside Plaza). Holabird and Root, 1929. Photo: Kaufmann and Fabry, courtesy The Burnham Library of Architecture, The Art Institute of Chicago.

8. North Michigan Avenue, Chicago, showing Illinois Center. Ludwig Mies van der Rohe, 1967, and 333 North Michigan, Holabird and Root, 1929. Photo: courtesy Illinois Center.

9. Three First National Plaza, Chicago. Skidmore, Owings & Merrill, 1982. Photo: Merrick, Hedrich-Blessing, courtesy Skidmore, Owings & Merrill.

10. 860-880 Lake Shore Drive, Chicago. Ludwig Mies van der Rohe. Pace Associates and Holsman, Holsman, Klekamp and Taylor, 1952. Photo: © Hedrich-Blessing.

11. John Hancock Tower, Chicago. Skidmore, Owings & Merrill, 1974. Photo: © Ezra Stoller, ESTO.

12. Sears Tower, Chicago. Skidmore, Owings & Merrill, 1969. Photo: Bill Engdahl, Hedrich-Blessing.

13. Penascola Place II Apartment Building, Chicago. Stanley Tigerman, 1981. Photo: Howard N. Kaplan, HNK Architectural Photography, courtesy Stanley Tigerman and Associates, Ltd.

14. Facade, 320 North Michigan Avenue, Chicago. Booth/Hansen & Associates, 1982. Photo: Steve Weiss, courtesy Booth/Hansen & Associates.

15. Addition to the Board of Trade with the original Board of Trade Building behind, Chicago. Helmut Jahn of Murphy/Jahn with Shaw, 1983. Photo: Keith Palmer and James Steinkamp.

THE PLAINS AND THE ROCKIES

by Richard Longstreth

The vast area lying between the central Missouri River Valley and the Sierra Nevada Mountains is not a region but many regions encompassing a broad spectrum of physical qualities. All of this territory was at first considered more an impediment to overland travel than an asset to the growing nation. With few exceptions, concentrated settlement in the area did not begin before the 1850s. Thereafter, thousands of immigrants from this country and Europe came west, lured by cheap land, mineral wealth, and speculative townsite promotion.

Intense urban aspirations marked the early development of communities in both the plains and mountain regions. Yet agriculture and mining formed the economic bases. Only a few centers grew to be metropolises, their primary function being to serve as entrepôts. Small town and rural settlement have always been the norm. In the twentieth century, these activities have been supplemented by tourism, generating resort communities from southern Colorado to northern Montana.

Residents of the plains and mountain states have almost never sought to develop a strong regional character for their built environment. On the contrary, early settlers tended to build according to known methods of former homelands to the extent that resources allowed. Later, prosperous segments of society usually sought to emulate fashionable models from other locales. These impulses still prevail in the twentieth century. Local pride can be fierce and is matched by a suspicion of other regions, the East in particular. Nevertheless, a sense of identity stems from intangible factors—occupations, recreational pursuits, and ancestral heritage—and from the natural landscape—plains, mountains, and desert.

Yet both aspirations and landscape have imbued the area's settlement with some distinct physical characteristics. Towns were generally platted on a grid of generous dimensions as a means of establishing visual order on the frontier and in the hope that the hamlet might someday become a great city. The geometry of plan is reinforced through the form of buildings, especially those in small towns. Whether freestanding or grouped in linear blocks, the rectilinear mass and pervasive plainness of the architecture accentuates its presence. Subtlety and sophistication in design are rare. Embellished buildings, or even those that are simply larger than the others around them, can become major landmarks. Likewise, the towns themselves, whether demarcated by plantations, grain elevators, or strip highway development such as that in Bosler, Wyoming, emphatically mark the open terrain. In the country, sectional divisions continue the geometric order. Farmsteads, rural schools, and other buildings stand isolated and assume a prominence far greater than their size or design alone would suggest.

While the West does not possess a unique architecture, there are several qualities that distinguish some of its buildings. Immigrant groups implanted forms that have become closely associated with regions here as with other parts of the country. In a few instances, Europeans brought folk patterns to the Plains that cannot be found elsewhere in the United States. Local materials such as sod can give a distinct identity to work. Some building types, such as stage stations and ranch complexes, experienced substantial modifications in the West. Other types, including standardized railroad depots and grain elevators, are more prevalent, or at least more conspicuous, in the area than elsewhere.

The conscious pursuit of regional expression in design, which began to interest East Coast architects in the 1880s and became an important concern after the turn of the century, never had a significant impact in this area. There are, however, some notable exceptions. As early as H.H. Richardson's Ames Monument in Wyoming, efforts were made to reflect the scale and ruggedness of the western landscape through abstract form. Since the 1900s, some architects have sought to develop rustic imagery, generally inspired by precedents elsewhere, that might become identified with a given region. Yet most such endeavors have stemmed from offices on either coast, not from those in the region itself.

More than a casual or antiquarian interest in archetypal images and select historic sites throughout these states has developed only in recent years. No other area's architecture has received so little detailed study. Yet the plains and mountain regions contain a rich, diverse legacy that holds great potential for broadening our understanding of American architecture.

THE COUNTRY

From the mid-eighteenth through the mid-nineteenth century, the "I" house—two rooms per floor, one room deep, two stories with end gables, and, often, a central hall—was one of the most common dwelling types in America. Originating in the Middle Atlantic region, it was employed by immigrants as they settled along the Appalachian axis, into the upland South, and through the lower Midwest. Early on, the "I" house became a symbol of economic prosperity.

During the mid-nineteenth century, the type was popular in Missouri, especially among transplanted southerners who sought to continue the traditions of a planter society. John Wornall's house was the hub of an 1,100-acre plantation. In its form and embelishment, the house is similar to examples erected during the previous decade in the owner's native Kentucky. Typical of ambitious architecture in newly settled areas, the design is grand but not sophisticated. The portico and other Greek Revival details are awkward in their proportions; they succeed, however, in making the front appear larger than it actually is.

The Mormon migration from Nauvoo, Illinois, to Utah in 1846–1847 initiated an infusion of eighteenth-century house types into the far West. Dedicated to an expeditious civilization of the wilderness, Mormon settlers left a rich if isolated legacy of domestic architecture in adobe, stone, and brick. While many Latter-day Saints originally came from New England and upstate New York, others had lived further south or immigrated directly from Great Britain and Scandinavia. As a result, early Utah houses embody a spectrum of cultural patterns. In form, many dwellings can be traced to the Middle Atlantic region. The "I" house without a corridor (also known as the hall and parlor house) was perhaps the most common. Later versions were often larger and contained a center hall.

H.P. Olsen's brick house is a good reflection of the state's diverse cultural origins. A native of Denmark, Olsen employed an English mason who used the prevalent hall and parlor plan. Proportions and detailing of the gable ends recall simple Greek Revival houses in New England. The facade's three-gabled half dormers, however, suggest a borrowing from more recent Gothic Revival motifs, here used in a manner probably unique to the state.

Logs and sod were standard building materials during the early phases of settlement in the Plains. The Ball house is larger than most of its type and a very rare surviving example of uncovered sod construction. For Ball and many other settlers, sod was more than a material of necessity. It offered thermal advantages, resistance to fire, and a sense of protection amid a vast, unvaried, windswept landscape. Sod became, in effect, a surrogate for masonry. As seen here, the material continued to be used into the early twentieth century, long after other building products became readily available. Both the attic story and barn are original to the compound.

Beginning in the 1870s, many portions of the Plains were settled by Germans whose ancestors had populated the lower Volga River and Ukraine regions. They brought their post-medieval German folk culture and continued to employ their native house types, most commonly in the remote farmsteads of the Dakotas.

House-barns were as prevalent in that region as they had been in the Old World. The Ziegler compound is among the best surviving examples. The residence has a typical plan of four rooms—two wide, two deep, with no corridor—and is constructed of wood frame and batsa (sun-dried clay) bricks. The attached barn is of batsa brick faced with clay. The house's clapboard veneer, used to protect the structure underneath, is a departure from tradition.

The Hutmacher house has a linear plan, also common to German-Russian dwellings. The finest extant example in North Dakota of stone-slab construction—another imported building technique—the house offers a good illustration of the persistence of tradition in folk architecture.

From North Dakota to New Mexico, numerous imposing ranch houses built during the late nineteenth century became oases of elegant living situated in remote areas. At once elaborate and awkward, these houses tend to depart from standard residential types, representing the personal, sometimes idiosyncratic visions of their affluent owners, and stand as monuments to rugged individualism in the West.

The HT Ranch was one of several very large tracts developed in western North Dakota by rich easterners during the late nineteenth century. Established in 1882 by Pennsylvanian A.C. Huidekoper, the main house, Shackford, employs an unorthodox mixture of precedents. A two-tiered porch, wrapping around the east and south elevations, recalls those of southern plantation houses, as well as those on some ranches in the Southwest. The square mass, capped by a pyramidal roof, on the other hand, was common to more modest dwellings in the South and the Plains. The log construction may reflect the survival of frontier building techniques in what was still a remote region. However, the house's name and its trunk porch posts suggest that a rustic appearance was also consciously sought.

During the mid-nineteenth century, hundreds of way stations were erected to service passenger and freight wagon trains along overland routes in the West. Spaced at approximately fifteen-mile intervals, these stops provided food, water and sometimes lodging. Linear in form and often not more than one room deep, their configuration was somewhat similar to that of numerous roadside motels that would appear in the 1930s. The Midway Station is among the few to survive unrestored and on its original site.

Rural churches have long been a common feature of agrarian settlement throughout the United States, but they are particularly prevalent and conspicuous in the Plains. While the first sanctuaries there were in makeshift quarters, by the 1890s, hundreds of permanent facilities were being constructed. Most examples are similar to counterparts in towns, yet the Plains rural church has a quality all its own, standing on an expansive, flat terrain. Erected by Swedish immigrants, the Salem Church is nevertheless characteristically American in its Gothic details, L-shaped form and modified Akron plan, with Sunday School rooms opening directly off the nave. In 1914, the interior was embellished with a low-cost ornament of stamped metal veneer.

Commissioned by the Union Pacific Railroad as a memorial to Oliver and Oakes Ames, the Ames

Monument in Albany County, Wyoming broke with convention in several respects. It is a tribute to entrepreneurs who were instrumental in realizing the transcontinental route's completion. It is built in a remote area, and eschews then-standard decorative trappings for a bold, two-step pyramidal mass. Built of rough-faced granite quarried from nearby outcroppings, the monument is much larger (60 feet square at the base) than most photographs indicate. Shape and materials are orchestrated in a magnificent response to the Rocky Mountain setting. This was probably the first occasion a designer sought to embody the vast rugged character of the western landscape through abstract form. H. H. Richardson was the logical choice as architect, given his close association with the Ames family. But in spite of his reputation, the monument was at best viewed as a local curiosity for many years, and was little known outside the region.

Following the creation of the National Park Service in 1916, systematic development programs were initiated for each property. Mesa Verde's administrative buildings were mostly designed by the park superintendent and his wife as a low-profile complement to the nearby cliff dwellings. The Nusbaums made a detailed study of Pueblo architecture in order to have their work serve as an educational resource. These buildings also became an important precedent for sensitive, site-specific design in the National Park system.

Established in 1872, Yellowstone is the oldest National Park in the U.S. With the construction of a branch railroad line in the 1880s, it became readily accessible to tourists. Soon the Department of the Interior began to press for entrepreneurs to develop good visitor accommodations. The Old Faithful Inn, the first large, permanent hostelry in the park system, set the standard for such facilities through the 1930s. As a result, the National Park hotel became a distinct and memorable place that could be nowhere but in the West.

Mesa Verde National Park contains over 4,000 sites built by the San Juan Anasazi Indians from as early as the sixth century until around 1300 when they abandoned the area. The most famous and distinctive remains are from the Pueblo III period and consist of large, concentrated apartments and kivas in cliff wall caves. These ruins comprise the most extensive, well-developed prehistoric cliff dwellings in the United States.

The Inn is rustic with a vengeance. Inspired by Alpine chalets, European hunting lodges and, perhaps, large summer camps in New York's Adirondacks, it achieves an even grander scale, with commensurately epic details. The multi-storied lobby, spun in a web of tree trunks and gnarled branches, with a gargantuan lava stone fireplace in one corner, is a remarkable "wilderness" counterpart to those of major hotels in Denver and San Francisco.

Since the introduction of commercial jet airplane

Superintendent's residence, Administrative District, Mesa Verde National Park, Montezuma County, Colorado. Jesse and Aileen Nusbaum, 1921, 1928. Photo: Colorado Historical Society.

travel and the development of the Interstate Highway system, the Rocky Mountains and other high peak regions in the West have experienced increasingly intense resort development. Although many of these new ventures were at first boomtowns, in recent years they have encouraged design and planning more compatible with the landscape. Most recent western resort architecture has relied on stereotypical imagery, either lapsing into rustic clichés or emulating stylish new buildings designed for very different parts of the country. The Centennial of Beaver Creek, near Avon, Colorado, designed by MLTW/Turnbull, is a noteworthy exception to the prevailing pattern. Consisting of twenty-nine condominium units, it is part of an elaborate complex still under development. The building possesses an elegance and sensitivity to its setting found in the best late nineteenth- and early twentieth-century resort hotels. While inspired by work in both the United States and Europe, the allusions remain vague, manifesting an idea rather than specific precedents. Many of Turnbull's houses are also echoed in the massing and spatial organization, here effectively translated to a grand scale.

The Silver Lake ski lodge is another distinguished example of new resort architecture. Here, however, specific western sources were tapped, including Timberline Lodge (1936–1937) on Oregon's Mount Hood, and Bernard Maybeck's fanciful castle Wyntoon (1902–1903) in northern California. Silver Lake, near Park City, Utah, also displays a studied casualness that has typified rustic design in the San Francisco area since the 1890s. Rugged, elemental and, at the same time, sophisticated, the design demonstrates how the approach taken with many Park Service buildings before World War II can be successfully applied to contemporary work.

THE TOWN

In an area where towns of 5,000 to 10,000 are considered important centers, substantially smaller communities constitute the norm. Since the turn of the century, many of these latter towns have enjoyed a stable population, and have experienced few extensive changes to their physical fabric. In their appearance, the settlements reflect early urban aspirations. Streets tend to be wide and, in residential quarters, lined with trees. Commercial buildings are concentrated in a linear core; public buildings are conspicuously placed along, or at the head of, principal streets. At the same time, the architecture is characteristically modest in size and treatment.

Cottonwood Falls, Kansas, was first developed as a river town. Its main street (Broadway) runs from the river bank to the courthouse (1871–1873). The flanking commercial buildings are mostly from the 1880s to the 1900s. A few of them, such as the paired bank and store represent substantial investments. Most businesses remain housed in one-story blocks erected as temporary facilities in anticipation of growth that never came.

Western mining towns, located near large mineral deposits, often became miniature instant cities. They were centers of intense activity. Their main streets were lined with pretentious commercial and civic buildings, yet the towns sat in barren landscapes, surrounded by the industrial complexes that were their raison d'être. Since a town's economy depended upon access to, and the demand for, a single resource, even the largest communities enjoyed prosperity for only a few decades.

No town has held a more important place in American mining history than Virginia City, Nevada. Following the discovery of the Comstock Lode in 1859, it became a proving ground for large-scale investment, speculation and technological experimentation. By the 1880s growth was arrested by economic decline. Revival of mining operations occurred sporadically over the next several decades; thereafter, Virginia City languished. Since 1960, tourist-oriented activities have considerably altered its character.

Recent intensified exploitation of mineral resources in the West has led to a new surge of boomtown development. This activity has generated soaring population growth, bringing with it various forms of visual and social chaos. A new town, Wright, Wyoming, reflects the concern for making future development more orderly. Planned under the auspices of Atlantic Richfield, it has open space, schools, a shopping plaza, recreational facilities and single-family houses, echoing the features of model early twentieth-century company towns, such as Sinclair, Wyoming, 150 miles away. At the same time, mobile home and recreational vehicle parks in Wright attest to the transient component that has always been a part of mining communities.

The enormous hotel rising above makeshift shelters was one of the many anachronisms found in the early development of western communities. Often large amounts of capital were invested by town promoters for erecting a hotel that might rival those in cities further east. These frontier palaces were conceived to foster land sales, house new residents, and serve as a center for the community. The Patee House's builder claimed that it was the largest hotel west of Chicago. But like many such establishments, its heyday was brief. Since the Civil War, the Patee House has served other uses. Today it stands as a rare survivor of a once common type.

During the mid-nineteenth century, most newly founded state institutions of higher learning in the West erected a single, large, multi-purpose edifice for their quarters. Kansas State Agricultural College's early physical development was an exception. The second president, John Anderson, believed the state's needs required a curricular emphasis on vocational studies, making the institution markedly different from counterparts further east. Likewise, the campus was developed to appear like "a village of thriving artisans," and given a simple, utilitarian character.

Most western universities in the twentieth century, no less than in the nineteenth, have sought to fashion their physical development in a manner patterned after fashionable East Coast models. The University of Colorado Regents in 1917 commissioned Charles Klauder, renowned for his work at Princeton, Wellesley, and other colleges, to create an elegant Gothic compound for their Boulder campus. Subsequently, Klauder proposed an alternative that would be more in keeping with the regional character and landscape. This plan guided campus development over the next several decades.

Since Klauder felt the region had no suitable historic precedents, he turned to the architecture of northern Italian hill towns for inspiration. Closely-knit buildings varying in size but more or less uniform in scale were placed around an existing quadrangle and in residential clusters beyond. Combining symmetrical and picturesque forms, high style and vernacular sources, the designs are composed to superb visual effect, framed by the Rockies and accentuated by the strong Colorado sunlight.

The 1919 master plan was continuously revised by Klauder over the next two decades. Rapid growth led to the development of a new master plan in 1960. Designed by Sasaki and Walker Associates, with Pietro Belluschi as architectural consultant, this scheme sought a new direction, yet one that would harmonize with the existing campus. The Engineering Sciences Center is the most dramatic component, and helped generate a shift in modernism toward again accepting regional expression.

The Germans were among the largest immigrant groups to settle in Kansas. The Catholics among them were ardent church builders. Most of their sanctuaries are located in villages and rural areas, providing a sharp contrast in size and sumptuousness to their surroundings. St. Fidelis is the largest, with a seating capacity of 1,100. Erected through local voluntary labor, the building cost around $132,000, a staggering sum for a community of 800 in 1910. The design is reminiscent of Rhenish Romanesque churches, perhaps reflecting the Palatine origins of many German-Russian families who settled in the vicinity.

The four Mormon temples erected in Utah during the nineteenth century are as unique in form and concept as the theology they represent. Built to accommodate secret rituals (considered requisite for partaking in the joys of afterlife), to hasten the millennium and, thereafter, to serve as suitable dwelling places for Christ, the temples were also seen by Church President Brigham Young as outpost bastions to foster the organized colonization of his theocracy. Thus they are more palatial and governmental than religious in character.

The Manti Temple is the most sophisticated of the four designs. While Young was responsible for the overall concept (officially, a divine revelation), the details were developed by William H. Folsom, then Utah's most experienced and well-trained architect. Manti is rendered in what was then a retardataire castellated mode; yet it possesses great strength and vigor, reflecting Mormon determination to transform the wilderness into an Edenic garden.

For western towns, especially, the railroad depot was long a major focus of activity and an important symbol of links to the outside world. Railroad companies took a very different attitude toward their buildings. Since the routes were expensive to construct, yet had relatively light traffic that was subject to considerable market fluctuations, early western stations typically constituted a minimal investment. By using standardized station designs, company architects could easily vary size and facilities according to the projected requirements of each stop. Accommodations for passengers, employees and freight were housed under one roof. The Ness City depot in Kansas is a large version of a standard wood-frame design used by the Santa Fe during the 1890s and 1900s.

Louis Curtis, the architect for the Union Depot in Joplin, Missouri, was part of a small outpost avant-garde who believed that the West offered opportunities for developing new architectural forms. He was strongly influenced by early modernists, including the Prairie school in the Midwest and the *Wagnerschüle* in Austria, but had no direct contact with them. He experimented with reinforced concrete and also looked to non-Western traditions—the architecture of the Pueblo Indians and, probably, of ancient Meso-America—for ideas. At the same time, Curtiss gave his work a compositional order that reflects his training at the Ecole des Beaux Arts. He combined these academic, modernist, and native American sources in a highly inventive, personal style.

The Joplin depot, among Curtiss's finest designs, is made of exposed reinforced concrete molded in a Beaux-Arts *parti*. The ornament seems Mayan in its scale and boldness, while it is abstracted in a manner that owes a debt to both Chicago and Vienna. Long vacant, the building is now threatened with demolition.

Corn Palace (first building), Mitchell, South Dakota. A. J. Kings, 1892–1893. Photo: courtesy the Goin Company.

Celebrations of seasonal events, particularly harvests, have long been a tradition in the West; yet these endeavors seldom resulted in distinct architecture. The numerous agricultural exposition halls and state fair buildings erected during the late nineteenth and early twentieth centuries gave little indication of regional qualities or their agrarian orientation. The Corn Palace in South Dakota was one of the few exceptions and the only such building to last for an extended period of time.

Conceived to house the Corn Belt Exposition (now Corn Palace Festival), the original edifice was a large hall accommodating product displays, stage entertainment and community events, as were its two successors. All three buildings have been lavishly adorned with turrets, cupolas, and domes to foster the idea of festival. But most unusual about the Corn Palaces is their annually changing decorative veneer of grain arranged in a panoply of abstract and representational patterns. No other buildings have used a regionally-oriented iconography with such élan.

THE METROPOLIS

The winner of a limited national competition, Goodhue's Nebraska capitol design is the first major American public building to reflect European modernist design. It is also a rare example of large-scale civic architecture that offers a distinct response to a regional setting.

The debt to Europe's avant-garde is most evident in the abstract modeling of forms. The tower was derived from recent work by Lars Sonck and Eliel Saarinen in Finland. Other sources are historical; the plan makes use of Beaux-Arts cross-in-square composition, while the massing, details and decoration have their precedent in the Roman baths, French Romanesque churches, Byzantine sanctuaries, and ancient palaces in the Near East.

From these diverse precedents, Goodhue developed a suave metropolitan building, yet one that converses with the small city in which it is located and with the Nebraska landscape beyond. The low base underscores the region's expansive, flat terrain. The

State Capitol, Lincoln, Nebraska. Bertram Grosvenor Good-hue, 1920–1932. Photo: George Condra, courtesy Nebraska State Historical Society.

soaring tower serves as a beacon of state, visible for miles around. This basic form, employed for many American public buildings and widely used in mid-western court houses, is here exaggerated, intensified and conceived at a grand scale comparable to that of the Plains. Nebraska's early history and the development of law comprise the subject matter of an unusually rich iconographic program integral to the conception of the building. Goodhue's design became popular at once among the citizenry. In few other instances has a government building fulfilled its symbolic function so effectively.

The introduction of the tall office building to metropolises from St. Louis to San Francisco occurred during the second half of the 1880s, soon after the type's seminal development had taken place. This phenomenon reflects not only the rapid growth of cities in the West, but also the insatiable appetite of their business leaders for a sophisticated urban appearance. At first local architects were seldom considered to undertake such work; prominent firms in Chicago and the East were commissioned instead. Kansas City initiated what quickly became a trend with Burnham and Root's Board of Trade Building, designed in 1886. A decade later, the practice of importing architects waned. However, the tendency of western cities to emulate as closely as possible new work in centers such as Boston, New York, and Chicago remained strong and has continued to characterize metropolitan architecture in the area ever since.

The New York Life Building by McKim, Mead & White was the largest commercial edifice in Kansas City at the time it was constructed. The elegant composition and rendering of Italian Renaissance details represented the most stylish design the East could offer. Yet the structural system is conservative: exterior masonry walls are loadbearing, and inside a cast iron frame is encased in concrete. Located at the edge of what was then the commercial center, the building stood in sharp contrast to its surroundings. Such pronounced juxtapositions were both typical of and unique to nineteenth-century urban development in the West.

The warehouse district embodies the key role played by the outpost metropolis as a supply center for the West. While such districts exist in cities throughout the country, Omaha's is particularly prominent in location and distinctive in treatment. Situated on a bluff above the Missouri River close to railroad lines and the commercial center, the district rises like a small city unto itself.

The quarter was mostly developed between 1898 and 1920, replacing an older assemblage of warehouses to the east. Both the swelling influx of immigrants to the Plains and the greater reliance on manufactured products contributed to the need for much larger facilities than had existed in the nineteenth century. The new buildings, designed by some of Omaha's leading architectural firms, are both utilitarian and elegant. With carefully composed elevations constructed of fine materials, they form an urbane ensemble that expresses their contribution to the region's economy in a grand, almost civic, gesture. Still active today, the district is among the best preserved of its type and period in the Untied States.

The intensity of urban aspirations in the western metropolis during the nineteenth century has been matched by a taste for lateral expansion and suburban-oriented development over the past sixty years. The Country Club Plaza in Kansas City, Missouri, was instrumental in redirecting local growth patterns, and became a paradigm for suburban retail centers across the country. It is probably the first such complex built according to a comprehensive plan and tailored to the automobile. Developer Jesse Clyde Nichols envisioned the Plaza as an integral component of an enormous residential area, the Country Club District, begun in 1907. The Plaza's organization, including street width and building size, was calculated for maximum light and ease of circulation. Offstreet parking and service stations were considered marketing assets, not just necessities. High-rise apartments were built on the perimeter to increase the local clientele and provide a buffer for the single-family residential enclaves beyond. The buildings allude to Spanish precedent, reflecting Nichols's fondness for Seville. This imagery also represents a trend in many western cities to implant associational ties to the Spanish-American Southwest in the alleged absence of suitable historic architecture locally.

THE PLAINS AND THE ROCKIES

Introduction
1. School District #11, Bent County, Colorado, 1899. Photo: Richard Longstreth.

2. Commercial district, Bosler, Wyoming, 1920s et seq. Photo: Mark Junge, courtesy Wyoming Recreation Commission.

3. Gano Grain Company elevator, Burdett, Kansas, 1947, annex 1981 (right). Farmer's Cooperative Grain Supply Company Elevator, Burdett, Kansas. Chalmers and Borton, 1947, annexes 1954 and 1959 (left). Photo: Richard Longstreth.

Country

1. John Wornall House, Kansas City, Missouri. Bright and Rogers, builders, 1858. Photo: Richard Longstreth.

2. Hans Peter Olsen House, Fountain Green, Utah. Thomas Morgan, 1877. Photo: courtesy Thomas Carter.

3. Charles Ball House, Box Butte County, Nebraska, c. 1913. Photo: David Murphy, courtesy Nebraska Historical Society.

4. Edwin Ziegler house-barn, Hutchinson County, South Dakota, c. 1880. Photo: Michael Koop, courtesy South Dakota Department of Education and Cultural Affairs.

5. Frank Hutmacher House, Dunn County, North Dakota, 1928. Photo: Kurt Schweigert, courtesy State Historical Society of North Dakota.

6. HT Ranch, Billings County, North Dakota, late 1880s. Photo: courtesy State Historical Society of North Dakota.

7. Midway Stage Station, near Gothenburg, Nebraska, c. 1859–1861. Photo: Richard Longstreth.

8. Salem Methodist Episcopal Church, Kearny County, Nebraska, 1898. Photo: Richard Longstreth.

9. Salem Methodist Episcopal Church, Kearny County, Nebraska, sanctuary as altered, 1914. Photo: R. Bruhn.

10. Ames Monument, Albany County, Wyoming. Henry Hobson Richardson, architect, Augustus Saint-Gaudens, sculptor, 1879–1882. Photo: Richard Longstreth.

11. Cliff Palace, Mesa Verde National Park, Montezuma County, Colorado, 1200–1276. Photo: William H. Jackson, courtesy CO Historical Society.

12. Superintendent's residence, Administrative District, Mesa Verde National Park, Montezuma County, Colorado. Jesse and Aileen Nusbaum, 1921, 1928. Photo: courtesy Colorado Historical Society.

13. Old Faithful Inn, Yellowstone National Park, Teton County, Wyoming. Robert C. Reamer, 1903–1904. Photo: courtesy Collections of Greenfield Village and the Henry Ford Museum, Dearborn, Michigan.

14. Interior, Old Faithful Inn, Yellowstone National Park, Teton County, Wyoming. Robert C. Reamer, 1903–1904. Photo: courtesy Haynes Foundation Collection, Montana Historical Society.

15. The Centennial of Beaver Creek, near Avon, Colorado. MLTW/Turnbull Associates, 1980–1983. Rendering: William Hersey, courtesy MLTW/Turnbull Associates.

16. Silver Lake Center, Dear Valley Resort, near Park City, Utah. Esherick Homsey Dodge and Davis, 1980–1981. Photo: © Peter Aaron, ESTO.

Town

1. Cottonwood Falls, Kansas, founded 1858. Photo: David Johnson, courtesy Kansas State Historical Society.

2. Virginia City, Nevada, founded 1859. Photo: Nevada Historical Society.

3. Wright, Wyoming, Community Development Group. Atlantic Richfield Co. and Harmon, O'Donnell and Henninger Associates, 1975–1976. Photo: Louie Psihoyos, courtesy National Geographic Society.

4. Patee House, St. Joseph, Missouri. L.S. Stigers, 1856–1858. Photo: courtesy Pony Express Historical Association.

5. Kansas State Agricultural College, Manhattan, Kansas. John Haskell and Erasmus Carr, 1872–1876. Photo: courtesy Special Collection, Kansas State University.

6. Engineering Administration Building, University of Colorado, Boulder, Colorado. Floyd Walters, 1938. Photo: courtesy Western Historical Collections, University of Colorado.

7. Engineering Sciences Center, University of Colorado, Boulder, Colorado. Associated Architects of Colorado, 1961–1965. Photo: courtesy Western Historical Collections, University of Colorado.

8. St. Fidelis Roman Catholic Church, Victoria, Kansas. John T. Comes and John Marshall, 1905–1911. Photo: Richard Longstreth.

9. Manti Temple, Church of Jesus Christ of Latter-day Saints, Manti, Utah. William Harrison Folsom, 1877–1888. Photo: George Anderson, courtesy Utah Historical Society.

10. Santa Fe Depot, Ness City, Kansas. Santa Fe Railway Company, 1903. Photo: Richard Longstreth.

11. Union Depot, Joplin, Missouri. Louis Curtis, 1910–1911. Photo: courtesy Spencer Library, University of Kansas.

12. Corn Palace (first building), Mitchell, South Dakota. A.J. Kings, 1892–1893. Photo: courtesy the Goin Company.

13. Corn Palace (third building), Mitchell, South Dakota. C.W. and George L. Rapp, 1920–1921, 1937. Photo: courtesy South Dakota Department of Education and Cultural Affairs.

Metropolis

1. State Capitol, Lincoln, Nebraska. Bertram Grosvenor Goodhue, 1920–1932. Photo: George Condra, courtesy Nebraska State Historical Society.

2. Plan, State Capitol, Lincoln, Nebraska. Bertram Grosvenor Goodhue, 1920–1932.

3. New York Life Insurance Company Building, Kansas City, Missouri. McKim, Mead & White, 1887–1890. Photo: MO Valley Room, Kansas City Public Library.

4. Elevation, New York Life Insurance Company Building, Kansas City, Missouri. McKim, Mead & White, 1887–1890.

5. Ninth Street Warehouse District, Omaha, Nebraska, early 20th century. Photo: Lynn Meyer.

6. Country Club Plaza, Kansas City, Missouri. Edward Delk and Edward Tanner, begun 1922. Photo: Tyner-Murphy, courtesy J.C. Nichols Company.

THE SOUTHWEST

by Lawrence Speck

In the southwestern United States, civilization still lies thinly over a vast landscape of broad prairies, lonely rolling hills and commanding promontories. This formidable terrain, the infinite sky and boundless horizons dominate even the most impressive human attempts to occupy the land.

Here in the long valleys that terrace away from the banks of the upper Rio Grande River in New Mexico, permanent human settlements were established as early as the tenth century. Still standing are ruins of structures built seven hundred years ago by sedentary, agricultural Indians dwelling in well-planned villages of stone and adobe. In his remarkable expedition across Texas in 1534–1535, the Spanish explorer Cabeza de Vaca found Indian communities that jealously guarded their claim to an indomitable land. In 1540 Coronado discovered in the Southwest a highly indigenous culture of some 20,000 to 30,000 people, living in seventy different settlements and speaking distinct languages.

Today, more than four hundred years later, the Southwest remains a frontier still being settled. Streams of migrants enter daily from the northern parts of the States, from the south (Mexico) and from places around the world, seeking the new opportunities that the natural resources of the area can offer.

The settlers of the region, coming first across the Bering Straits from Asia, later from Spanish colonies in Mexico, still later from Europe and Colonial America, matched the toughness and grandeur of the landscape in their architecture. Often third or fourth generation migrants, these settlers in the Southwest carried with them rich and diverse architectural traditions, but traditions that commonly had no *single* culture source. Thick earthen masonry wall techniques brought from Mexico in the seventeenth century, for example, had come from Spain earlier, where in turn they had been imported by the Moors from the Middle East. The nineteenth-century Greek Revival architecture of Austin, Texas, and the Victorian architectural styles one sees in Galveston, Texas, came indirectly from their original British sources, by way of Virginia, the South, the Midwest and even California.

Building traditions introduced to the Southwest were thus notably impure—already modified and enriched by diverse experiences and circumstances of other places. When applying these traditions in a new and alien setting, settlers often varied and combined elements inventively. The result is an intermingling of architectural forms—heavy adobe walls alongside thin Anglo-Colonial wood detail, delicate Victorian ornamentation alongside robust Germanic masonry. These stratifications of diverse human occupancy,

from the earliest Indian pueblos to the most recent sunbelt towns, grew in much the same way as the geographical formations on which they rest. Elements drawn from divergent, even conflicting, sources were modified according to the climate, the availability of materials and the practicality of indigenous building techniques—as well as the region's own sense of place.

Southwesterners have long valued utilitarian solutions in design—objects, buildings, cities—but do not seem satisfied with usefulness alone. Primitive Indian crafts, such as the coarsely woven but inventively patterned crafts of the New Mexico Indians, indicate a rugged pragmatism along with a gentle spirit. The traditional cowboy boot has long been standard footwear because of its practicality and comfort. Ornamental features, however, are generally applied to these durable shoes in a manner that fashion designers have now usurped. Less fashion than function, the Adams Extract label and packaging eschew trends and fads in favor of a simple legibility that has served its company for 75 years. Architect Mike Lance's cowhide folding chair of 1977 also mixes down-to-earth pragmatism (it can fold flat to the thickness of the tube frame) with consciously aesthetic appeal.

THE COUNTRY

Physical isolation has always characterized the population distribution in the Southwest. Unlike most parts of the U.S., the Southwest never supported self-sufficient farming. Because of limited arability, the only economically viable agriculture available to early landholders was extensive grazing or, where soils and rainfall permitted, generally single-crop farming on a broad scale. Ranches and homesteads were large and widely dispersed. Country towns, which served as collection and distribution points, were remote and isolated. Only with the advent of railroads in the mid-nineteenth century did settlement of areas become feasible.

Buildings in the landscape become isolated objects, as can be seen by the Lotthouse of 1890, or the "Peaceable Kingdom," an educational crafts facility in Texas designed by Taft Architects (formerly "In Cahoots") in 1972. Treated as discrete pavilions rather than space-making agglomerations, structures in the Southwest have continued to demonstrate the ability of manmade objects to dominate visually huge expanses of space. One sees this in the Choctaw Chief's House in Swink, Oklahoma, of 1837, with its simple log construction and double porches, as well as in the austere clapboard Columbus Church built in Hempstead County, Arkansas, around 1875.

THE TOWN

Even when multiple buildings were needed and towns began to spring up, the southwesterners's predilection for buildings as single visible objects prevailed. Simple, primal forms, such as the West Eufala Burying Ground in Oklahoma, retained a sense of independence and completeness even when grouped together. At a larger scale, the three houses in Little Rock, built around 1890, similarly maintain an individual identity by their gables, porches and long rectangular "shotgun" plans.

When land was subdivided, the methods chosen were generally as unrestrictive as possible. A loose framework allowed development to take place and still accommodate the desire for independence and individuality among the settlers. While the grid plan characterized development patterns of most nineteenth-century American cities, in towns like Austin, Texas, the grid was especially neutral. Here the square, not the rectangle, formed the geometric basis for the plan. The filling out of blocks with uniform rowhouses seldom occurred in the Southwest. Even when it did, development was not necessarily systematic, as a country store in Nathan, Arkansas, illustrates. When real estate values rose and full land use required close packing of buildings on blocks, individual expression still prevailed. The main street of Houston, dating to the nineteenth century when this metropolis was a town, shows how conformity in material, cornice line or style was rejected in favor of uniqueness and distinction.

Public buildings took the meaning of the phrase "building as object" to a new level of interpretation. The most common town plan for county seats in Texas in the nineteenth century isolated an entire block in the center of town for the courthouse. The need to create a strong identity for maturing settlements is shown by the exuberant Richardsonian Romanesque forms of patterned stone in James Riely Gordon's Ellis County (Texas) Courthouse, built in 1895.

Just as towns became amalgams of disparate elements, the architectural styles developed for individual buildings similarly acknowledged the society's historic diversity. The Church of San Felipe de Jesus and its adjacent pueblo built in 1706 demonstate a synthesis of Indian and Spanish building traditions. Sometimes the building methods of two cultures are juxtaposed, as seen in the typically Indian use of flat roof terraces and the overtly Spanish steeples that were added in 1808. Sometimes traditions are merged: both Indian and Spanish architecture, for instance, employ massive masonry walls with tiny pierced openings.

La Villita in old San Antonio, built around 1790, first restored in 1936 by O'Neil Ford and more recently restored and renovated by Ford, Powell & Carson, demonstrates the same sort of merging of cultural influences. But here the range is even greater, reflecting the fact that the Indian, Spanish, Mexican, German, French and Anglo-Colonial people who settled

Grain elevator, Optima, Oklahoma, ca. 1924. Photo: Arn Henderson.

That same sense of isolation and focused energy is shown in the grain elevators of 1924 erected in Optima, Oklahoma.

The tension created between landscape and built form lends added potency to the experience of both elements, as seen in the Kitts Peak Observatory designed by Skidmore, Owings & Merrill in 1961. On the other hand, the Herb Greene House, built in Oklahoma in 1959, illustrates an example of nature being reinterpreted through the man-made artifacts.

In the Southwest a most surreal effect is often created in the relationship between architectural form, light and space, as illustrated in the Morton House, built in 1980 in San Antonio. The architectural expression emerging from the landscape's emptiness has a severity and subtlety about it, as seen in both Fort Ben Leaton in Presidio, Texas, built around 1830, and J.B. Jackson's house built thirteen years ago in Sante Fe. The house that architect Judith Chafee designed in 1976 for clients living outside of Tucson convincingly occupies its powerful site. It captures the stark textures and quality of light of southern Arizona, taming them for human habitation.

Texture and detail give added dimension to prosaic objects and a palpability to structures, evoking an emotional response. Southwestern architecture appeals to the mind's power to *touch*. The basic primal qualities of buildings become most appropriate in this setting, as the direct, simply constructed barn in southeast Arkansas shows. Such structures, whether conceived as shelter in a benign climate or as an assembly of constructed parts, can also become a stark symbol of human presence, exemplified by the Thorncrown Chapel designed by Evine Fay Jones in Arkansas in 1980.

Barrio de Analco, Santa Fé, New Mexico, ca. 1810, additions ca. 1890, renovation and restoration by William Lumpkins, 1968. Photo: © Lloyd Herman.

in San Antonio had not separated into ethnic communities but had intermingled. In the seven small original houses of La Villita, there are combined traces of building traditions from several different cultures: adobe, earth, half-timber, field stone and caliche, a clay-like and stone masonry block. Forms and technologies from widely divergent cultures are mixed into a new composite in response to the uniquely southwestern setting.

Similarly, in the Barrio de Analco in Santa Fe of 1810, restored and renovated in 1968, thick adobe is combined with thin porch rails; fluid earthen shapes mix with precisely milled detail. Not only are Indian, Latin and Anglo cultures merged, but eighteenth-, nineteenth- and twentieth-century elements are layered on top of each other. In these rich amalgams—such as the Wulff House in San Antonio dating to about 1870, with its plain heavy limestone and delicate Victorian trim—is found a truly American expression. In structures like these, the melting pot is given physical form. Nowhere in the United States was the appropriateness of this new composite architecture more evident than in the Southwest at the turn of the century.

Even as doctrinaire a stylist as Ralph Adams Cram noted of his commission to execute the Rice University campus in Houston (1909): "On abstract principles, we were convinced that our own type of transmuted Gothic was the right thing; but in this particular case it was manifestly out of place . . . as were all other styles."

Cram and his contemporary Cass Gilbert, who designed Battle Hall at the University of Texas in Austin in 1912, strained to "regionalize" their sophisticated northeastern academic style when

working in the Southwest. They found new freedom to bring together Byzantine elements with those from other sources, including early medieval Italy, southern France and northern Spain, resulting in work that was more original, if less refined, than similar commissions they executed elsewhere.

THE METROPOLIS

The Southwest is today the most rapidly growing region of the United States. Eighty percent of the population lives in cities, much of it in the vast sprawling metropolises that now typify the region. These new gargantuan urban forms also reflect the character and tradition of the Southwest. The sense of isolation and the perception of great distances between places are still dominant impressions: where once the cowboys spent long days in the saddle, urban commuters spend long hours behind the wheel.

The discrete nodes of houses, barns and churches in the country, or courthouses, schools and grange halls in the town, have their correlative in urban centers linked by freeway arteries. In Houston there are four such satellite centers that compete with the original downtown center. Individual buildings, such as Caudill Rowlett Scott's US Homes Building of 1978, assert the independence of their small town predecessors. Isolated forms, like the Post Oak Towers in Houston designed by Philip Johnson and John Burgee, assert their autonomy as singular, precious objects.

The southwestern metropolis as an emerging form can be seen clearly on Louisiana Street in downtown Houston. Towering behemoths line a canyon that was once a broad open street. As the Pennzoil Building by Philip Johnson and John Burgee shows so well, the gigantic objects retain their own identities where other buildings by well-known architects also vie for attention. The Pennzoil in particular expresses that glamorous flashy Houston style, in which simple obvious forms can be seen at a great distance—even from the highway—until new buildings come along to block the view.

The deep urban canyon-like streets of the burgeoning southwestern cities are matched by vast urban caves inside buildings—enormous interior spaces that maintain the scale of the outdoors in perfect climate-controlled comfort. Harwell Hamilton Harris's pioneering Trade Mart in Dallas of 1960 created a "pre-Portman" urban outdoor room. But the Astrodome of 1965 and the Galleria of 1973, both in Houston, took the giant step toward creating complete interior worlds. Football fields, baseball fields, nightclubs, restaurants, hotels, department stores, recreational facilities and parking are all connected under one roof or series of roofs.

The recent dynamic growth of southwestern cities has over shadowed another side of the urban environmental character of the region, which is equally compelling. Beyond the towers and highways, beyond the shops and parking lots, lie gentle enclaves of gracious urban and suburban life.

This grace is evident in the lavish suburbs of Houston of which Bayou Bend, designed by John Staub in the 1920s, is a prime example. It is also in evidence in San Antonio, Phoenix, Oklahoma City or Fort Worth, where grand houses assert the same need for individual identity that pioneer homesteads, such as the Kellum-Noble House of 1847, once displayed. The longstanding emphasis on the home is seen in all levels of the economic spectrum, as the modest but stately architecture of Frank Welch's O'Donnell House built in Dallas in 1979 indicates.

The pleasant urban graciousness of southwestern residential sections can also be found in public places, such as San Antonio's Paseo del Rio. This riverwalk, located on a level below the city's grid of streets, was first designed in 1936 as a landscaped *quai* as part of the WPA program. Its garden-like quality has remained, but shops and cafes have been added, many since the 1960s. Today the timeless quality and captivating charm of its architectural street lamps, bridges, stairs and amphitheater make it truly unique, but still very much of its region. Shopping districts such as Dallas's Quadrangle, designed in 1969, also create a special blend of architecture, nature and human activity.

Institutions like Fort Worth's Kimbell Art Museum of 1972 also create an extraordinary architectural environment. The Kimbell Museum may have an international reputation as one of Louis Kahn's finest works, but it is also a building in harmony with its place. Its parched flatness and tawny naturalness of surface and color, as well as its response to the brutal Texas sun, all tie it strongly to the Southwest tradition.

Whole communities for living and working, such as Trinity University in San Antonio, merge simple, finely crafted buildings and sensitively scaled outdoor spaces with rugged natural terrain.

Trinity University, San Antonio, Texas. O'Neil Ford and Barlett Cocke, 1951–1979. Photo: © Richard Payne.

Country

1. Henry Lott Ranch House, near Goliad, Texas, c. 1890. Photo: © Rick Gardner.

2. Peaceable Kingdom Barn, Novasota, Texas. Taft Architects (formerly "In Cahoots"), 1973. Photo: Taft Architects.

3. Choctaw Chief's House, near Swink, Oklahoma, 1837. Photo: Arn Henderson.

4. Columbus Church, Hempstead County, Arkansas, c. 1875. Photo: © Geoff Winningham, courtesy First Federal Savings and Loan Association of Little Rock.

5. Grain elevator, Optima, Oklahoma, c. 1924. Photo: Arn Henderson.

6. Kitts Peak Observatory, Arizona. Skidmore, Owings & Merrill, 1961. Photo: © Ezra Stoller, ESTO.

7. Herb Greene House, near Norman, Oklahoma. Herb Greene, 1959. Photo: Arn Henderson.

8. Morton House, near San Antonio, Texas. Frank Welch, 1980. Photo: © Rick Gardner.

9. Fort Ben Leaton, Presidio, Texas, c. 1830. Photo: © Eugene George.

10. Private Residence, Tucson, Arizona, Judith Chafee, 1976. Photo: © Glen Allison.

11. Jackson House, Santa Fe, New Mexico. J.B. Jackson, 1970. Photo: Barrie B. Greenbie.

12. Barn, southeastern Arkansas. Photo: Geoff Winningham, courtesy First Federal Savings and Loan Association of Little Rock.

13. Thorncrown Chapel, Eureka Springs, Arkansas. Evine Fay Jones, 1981. Photo: © Hursley/Lark/Hursley.

THE SOUTHWEST

Introduction

1. Indian Crafts, New Mexico. Photo: courtesy Humanities Research Center, University of Texas at Austin, Frederick A. Williams Collection.

2. Custom cowboy boot, Austin, Texas. Charlie Dunn, craftsman. Courtesy Ch. Dunn Boot Company.

3. Packaging for Adams Extract. Fred W. Adams, designer, 1909. Photo: courtesy *Texas Architect*.

4. Folding chair, San Antonio, Texas. Mike Lance of Lance, Larcade & Bechtol, architects, 1977. Photo: courtesy Mike Lance.

5. Oil derrick-styled rest area near Tyler, Texas. Photo: courtesy Texas Highway Department.

Town

1. West Eufala Burying Ground, near Eufala, Oklahoma, c. 1900. Photo: Art Henderson.

2. Three Houses, Little Rock, Arkansas, c. 1890. Photo: © Geoff Winningham, courtesy First Federal Savings and Loan Association of Little Rock.

3. Bird's eye view of Austin, Texas, 1873. Photo: courtesy Miller Blueprint Co.

4. Country Store, Nathan, Tike County, Arkansas, c. 1905. Photo: © Geoff Winningham, courtesy First Federal Savings and Loan Association of Little Rock.

5. Main Street, Houston, Texas, showing late 19th century buildings. Photo: © Richard Payne.

6. Ellis County Courthouse, Waxahachie, Texas. James Riely Gordon, 1895. Photo: courtesy Archives Collection, School of Architecture, The University of Texas at Austin.

7. San Filipe de Jesus, San Filipe, New Mexico, 1706 (steeples added 1808). Photo: courtesy Humanities Research Center, The University of Texas at Austin, Frederick A. Williams Collection.

8. La Villita, San Antonio, Texas, c. 1790. Restoration by O'Neil Ford, 1936, and Ford, Powell & Carson, 1982. Photo: Lawrence Speck.

9. Barrio de Analco, Santa Fe, New Mexico, c. 1810, additions c. 1890, renovation and restoration by William Lumpkins, 1968. Photo: © Lloyd Herman.

10. Wulff House, San Antonio, Texas, c. 1870. Photo: © Rick Gardner.

11. Lovett Hall, Rice University, Houston, Texas. Cram, Goodhue & Ferguson, 1910. Photo: © Richard Payne.

12. Battle Hall, The University of Texas at Austin. Cass Gilbert, 1912. Photo: © Debbe Sharpe.

13. William M. Rice Institute. Houston, Texas. Cram, Goodhue & Ferguson, 1929.

Metropolis

1. US Homes Building, Houston, Texas, Caudill Rowlett Scott, 1978. Photo: courtesy Texas Highway Department.

2. Post Oak Towers, Houston, Texas. Johnson & Burgee, 1981. Photo: © Richard Payne.

3. Louisiana Street, Houston, Texas. Photo: © Paul Hester.

4. Pennzoil Building, Houston, Texas. Johnson & Burgee, 1976. Photo: © Richard Payne.

5. Trade Mart Court, Dallas, Texas. Harwell Hamilton Harris, 1960. Photo: courtesy Harwell Hamilton Harris.

6. Astrodome, Houston, Texas. Wilson, Morris, Crain and Anderson, 1965. Photo: Lawrence Speck.

7. Galleria, Houston, Texas. Hellmuth, Obata & Kassabaum, Neuhaus and Taylor, 1973. Photo: Lawrence Speck.

8. Bayou Bend, Houston, Texas. John F. Staub, 1926. Photo: © Richard Payne.

9. Kellum-Noble House, Houston, Texas, 1847. Photo: © Richard Payne.

10. O'Donnell House, Houston, Texas. Frank Welch, 1979. Photo: © Rick Gardener.

11. Paseo del Rio, San Antonio, Texas, 1930s. Photo: Lawrence Speck.

12. Quadrangle Shopping Center, Dallas, Texas. Pratt, Box, Henderson, 1969. Photo: courtesy Pratt, Box, Henderson.

13. Kimbell Art Museum, Fort Worth, Texas. Louis I. Kahn, 1972. Photo: courtesy Kimbell Art Museum.

14. Trinity University, San Antonio, Texas. O'Neil Ford and Bartlett Cocke, 1951–1979. Photo: © Richard Payne.

THE WEST COAST

by Sally Woodbridge

In 1769, the Spanish began to colonize the West Coast, founding the first of the twenty-one Franciscan missions that stretched from San Diego to Sonoma, near San Francisco. The Mission style, as generally illustrated by the Mission San Antonio del Padua near Jolon of 1810–1814, was to gain a foothold in California architecture by the end of the nineteenth century, and was adapted to any number of diverse building types.

During the Mexican rule of California between 1822 and 1848, over 500 land grants were given, grants that spurred development of the fertile land along the central and southern California coast. By the early 1840s United States settlers began to penetrate the northwest region. In spite of the colonists's perception that the land was unoccupied, the entire West Coast had been settled as long as 20,000 years previously by ancestors of the so-called "Indians." By the time white men arrived, the native culture, particularly that of the northwest coast, had reached a highly sophisticated level. The pioneers did not choose to learn much from the local tribes's building methods.

The settlers, using their own building techniques and the materials at hand, evolved a number of architectural forms. The abundance of wood and lack of suitable building stone in most of the central and south coastal area produced a predominantly woodsy style emphasizing such elements as broad gable roofs. In the southern portion of the coast the adobe construction of the Colonial period evolved into stucco on wood frame. This construction technique assumed prominence because of the more benign climate, which permitted lighter materials.

Because the climate of the West Coast varies more dramatically in rainfall than in temperature, the most extreme differences in building relate to this climatic factor. The economy has always depended heavily on agriculture—even in the arid eastern parts of the coastal states, where irrigation and mechanized farming occurred earlier than in the rest of the country. Other economic factors have affected patterns and types of settlement: the development of the film and television industry around Los Angeles; the growth of viniculture, now experiencing considerable expansion in the Northwest as well as California; and the development of aerospace and high-technology industries since World War II in southern California and Washington, and of the micro-electronic industry in "Silicon Valley" south of San Francisco. Recreational activities also have had their effect on built form in resorts and skiing lodges.

In the mountainous area extending from Canada to northern California are many ski resorts; the Tim-berline Lodge built at Mount Hood in 1937 by the Mt. Hood Development Association and the WPA is an outstanding example of the type. Designed by architects from the U.S. Forest Service, the building is executed in the modified chalet style, with two wings spreading out from a massive core. The entire assemblage—a three-story hexagon with a pyramidal roof—sits on a rubble-masonry base surmounted by two stories clad variously in board-and-batten, shingles and clapboards and capped by a hipped, shake roof.

Of quite another genre, but equally emblematic of West Coast regional architecture, are the Case Study Houses built in Los Angeles in the late 1940s. European-influenced Modern movement architecture had been introduced to the area in the 1920s by immigrants such as Rudolph Schindler and Richard Neutra. In 1945 John Entenza, editor of *Arts and Architecture* magazine, initiated the Case Study Houses problem, which advanced the use of industrial materials, notably steel, and other technological elements for residential architecture. Among the earliest examples were a house designed by Charles Eames for himself and his wife Ray in Santa Monica in 1949, and a house Eero Saarinen and Eames designed for Entenza in the same year.

Today architects are looking back to vernacular traditions as well as to more self-consciously developed styles. The Fisher Winery in Sonoma Valley by MLTW/Turnbull Associates uses vernacular barn-like construction of redwood and fir for a wine making facility. Architects such as Batey/Mack of San Francisco have turned to even more archetypal forms—as shown in their 1981 design for a courtyard-house in Napa Valley made of concrete block with a stucco finish.

THE COUNTRY

Wherever colonists settled on the West Coast, they built as closely to the tradition of their origin as technology and skill permitted. Their eighteenth-century dwelling places showed influences mainly of Hispanic or "eastern American" (meaning east of the Mississippi) derivation. As the William Case House built in Willamette Valley, Oregon, in 1852–1859 illustrates, a variety of materials and a range of building methods—from mortise-and-tenon, to log, to stud construction—were used. In his temple-form house, Case, a carpenter, turned his porch columns from single logs, notched them to suggest a base and milled them at the top to create a modified Tuscan capital. The house is a monument to frontier technology in the service of cultural memory.

The house that Samuel and Joseph C. Newsom designed for William Carson, built in Eureka in 1884–1886, is a baronial castle in redwood, the major regional building material and the source of Carson's wealth. The illusion of grandeur in the house is heightened by the play on scale, the use of fanciful detail and the handling of mass as separate volumes topped by a lively roofscape.

Architecture's ability to express personal dreams and fantasies is emphatically illustrated in Cuesta Encantada, San Simeon. Here the power of oratory is translated into architecture. William Randolph Hearst built this country seat on the site of his father's 240,000-acre ranch on California's coast. In 1919 he told his architect, Julia Morgan, that he wanted a "Jappo-Swiss" bungalow. By Hearst's death in 1951, however, the complex of buildings included the 150-room Casa Grande with its cathedral-like facade in an amalgam of Mediterranean-Renaissance styles, three Italian villa-esque guest houses, a pool worthy of a Roman emperor, extensive outdoor terraces and gardens, a menagerie, a private dock on a 50-mile private stretch of ocean frontage and an airfield.

When Thomas D. Larkin, the American Consul in Mexican Monterey, built the first two-story house there in 1835, he added such eastern amenities as an interior staircase and glazed windows. Still, the house with its adobe walls and broad verandas shared strongly in a tradition that stretched across the southwestern part of the country, where it was called the "Territorial" style. Not only did Larkin's house set the style in Monterey, where it was much copied, but it also influenced the Monterey Revival of the 1920s and 1930s.

Much larger, but still domestic in scale, was General Mariano Vallejo's Petaluma Ranch headquarters in Monterey. Vallejo's headquarters buildings for a ranch that covered 100 square miles originally formed a quadrangle over 200 square feet. Made of adobe bricks and hand-hewn redwood timbers and whitewashed with lime, the structure cost over $80,000 to build during the decade it took to complete. The ranch deteriorated for nearly 100 years, until it was acquired by the state in 1951 and restoration was completed.

The influence of the Anglo-Mexican period of the 1830s and 1840s extended to country as well as suburban houses. California's leading native-born modern architect, William Wilson Wurster, saw the ranchhouse with its simple volumes and straightforward use of materials and structural detail as a proper wellspring for a modern regional architecture that was attentive to landscape and climates. His first residential commission was for a vacation farmhouse for the Gregory family, built in Santa Cruz in 1926–1927. The living quarters form two sides of the courtyard plan; a water tower marks the entrance and low walls form the rest of the enclosure. As in Anglo-Spanish ranch houses, the interior of the house is accessible by doors opening onto the corridor around

Bonham House, near Santa Cruz, California. MLTW, 1961. Photo: Morley Baer.

the court side or the terrace on the south side of the compound.

The Pope Ranchhouse in the Central Valley, designed by Wurster, Bernardi and Emmons in 1958, makes a conscious use of vernacular materials, adobe and a red-painted metal roof. It offered Wurster's vision of what regional architecture could be: a careful restatement of the past with forms and materials still appropriate to the present.

An example of a vanishing vernacular form is a great domed barn located east of Steptoe Butte, Washington. This structure stands as a monument to man's innovative response to the region's agricultural potential and to early technology. The heavy braceframe method of barn building, traditional in the East, was replaced around 1920 by balloon framing methods. The relative lightness of studs, as compared to the heaviness of timbers, made domed structures of maximum storage capacity possible.

The cabin-in-the-woods is a house type that Moore/Lyndon/Turnbull/Whitaker explored successfully in 1961 in the Bonham House in the Santa Cruz mountains. Designed around a 14-foot square central space, the house has window seats and a short flight of steps leading to a sleeping platform. Two saddlebag spaces contain bath and kitchen, screen porch, and fireplace area. The architects exulted in expressing the house's tiny budget, using asphalt roll-roofing with battens, plywood siding, a flimsy chimney, and industrial sash. But they also attempted a sense of grandeur in the height of the main space and the tower-like form.

The northwest coastal tribes had developed a timber building style with post, beams, and plates of staggering dimensions and heights, gable or half-gable roofs, and plank walls, set in an interlocking frame. The Haida long house, reconstructed at the Museum of Anthropology in Vancouver, B.C. provides a straightforward example of the type.

A reinterpretation of the long house was designed in 1974 by the Bumgardner Partnership for the Tulalip Reservation Community Center near Seattle. Housing a gym, library, kitchen, offices, and meeting rooms, the building is an immense, shingled wooden hive that fits as naturally into the landscape as the two ceremonial long houses nearby.

A major landmark in the tradition of buildings being carefully inserted into the landscape is the residential condominium complex Sea Ranch in northern California. Few, if any, West Coast buildings have had the influence of the Sea Ranch Condominium, designed in 1964 by Moore/Lyndon/Turnbull/Whitaker. The concept also marks a shift in the market away from single-family houses to cluster housing. Like a Russian Easter egg, each dwelling unit contains spaces within spaces. Abandoned mines in the Gold Rush country, barns, and other utilitarian structures were assumed to be prototypes for the condominium buildings's spartan, planar character. By the architects's account, they were less influenced by history than by environmental factors such as high winds.

THE TOWN

West Coast towns have usually been considered potential cities. The escalating population growth of the past seven decades has proven that prediction accurate, generating a "no growth" movement in many communities. Some towns, treated by their inhabitants—many of whom moved there from cities—as "frozen," derive income from tourists who come to savor their preserved historic status. Such a town is La Conner, located in the Skagit River Valley of Washington, one of the Northwest's most serene and lovely landscapes. Originally established as a trading post in 1867, much of the town is now an historic district.

The search for appropriate forms for southern California produced a range of architectural solutions still in use. Because there was so little architecture left from the Colonial period, there was little to impede imagination. The simple and fragmentary remains furnished a code of forms. Arcades, towers, tile roofs, white walls, and simple, often linear details composed the basic lexicon. No one used these elements more simply and eloquently than Irving Gill, represented by his Women's Club of 1913 near the La Jolla community center, which he also designed. Though evocative of the past, the pristine arcade was built with the latest technology of the time: a concrete slab cast in a frame on the ground—with arches, metal doors and windows inserted in place—was tilted upright to form the wall.

One of the most fanciful agglomerations of historic fragments is the Glenwood Mission Inn in Riverside, California. When construction began in 1902, A.B.

La Conner, Washington. Photo: Art Hupy.

Benton was the architect, but by the time the inn was finished in 1931, Myron Hunt, Elmer Grey, and B. Stanley Wilson had also designed pieces of this picturesque concrete composition.

The Santa Barbara County Courthouse and the Pasadena City Hall illustrate two sorts of Mediterranean styles architects drew on in southern California. In the case of the Santa Barbara courthouse, designed in 1929, the architects from William Mooser's office and the Santa Barbara Advisory Committee inflated the Andalusian frame house to inordinate proportions and added elements typical of the Franciscan Mission style. The portal, like a stage flat, permits a view of the landscaped open court beyond.

Pasadena's city hall was designed in 1923 by Bakewell & Brown, architects of the San Francisco City Hall of 1913. In contrast to the San Francisco City Hall, a more faithful representative of the Beaux-Arts classicism of the late nineteenth century "City Beautiful" movement, the Pasadena building is scenographic, its neo-Baroque dome rising above the entrance opening to a lush tropical garden.

Leaping from hill to hill on an arcaded base reminiscent of a Roman aqueduct, the Marin County Civic Center is a masterful work of scenography like the Pasadena City Hall or the Santa Barbara County Courthouse, but is executed in a futuristic vein. Frank Lloyd Wright, with Aaron Green as associated architect, designed the building in 1957, but its construction was executed in stages and not completed until 1969.

Mediterranean hill towns provided the model for the town-like setting of Kresge College at the University of California, Santa Cruz, designed by Moore and Turnbull in 1966–1973. Departing from the usual campus segregation of living and working spaces, the architects created a one-street town with various components intermixed along a processional route. To play up the quality of the college as a settlement in the wilderness, the architects painted the buildings white on the inner street side of the campus and brown on the side facing out to the forest. Perforated walls, like the false fronts of buildings in western frontier towns, give the street an urban order.

In San Francisco a cluster of twelve housing units designed for single persons sharing the units exemplifies one approach to building for a dense but low-rise townscape. Architects Daniel Solomon and Paulett Taggert have designed a series of clapboard cubiform walk-ups to fill in the city's grid-like pattern and have used frame-like gateways to acknowledge the street running diagonally at the edge.

Two mainstays of the traditional affluent American suburb are the country club and the church. The Seattle Country Club, designed by Cutter & Malmgren with Andrew Willatsen in 1909–1910, reveals a strong regional use of wood, the basic material of the central and northern part of the coast. The country club's Swiss-Alpine chalet style, a favorite of the turn-of-the-century Arts and Crafts movement, proved appropriate for the mountainous region of Washington.

California architect Bernard Maybeck also admired the architecture of heavy timbers and wood joinery. In the First Church of Christ Scientist he designed in Berkeley, California, in 1910, he fused Alpine and Oriental motifs with his personal version of Gothic tracery inset with industrial sash. Maybeck's genius for stylistic invention was most evident in his manipulation of traditional forms and materials to create buildings that were and are "of this place."

Ellsworth Storey and Bernard Maybeck had much in common in their approach to architecture. Deeply influenced by the Arts and Crafts movement, they used local wood materials with particular reverence in their designs for economical houses that are monuments to the ideal of "the simple life." Storey's cottages for small parcels of land in a wooded Seattle suburb were straightforward yet structurally sophisticated. The 20-by-32 ft., four-room units were set with timber posts and beams on concrete foundation blocks. Walls are a single thickness of 1-by-6 in. tongue-and-groove boards set inside the studs; front porches have slatted screens. The exposed roof framing and casement sash set in the structural modules complete the "good carpenter" image.

The peak of craftsmanship in wood was reached in the work of the Greenes, whose Gamble House built in Pasadena, California in 1908, is a well-known masterpiece. In addition to the wealth of wood joinery in the building's fabric, the Greenes also designed the furniture and lighting fixtures, which were produced in their Pasadena workshop.

Nature's generous endowment of most of the West Coast with trees perfectly designed for milling led to the dominant building tradition. John Yeon's 1946–1947 Watzek House, built—like the Newsoms's Carson House—for a lumber baron, is an understated yet elegant temple in wood. Like the best of the post-World War II modern movement work on the West Coast, this house escapes the dated quality that comes with time.

Clearly tied to the influential timber building tradition of Japan is the 1960s guest house for the Bloedels, designed by Paul Hayden Kirk. The house in Seattle illustrates how Japanese architecture has enriched contemporary regional design.

In the southern coastal area, wood for building was not plentiful. (The lush vegetation in the area had resulted from irrigation measures.) The indigenous materials here were adobe, reinforced mud and stone. Even river boulders shaped by water currents were lavishly used by the Craftsman designers because of their natural forms.

Although other architects looked to Spanish colonial styles in the 1920s, Lloyd Wright created a Mayanesque masterwork in concrete "textile" block. The Sowden House is walled off from the street and dominated by a grotto-like entrance form duplicated on the courtyard side.

While others worked changes on historic tradition, the Viennese-born Modern architect Rudolph Schindler designed a beach house in 1926 in what was soon to be called the International Style. Five vertical concrete frames contain the two-story living space, lifted above ground to gain the ocean view. On top is a sunken sunbathing deck; on the ground below is an outdoor "living" room with fireplace.

A few years later, for the same clients, Schindler's fellow countryman Richard Neutra designed the first completely steel-framed house in the U.S. The prefabricated frame was bolted together on the site, casement windows were clamped on, and concrete gunite was shot onto wire lath for the exterior walls. With its crisp geometry and non-traditional use of materials, the so-called Lovell Health House brought the European modern movement directly to the West Coast.

European-influenced Modern architecture, inaugurated in southern California by Schindler and Neutra, won the allegiance of the generation of architects practicing after World War II. Contemporary residential architecture has generally pursued goals different from the technological ones of the 1940s modern movement. A renewed interest in regionalism or "contextualism" has prompted young architects such as Rob Quigley in San Diego, Michael Rotundi and Thom Mayne of Morphosis in Los Angeles, and Dan Solomon in San Francisco to design buildings that reflect architectural styles of their particular locale. Dan Solomon's Glover Street Condominiums fit into the San Francisco streetscape with the ease, if not the stylistic eccentricity, of Bernard Maybeck's shingled Goslinsky townhouse of 1909.

Architecture is always in transition, reflecting tradition while introducing change. Nowhere is this more explicit than in Frank Gehry's 1980 house in Santa Monica where the architect has articulated the tension between old and new by wrapping a new and highly personal shell around a partially dismantled Cape Cod style contractor's cottage.

THE METROPOLIS

To a large extent the western coastal states skipped the agrarian stage of settlement, moving directly into an urbanized, commercial economy. The first cities—San Francisco, Portland and Seattle—were colonized by eastern urbanites and served as bridgeheads from which the hinterlands were settled. Los Angeles, the great exception, experienced its largest immigration later, from the Midwest.

For most of the nineteenth century San Francisco was simply called "the city." As the West Coast nexus of cosmopolitanism and wealth, downtown San Francisco was first built and then rebuilt—after the 1906 earthquake and fire—to eastern standards of taste. Today, with the downtown once again renewed, the street pattern is virtually the only remnant of the city's early form.

Portland's grid of small 200-by-200 ft. blocks and the narrow strip of 100-ft. wide park blocks running east-west across the old part of the city distinguish it from other West Coast cities and contribute to a sense of urbanity associated with old eastern cities.

Like its plan, Portland's buildings are designed in architectural styles imported from elsewhere. The two buildings that illustrate this tendency best and have earned for Portland the reputation of being architecturally up-to-the-minute are Pietro Belluschi's Equitable Building of 1948 and Michael Graves's Public Services Building of 1982.

Excited by the potential for using the lightweight metals of wartime in post-war building, Belluschi clad this concrete frame structure with aluminum—in natural sheets on the frame, cast and anodized in the spandrels, and extruded for the mullions. By 1982, architectural fashion had changed. In his Portland Building, Graves employed concrete in a centralized, axially-ordered mass, embellished with color and abstract references to Classical detail.

As early as 1909, Los Angeles restricted the height of buildings and used zoning to segregate industry from residences. These actions furthered a "horizontal spread" and blessed the continuation of what was already a loose aggregation of communities masquerading, some said, as a city. The freeways have not really changed the lay of the land, nor have they forged new paths in most cases. The Los Angeles basin was crisscrossed with long routes before white men came: Wilshire Boulevard roughly follows El Camino Real, the colonial road of New Spain, from the original pueblo to the La Brea tar pits. The creation of the "Miracle Mile" in the late 1920s and '30s launched Wilshire as L.A.'s linear downtown. Now, in the '80s, the line of towers is nearly continuous.

Bullock's Wilshire, designed by John and Donald B. Parkinson in 1928, was the most dazzling retail palace on the Boulevard's Miracle Mile. It boasted two main entrances—one on Wilshire and one on the large parking lot on the opposite side, which had a *porte cochère* embellished with murals devoted, appropriately, to the theme of transportation.

Equitable Building, Portland, Oregon. Pietro Belluschi, 1948. Photo: Walter Boychuck, courtesy Oregon Historical Society.

Modern architects were rarely asked to design buildings for the older, more traditional West Coast industries. A notable exception is William W. Wurster's office building for the Schuckl Canning Company—a masterful blend of regional and International Style motifs built in 1942.

The early development of high technology industries on the West Coast, resulting partly from heavy concentration of aircraft and allied industries during World War II, has spurred "high tech" designs for office buildings and laboratories. IBM's Santa Teresa Laboratory, built in 1977 in "silicon valley" at the southern end of the San Francisco Bay, is one example. Here McCue, Boone and Tomsick clustered repetitive structures around a sunken computer center with a rooftop plaza. The gleaming aluminum curtain wall with flush-glazed reflecting glass windows shifts to color-coated panels in the courtyards.

THE WEST COAST

Introduction

1. Orange crate label, California, 1930s. Photo: Steven Lewis, courtesy Robin Parker.

2. Timberline Lodge, Mount Hood, Oregon. Mount Hood Development Association and WPA, 1937. Photo: courtesy Oregon Historical Society.

3. Fisher Winery, Sonoma Valley, California. MLTW/Turnbull Associates, 1982. Photo: © Rob Super.

AMERICA AS A REGION

by Ann Kaufman

. . . In aristocracies, a few great pictures are produced, in democratic countries, a vast number of insignificant ones. In the former, statues are of bronze; in the latter, they are modeled in plaster.

When I arrived for the first time at New York, by that part of the Atlantic Ocean which is called the East River, I was surprised to perceive along the shore, at some distance from the city, a number of little palaces of white marble, several of which were of ancient architecture. When I went the next day to inspect more closely one which had particularly attracted my notice, I found that its walls were of painted wood. All the edifices which I had admired the night before were of the same kind.

Alexis de Tocqueville
Democracy in America, 1840

The observation that American architecture is often characterized by mimicry, repetition, and illusion was as true in the nineteenth-century settings viewed by Alexis de Tocqueville as it is in a contemporary American landscape of McDonald's, Amoco stations and Tudoresque condominiums. The unique regional developments contributing to the vigor of American architecture exist within the framework of a nation whose history and structure have created patterns of settlement, planning and building uniformly found throughout the country. The integration of the local and the individualistic with the general and commonly shared is a characteristic value fundamental to American democracy. It is evidenced in architecture as well, as illustrated in de Tocqueville's analysis of the villas on the East River.

In the last century industrial production has made the creation of repeatable building types possible and has helped contribute to a common language of structure and style in architecture. At the same time "hybrids"—created through the interaction of standardized production and local modifications—reflect shared tastes, values and ambitions of the American public.

The home, the factory and the place of recreation have been the primary settings for the development of these shared values, which have been made more recognizable as a result of industrialization. America's central position in the development of building technology has led to the creation of a powerful language of modern architecture that has been spread through-

out the world. This country's burgeoning communication industry has furthered the dissemination of images and information about this architecture. The resulting aesthetic can be seen particularly in the modernist-influenced house, in the factory and in the American hotel. The houses of Richard Meier, the factories of Albert Kahn, and the hotels of John Portman, for example, articulate a clear architectural style that transcends place. They stand out from local and familiar images of home, work and recreational settings that have evolved traditionally in various regions.

Nevertheless, these building types have developed from a context of both shared values and specific methods of construction and planning that created similarities in the built environment long before "modern" architecture arrived. For example, the strength of Protestant ideals regarding the ties between church and state in the early colonies generated close groupings of important cultural and civic institutions regardless of local physical conditions. In the country and suburb, more elusive factors, such as the attraction to open space, the desire for private ownership of land and the quest for health, expressed the "pastoral ideal" that has persisted in the American psyche. In the American city, the practice of dividing land according to an orthogonal grid led to the development of uniform physical patterns that spurred specific building types such as the skyscraper.

Aspects of the American built environment that transcend regions are the result of a complex interaction of necessity, economy and desire. Thus the buildings and objects that are uniquely American often combine seemingly diverse and sometimes opposed intentions. The American diner, for example, both solves the problem of reusing an obsolete object and finding an appropriately functional form for a roadside structure. Perhaps unlike any other country's architecture, innovations in American building include not only the elegant and functional results of studied design, but also the exceptionally pragmatic and often humorous works of the untrained.

THE COUNTRY

. . . important evidence of a genuine longing for the beautiful may at once be pointed out. Almost every American has an equally unaffected, though not, of course, an equally appreciative, love for 'the country.' This love appears intuitive, and the possibility of ease and a country place or suburban cottage, large or small, is a vision that gives zest to the labors of industrious thousands.

Calvert Vaux
Villas and Cottages, 1857

The American countryside has been an important image in art and literature and has become a symbol of an ideal structure in which God, man and nature are united through the institutions of the home, school and church. Although other expressions of nature—the "wilderness," the "frontier" and the "land"—have had particular meaning to Americans historically, the small country farm perhaps best symbolizes the resolution of the struggle with the American land that was the basis of our early economy. The suburban home now bears the meaning of this ideal for the modern man who straddles the urban and rural worlds.

The rural American home, long a subject of concern to architects, writers and social critics, has taken many forms—as cottage, villa, estate or rustic cabin. The country home bears a special external relationship to nature, but with the advent of mass production, an interior environment, equipped with all manner of domestic conveniences, became possible in even the most isolated country settings. The film industry has reinforced popular images of the home in all its forms, including the rustic, the spare and the craftsy expressions of the ranch house, saltbox and bungalow.

Since the early twentieth century, the countryside has been penetrated by the road, leading to the development of an entirely unique and dynamic culture overlaid across the static harmony of rural America. The national system of highways crossing the land provides a structure of signage and events meant to engage and capture the attention of the traveller. Important services—food, lodging and provisions for the automobile—are offered in clever adaptations of existing building types. Buildings along America's roadsides have redefined the possible images of a building. These commercial vernacular structures attract attention by looking like well-known objects

such as a hat, or symbolize their function by looking like the wares they purvey. Roadside architecture has often adapted recognizable vernacular types, such as the wigwam or log cabin, or American institutions like the schoolhouse for new uses. The motor court motel, the gas station, and the drive-in building are unique institutions of the road and form America's most uniquely symbolic landscape.

THE TOWN

Now if we can, with a knowledge of true architectural principles, build one house rightly, conveniently, and elegantly, we can, by taking it for a model and building others like it, make a perfect and beautiful city; in the same manner, if we can, with a knowledge of true social principles, organize one township rightly, we can, by organizing others like it, and by spreading and rendering them universal, establish a true Social and Political order.

Albert Brisbane
A Concise Exposition of the Doctrine of Association, 1843

The orderly town represented a scale of intervention in the landscape that satisfied the utopian spirit of nineteenth-century idealists. But almost from the beginning of Colonial America, significant agglomerations of people and resources in towns formed a network of communication and exchange along the Eastern seaboard. Whereas the countryside was the symbolic setting for the American ideal of individualism, it was in the town that the social principles of democracy were to be established.

A grid arrangement of streets and parks was the most common pattern of both planned and unplanned towns in the developing nation, and specific institutions, including the town hall, courthouse, school, post office, library, general store and railroad station, provided important services along the circulation spine of the main street. Most of these were directly or indirectly regulated by the national government, and therefore became clearly recognizable images of the American town. The movie theater and the luncheonette, settings for the presentation and sale of important American industries, sprang up along with other mercantile establishments on the town's main street.

America's long-standing interaction with nature has led to the development of a great variety of distinctive settings. The county fair introduces a temporary structure of exchange and recreation for the farmer; the American urban park, best exemplified by Central Park in New York, but also represented by many of the projects of the Works Progress Administration, offers an opportunity for the urbanite to retreat to a temporary natural world. In like manner, the

Prefabricated house, 1940s. Photo: Courtesy Venturi, Rauch and Scott Brown.

Railroad station, White House, New Jersey, 1963. Photo: David Plowden, courtesy Hardy Holzman Pfeiffer Associates and Educational Facilities Laboratory.

urban pleasure palace, a late nineteenth-century type including theaters, restaurants and vaudeville, served escapist needs.

The American resort is another inter-regional development that has developed quite distinctly from European phenomena of a similar type. The country inn, the motor court motel and the resort town with its typically playful wood-frame buildings are expected way stations for the traveller in America.

THE METROPOLIS

> The wild life of the streets has perhaps as unforgettable a charm, to those who have totally imbibed it, as the life of the forest or of the prairie.
>
> Nathaniel Hawthorne

Despite the persistence of the rural ideal, the American city has developed unique qualities that express a vigorous image of this country world. The scale of American urban architecture, the presence of highway interchanges at the edge of cities and unique building types such as the civic center, the garden apartment, and the urban galleria are striking images of the contemporary American city.

Important public institutions, including the museum, hotel and department store, developed a stylistic clarity in many large cities of America around the turn of the century. A Beaux-Arts plan configuration was frequently adapted for public buildings on a grand scale, recalling either similar contemporary European types or earlier precedents, such as the urban palazzo. Like the typical American museum or department store, Henry Hardenbergh's Plaza Hotel in New York dominates its setting both by means of a striking French mansarded facade and through the command of an unusual urban site. The use of gigantic Classical columns, both in Trowbridge and Livingston's B. Altman store and in John Russell Pope's later National Gallery, express architectural language that remains throughout America's cities as vestiges of this confident age.

The American suburb in many ways summarizes certain unifying themes in American architecture. Resolving the conflicting desires to live both close to nature and to draw income from the commercial life of the city, the suburb has accepted America's fantasies of wealth, status and luxury and continues to be the preferred setting of most citizens for the establishment of family and community. The planned suburb, perhaps represented most purely by Llewelyn Park, New Jersey, designed in 1853 by Andrew Jackson Downing, has taken many and varied forms. It provides an alternative to the sprawl induced by low land values around cities, as seen in developments like San Mateo, California, and to the high-density rowhouse developments of the first ring of suburbs formed in the early years of this century, seen in the example of Queens, New York, around 1920.

The bungalow courtyard, such as Arthur Heineman's Bowen Court in Pasadena, developed primarily in California during the 1910s and '20s, was one expression of the "middle landscape" of mediation between settlement and nature that exemplifies the suburb. As computer technology increasingly frees business from the infrastructures of the city, the suburb takes on import as a new frontier of architectural development. It is perhaps in this setting that new hybrids as rich as the diner, the garden apartment or the American park may be developed. The strength of the suburban ideal may spur the unique synthesis of innovation and tradition that characterizes this country's architecture.

Interior, I.D.S. Center, Minneapolis, Minnesota. Johnson/ Burgee Architects, 1973. Photo: © Richard Payne.

273

AMERICA AS A REGION

Introduction

1. Smith House, Darien, Connecticut. Richard Meier, 1967. Photo: courtesy Richard Meier & Partners.

2. Saltzman House, East Hampton, New York. Richard Meier, 1969. Photo: © Ezra Stoller, ESTO, courtesy Richard Meier & Partners.

3. Douglas House, Harbor Springs, Michigan. Richard Meier, 1973. Photo: © Ezra Stoller, ESTO, courtesy Richard Meier & Partners.

4. Buick Plant, Melrose Park, Illinois. Albert Kahn, 1942. Photo: Ken Hedrich.

5. General Motors Technical Center, Warren, Michigan. Eero Saarinen, 1949. Photo: courtesy Kevin Roche John Dinkeloo and Associates.

6. Cummins Engine Co. Inc. Components Plant, Columbus, Indiana. Kevin Roche John Dinkeloo and Associates, 1973. Photo: courtesy Kevin Roche John Dinkeloo and Associates.

7. Renaissance Center, Detroit, Michigan. John Portman & Associates, 1976–1981. Photo: Alexandre Georges.

8. Hyatt Regency O'Hare, Chicago, Illinois. John Portman & Associates, 1971–1979. Photo: Alexandre Georges.

9. Peachtree Plaza Hotel, Atlanta, Georgia. John Portman & Associates, 1967. Photo: Stewart Bumgardener.

Country

1. Garden, Cornish, New Hampshire. Photo: courtesy New Haven Historical Society.

2. Country church and cornfield, Monona County, Iowa, 1940. Photo: Library of Congress, courtesy Peter M. Wolf.

3. Prefabricated house, 1940s. Photo: Library of Congress, courtesy Venturi, Rauch and Scott Brown.

4. Interior, prefabricated house, 1940s. Photo: Library of Congress, courtesy Venturi, Rauch and Scott Brown.

5. Film still, house exterior from *Bringing Up Baby*, R.K.O., 1938. Photo: courtesy Donald Albrecht and John Mansbridge.

6. Film still, house interior from *Bringing Up Baby*, R.K.O., 1938. Photo: courtesy Donald Albrecht and John Mansbridge.

7. "Radford's Bungalows," advertisement. Photo: courtesy Venturi, Rauch and Scott Brown.

8. Amoco sign. Photo: courtesy Venturi, Rauch and Scott Brown.

9. IH 610, Houston, Texas, 1964. Photo: Texas Highway Department, courtesy Lawrence Speck.

10. Sioux Chief Train Motel, Sioux Falls, South Dakota, 1963. Photo: © John Margolies, ESTO.

11. The Wigwams Free Museum, Route 17, Jasper, New York. Photo: courtesy Venturi, Rauch and Scott Brown.

12. Big Hat Restaurant. Photo: Library of Congress, courtesy Venturi, Rauch and Scott Brown.

13. Schoolhouse building, Common on the Green, Hartford, Connecticut. Photo: © John Margolies, ESTO.

14. Benewah Dairy No. 1, Spokane, Washington, 1935. Photo: © John Margolies, ESTO.

Town

1. Main street, Nevada City, California, 1982. Photo: © Robert Likter, courtesy Mother Lode Views.

2. U.S. Post Office. Photo: courtesy Venturi, Rauch and Scott Brown.

3. Martin Theater, Talladega, Alabama. Rufus Bland, 1936. Photo: © John Margolies, ESTO.

4. Railroad station, White House, New Jersey, 1963. Photo: David Plowden, courtesy Hardy Holzman Pfeiffer Associates and Educational Facilities Laboratory.

5. Film still, main street from *Tomorrow the World*. United Artists, 1944. Photo: © United Artists Corporation.

6. White Tower #19, New York, 1936. Photo: courtesy Steve Izenour.

7. White Tower #xx, New York. Photo: courtesy Steve Izenour.

8. Boathouse and lake, Mineral Palace Park, Pueblo, Colorado, 1940. Photo: Library of Congress, courtesy Venturi, Rauch and Scott Brown.

9. Granville, on Scott's Run, West Virginia, 1938. Photo: Marion Post Wolcott, Library of Congress, courtesy Venturi, Rauch and Scott Brown.

10. The Beekman Arms, Rhinebeck, New York, c. 1700. Photo: courtesy The Beekman Arms.

11. Street, Cape May, New Jersey, 1983. Photo: © Laura Rosen.

12. View from the Ramble, Central Park, New York, 1860. Photo: courtesy the New-York Historical Society.

13. Proctor's Pleasure Palace, New York. J. B. McElphatrick and Sons, 1894. Photo: courtesy Claudia Hart.

Metropolis

1. The National Gallery of Art, Washington, D.C. John Russell Pope, 1941. Photo: courtesy the National Gallery of Art.

2. B. Altman & Company, New York. Trowbridge & Livingston, 1914. Photo: Museum of the City of New York, courtesy Robert A. M. Stern.

3. The Plaza Hotel, New York. Henry J. Hardenbergh, 1907. Photo: courtesy the Plaza Hotel.

4. Union Passenger Terminal, Los Angeles, California, 1939. Photo: courtesy Educational Facilities Laboratory.

5. Central Expressway, Dallas, Texas, 1972. Photo: Bob W. Smith, U.S. Environmental Protection Agency-Documerica, courtesy Peter M. Wolf.

6. Las Vegas, Nevada, 1972. Photo: Charles O'Rear, U.S. Environmental Protection Agency-Documerica, courtesy Peter M. Wolf.

7. I.D.S. Center, Minneapolis, Minnesota. Johnson/Burgee Architects, 1973. Photo: © Richard Payne.

8. Interior, I.D.S. Center, Minneapolis, Minnesota. Johnson/Burgee Architects, 1973. Photo © Richard Payne.

9. Llewelyn Park gateway, Orange, New Jersey. Andrew Jackson Downing, 1853. Drawing: courtesy Andrew Jackson Downing, *A Treatise on the Theory and Practice of Landscape Gardening*.

10. Northwestern plan, Llewelyn Park, Orange, New Jersey. Andrew Jackson Downing, 1853. Drawing: courtesy Andrew Jackson Downing, *A Treatise on the Theory and Practice of Landscape Gardening*.

11. Dezenoorf's Delightful Dwellings, Queens, New York, 1920–1930. Photo: Library of Congress, courtesy Peter M. Wolf.

12. Bowen Court, Pasadena, California. Arthur S. Heineman, 1912. Photo: courtesy Greene and Greene Library, University of Southern CA.

13. Housing, San Mateo, California, 1956. Photo: R. J. Wagner, U.S. Department of Agriculture, courtesy Peter M. Wolf.

14. Foxhall Crescents, Washington, D.C. Arthur Cotton Moore/Associates, 1982. Photo: courtesy Arthur Cotton Moore/Associates.

15. Plan, Foxhall Crescents, Washington, D.C. Arthur Cotton Moore/Associates, 1982. Drawing: courtesy Arthur Cotton Moore/Associates.

FIGURE CREDITS

VINCENT SCULLY, "AMERICAN ARCHITECTURE: THE REAL AND THE IDEAL."

1 Photo: René Taylor.
2 From George Kubler, *The Art and Architecture of Ancient America* (Baltimore, Maryland: Penguin, 1962).
3 Photo: Mary Elizabeth Smith.
4 From Rem Koolhaas, *Delirious New York* (New York: Oxford University Press, 1978).
5 From H. H. Arnason, *Modern Art: Painting, Sculpture, Architecture* (New York, Abrams, 1968).
6 From Samuel Chamberlain, *Beyond New England Thresholds* (New York: Hastings House, 1936).
7, 9 Courtesy of The Henry Francis du Pont Winterthur Museum.
8, 11, 12, 14, 18 Courtesy of Yale University Art Gallery.
10 Courtesy of Bowdoin College Art Museum.
13 From Samuel Chamberlain, *Portsmouth New Hampshire: A Camera Impression* (New York: Hastings House, 1940).
15, 21, 24 Courtesy of the Metropolitan Museum of Art.
16, 17 Courtesy of the Boston Museum of Fine Arts.
19 From Vincent Scully, *The Shingle Style* (New Haven, Conn.: Yale University Press, 1955).
20 From Andrew Jackson Downing, *The Architecture of Country Houses* (New York: D. Appleton & Co., 1853).
22 Courtesy of the author.
23, 27 Courtesy of Columbia University.
25, 26 Courtesy, Venturi, Rauch and Scott Brown.
28 From Michael Graves, *Buildings and Projects 1966–81* (New York: Rizzoli, 1982).
29, 30 Courtesy of Columbia University Slide Library.

DAVID HANDLIN, "BETWEEN SUBJECT AND OBJECT."

1–15 Courtesy of the author.

ARTHUR PULOS, "THE OBJECT: A SEARCH FOR FORM."

1–20 Courtesy of the author.
1 From *Arts and Decoration,* November, 1933.
2 From *Architectural Record,* March, 1907.
5 Metropolitan Museum of Art, New York.
6 Henry Ford Museum, Dearborn, Michigan.
8 Chrysler Museum, Provincetown, Massachusetts.
9 Harris Gallery.
12 California College of Arts and Crafts.
13 From *Saturday Evening Post,* May 6, 1983.
14 From Henry-Russell Hitchcock and Arthur Drexler, ed., *Built in U.S.A.: Post-war Architecture* (New York: Museum of Modern Art; Simon & Schuster, 1952).
15 IBM Corporation.
16 American Airlines.
17 Photo: Raymond Loewy.
18 Chrysler Corporation.
19 From *Architectural Forum,* September, 1938.
20 From *Pencil Points,* September, 1937.

THOMAS HINES, "LOS ANGELES ARCHITECTURE: THE ISSUE OF TRADITION IN A TWENTIETH-CENTURY CITY."

4–16 Photographed by and courtesy of the author.
1 Columbia University Slide Library.
2 From *Greene & Greene: Architects in the Residential Style* (Fort Worth, TX: Amon Carter Museum of Western Art, 1974).
3 From *Irving Gill: 1870–1936* (Los Angeles County Museum; Art Center in La Jolla, 1958).

DONALD HOFFMAN, "CHICAGO ARCHITECTURE: THE OTHER SIDE."

1–13, 15–19 Photographed by and courtesy of the author.
14 American Institute of Architects, Washington, D.C.
20 Chicago Tribune.

JAMES O'GORMAN, "AMERICA AND H. H. RICHARDSON."

1–9 Courtesy of the author.
1 Chicago Historical Society.
3 *Gleason's Historical.*
4 Photo: Jean Baer O'Gorman.
7 From W. C. Bryant, ed., *Picturesque America, 1794–1878* (New York: Appleton and Company.
9 Reynolda House Museum of American Art, Winston-Salem, North Carolina.

JOHN COOLIDGE, "AMERICAN ARCHITECTURE: THE SEARCH FOR TRADITION."

1–14 Courtesy of the author.

DOLORES HAYDEN, "THE AMERICAN SENSE OF PLACE AND THE POLITICS OF SPACE."

1, 3–5, 7–14 Courtesy of the author.
2 From William Morgan, *Prehistoric Architecture in the Eastern United States* (Cambridge, Mass.: MIT Press, 1980).
6 Photo: William Garnett.

CHARLES GWATHMEY, STATEMENT.

1–32 Courtesy of the author.
1, 2, 33 Photo: David Hirsch.
3–5 Photo: Bill Maris.
6 Photo: Louis Checkman.
7–9 Photo: George Raustiola.
10, 11 Photo: Marvin Rand.
12, 13, 15, 16, 18–31 Norman McGrath.
14, 17, 32 Photo: Roberto Schezen.

KEVIN ROCHE, STATEMENT.

1–13 Courtesy of the author.

ALLAN GREENBERG, STATEMENT.

1–30 Courtesy of the author.

INDEX